FINANCIAL ADMINISTRATION
IN LOCAL GOVERNMENT

The work has been prepared under the auspices of
THE ROYAL INSTITUTE OF PUBLIC ADMINISTRATION
which has also been responsible for

Budgeting in Public Authorities
by a Study Group of the RIPA

New Sources of Local Revenue

of similar interest
The British Budgetary System
by Sir Herbert Brittain

Other books by A. H. Marshall

Local Authorities: Internal Financial Control (1936)

Consolidated Loans Funds of Local Authorities (1938)
with J. M. Drummond

Report on Local Government in the Sudan (1949)

Report on Local Government in British Guiana (1955)

FINANCIAL ADMINISTRATION IN LOCAL GOVERNMENT

by

A. H. MARSHALL

C.B.E.

City Treasurer, Coventry,
One-time President of the
Institute of Municipal Treasurers
and Accountants

Published for the Royal Institute
of Public Administration

UNIVERSITY OF TORONTO PRESS

Reprinted in 2018

ISBN 978-1-4875-8097-1 (paper)

PRINTED IN GREAT BRITAIN
in 10 *on* 11 *point Times type*
BY SIMSON SHAND LTD
LONDON, HERTFORD AND HARLOW

ACKNOWLEDGMENTS

IT is scarcely possible to write about the work of a profession without incurring pleasurable obligations to one's colleagues. I am, therefore, indebted first to the accumulated skill and proficiency of those who follow the calling of local government finance. The store of knowledge at their disposal, built up over several generations, is to be sought in current practice and in the domestic literature of the profession. Happily, our customs decree that it shall be freely available to all enquirers.

My debt to individuals is equally heavy. Many of my own staff, both professional and secretarial, have, over the years that the book has been in preparation, cheerfully and generously given of their leisure time. Their names would make a list too long to set out here. Among those outside Coventry who, at some stage or other, have read practically the whole of the book and made useful suggestions are: Mr John Steane, Mr Raymond Nottage (the Director of the Royal Institute of Public Administration), and the following members of the Institute of Municipal Treasurers and Accountants—Messrs George Esslemont, W. H. Foakes, Richard Marshall, J. V. Miller, Alexander Philip, E. T. Stenning, L. E. Taylor and J. B. Woodham.

The Institute of Municipal Treasurers and Accountants kindly allowed their assistant secretary, Mr R. A. Emmott, to work on Appendix B, to check the index and to read both manuscript and proof. The Royal Institute of Public Administration graciously placed their publishing arrangements at my disposal.

Finally there is the Coventry City Council whose open-mindedness in financial administration has made it possible for me to write from experience about so many of the techniques of financial administration which I have advocated.

All this unstinted assistance has saved me from a number of errors and enabled me to improve the arrangement and contents. The reader's path has thus been smoothed. In offering grateful thanks I would add that the responsibility is mine alone.

Chapter X includes passages from a paper I read before the I.M.T.A. in 1957, and elsewhere there are a few sentences from my 'Local Authorities: Internal Financial Control' (1936). Otherwise the book is entirely new, despite some similarity in arrangement to the earlier publication.

A. H. MARSHALL

Coventry, November 1959

FOR MARGARET
who understands so much

PREFACE

THIS book is about the organization of the financial work of local authorities. It describes the ways in which elected members ensure that proper respect is paid to finance; it shows how officials keep accounts and prepare information; and it deals with methods of avoiding dishonesty, laxity and abuse. The subject matter is financial administration and not finance, accounting or auditing. Consequently the organization of an accountancy section is discussed, but not the form of the accounts; the procedure for making a budget is treated, but not its contents.

The place of financial organization in a local authority is much the same as in other kinds of enterprise, such differences as exist being due to the special features of local authorities as administrative units. These distinctive characteristics are brought out in the first chapter. They form the background for the discussion of the principles of financial administration in the second chapter. Chapter III is concerned with the finance committee, the lay organ of financial administration. The professional element—the chief financial officer and his staff—is considered in Chapters IV to XII. Not all the financial work is done in the finance department so there are chapters (XIII and XIV) defining the part in financial administration played by other departments. All but one of the remaining chapters are devoted to individual aspects of financial work. Thus, Chapter XV deals with Payments, Chapter XVI with Income, Chapters XVII and XVIII with Purchasing and Contracting, and Chapters XIX–XXI with the Budget. These chapters are concerned with those processes and procedures which are not solely, or even mainly, the function of any one branch of the organization, and therefore could not conveniently be dealt with in the earlier chapters. The last chapter deals with the internal rules needed to provide a formal framework for the organization recommended throughout the book.

In general, references to England can—with apologies to the author's Scottish colleagues—be taken to cover Scotland. Major divergencies have been specifically noted, but a few minor differences have been ignored in the belief that they are of insufficient importance to warrant the further complication of the text. The word Clerk (with a capital C) is used to denote the County, Town or District Council Clerk.

A work on financial administration has inevitably to be written primarily for the professional reader—the practitioners and students in finance departments. But it should also be used by members of local authorities, especially those who serve on finance committees, and by the officers of other departments to whom finance is supremely important. For this reason technicalities have been avoided and an attempt has been made to make the book understandable by professional and lay reader alike.

Contacts over a number of years with accountants and financial officers have impressed upon the author the extent of the common ground between the work of financial officers of all kinds. A work on financial administration in any particular field should, if it is intelligibly written, be of value to financial administrators serving other kinds of organization. By setting the work of the financial officer in the context of the distinguishing traits of local government administration, the author hopes he has made the book useful outside as well as inside the service, and enabled those familiar with financial procedures to appreciate the reasons for the particular pattern of financial administration in local government. They may even be able to sympathize with what the chief financial officers of local authorities are pleased to regard as their special difficulties.

If there is a central theme running through the pages which follow, it is the need for the financial arrangements to be an integral part of the work of an organization. Finance is not a rite peculiar to the finance department, nor is financial administration an end in itself. Financial factors have to be considered along with others, not independently of them; the financial work is dispersed throughout the whole organization; and neither the most vigilant finance committee nor the most efficient finance department will be of much avail unless those responsible for directing the operations of the authority interest themselves in finance. Hence the stress which is laid on such matters as the need for using a centralized financial administration to strengthen rather than weaken the sense of financial responsibility of the departments, the desirability of a proper distinction between the 'control' and the 'service' aspects of the work of the chief financial officer and the importance of interdepartmental co-operation.

CONTENTS

CHAPTER I

INTERNAL ORGANIZATION OF LOCAL AUTHORITIES

(1)

BEING a practical treatise designed to help local authorities to do their financial work in the best way, this book is almost entirely concerned with administrative processes. It has been arranged so that the subject matter of each chapter can at once be related to the organization of the average local authority. But such a book must include some description of the administrative framework into which the financial arrangements must fit. The first chapter therefore attempts to explain the main features of the internal organization of local authorities, and to draw attention to the administrative traits of most significance to those charged with the direction of financial affairs. There follows in Chapter II a statement of the fundamentals of financial administration. Thus the way is cleared for the main purpose of the book—a detailed study of the application of these general financial principles to local government administration.

(2)

Were English local authorities charged with the provision of a single service, or even a group of homogeneous services, one might fairly expect their administrative arrangements to be simple to work and easy to describe. Such, however, is not their lot. The State has assigned to them a varied range of duties, each with its own aims, ideals, methods and criteria of success. Appendix A, where the work of local authorities is briefly summarized, shows that under one administrative roof, engineering, social, educational, cultural, amenity, trading and even minor law-making services have to be catered for. To expect a simple clear-cut administrative pattern for an organization which has to cope with so many services would be unreasonable: local government inevitably presents difficult problems to those responsible for its management, and interesting features to the student of administration. The unique form of the administration of English local authorities provides added interest. Rooted

13

in the committee system, it differs from that of local authorities in other countries, and from that of other large-scale organizations, and it is strange that, though so much has been written about the work of local government, little has been said of the administrative consequences of the constitutional principles upon which it has been built.[1]

English local authorities lack the varied forms of organization found in American local government, many devices common in the States, e.g. a central executive, being regarded as incompatible with the committee system, the cornerstone of English local government. In patterns of internal organization, as in functions performed, English local government exhibits a uniformity which, though it makes the system dull in comparison with that of some foreign countries, at the same time lightens the task of description. Studies of English local government administration are therefore concerned, not with comparative systems, but with variations within a traditional framework, differences in the quality of administration, the quest for efficiency, the search for refinements in procedure and so forth. Moreover this basic uniformity of structure applies irrespective of size. If one ignores the parish councils as being too small to need administrative machinery of the kind discussed in this book, one can assume that all local authorities set about their duties in much the same way, notwithstanding the great differences in their size and importance.

(3)

The structure of the English system of local government is straightforward. There is no pyramid of authorities with each layer of government subject to the one above. In the areas of county boroughs there is but one authority for all purposes; in other areas there are either two or three tiers, but each has its clearly defined duties, the more lowly being in general independent of the more exalted, though some services are carried out as a partnership between the tiers. Though they are greatly influenced by the central government, English local authorities do not act as its agents, except for a few easily defined tasks, notably the construction and maintenance of trunk roads and the collection of vehicle excise duties. Their officials receive no directions from the central government and, unlike some

[1] There is now a book—*The Machinery of Local Government*—by R. M. Jackson, (Macmillan 1958)—which caters for the general student who wants to know about the structure and organization rather than the nature and extent of particular services.

of their continental counterparts, they escape the hazardous task of serving two masters. English local authorities possess the characteristics of true self-governing bodies. They are democratically constituted, accessible to the people, sensitive to local opinion and they employ their own officials. They have a very considerable range of duties and responsibilities and dispose of about 6 per cent of the national income. Local authorities have their own local tax—the local rate. They enjoy autonomy in budgeting and except in parishes, and for certain services, there is no statutory limit to their rates. Finally, and perhaps most important for the purpose of this book, there is little statutory regulation of their internal management.

There are, however, disturbing trends in English local government of which the most serious is the inroad into local autonomy brought about by supervision from Whitehall and greater dependence upon the central government for funds. Limited to one local tax, that on the occupancy of real property, and compelled to accept the gradual whittling away of the basis of this tax by legislation—a process with scarcely a parallel in other countries—English local authorities in the aggregate now depend upon the central treasury for about half of their funds, and the less wealthy counties and county boroughs for a much greater proportion. That this is not a healthy state of affairs is generally recognized, but its significance for our present purpose—internal administration—is its tendency to weaken the sense of responsibility of the members and encourage them to look to the government departments for leadership. This tendency has been reinforced by the prevailing desire for uniformity of public services. The general acceptance of the aims of the welfare state has encouraged the citizen to expect identical public services from Land's End to John o' Groats. In the Scandinavian countries the central governments allow, and the public accepts, some latitude in the payment of benefits and in the nature of the social services rendered by the local authorities. In England anomalies and local differences are less readily tolerated so that, notwithstanding their desire for autonomy, local authorities pay great regard to the actions of other local authorities, an attitude which of itself militates against experiment and variety.

Nervous though they may be about the encroachment of the central government, local authorities may, however, still claim to possess a considerable degree of self government.[1] At any rate,

[1] But Great Britain does not show up well in comparison with other countries In September 1955, the International Union of Local Authorities collated the

sufficient powers of decision remain with a local authority to allow of marked differences in the extent and quality of services provided. For this reason, and because the local authority is largely free to order its own internal management, the subject of local administration is one of importance to the practitioner and of moment to the citizen.

(4)

The feature which distinguishes English local administration from that of other countries and from that of nearly all other large-scale organizations, whether public or private, is the merging of the responsibility for the determination of policy and for the supervision of its execution in one body—the council itself. Continental and American practice is, in the main, different, for there is often a council to define the aim, and a separate executive to attain it. Such an executive may be a 'college', e.g. in Hamburg or Montreal; or it may be an individual, e.g. the pre-war Rhineland Burgomaster or the American City Manager. It may have independently derived authority (being either appointed by the central government or separately elected) or it may be appointed by the council. It may have power to refer the decisions of the council to higher authority; it may even have power to veto the council's decisions; or it may be appointed

---

financial practices of twenty-four countries and classified the data, first according to the relative importance of the part played by local government, and secondly according to the degree of financial autonomy enjoyed by the local authorities. Countries were first placed in groups according to the proportion of total government expenditure incurred by the local authorities: greater than the norm, within the norm, and less than the norm. Great Britain fell into the middle group, that is to say, local authorities here had broadly speaking an average range of duties. Countries were then grouped according to the proportion of local expenditure which they were able to meet from their own taxes. Again, they were divided into three groups, the classification being: high, average and low. Great Britain fell into the last class. If the basic assumption of the report is accepted, i.e. that a high degree of dependence on the central exchequer tends to reduce local autonomy, our local authorities can no longer be held out as being in an enviable position. Indeed, a third table in the report which combines the two classifications described above, shows local authorities in Great Britain as being in effect in the bottom class, described as 'Countries in which local authorities have an average share in expenditure and derive a low percentage of their revenue from their own taxes'. See *Local Government Finance and its importance for local autonomy*—reports prepared for the International Union of Local Authorities Rome Congress, September 26th–October 1st, 1955 generally, and particularly pp. 16–20.

merely to carry out without question the council's policy. But, whatever the precise position of a separate executive, it has a direct responsibility for *execution* of policy. The council, though they criticize the executive, do not control its day to day acts, but in case of extreme dissatisfaction they can, in some countries, appoint a new executive. A possible consequence is that in the eyes of the public the executive may dwarf the policy-forming organ. The executive, being the professional, permanent element, and having continuous contact with the public, may easily come to be regarded by the man in the street as the local government or local authority. It is this which partly accounts in some countries for the awe towards the officials and for their isolation from the public. Only those who have seen officials dominating a meeting of respectful elected representatives can fully realize the gulf between English and continental practice!

This idea of a separation of powers under which an official bears a direct responsibility to the electors for any of his acts is foreign to our local government institutions. In England, therefore, the elected council must be answerable not only for policy but also for supervising its execution. The council must employ paid officials who collectively form the 'administration'. This corps of paid servants is of immense importance, for without an efficient administration the council can accomplish little. Nevertheless the responsibility of the council to the electors remains intact. Should the official err, the council must accept the blame, and afterwards settle its account with him. A Dutch driver finding a stretch of bad road will remark, 'There must be a poor Burgomaster here.' In similar circumstances in England the driver would say, 'This council is doing a bad job.' Both statements are correct reflections of the differing constitutional positions. This distinction in outlook is of both constitutional and administrative significance, but it is only with the administrative consequences that this chapter is concerned.

The vesting of executive responsibility in an elected body is of importance because it gives members—in their corporate capacity and not as individuals—opportunities for participation in administration rarely found elsewhere. But it places upon them obligations of a high order. They must evolve a way of keeping in touch with everyday administration without hindering the despatch of business or destroying the official's sense of responsibility; they must control, stimulate and, if necessary, defend the official; and they must account to the ratepayer, not only for what has been done, but for the manner in which it has been done. They must also do their part in establishing between the council and its officials one of those intimate and intangible relationships, so prominent in our political system, but eluding satisfactory analysis or explanation and beyond the understanding of all but the most astute foreign observers.

Some division of labour between the elected members is necessary. This is accomplished by an intensive use of the 'committee system' which takes the form of a number of committees composed, subject to a limited use of co-optation, of members of the council, each committee having charge of the work of a department or group of departments or being responsible for some specialized function, e.g. establishment matters. The committee have the dual function of making recommendations to the council and of supervising the administration.[1] Whilst there is among local authorities considerable difference in the extent of formal delegation to committees, major matters of policy or of acute controversy are in practice settled by the council, which is also kept informed by periodical report of the activities delegated to committees. Chairmen of committees occupy a coveted position, leading the committee's deliberations, influencing its decisions, answering for the committee in public, acting as the link between the committee and the administration, and dealing with emergencies. Committees mostly sit in private, the officials attending not as members with a right to vote, but as the servants of the committees. The extent of the officials' participation in the discussion depends on local tradition and the interplay of personalities, but whatever the committee procedure, the official, being both permanent and professional, has naturally a good deal of influence. Frequently he suggests, though he cannot determine, new policy. Whilst he must zealously carry out the decisions, he can, if asked, freely express his opinion on matters of policy within the committee room, but not outside.

The contrast between the council and its committees and the governing bodies of other types of large-scale organization, including other systems of local government, could hardly be greater. Most large organizations are guided at the top level by a handful of people who concentrate upon major policy questions. The larger English local authorities, on the other hand, have a considerable membership—thirty to eighty persons, sometimes even more. An

[1] For a detailed description of committees in local government functioning as examples of 'committees to administer', see *Government by Committee* by K. C. Wheare (Oxford University Press, 1955), Chapter VII.

authority, especially a county borough which performs all the local government services, may have up to twenty main committees which usually meet once a month, and many sub-committees in addition. Meetings may last from one to several hours, the agenda being laden with items of an administrative nature as well as with matters of policy. Returns summarizing the routine work of the departments since the last meeting, requests for instructions on the application of policy to individual cases, e.g. giving planning permission, negotiations for the purchase of goods, appointment of staff, wages and conditions of service of employees, invitations to attend conferences, recovery of debts, allocation of tenancies, furnishing, repairs and alterations of property, arrangements for Christmas celebrations at a Children's or Old People's Home, taking proceedings for minor infringements of regulations—these items and many more of a similar nature are regularly to be found set out in detail upon the agenda papers of committee meetings.

Many of the effects of such a system, such as the demands on the time of the members,[1] and the consequent reluctance of busy citizens to stand for election to local councils, are outside the scope of this book. The administrative results of the existence of a governing body which deals both with policy and with small day-to-day affairs are, however, highly relevant to a study of local government financial administration.

(5)

A consequence of the English local government committee system is that it creates, in the realm of policy making, a need for co-ordination. Committees tend to think of themselves as separate entities, and thus need to be continuously reminded that they are but parts of a whole. The dangers of insularity and the difficulties of securing co-ordination between committees are well known and many remedies and devices, formal and informal, have been propounded and tried.

The committee system itself can be moulded to assist co-ordination. The allocation of duties to committees can be so done that the

---

[1] Statistics collected in 1952 showed that in three counties the number of meetings to which a member was called in a year varied from thirty-one to eighty, and in three County Boroughs from sixty-one to ninety-one (Presidential Address of Mr J. Whittle to the Institute of Municipal Treasurers and Accountants Conference, June, 1952, pp. 107–8).

fewest possible problems of co-ordination are created, and membership can be so arranged that committees with related functions have common members who form a liaison. 'Functional' committees such as Finance, Establishment or Central Purchasing can be set up to carry out duties common to all services. These committees are to be contrasted with those set up to run the services of the authority and alluded to in this book as the 'operating' committees. Sometimes a single committee will combine two or more of these horizontal functions, e.g. combined finance and purchasing committees occur. 'Policy' committees to sift all major matters affecting more than one department, and to initiate changes in the administrative structure are also found in local government, though they are not as well known as they should be. On the other hand, 'general purposes' committees, sometimes confined to smaller matters common to more than one committee and sometimes with a much wider mandate, are in general use. Personal co-ordination by the mayor, the chairman or a leader, is frequently an important factor; and where a political party with a tight organization has a majority, a measure of policy co-ordination will take place within the party organization.

Most local authorities adopt some of these ways of counteracting the fragmentation to which the committee system tends. Complete integration can hardly be expected, but the best authorities have succeeded in overcoming many of the shortcomings of the local government administrative system, a result achieved as much by encouraging the right attitude in the members and officials as by the adoption of more formal means.

(6)

The dominant role played by committees, and the lack of an independent executive, are together responsible for another interesting feature—the absence of centralized management. The council, through its committees, holds the head of each department directly responsible for his department. They are not, as in other large-scale concerns, responsible to a general manager or central executive. A general manager might be able to work with a score or so of separate committees if they were concerned with policy formation only. But to have to deal with so many different committees, each of which interests itself so intensely in administrative detail, would be impracticable. The committee system and the tradition of direct responsibility of heads of departments to the council and its committees are thus interlocked. A related feature of English local government which is also important for the student of administration is the almost universal insistence on a technical qualification for heads of departments. Local authorities do not follow the practice prevailing in the central government of making the technical expert subordinate to an administrator. The technical officer must serve both as professional expert and as administrator. This holds in the Clerk's department (the Clerk usually being a lawyer), and in the finance department (the chief financial officer being usually an accountant), as much as in the operating departments—medical, engineering, education, etc. The arrangement works well in most cases because councils, when making the appointment of a chief officer, have regard to his administrative experience and ability. But there remains the potential danger of the professional man without administrative ability reaching the top. The absence of administrators as such, also accounts for the continued existence of a large number of separate departments. This is another distinguishing feature of our local government: if non-professional administrators were employed, there could be a grouping of departments.

(7)

If each department could function as a separate entity, the system would, from some points of view, be easier to work. The administration of local authorities however cannot be divided into separate water-tight departments: departmental functions overlap; initiative has to be taken on behalf of the local authority as a whole; there must be common legal, financial, architectural and engineering services; and finally there are many matters in which there must be uniformity of procedure among the departments. The need to make sure that the administration functions as a whole, instead of as a series of separate units, is the counterpart on the administrative level of the need for co-ordination at committee level which we have already considered.

The existence of two officers who serve all committees and all departments—the Clerk and chief financial officer—helps to secure co-ordination. The Clerk (of either town or county) is the council's senior officer; he advises the council and its committees on general matters, he is the official channel of communication between the council and the outer world, and he must shoulder the responsibility for seeing that arrangements for co-ordination of policy and efficient

21

organization exist and are continuously operated. The Clerk is also usually the council's legal adviser. Although he does not control the work of the departments, his responsibility is heavy, for the varied work of the local authorities and the nature of the administrative organization makes the task of co-ordination exceptionally intricate and delicate. The relationship of the Clerk with the other officers is as difficult to appraise as that between the committees and their officers: it depends on what H. J. Laski called 'the ability to compromise at pivotal points'. Whilst leaving intact the responsibility of the heads of departments for operational, technical and departmental efficiency, the Clerk must hold a watching brief for the council as a whole. The chief financial officer too exerts a co-ordinating influence on the administration. First in so far as he insists on uniformities of procedure in financial matters, and secondly because an integrated financial system, as is explained in the next chapter, encourages co-ordination in other spheres of the council's work.

The centralization of matters concerning the staff or staffing establishments of the various departments is another method of co-ordination. Nationally negotiated scales of pay and conditions of service have accelerated the movement towards centralization of establishment work within local authorities and, though many local authorities' arrangements are far from ideal, the best authorities are now regulating centrally the numbers and grades of staff, recruitment, training and interchangeability between departments. As an offshoot of establishment work, or independently, a growing number of local authorities employ an organization and methods officer whose services are available to all departments to advise on office procedures and the use of office equipment. Similarly central purchasing of goods which are used by more than one department and the supply of common services—duplicating, typing, printing and the like—help to break down departmental barriers as well as making economies possible. Unfortunately such arrangements are by no means general.

(8)

The main features of English local authorities, as they appear to students of administration, are, therefore, as follows. There is no separate executive, the council taking responsibility for both policy and the supervision of its execution. The council functions through committees of unpaid, elected members, advised by permanent officers, each committee having charge of some branch or branches of the council's work. The committees act as the channel through which business reaches the council, for the council itself initiates practically nothing. The committees control the administration and maintain a general oversight of the work of the paid officials. The permanent heads of departments are highly trained in the work of their departments rather than in administration generally, and are responsible to the council (through its committees) and not directly to the ratepayers.

Such a structure exhibits many characteristics of significance to those charged with the task of devising the administrative arrangements. The purpose of this section is briefly to set out those which appear to the author to be of particular importance to students of financial arrangements. They are:

(a) The danger of confusion between the role of the member and that of the officer.
(b) Diffuseness of purpose.
(c) Dispersion of responsibility.
(d) Departmentalism.
(e) A lack of independent criticism from within.

(a) *The danger of confusion between the role of the member and that of the officer*
The concentration in the council of responsibility for both policy and the supervision of its execution may induce members and officers to forget that their functions are distinct; policy is for the members, and administration for the officials, even though the members are ultimately accountable. If this distinction is forgotten, members tend to occupy themselves too much with detail, whilst officials are discouraged from taking responsibility. No small part of the variations in the quality of the administration in different areas can be attributed to the relative success or failure of members and officers in observing the correct dividing line. The financial procedures recommended in subsequent chapters for such purposes as making the budget, scrutinizing proposed new projects or selecting contractors, can work satisfactorily only if both members and officers understand the principles underlying the division of duties between them.

(b) *Diffuseness of purpose*
Within a local authority many influences combine to make concen-

tration of effort difficult. The duties laid upon local authorities by Parliament are many and varied, and their quality cannot be measured on a profitability basis like the activities of commercial concerns. Further, the members of the authority are drawn from many walks of life, are actuated by differing motives and approach their tasks in widely contrasted ways, thus making clashes of opinion and political divisions inevitable. Finally, the local authority conducts its business in public with the local electors ever at hand, watchful, critical and, in the last analysis, all-powerful. This affects the attitude of both members and officials who know that there is a risk of their smallest acts becoming local—or even national—news. For several reasons, therefore, it would be unreasonable to expect in town and county halls, the singleness of purpose displayed by a board of directors making broad decisions of policy behind closed doors.

(c) *Dispersion of responsibility*
English local government is essentially committee government, and some dispersion of the sense of responsibility is inevitable because the members of a corporate body tend not to feel their responsibility as keenly as an individual. There is the further danger that the council may cease to trust the committees, interfere with their business or arbitrarily discard their recommendations. Also, because members must account to the electors for the executive acts of officials, they are liable to operate the committee system in a way that relieves the administration of its proper obligations. Several influences thus combine in local government to reduce the sense of individual accountability, a feature which leaves its marks upon the administration. For instance, the best industrial practice is to place responsibility for each item of expenditure in the budget on the individual who will actually incur it, whilst local authorities are content to make the head of the department generally answerable.

(d) *Departmentalism*
Closely allied to the diffuseness of purpose and dispersion of responsibility is a fourth obstacle to a rational organization of local government financial administration: departmentalism. The slow acceptance of common services and functional committees which cut across departmental boundaries, has already been noted. The spirit of departmentalism has ever been at war with the idea of an integrated financial system. Local government has consequently suffered

from the erroneous notion that finance is a separate feature which is the business of the financial officer alone, a notion which financial officers themselves can so easily foster by a wrong emphasis on their own duties. Not a small part of the book will be concerned with ways, direct and indirect, in which the financial organization can be used to counteract departmentalism.

(e) *A lack of independent criticism from within*
Finally, the merging of responsibility for policy making and administration implies a lack of detached and impartial criticism from within. This little realized defect applies to many aspects of local government administration, but is specially noticeable in the financial sphere. To appraise results—financial or otherwise—there must be that independence of outlook and freedom from responsibility for detailed administration with which a board of directors can judge the work of its administration. To present to a committee of a local authority a report which could be construed as critical of the administration, is to criticize the committee itself, and to risk the resentment of members, who may be disinclined, because of the nature of their responsibility, to consider such criticisms impartially. Even if the members are able to overcome their natural reactions, it is well nigh impossible for them to discount the inevitable bias of one who has been a party to actions which are being appraised, or perhaps questioned. Thus officials, auditors and even outside consultants called upon to report can be easily deterred from plain speaking if they are not both zealous and fearless, and when they speak plainly they may be resented, misunderstood or ignored.

(9)

However effective it may be for its purpose, every form of organization has its shortcomings, and the purpose of the preceding pages has been to throw into relief the special problems which our English brand of local government offers to the administrator. The pages which are to follow discuss how these defects and disabilities can be overcome or circumvented in one branch of the local administration—that of finance. Already the emphasis has been upon the difficulties of local authorities, a tendency bound to persist throughout a book aimed at the improvement of local financial administration.

To leave an impression that English local government is inefficient or inferior to other types of organization, whether public or private,

25

would, however, be false. The English local government services themselves are generally acknowledged to be as good as any in the world. In local government techniques, too, English local authorities are in the forefront. Thus, to take an example from the financial field, budgeting and accounting methods in English local authorities have, generally speaking, been developed further than on the continent, and compare favourably with those adopted by our own central government. There are also some features of long standing in local government which have only relatively recently been developed in industry. Budgetary control, common services, intensive professional training, cultivation of public relations, formulation of a judicial rather than a personal touch, were cited as illustrations in a paper delivered to the Institute of Municipal Treasurers and Accountants.[1]

But, judged by the crispness of the administration or its costs, English local government does not come out of the test quite so well. For, as the reader will have suspected from the preceding pages, local councils are not always completely successful in surmounting their administrative handicaps. There is considerable room for improvement. It is this which should make worthwhile the attempt to consider critically but constructively the financial administration of local authorities and should justify—if justification is needed—a book upon the subject.

[1] See paper *The Financial Officer in the Public Service* by the late Alderman Arthur Collins delivered at the 64th Conference of the Institute of Municipal Treasurers and Accountants (1949).

CHAPTER II

THE PRINCIPLES OF FINANCIAL ADMINISTRATION

(1)

THE purpose of this chapter is first of all to expand the brief description of financial administration given in the preface, and then to explain the principles governing its organization. After an exposition of the basic idea around which the book has been written—that of integration of financial arrangements—the chapter proceeds to a study of the theoretical implications of this notion. Attention is then drawn to the incidental contribution of an integrated system of finance to the general administration of the authority, and a concluding note reminds the reader of the close connexion between finance itself and financial administration.

The propositions stated here in general terms are used in later chapters as the touchstone for deciding the working arrangements, and the reader who finds the concentrated matter of the chapter hard reading can seek comfort in the thought of the less exacting, simpler and more practical chapters to come.

(2)

Financial administration consists of three kinds of activity. The first and the most dynamic is the giving of financial advice. Members of the governing body must be kept continuously alive to their commitments; they must be encouraged to judge proposed expenditure in the light of resources and the merits of alternative schemes; they must not be allowed to become preoccupied with current problems to the exclusion of long term aims and plans; and they must not take decisions in the absence of unbiased advice about finance.

Secondly, management must be supplied with financial information in the most suitable form. All levels of management need information: the governing body in making policy and in judging to what extent their objectives have been attained; departmental heads in the control of operations; subordinate staff for guidance in their daily work. Each level of management needs its own kind of data: policy makers are concerned with broad measurements of past results and forecasts of the effects of future action; departmental heads want to know the current position of each part of their activities so that they can make any necessary adjustments, e.g. in the rate of expenditure; individual members of the staff must be told how they stand in comparison with their standards. The form of the information will vary according to the person for whom it is intended. Policy makers will expect complete reports with reasoned inferences, suggestions and advice about possible future courses of action; reports at this level will vary according to the nature of the subject matter. Reports to the departments, on the other hand, will generally be of a regular routine nature; here speed of preparation is of more importance than absolute accuracy, and the statements should be in such a form that they can be understood without explanatory details. Reports must also be exactly suited to the type of officer who is to study them. Thus, statements sent to the head of a department will differ in style from those supplied to a canteen supervisor or works foreman. Both those who prepare and those who use the statements must understand the purposes for which they are designed, the nature of the inferences which should be drawn from them and, in particular, the limitations of the data. As in other aspects of financial administration, the closest co-operation is therefore essential if the best use is to be made of the data. In the preparation of statements every possible measuring rod should be exploited to the full, and the utmost use should be made of the techniques of accounting and costing, some of which, such as standard costing, are as yet little developed in local government.

Another, and different, kind of financial information is that which appears in the final accounts. This information must be absolutely accurate and complete, for it is one of the media by which the elected body accounts to the public. Final accounts will be audited, and sometimes may be made the subject of enquiries, such as those conducted in the central government by the Public Accounts Committee. A subsequent chapter will however show that they are of limited use in financial control, being prepared *post mortem* and cast in terms of ultimate accountability rather than of day-to-day management.

The third aspect of financial administration is routine control. Its aim is to secure purity of administration. There must be machinery for ensuring that responsibilities are clearly defined, that financial duties are properly distributed, that expenditure is properly sanctioned, that outlays are wisely made, that collection of monies is carried out with diligence and honesty, that precautions for the custody of cash, the protection of property or financial interests are not overlooked. In short the financial administration must ensure regularity and enforce accountability.

(3)

In industry and commerce there has been in recent years a live interest in financial management. Stimulated by American practice English accountants have, since World War II, paid increased attention to 'Management Accountancy' by which is meant 'the application of accounting skill to problems of management';[1] or more fully '. . . a comprehensive scheme for reporting on all the activities of a concern in line with certain established budgets and standards to provide effective information at frequent and regular intervals for all levels of managerial and policy-making responsibility'.[2] This tendency implies not so much a revolution in accountancy techique as a growing awareness in modern business management of the value of accountancy records and of the distinctive role of the accountant, though naturally the methods of preparing information to assist the management in making decisions have at the same time improved.

In English government, both central and local, neither the idea of management accountancy nor the notion of the accountant or financial officer as the handmaid of the policy-forming body are new. Indeed the central government has always laid the emphasis on the financial control and on the accountability aspect of the work of their finance officers rather than on their duties as accountants, and the present author's 'Local Authorities: Internal Financial Control' contains sufficient evidence to show that the chief financial officer of a local authority has for years been regarded, except in backward authorities, as a financial adviser as well as an accountant. None the less, the ferment of ideas in industry, like the development of financial administration in the public boards, has lessons for local authorities. The most cursory examination of the methods of management accountancy brings to light shortcomings in local authority practice, such as too much reliance on final accounts, failure to use budgets fully to enforce individual responsibility and a tendency to allow departmentalism to prevent the full fruits of management accountancy from being reaped.

[1] Notes on *Management Accounting* issued by the Institute of Chartered Accountants, June 1954.

[2] *Management Accounting for Public Administration*, an address by Lawrence W. Robson reprinted in *Local Government Finance*, March 1954.

Differences in constitution, aims and organization, encourage administrators to discount the advantages of applying industrial methods to local authorities. Often there is justification for this reluctance. But in the case of financial administration it happens that industry has recently made considerable advances which local government cannot afford to ignore. In the formulation of principles, to which we now proceed, and in their working out in later chapters attention has therefore been paid to commercial methods.

(4)

Having discussed the nature and scope of financial administration, we must consider the guiding principle by which a local authority should order its financial arrangements. This principle will be alluded to throughout the book as that of integration. It will be briefly defined in this section, examined in more detail in the remaining sections of the chapter and it will form the unifying and connecting thread for all the remaining chapters. Many of the points dealt with generally in this chapter will recur later in a variety of practical applications.

According to the dictionary, to 'integrate' is to combine parts into a whole. The word has already been used in the preceding chapter, when discussing the difficulties of making local authorities with their many separate departments, each with its own ideology, work as one unit. It will be used in connexion with the financial organization of local authorities to mean:

(*a*) That at the policy-forming level finance is conceived not as a separate matter but as one of a number of aspects each of which must have proper consideration. A good financial administration is one which ensures that finance carries its due weight: no less, no more. Finance thus cannot be divorced and treated separately and the responsibility for financial consequences must go hand-in-hand with the making of policy.

(*b*) That a sense of financial responsibility is not something applicable only to the finance committee or finance department, or to those officers in an operating department specially charged with financial duties. Every member and every employee must feel financially accountable for his use of the authority's time or goods, or his responsibility—whether exalted or humble—for ordering materials, controlling labour or directing operations.

30

(c) That a single officer should be charged with the responsibility for the financial work, which should be conceived as one piece of machinery serving the whole of the authority and not a number of unco-ordinated units varying in aim and subject to different direction. The form of the accounting and other financial records, the clerical procedures, the methods of controlling income and expenditure, the principles upon which estimates are made or reports constructed—all these should be, as far as is appropriate, uniform throughout the authority and should be centrally supervised.

(d) Finally—but by no means least—that the financial organization is not an end in itself. It should therefore be closely woven into the administration of the authority and not remain on the outside as an extraneous influence, unsympathetic to the aims of the various services. Its aim should be to serve the departments, whilst preserving the independent outlook of the financial staff and their right to express their views on financial matters at the highest levels. Financial staffs should remember that their function is to advise, to suggest implications, to warn and to persuade, but not to dictate; for financial administration is part of a larger whole, and financial considerations are not necessarily paramount.

We now proceed to discuss some general considerations of financial administration which have to be borne in mind in applying the principle of financial integration to local authorities.

(5)

There is general agreement among writers on administration that the financial arrangements should not be operated to divest management of its responsibilities: financial factors are there merely to be weighed, together with others, by the policy makers; and the advice given by the financial officer, like the documents he prepares, is best regarded as a tool of management. In the title of the present book the words 'financial administration' appear in place of 'financial control' used in the author's earlier work. The word 'control' is apt to imply, at the best, a well-meant but probably misguided restraint exercised by an outside agency and, at the worst, irksome interference. Such impressions would be unfortunate in a treatise, the keynote of which is that the financial organs of local authorities, whether committees of elected members, or paid officials, should

31

serve rather than control. Financial administrative devices are not for discouraging initiative but for making sure that financial aspects are considered in their proper context.

Nevertheless control *is* an essential part of financial administration, especially in the public services where so much of the work is concerned with the allocations of public funds and the working of an inevitably elaborate system of safeguards to ensure that money is spent only on the authority of the elected body. Most of the expenditure on public services is met by taxation and—apart from ultimate economic limits—the expansion of the public services stops at the point where the supreme authority decides that taxation cannot be pushed further. Within the yield of taxes, the governing body has to allocate the total sum under its control on a basis which cannot be determined by formula but must be settled by more or less arbitrary decision. In both these respects, in the determination of the sums to be raised by taxation and in its allocation over the services, it is correct to speak of financial control.

Moreover, public funds being taken from the citizens compulsorily by taxation, accountability is of supreme importance. In business a subordinate has normally to account to the management in terms of profits; in public life his stewardship takes the form of answering for the expenditure of given sums of money on closely defined objects. In a private concern each management can determine for itself the extent of the precautions to be taken to ensure honesty, regularity and conscientious use of money and property. In government, whether central or local, because the monies and goods are held on trust for the public, the precautions must be more elaborate. They must not only be sound but their soundness must be capable of easy demonstration, if only because of the shock brought to public opinion by the lax use of goods and misapplication of funds. Devices unknown in commerce, such as the Public Accounts Committee, exist to foster in the central government a high standard of conduct on the part of officials, and to assure the public that shortcomings will be brought to light.

Therefore, though other more comprehensive and more positive aspects of financial administration make the title 'Internal Financial Control' unsuitable to cover the contents of this book, the special importance of the 'control' element in the financial administration of public authorities should not be overlooked.

(6)

The existence of the control element in financial administration, notwithstanding the current tendency to lay emphasis on the service aspects, must colour the financial arrangements. Some check on departments is essential in goverment, for those responsible for the services have every incentive to expand them, and at the same time are not subject to a profits incentive, or automatic test of efficiency. The Haldane Committee remarked, 'On the whole experience seems to show that the interest of the taxpayer cannot be left to the spending Departments'.[1]

Financial advice and control must therefore be unbiased, independent and firm. Attention has already been called to the danger of allowing the financial branch of an organization to have the last word. But finance has none the less a specialized function to perform. The finance department sees affairs in perspective and accumulates a wealth of experience to guide the management in making choices between alternative schemes or in gauging the validity of objectives. By long practice it can sense when things are out of scale, detect estimates which are too optimistic, prevent one department encroaching upon another, and often predict when the governing body is likely to call a halt. The independence of the financial administration must therefore be inviolate, and nothing is gained by disguising the fact that the task of the financial officer, however constructively it is done, is sometimes unpleasant and unpopular.

Unhappily the qualities needed for financial work—an independent impartial outlook, and prestige to ensure that sufficient weight is given to finance—tend to encourage aloofness: those engaged on finance can so easily become unhelpful and even ignorant of the business of their councils. In local government there is little danger of this with the elected members of finance committees who, so far from being exclusively concerned with finance, will almost always have an interest in the work of the authority; usually they will be active members of other committees and in any case, as members of the council, will be regularly adjudicating upon committee recommendations of all kinds. With the officials it can be otherwise: a chief financial officer and his staff may be discouraged, especially in a large authority, by the wide range of a local authority's work from making the effort needed to keep in touch with the aims,

[1] *Report of the Machinery of Government Committee, 1918.* Cmnd. 9230, p. 18.

activities and techniques of the services. Hence the need, which will be emphasized many times throughout this book, for the chief financial officer never to lose sight of the service aspects of his work.

(7)

A local authority will find its task of securing a balance between the control and service aspects of its finance department easier if there is a widespread sense of financial responsibility. The finance department does not directly spend monies, or control the use of goods or supplies. Though it may influence the governing body in determining policy and comparing the results with the plan, it cannot itself—except at second hand through audit and otherwise—ensure prudent housekeeping. This can be done only if every employee in every department who is concerned with the formulation of policy, the control of personnel, the expenditure of monies, or the use of goods is imbued with a desire to disburse public money wisely and economically. Therefore, when policy is to be formulated departments should be encouraged to work out the financial aspect of their proposals for themselves, leaving to the finance department the task of supplying technical information and advice, adding any independent comments needed, checking figures and verifying that no financial consideration has been omitted. When the time comes for the policy to be translated into action, every individual whose activities affect the public purse should be clothed with all the authority, provided with the tools, and stimulated with information necessary to enable him to be as zealous in protecting the ratepayer's financial interest as is the chairman of the finance committee himself.

Related to the need for a widespread sense of financial responsibility is the need for clear definition of individual responsibility. The doctrine that the departmental head is ultimately responsible for everything that happens in his department is sometimes allowed to obscure the necessity to define financial responsibilities lower down. Mr E. H. Davison in an article on 'The Accounts Organization in a large Industrial Concern' pointed out that only persons, not expenses can be controlled.[1] Statements of expenditure or costs which cannot be related to the responsibility of an individual are therefore of limited use as instruments of control. Enjoying by the very nature of their services only intangible means of gauging results, local authori-

[1] *The Accountant*, March 31, 1951.

ties might have been expected to be particularly careful in laying down the responsibilities of individuals, but in fact they are not. They are prone to depend over-much on the good sense of their officials and on traditions of co-operation which, though valuable and indeed indispensable, are not in themselves substitutes for a strict definition of responsibility and codification of procedure.

(8)

Critical observers have been known to represent English local government administration as a somewhat rickety structure in the hands of fumbling officials. This view has its origin in the difficulties of co-ordinating so many types of service without a central executive, rather than in any lack of faith in the competence or diligence of those responsible for individual services. Any administrative device which helps to bring cohesion has therefore indirect value in addition to its primary purpose. Accordingly this chapter would be incomplete without some discussion of the incidental advantages of an integrated financial organization to the local administration as a whole.

Obviously a good financial system will exert a direct influence towards rationalization by bringing deficiencies in the local administration to the notice of members. Thus a central system of scrutiny of bills for payment may well draw attention to the need for better purchasing arrangements; examination of transport costs may emphasize the need for standardizing of types of vehicles; and variations in the costs of repair and maintenance of buildings may show the desirability of the departments making better use of the specialized skill of engineers or architects.

The indirect influences of an integrated financial system are perhaps even more important. It will, for instance, spread the habit of co-operation, for if so many committees, departments and officials come together to discuss financial matters, and become accustomed to uniform financial procedure, they will be more willing to do the same in other branches of local government. A first step will have been taken towards the evolution of that corporate spirit without which no local authority can function as a unit. But it is unlikely that this will be all, for committees enjoying the advantages of joint financial reports will look to joint reports on other matters. Further, having come to expect uniform presentation of financial data they will all the more readily accept other co-ordinating measures—

35

central purchasing, central printing, etc.—and activities embracing the whole of the authority such as those of establishment officers and organization and methods officers. The institution of such arrangements is often preceded by bitter departmental opposition to the inroads into departmental sovereignty, and all too often followed by a period of perfunctory acceptance. Once unification is established in the pervasive sphere of finance the way is paved for further instalments. There is, of course, no reason why the tidying of financial administration should come first, though in practice it has usually done so, the initial struggle for reform having fallen mainly upon the chief financial officer. Chief financial officers as a class have had little credit for their efforts over the last forty years to secure co-ordination, though they may console themselves with the knowledge that integration of financial arrangements is so often followed by integration of other kinds.

The existence of one financial adviser for all committees also helps to break down that curious tendency for each committee to evolve a corporate spirit of its own, and to go its own way regardless of the others, an attitude responsible for not a little bickering in local councils. For instance, a committee's worst instincts are roused over inter-committee transactions, especially over the amounts to be 'paid' for services rendered by one committee to another, a matter which to the ratepayers often means little more than a transference of money from one pocket to another. To committees such matters are apt to appear to be vital, the classic instance being of a town which went to the length of calling in an outside financial adviser to settle the amount to be transferred from the tramways committee to the highways committee in respect of the cost of abandoning the tramway tracks. One likes to think that if this town had enjoyed an integrated system of finance it would hardly have gone so far.

It is hardly necessary to enlarge on the advantages to inter-departmental relations of making sure that, at least in one important aspect of administration, officers are working closely together on a common plan: a greater understanding and tolerance of other people's work can hardly fail to follow, whilst the burden of the work of the Clerk of the authority is eased.

Co-ordination of financial work is thus something more than a means of carrying out financial tasks more efficiently and more economically: it is a way of counteracting the inevitable weaknesses of an organization with such varied tasks and no central executive.

(9)

Our concern is not with the finances of local authorities but with financial administration. The two are, however, connected: indeed the need for a specialized branch of the administration whose sole duty it is to think of finance, is a direct consequence of the growing complexities of finance itself. No longer does the light of nature suffice. The amount spent by government, central and local, serves to emphasize the need for financial control and scrutiny, and the importance of the subjects discussed in these pages.

'The art of finance ranks, in my view, with (*a*) the art of selecting the right men and handling them properly and (*b*) the art of public relations in the widest sense. It is finance which acts as midwife at the birth of an enterprise, which watches over its health during maturity, and which sounds the warning knell when decay sets in; it is finance which often forces the final dissolution; throughout the life of the enterprise its shape is fundamentally influenced by decisions which are largely financial . . . Finance can often be made into a greater and more effective disciplinary force than any administration "Diktat" and it has the merits of being less obvious and less offensive . . . A green bay tree may flourish for a long time but it does not last for ever. Everything has to be paid for in the end, and if the principles of finance and of financial management grind slowly, they also grind small enough to reduce to dust, eventually, any public administration which persistently ignores them.'[1]

The value of finance as a discipline, and the importance of financial integrity, could hardly be more eloquently or thoughtfully set out than in these remarks by Sir Reginald Wilson.

---

[1] Extract from *Passenger Transport*, a paper delivered by Sir Reginald Wilson, Member of the British Transport Commission, at the conference on *The Place of Finance in Public Administration* held by the Institute of Municipal Treasurers and Accountants at Balliol College, Oxford, March 1954, and published by the Institute, pp. 46–7.

37

CHAPTER III

THE FINANCE COMMITTEE

(1)

A LOCAL authority needs two specialized internal financial organs: a finance committee consisting of members of the authority and a chief financial officer. The latter is dealt with in the chapters immediately following; this chapter is concerned with the finance committee and its chairman.

English county councils and metropolitan borough councils are required by statute to appoint a finance committee for 'regulating and controlling the finances' of the authority. In the case of the vast majority of authorities—including all provincial urban authorities—the appointment of a finance committee is optional, but finance committees, if appointed, cannot include co-opted members. All Scottish local authorities, however, must appoint a finance committee charged with the tasks of advising the council on financial matters and of supervising the financial arrangements of the authority.

Whether statutory or not, finance committees are well nigh universal in all types of authority, and the belief in their indispensability is so strong that for many years there was persistent pressure for the appointment of finance committees to be made compulsory by statute. This pressure bore fruit when the Local Government (Scotland) Act, 1947, made finance committees compulsory in Scotland. In England the demand for statutory finance committees seems to have died down: presumably their advocates have been influenced by the Manpower Committee's recommendations in favour of leaving local authorities to decide for themselves the distribution and the grouping of services for the purposes of the appointment of committees.[1]

(2)

As has been made plain in the introductory chapters, a local authority is an assemblage of quasi-independent committees coming together only at the very highest level, the council itself; a body which meets

[1] *Second Report of the Local Government Manpower Committee.* Cmnd. 8421. December 1951, pp. 36–7.

in public and is for the most part a debating chamber unsuited to the task of co-ordination. For this reason there have come into existence those 'functional' committees mentioned in the first chapter which cut across the vertical organization by insisting on uniformities of practice and by reviewing—at times even regulating—aspects of the work of operating committees. Inevitably, horizontal contrivances of this kind complicate the administrative machinery, restrict the freedom of committees and, however well-conducted the local authority's business may be, bring occasional irritation or friction. Local authorities have therefore to satisfy themselves that the blessings outweigh the more roundabout processes of administration. What then is the case for the finance committee, the most common of co-ordinating devices?

At the outset one must note its distinctive character. Other functional committees are set up either to ensure standardized practice in such matters as rates of pay and conditions of appointment, or else to provide services such as central purchasing. Whilst a finance committee also promotes uniformity and provides a common service, the main reason for its existence is of a different and more imperative kind, springing from the very nature of a local authority as a taxing body maintaining a number of different activities. Each claimant committee can show the desirability of spending ever increasing sums upon the services under its control. Seldom will there be a profit and loss test and the council—the supreme governing body—has the task of weighing one marginal benefit against another. A small discriminating, impartial, influential and well informed group from among the members must examine the evidence and make recommendations to the council; for such complex, controversial and intangible matters cannot be sifted in an open debating chamber, though they have ultimately to be decided there. The first and most cogent reason for the existence of a finance committee is, therefore, that a local authority must have a body to consider its finances as a whole, to weigh the merits of one scheme against another, to arrange priorities and to advise on the level of local taxation.

There is in local government, as in central government, what Lord Bridges called an 'inevitable dualism'. Whilst committees and departments desire and plan, they can proceed only to the extent that they can persuade the council (advised by the finance committee) to provide the money.[1] A department and committee urging a scheme

[1] See *The Place of Finance in Public Administration* (Institute of Municipal Treasurers and Accountants, 1954), p. 19.

upon the council have not the responsibility of suggesting how the money shall be provided and, unlike their counterparts in productive industry, they can rarely bring forward self-supporting schemes. Some other branch of the administration—in practice the finance committee—has to see its way to recommend the governing body to provide the money by taxation. Indeed a committee advocating new expenditure has often in effect to persuade the finance committee and ultimately the council to prefer its scheme to others which may well be equally worthy. To counter the effects on morale of this dualism—the divorce of responsibility for getting money and spending it is one of the chief tasks of financial administration.

A strong finance committee is also the only way of ensuring that, at all stages in formulating and reaching decisions, adequate attention has been given to finance. Operating committees are apt to let zeal run away with them and their major recommendations need to be passed through the sieve of a specialized committee.

The other reasons for the existence of a finance committee are more obvious. One is the existence of purely financial work—raising loans, collecting monies, managing reserve, renewals and insurance funds, arranging insurances and the like—which of itself warrants a specialized committee. Then there is need for continuous oversight of the finances and financial machinery: examining the financial position of the council, comparing financial performances with the budget, devising and supervising the financial administration including the financial records and arrangements for the receipt and payment of monies. If a single committee is not charged with this responsibility, the local authority cannot make full use of accounting techniques and appliances, and cannot have those uniformities of financial practice so difficult to attain, yet so necessary if wasted effort and public criticism are to be avoided. Nor is the authority likely to employ those devices of management accounting—so much improved in recent years—designed to ensure that every level of management is supplied with appropriate information.

Finally, an alert finance committee is the best way of making sure that a permanent watch is kept on the opportunities for economies and improvements. No finance committee worthy of the name will be satisfied until the council is making the most of the economies of such central purchasing and common departmental services as are appropriate to the size of the authority. Local government has no counterpart to the Estimates Committee of the House of Commons or to the Public Accounts Committee. The finance committee, as the only organ at member level charged with the oversight of financial matters, can therefore reasonably claim a wide mandate from the council.

These reasons for the existence of finance committees are not invalidated by the temporary allocation upon occasion to another committee of some of the functions normally falling to the finance committee, e.g. in times of economic stress a council may appoint an *ad hoc* economy committee or, if labour and materials are in short supply, a committee to decide priorities of capital expenditure. All that has happened is that some aspect of financial work has become so important, so controversial or so much in the public eye that the council has deemed it desirable to establish a special means of dealing with acute temporary difficulties or problems. When the crisis is over the duties revert to the finance committee, the permanent watchdog of finance.

(3)

Judged by continental standards, committees of English local authorities are large, and finance committees are no exception, the majority having between ten and twenty members. In a few instances all the members of the council serve upon the committee, a tribute to its importance in the eyes of the members.

A very small committee would be a mistake, for the finance committee needs to reflect the opinions of the members of the council and to be sufficiently sure that, save on the exceptional occasion, its acts will be approved by the council. A finance committee regularly defeated on the floor of the council chamber would soon carry little weight, and one without a wide knowledge of, and sympathy with, the services of the authority would be seriously hampered when making recommendations about the allocation of the rate or the arrangement of priorities. Any committee whose prestige depends on the acceptance by the council of its recommendations must have a sufficient membership for the committee's views to permeate the council. Moreover the judgment of the members must be based on knowledge, and it must be manifest to all that this is so : the members should, therefore, collectively have first-hand experience of the major services.

What should be the qualification of members? Do accountants and stockbrokers make a better contribution than members without specialized knowledge? Certainly the specialist can make a unique contribution for he can apply professional experience and a readier understanding of financial problems. But he may also bring limitations; for example, he may find it more difficult than the layman to rid himself of preconceived notions about financial matters, and he may suffer from a tendency to go beyond the function of the elected member into that of the paid official, thus antagonizing both the official and the other members who may be fearful of his acquiring too great an influence. In short he may not be able to bring to bear that distinctive layman's judgment which is the essence of the contribution of the member. Nevertheless, on balance, the specialized contribution of an accountant is found to be valuable, and often the membership of the finance committee includes the accountants on the council. For the rest, there is every possible method of selection. In some authorities membership of the finance committee is a prized position, liable to be awarded mostly on seniority. In others great weight is given to the predilections of the members; the committee then tends to comprise those who have a bent for the subject. In most cases at least a sprinkling of the most influential members is put on the committee to ensure that it carries conviction with the council.

A practice more common than one might suppose is to have a finance committee composed of the chairmen of the other most important committees. This simple method has one supreme advantage: the committee cannot act in ignorance of the work of the authority. It is moreover useful to have all the chairmen kept abreast of the financial position of the authority, and helpful from the point of view of the chairman of the finance committee to make them responsible, through their membership of the committee, for unpalatable recommendations such as reductions in estimates. There is ample evidence that the system is in successful operation in many local authorities. Nevertheless it has important disadvantages: it encourages log-rolling; it may exclude able and suitable members who do not happen to be chairmen; and it may include some with little aptitude for finance.

At the opposite pole is an authority where the chairmen are *forbidden* to belong to the finance committee. This certainly prevents log-rolling, but has all those disadvantages associated with the automatic exclusion of what are presumably the most able members of the council, some of whom will have in addition a flair for financial matters. It seems a pity for the council to lose their services in the capacity of finance committee members.

A finance committee composed of all the members of the council is still more difficult to defend. It is cumbrous, it suffers from a diffusion of responsibility and it can hardly be a committee in which opinions are freely and easily exchanged, but rather a meeting which members 'address'. So large a body cannot be called together in a hurry to meet emergencies, and would be much too unwieldy for such purposes as sifting a budget. What happens usually is that there is a sub-committee carrying out many of the normal functions of the committee. The full meeting then becomes a way of allowing all the members of the council to discuss financial matters in the freer atmosphere of committee procedure, and probably in private. If one regards it as necessary for all the members of the council to have such an opportunity, then there is something to be said for the method.

There probably is no 'best' method of constituting a finance committee but the foregoing brief description of the chief methods in vogue and their pros and cons does suggest a few tentative generalizations. Successful participation in financial administration calls for a combination of qualities—a certain austerity of outlook combined with a deep understanding of the affairs of the authority, a capacity to stand back and look at the picture as a whole, discretion, firmness, willingness to face unpopularity and an absence of undue leanings towards particular services. Surely, therefore, personal sympathies, qualities and aptitude should play a large part in the selection.

There are likely to be on every council some members who have little interest in finance, and some who find it distasteful to have to take even that general interest in the subject expected of every conscientious member of the council. Such members—though they cannot divest themselves of their share of responsibility for finance as members of the local authority—are not likely to make an effective contribution to a committee whose sole function is finance, and whatever the system of selection it should be designed to exclude them. Any method of selection which automatically includes a particular class of councillors, e.g. chairmen of committees, offends against the principle that weight should be attached to personal qualities; it should not, therefore, be condoned. In a well regulated authority a committee should not need direct representation on the finance committee to ensure fair treatment. There are other ways of ensuring that the finance committee does not act in ignorance, e.g. by a regulation that a committee unrepresented on the finance committee may send a representative when questions concerning that particular

43

committee are under consideration. Much the same result can also be achieved by informal discussion between chairmen.

On the other hand there will be members with a taste for the work of the finance committee. This attraction may spring from a number of causes—a liking for figures, a desire to be associated with the determination of priorities, specialized training, or even just an appreciation of the importance and significance of the work. Such members should be given an opportunity to serve.

There is no easy formula for making a finance committee representative of the experience of members. Indeed it never can be completely representative. But it should at least have among its members those who specialize on the social services as well as those whose main interest is in the business enterprises, and it should include younger as well as older members. It must appreciate, if it cannot reflect, all shades of opinion on the council.

A finance committee, as has been noted earlier, must carry the council with it on all but the exceptional matters. Otherwise, not only will the council lose the advantages of having a mechanism for sifting the financial aspects of its business, but in addition the members of the committee will not feel a proper sense of responsibility. They will tend to shirk decisions on controversial questions, knowing that the council may not adopt their recommendations.

Powerful, influential members of the council, able to lead the council in financial matters, must therefore serve upon the finance committee. For this reason local authorities may make the chairman of the council automatically the chairman of the committee or may put the party leaders on the committee, whilst most committees have persuasive members who have specialized for many years on finance and whose opinions are widely respected.

To be avoided almost above all other types are the log-rollers and those who cannot resist the temptation to use their power as members of the committee to advance their pet projects, for such persons— who often make excellent members of the council in other respects —are constitutionally incapable of forming those dispassionate judgments which are the very essence of finance committee work.

(4)

In so far as the finance committee is concerned with business exclusively financial, e.g. the raising of capital monies, its relation to the council is identical with that of the operating committee. Its position on matters where finance is one aspect of a larger issue, other committees being also concerned, is not so easy to determine with exactness. In pure theory the role of the committee is not to usurp the powers of the council but to comment from the financial point of view on all major projects, changes of policy and so forth, theoretically leaving to the council the task of weighing the pros and cons. On proposed new expenditure, for instance, the council has to decide, before involving the ratepayers in extra expense, that the benefit of the additional service justifies the extra financial burden. This decision is the prerogative of the council. Finance committees, therefore, should refrain from expressing opinions about the merits of schemes, but should confine themselves to comments upon the council's capacity to afford them and to observations upon the economic aspects. It would, for example, be proper for the finance committee to draw attention to what they deemed to be extravagant planning of a project, or a failure to make proper charges for services rendered, but wrong for them to comment upon the architectural quality of a building or the design of a sewerage system. Some writers think it so important for finance committees to dissociate themselves from questions of desirability that they do not advocate the attendance of representatives of operating committees at meetings of the finance committee when their projects are under discussion. Their presence is thought to encourage the finance committee to stray from the field of finance into that of the merits of the proposals. Wise finance committees keep as near to pure finance as they can, carefully refraining from giving opportunities for their actions to be construed as meddling with other people's affairs.

But in practice the pure milk of the theory becomes watered down, first because the distinction between financial considerations and others, and hence the line of demarcation between the finance and other committees, is not always clear, and secondly because there are important occasions when the finance committee can hardly refrain from expressing, if only by implication, judgment on desirability as well as on financial feasibility. Whenever the finance committee recommends an order of priority, or suggests what rate should be levied or how it should be allocated, it is, in effect, exercising a judgment on relative merits if not on absolute merits. There is of course no escape from this position, for, as has already been explained, there comes a stage at which some group smaller in size than the council must sift complicated proposals and conflicting claims and make firm recommendations, the council itself being much too unwieldy a body for the task. Even so, the finance committee should recognize that the less it becomes involved in the merits of schemes, the better. Thus it would, for example, when suggesting 'cuts' in estimates, leave the individual committees to decide where the axe can be least painfully employed, a theme which is developed in a later chapter.

In fact finance committees exercise to some degree all four of the different levels of treasury control as they have been recently defined: (a) playing a part in deciding the total amount of expenditure; (b) securing a proper balance of expenditure between services; (c) helping to determine the total expenditure on individual policies and services; and (d) making sure that there is a proper balance within services.[1]

The impossibility of laying down with strictness the limitations of a finance committee's responsibility offers difficulties both to the student seeking to explain the working of English local government and to the administrator looking for a proper working relationship between a particular council and its committees. But, like so many things English, finance committees in the main work happily notwithstanding a certain vagueness in their position. Presumably finance committees are normally discreet and careful, and operating committees tolerant and conscious that the dualism discussed earlier in the chapter must inevitably involve some abrogation of their sovereignty.

In appraising the position of the finance committee as the adviser of the council on priorities, regard must be had to a post-war trend which has added materially to its difficulties—the alterations of the pace of local expenditure at the behest of the central government. Revenue expenditure of governments, both central and local, has always been liable to retrenchment in times of economic crisis. For instance, the two decades before the war produced two 'economy' committees: the May committee[2] and the Ray committee.[3] But the post-war period has seen the governments of the world assume a much wider responsibility for economic well-being and for the rate of spending on capital and revenue accounts by both public authorities and private concerns. In the United Kingdom the new era was ushered in by the White Paper on Employment Policy.[4] Public expenditure is now liable to fluctuate not only in times of crises, but

---

[1] See *Sixth Report from the Select Committee on Estimates, 1957–58*. Cmnd. 254, pp. VI and VII.
[2] Cmnd. 3920, 1931.   [3] Cmnd. 4200, 1932.   [4] Cmnd. 6527, 1944.

also to correct maladjustments in the national economy, even though they may be marginal. It may well be, therefore, that the task of reviewing the expenditure of a local authority as a whole to conform with current government economic policy will have to be performed more frequently in the future, and will depend upon the state of the national economy rather than that of the locality. Finance committees are in the future likely to have frequent recurrences of the delicate task of suggesting ways of gearing the local machine to the current pace of that of the nation. Expansion and contraction of expenditure for reasons extraneous to the local authority are never popular with those engaged in local government. Administratively tiresome and politically embarrassing, they make planned development difficult. A proper attitude on the part of the council, forbearance on the part of the operating committee, and the utmost wisdom on the part of the finance committee are desirable if the local services are not to be discomfited, perhaps even thrown out of gear, by these periodic exercises.

(5)

One principle governing the relationship of the finance committee to the operating committees, overshadows all others; the finance committee must aim at reinforcing their sense of financial responsibility, not reducing it. It should take into its hands, apart from exclusively financial duties, only functions which an operating committee cannot carry out, i.e. those concerned with a general oversight in the light of the financial position of the authority as a whole. Each committee must feel the full financial responsibility for its own operations and must have access to all the information about its functions. The documents which are peculiar to the finance committee are merely those which transcend the finances of a particular department. It is for this reason that later in this book a system of reports is recommended which ensures that the documents supplied to the finance committee are, in the main, those which the operating committees have already had.

As much financial discretion as possible should be left with the committees. Watching the progress of expenditure against budgets, controlling the costs of plant and vehicles, fixing charges to be made for services rendered, regulating stocks of materials, even writing off bad debts —all these matters should be within their prerogative, subject to any necessary review or general direction of the finance committee.

47

To promote co-operation between operating committees and the finance committee, the standing orders of the council should provide for joint conferences in extreme cases and for the interchange of views through the chairmen in day-to-day transactions. Thus, the practice of allowing the chairman of a controlling committee to attend meetings of the finance committee to explain his committee's projects is sound; so is that of giving the chairman of the finance committee the right to attend other committees to put the financial point of view, either on specified occasions, e.g. when the budget is being considered, or, as is the case with some authorities, on any appropriate occasion. For harmonious co-operation and understanding, the chief financial officer must be in close touch with all the committees and must take scrupulous care that he gives to operating committees all the information he will give later to the finance committee.

There used to be much discussion whether the Local Government Act, 1888, gave the finance committee in counties a power to 'veto' expenditure. Whether the finance committee of a county legally possessed a power of veto or not was really of little importance, because there has been for many years general acceptance of the supremacy of the council. In practice finance committees do not claim power to prevent other committees bringing to the council propositions of which they disapprove. Every local authority therefore needs arrangements to regulate disagreements between the finance committee and other committees. A disputed proposition will be decided by the council after hearing the views of both committees. Many local authorities provide in their standing orders as much encouragement as possible for differences of opinion to be resolved before they reach the council. For instance, the finance committee may be given power to refer a proposal back to the operating committee for reconsideration. If the latter persists in its attitude, and if no compromise can be reached, then the dispute must go forward to the council for determination.[1]

[1] It is interesting to note that a power of veto has been successfully operated by the finance committee of Johannesburg for fifty years. 'The system has worked well, mainly because the council has been fortunate in having suitably qualified and experienced members from which to constitute its finance committee, particularly its chairman, and because there has been, on balance, co-operation and goodwill between the finance and other committees.' One of the most valuable features of the veto system is the opportunity for further consideration, the views of both committees being fully sifted before the proposals are either abandoned or re-submitted in an amended form to the finance committee. 'In practice, the

(6)

Descriptions of the part played by the finance committee in individual aspects of financial administration will be found scattered throughout the various chapters of this book, and the chapter on internal rules calls attention to those aspects of its work which need formal regulation. The position in any individual authority will be partly governed by the extent of delegation of day-to-day business to committees: precise prescriptions in either this chapter or later chapters would be impracticable. The purpose of this section is broadly to summarize the principal duties of the committee in the light of the preceding discussion.

Every finance committee should be specifically charged with the task of supervising the finances and financial administration of the authority. To this end it should be given adequate power of supervision, of representation and of reporting default to the council. The finance committee must make the council aware of its financial position and of the extent to which financial aims have been achieved. In short it must make sure that the council has all the data and advice appropriate to the top level of management. It must have power to comment upon all proposed actions involving finance and to appraise the financial results of all branches of the council's activities. Upon it falls the duty of collating the annual rate estimates, presenting them to the council with recommendations, and sifting all proposed additional or new expenditure outside the budget. It must be responsible for the exclusively financial work including the raising of capital monies, the management of funds, the supervision of the financial records, the making of payments, the collection of monies, internal audit, the management of insurances and so forth.

(7)

The finance committee, being a horizontal or functional committee whose work is mostly that of reviewing or commenting upon the projects initiated by other committees, has to guard against the

effect of the veto system is that items which are not viewed favourably by the finance committee are not rejected out of hand, but are referred back to the committees concerned for further consideration. Only in exceptional cases is it necessary to apply the veto.'

See I. Q. Holmes, *Local Government Finance in South Africa* (Butterworth, 1949), pp. 202-3.

danger of becoming a delaying mechanism. An operating committee naturally expects its proposals to come before the next council meeting. Most finance committees, therefore, meet in the interval between the end of a cycle of committee meetings and the meeting of the full council. Normally this means a monthly or quarterly meeting of the finance committee. Such a meeting lasting perhaps for an hour or two implies a very limited time for discussion and, if the committee is to carry satisfactorily its responsibilities, its business must be conducted in a manner calculated to make the best possible use of the time.

How can this be achieved? The answer lies in the realization that the meetings of the finance committee correspond to a meeting of directors devoted to financial matters. The documents and data should therefore correspond to those which directors are accustomed to receive, i.e. those which relate to the big issues—condensed statements summarizing the council's financial position, reports setting out the financial effects of new proposals and calling attention to any serious failures in financial performances. Purely financial matters—loans, funds, etc.—should be put before the committee in succinct form, preferably in a short report. The main part of its work will however be to adjudicate on the proposals of other committees, the committee relying on the same data as was submitted to originating committees. The committee can justifiably expect the chairmen and officers of such committees to be available to substantiate important proposals, but should be careful not to antagonize chairmen by requiring their attendance for trivial matters or for proposals which might reasonably be accepted without question.

A committee should never allow masses of information which it cannot possibly scrutinize to be prepared month by month. Finance lends itself with fatal readiness to the preparation of statistics, and the documents submitted to finance committees are often heavy with indigestible figures. Superfluous statements have a demoralizing effect on the staff, who know full well that they are not looked at, and naturally resent the waste of time spent in their preparation—an attitude which soon spreads towards other and more important work. The effect on the members is equally bad. Every statement presented to a committee should contain only information so important that it cannot be disregarded.

(8)

In most local authorities there will be from time to time urgent financial matters which cannot await a monthly or quarterly meeting: money is needed for emergency expenditure, superannuation or renewal funds must be invested and the terms to be offered to lenders must be settled. How can such business be dealt with? The common method of referring urgent matters to the chairman is not always appropriate because of the importance of the business. One method is to have meetings of the full committee more often than monthly or quarterly, e.g. fortnightly. A more common practice is to have a sub-committee, which can be quickly called together. Some authorities have a regular finance sub-committee which, in addition to coping with the emergency work, examines payments and follows up queries in the way described later in the chapter on the payment of accounts. This practice has much to commend it, for it assures the automatic availability each week of a sub-committee to which the officers can turn for instructions.

Some authorities make even greater use of finance sub-committees, allowing them to deal on behalf of the full committee with minor problems of many kinds. Thus they may examine costs of direct labour work or enquire into discrepancies between local costs and those of other authorities. Sub-committees may even be used to sift the proposals coming before the full committees or to make special investigations. If a sub-committee is to be effective, the main committee, whilst retaining the right to revise its work, must resist the temptation, save on the exceptional occasion, to traverse the whole of the ground again.

The author's experience is that a finance sub-committee carrying out the kind of tasks referred to above is a useful link in the financial organization. It exerts a salutary influence on committees and departments, and is a small body meeting regularly and conducting its business in as informal a way as possible, so that its members come to know the financial organization of the departments and the staff who deal with finance. If the system of departmental finance officers described later in the book is in operation, the members of the finance sub-committee become closely acquainted with them, for it is of the essence of a proper financial system that these officers should attend personally to deal with routine questions of financial organization. Attendance at the meetings of the finance sub-committee is in fact one of the ways in which departmental finance officers develop a loyalty to the council's financial system as a whole.

(9)

This chapter concludes with a short description of one of the most vital links in the chain of financial administration—the chairman of the finance committee. We noted in the first chapter that the position of chairman of *any* major committee of an English local authority is one of very considerable responsibility.[1] He has to act as the link between the department and the committee, and between the committee and the council: he will also have to defend the committee before the public. A good chairman will keep in close touch with the chief officer of the department, making a point of discussing with him business coming before the committee, and therefore attending meetings with a marked advantage over other members. He can guide discussion by his power to intervene at any time, call on speakers, sum up debates and so forth. He thus exercises a great influence on the decisions. His potential for good is enormous and so also is his power for doing harm. The latter may spring from incompetence, weakness (allowing himself to be 'run' by either the committee or the officers) or autocracy, when he may come to regard himself as the committee, brooking no opposition, stifling discussion and even keeping matters away from the committee. Mr Wheare thinks that one of the gravest dangers is that of his becoming a 'mere echo or a sworn companion-in-arms of the officials', which as he says is 'treason to the whole idea of government by committee'.[2] A chairman who can strike the right note in his relationships with the officials makes a positive contribution to the solution of one of the central problems of local government administration. On this point Dr R. M. Jackson says:

'A committee chairman must always remember two things. The first is that officials have no right to speak in meetings, and therefore they cannot answer back if they are attacked: the chairman *must* protect them against abuse and provide an opportunity for them to reply on matters of substance. The second is that the maintenance of good personal relationships is a continuing process, calling for tact and sympathy as well as for firm leadership.'[3]

[1] For an illuminating discussion on the role of the Chairman see K. C. Wheare's *Government by Committee*, pp. 36–42 and 179–84.

[2] *Op. cit.*, p. 182.   [3] R. M. Jackson, *The Machinery of Local Government*, p. 77.

Important though other chairmanships are, that of the finance committee has a very special significance for, whilst the effect of an unsuitable chairman of an operating committee is felt in a single part of the council's work, the failings of a weak or an incompetent finance chairman can prejudice the whole of the council's administration. The chairman's influence at budget time will usually be decisive, and during the year he will constantly be asked to pass judgment on affairs affecting many departments and services. That he should have sympathy, knowledge, firmness and impartiality hardly needs to be stressed, for the potential dangers of a chairman who cannot hold the balance between departments are self-evident. He also needs natural ability for explaining the intricacies of finance in simple terms. The official's task of producing and explaining a document at committee is one thing: that of the chairman, speaking in open council, subject to interruptions and hostile comments is another. Less obvious, but equally important, is the need for discretion, for in the course of the years the chairman of the finance committee will have to deal with confidential reports on cases of suspected irregularity, preliminary negotiations in respect of forthcoming stock issues and other matters which for the time being at any rate are confidential. There will also be times when the chairman of the finance committee has to deal with breaches of financial regulations by departments or committees who have proved resistant to administrative action, tasks which he has to try to carry out without antagonizing committees or departments. The references to the chairman of the finance committee in other chapters of this book attest his importance in financial administration and serve as a reminder that this chapter has been confined to a general description of his position.

The chairman's relations with the chief financial officer are governed by well-understood traditions, but they are none the less difficult to describe, for in no two authorities will they be exactly the same. The relationship cannot help but be close for the chief financial officer has to acquaint his chairman with the general trend of the finances of the authority, call his attention to breaches of the council's financial regulations and seek his approval for the dispatch of urgent business. But, because the chairman has the whole of the activities of the council for his province, he will not wish to be worried with the domestic problems of the finance department, nor with the more trivial of the authority's financial problems. The success of the relationship between the two will largely depend on the chairman's willingness to leave the details to the chief financial officer, and the ability of the latter to present major matters to the chairman in tabloid form. If chairman and chief officer are of the same cast of mind so much the better, but observance of the traditional line of demarcation between the roles of member and officer should make the relationship workable and effective whatever the differences in their outlook and predilections.

How should the chairman of the finance committee be selected? The method of selection by seniority hardly seems appropriate because of the responsibilities of the position and the influence he must wield if he is to succeed. He must be a leading member of the council if he is to be heeded, and for this reason chairmen of finance committees should be chosen for their personal qualities rather than on grounds of seniority. In some authorities the chairman of the council is by tradition also the chairman of the finance committee, a practice which has many disadvantages, but it does at least guarantee, save in exceptional cases, that the chairman of the finance committee will be influential.

Whilst the chairmanship of committees is an annual affair, reelection is common. Should a finance committee chairman hold office for a limited period—say three or four years? Should the office be a virtual freehold? Or is some intermediate course desirable? The relative merits of short and long chairmanships are the subject of perennial debate in local government and cannot be fully discussed here. Obviously long chairmanships make for greater knowledge and smoother working, and enable the services of exceptional members to be retained; on the other hand they tend to frustrate other aspirants, and they encourage autocracy. Each council has to strike for itself the balance between these advantages and disadvantages. It may well be, however, that a special case could be made out for not too frequent changes in the chairmanship of the finance committee. There should surely be at least some continuity in a post which demands a working knowledge of the whole of the council's services and a grasp of intricate financial matters. A three year tenure, with possibility of renewal, has much to commend it.

In conclusion the reader is reminded that in Scotland the legislature has seen fit to prescribe certain statutory duties for the chairman of the finance committee in addition to laying down the main responsibilities of the committee. These provisions are set out in detail in Appendix B. Briefly the Act provides that the chairman shall be appointed to the office of 'honorary treasurer' and must, subject to the directions of the council, exercise general superintendence over the finances of the council. The intention is not to create a new relationship between the chairman of the finance committee and the council, or between him and the officials, but to give statutory backing to what is already the practice in the best administered authorities in both England and Scotland.

CHAPTER IV

THE CHIEF FINANCIAL OFFICER

(1)

THE purpose of this chapter is to explain in general terms the part played by the chief financial officer in the affairs of his authority; later chapters contain a more detailed study of the various aspects of his work. Beginning with a short description of his duties, and the nature of his contribution to the local administration, the chapter continues with a broad analysis of the way in which his differing tasks should be approached. This is followed by a discussion of the relevant legal provisions, which are very few. The role of a chief financial officer is therefore settled by his conditions of appointment, expressed or implied, and the next section of the chapter gives a summary of his duties in a form suitable for embodiment in a contract of service. This list is intended both as a practical guide for local authorities and as a help to the student desirous of obtaining a bird's-eye view of the place of the chief financial officer. The chapter concludes with a short discussion of the situation in those authorities where the chief financial officer is not charged with the full range of responsibilities appropriate to the post.

(2)

One of the most interesting features of the financial adminstration of local authorities is the startling contrast in the position accorded to the chief financial officer in different localities. In some places, backed by an understanding council, he plays a weighty and effective part; in others he is little more than a book-keeper with a few additional responsibilities, such as those of advising the council on money market transactions or on the management of funds. In between these two extremes, almost every possible variation is to be found. Fortunately his position steadily improves as more and more authorities, both large and small, come to appreciate the value of an integrated financial system and a fully fledged financial officer. But in all too many places he has yet to come into his own. In this chapter are described the duties of a 'fully fledged' chief financial officer, i.e.

56

one carrying responsibilities normally associated with a chief financial officer in other types of administration.

Data collected by the author for an international conference in 1952 showed that, in general, the central government and the public boards combine, at the top level of administration, the work of accountancy with that of giving financial advice.[1] The titles 'financial officer', 'financial controller', 'director of finance' are common. Even when the terms 'accountant' or 'accountant-general' are employed, the individuals so designated are prone to regard their duties as financial adviser or controller as of no less importance than their responsibilities as accountants.

Similarly in local government, those authorities who have developed their financial administration have a 'chief financial officer' who combines the functions of financial adviser, accountant, collector of income, paymaster and internal auditor. This officer is most commonly called 'treasurer', other designations in use being 'accountant', 'chief financial officer' or in Scottish burghs 'chamberlain'. Where the term 'controller' is in use, it is usually spelt 'comptroller', for the head of the finance department controls only in the sense that he supervises the financial administration; in local government the elected members themselves control policy.

(3)

The duties of a chief financial officer are briefly as follows. First he is the financial adviser of the council, its committees and its officers on all aspects of the council's work. In so far as he advises the council upon financial control—deciding on the allocation of funds, approving new projects, determining the priorities of schemes, disciplining those committees or officers who do not abide by the council's rules—he tends to become identified with the finance committee, and to be thought of—erroneously if he is doing his job correctly— as the man who exercises the control. For this reason he will often find himself sharing the finance committee's unpopularity and the strictures showered upon it, a situation he must accept as one of the normal hazards of his post.

Next he will be the council's accountant, keeping the major records in his own department and settling the form of all financial records wherever they are kept. It is in his capacity as accountant that he must

[1] See report of the *Sixth International Congress on Accounting, 1952*, pp. 349–63.

supply to the council, its committees and its officers all the information needed for management.

Then there are his duties as internal auditor. The work of local authorities is so dispersed, so various and of such a kind, that much of the subsidiary financial work, e.g. the collection of incidental income and the ordering and custody of goods, will be done outside the finance department. Though these operations will be the immediate responsibility of operating departments, the chief financial officer must exercise general oversight. Internal audit provides him with the means.

The chief financial officer is also the treasurer. In this capacity he will be the channel of receipts and payments, and if he is the chief financial officer of a county or county borough he will usually collect the vehicle excise duty on behalf of the Ministry of Transport. Even in a town of 50,000 or so inhabitants, some millions of pounds will pass through his hands each year. His obligations partake of the nature of trustee with an independent direct responsibility to the ratepayers and he must exercise all the vigilance expected of anyone who handles public funds.

The chief financial officer has also to act as the council's officer for a wide range of purely financial work—raising capital money, negotiating financial business (as well as joining with other officers in the negotiation of affairs which may not be exclusively financial but have financial implications), effecting insurances, managing reserve, renewals and other funds, acting as receiver to estates, giving financial evidence on behalf of the council, and many other similar tasks.

Finally, the chief financial officer is often asked to do work which is not primarily financial—act as establishment officer, supervise housing management, maintain printing and stationery departments, carry out central purchasing. These tasks are outside the scope of a book concerned only with financial administration. They come to the chief financial officer for a variety of reasons: the council may think his department the most appropriate for some particular function for which they are seeking a home; they may regard it as his share of the responsibilities they are apportioning between the departments; they may wish to take advantage of his administrative arrangements, usually comparatively extensive because of the volume of routine work he has to organize; or tasks may be assigned to the chief financial officer for personal reasons.

Work of this kind is found in most chief financial officers' departments, and will continue so long as local authorities sensibly adhere to the idea that the fewer separate departments they have, the better the administration. It does, however, bring its own problems. It may involve the recruitment and control of specialists in fields other than finance and a crop of responsibilities of a novel kind. It also makes imperative an even sharper distinction between these extraneous duties and the financial work than is the case in the financial sphere between the duties as a watchdog of finance and those as an agent supplying the departments with a service in accountancy and financial advice. A central printing and stationery department, for instance, exists to supply its customers with the goods they want, not to control their expenditure. That chief financial officers in so many places are doing the extraneous tasks satisfactorily is evidence of the absence of any real difficulty in organizing the various sections of a department to reflect the different capacities in which they act. This is not surprising because a chief officer to a local authority is—or should be—an administrator able to take charge of a variety of work, as well as a technical expert in his own sphere.

(4)

In the financial sphere the tasks of the chief financial officer differ widely and cannot all be approached in the same way. From the point of view of the attitude he should adopt his duties can be divided into three main classes: first, those concerned with advice and control, either his own technical control of records, or the control which is exercised by the members of the council on the strength of reports and data he provides; second, the work he does as agent for the departments, e.g. provision of an accounting service; and finally, purely financial tasks—looking after funds, cash investments, etc.

The first two—the control functions and the agency functions—though they can both be properly discharged only in a spirit of helpfulness and co-operation are essentially dissimilar in nature. When carrying out the first, the chief financial officer is concerned, either directly or through the members, with regulating, controlling, curbing and checking. This is unpopular work, bound to arouse some resentment, because, however tactfully done, it involves restraint. When, on the other hand, he is supplying departments with data he is acting as an agent whose task it is to give the heads of the operating departments and their staffs the information they want. He is the specialist putting the technique and resources of his department at the disposal of his colleagues, realizing that accounts are not ends in themselves, but tools to be used, and remembering that the departments are entitled to insist on having the best available tools.

These kinds of activity both have their characteristics: the exercise of control calls for courage, firmness and tact; whilst the agency function demands a sense of service. The chief financial officer, both in his thinking and in his organization, must make a distinction between the two, so that no department is in doubt on any occasion about the capacity in which he is acting. Further, departments must have sufficient confidence in his goodwill never to feel inhibited from making requests to him as their agent because he has criticized their financial administration, or differed about the advice to be tendered to the council on some matter of policy. The chief financial officer—and for that matter the Clerk to the authority— exist, not in their own right, but because there are other departments providing services, educating children, building roads, etc., an aspect of local administration which is developed in a later chapter. In the meantime the point to note is that for this reason the chief financial officer's is primarily a service department. When he is operating a control, or prodding a committee to restrain a department or an official, it is all too easy for the chief financial officer to become the death's head at the feast, damping down the enthusiasm and curbing the activities of the idealist.

The third kind of work—investments, raising loans and the like— does not call for extended comment because other officers are not usually concerned. The chief financial officer's task is simply that of making diligent use of his professional skill on behalf of his authority.

(5)

Appendix B shows that the chief financial officer as described in these pages is practically unknown to the law. A 'treasurer', who must be a different person from the town clerk, must be appointed by local authorities in England and Wales, but apart from making him responsible for the supervision of the arrangements for the payment and receipt of monies, the law does not define his duties. It is possible to fulfil the statutory requirements by confining the treasurer's work to this task, leaving the bulk of the financial work to other officers. Chief financial officers themselves have always fancied the title of 'treasurer', presumably because of its historical overtones, rather than the more comprehensive one of 'chief financial officer' which is used in this book. The passing of the Local Government Act, 1958, which for the first time places a specific responsibility on the treasurer for supervision of receipts and payments—under the old law he was merely the channel through which the money had to pass—will presumably give further impetus to the preference for the title of 'treasurer'. At the same time it should give the death-blow to the practice of appointing a bank manager as treasurer, because, whilst such a person could act as a conduit for receipts and payments, he could not supervise the arrangements as required by the Local Government Act, 1958.

The specific responsibilities of the treasurer, clearly set out in the case of *Attorney-General v. de Winton*, have been the cause of much comment.[1]

Mr Justice Farwell in the course of his judgment in this case observed that the treasurer was not a mere servant of the council. He stood in a direct fiduciary relationship to the burgesses and could not plead the orders of the council as an excuse for an unlawful act. Mr Justice Farwell also cited with approval the following observations made by Earl, J., on R. *v.* Saunders[2] which related to a county treasurer: 'If an order be made on a county treasurer to repay expenses wholly disconnected with county matters such an order is without jurisdiction and one which the treasurer would be bound to disobey.'

This is a heavy responsibility which no action of the council can alter or diminish. This special responsibility is naturally ever in the minds of treasurers of boroughs and counties, and also in the minds of district auditors. The mere existence of a responsibility independent of the council can create a delicate situation, and few treasurers can relish those occasions upon which they have to remind their councils of the position. That major conflicts are so rare is attributable to the good sense of the local authorities who shrink from pursuing courses which force their officers to decline to follow their instructions and to the sense of balance which treasurers, in general, show in exercising the personal responsibilities of their office. Nor do local authorities normally place their treasurers in the other dilemma of his position, i.e. that of not having sufficient or proper staff to carry out his duties. The dilemma stems from the anomaly that whilst the treasurer's fiduciary relationship to the ratepayers clearly implies that he must look after their monies, he has, according to counsel's opinion given to a metropolitan borough in 1932, no way of com-

[1] See (1906) 2, Ch. 106.   [2] See (1854) 24, L.J. (M.C.) 45, at p. 48.

pelling his council to provide him with the means to carry out his duty. The metropolitan borough asked counsel whether internal audit was an integral part of the borough treasurer's duties and whether he could insist, in the light of the decision in *Attorney-General v. de Winton*, on having the necessary staff to carry out the audit. They also asked whether, by appointing an outside firm of accountants to carry out the internal examination of its accounts, the council had relieved the borough treasurer of the responsibility for the correctness of the accounts and whether it would be competent for the council to attempt to relieve him of such liability. Counsel's reply was to the effect that the internal running audit of the council's accounts was an integral part of the duties of a borough treasurer and that the council were under an obligation to appoint the necessary staff, though the treasurer was not entitled to dictate to the council about the staff he required. The council could not relieve the borough treasurer of his responsibilities by appointing an outside firm of accountants. Further, they could not modify any of the liabilities attaching by statute to the office and no action of the council could affect the fiduciary relation in which the treasurer stands to the burgesses as a body.

The position of the treasurer of a county or county borough is somewhat difficult to assess. On one view he has independent responsibilities, with no guarantee that he can carry them out.

On an alternative view, there is no anomaly. Notwithstanding the judgment in *Attorney-General v. de Winton*, Dr R. M. Jackson considers that the position of treasurer to local authorities is not substantially different from that of other officers. He says 'In fact a treasurer is in no different position from any other officer or, indeed, any other citizen, for none of us is entitled to break the law . . . The reason why the treasurer appears to be in a special position is that by the nature of his office he may have to decline to do something, whereas it is unlikely that other officers will find themselves in that position.'[1] A similar view is taken in an unsigned article in 'Local Government Finance'.[2] The writer says: 'The responsibilities of Treasurers have derived from the ordinary application of the Rule of Law and are shared by other officers of local authorities as well as by members, but are underlined by the fact that the Treasurers are the custodians of the cash. The Treasurers

[1] *Op. cit.*, p. 146.
[2] Local Government Finance—*Journal of the Institute of Municipal Treasurers and Accountants*. Vol. LXII, No. 12, p. 280, December 1958.

are apt, therefore, to find themselves with final responsibility on their shoulders. The readiness of the Courts to enforce the Rule of Law in the case of Treasurers was strikingly and directly evidenced in the De Winton decision.'

It is not for a layman to express an opinion on the correctness of the view of some lawyers that the 'Treasurer' is in a special position and that a chief financial officer not designated by this title might be better able to plead the order of his council if a payment were questioned. But what is clear to the layman is that it will normally be the chief financial officer, by whatsoever name he be called, who will have the invidious task of declining to make an illegal payment.

It is interesting to note that in Scotland all officers are at least protected against surcharge (by the Secretary of State for Scotland) if they have advised their authority in writing that a proposed payment was illegal. Section 201 of the Local Government (Scotland) Act, 1947, reads as follows:

'A surcharge shall not be made under this section upon an officer of a local authority by reason only of his signing a cheque or order in respect of any illegal payment, if he satisfies the Secretary of State that before signing the cheque or order he advised the authority in writing that in his opinion the payment was illegal.'

(6)

We have seen in the previous section that the English statutes do not use the term chief financial officer, and that the only statutory provisions which could be held to imply the existence of a separate finance department are the limited references to the duties of treasurers in the Local Government Act, 1958. Nor are the statutory orders more helpful, for the only reference to the chief financial officer in a statutory order which the author has been able to find, other than the unsatisfactory position under the 1930 Regulations discussed below, is in the Rate Accounts Order, 1926, and the corresponding statutory regulations of 1953 applying to the metropolitan boroughs. But the existence of a finance department is assumed by the government departments who when sending out to Clerks of local authorities circulars bearing on finance include an extra copy for transmission to the finance officer.

That it has never been possible in any statutory order to indicate the scope of the work of the finance department has been largely due to the lack of uniformity among local authorities in the distribution of duties and in the importance they ascribe to unified financial administration. This was largely responsible for the unsatisfactory definition of chief financial officer when the Accounts (Boroughs and Metropolitan Boroughs) Regulations, 1930, were drafted. The result is that though the Regulations do attach certain duties to the chief financial officer (notably the 'punctual keeping of a balancing system of double-entry ledger accounts recording all transactions which should be recorded in the accounts of the council') the council may delegate these duties to departmental accountants. It is thus possible to comply fully with the regulations even though a chief financial officer as such does not exist. The regulations apply to the whole of the accounts of metropolitan boroughs and to such accounts of a municipal borough as are subject to audit by the district auditor appointed by the Ministry of Housing and Local Government, e.g. education and rate collection accounts. However, in the memorandum which accompanied the regulations, the following remarks appeared:

'General Provisions—

13 The Regulations do not contain any provisions which would limit the discretion of a Council in regard to the officers it employs or the duties it assigns to each. But in view of the important bearing which wise allotment of duties has upon the efficiency, economy and security of the account-keeping, it is thought desirable to refer here to the principles which appear to be of chief value in this connexion.

13 (iii) That responsibility for the maintenance of current supervision of all accounts and records relating thereto should rest upon one chief financial officer, even when a separate departmental accountant is employed, as the efficiency of internal audit depends largely upon its independence. And that the officer charged with this duty of supervision should have access at any time and authority to apply any test or check to the accounts and records.

(iv) That responsibility for the organization of efficient accounting systems should also rest upon this officer. But that he should in all cases consult the chief officer of the department concerned as to the form and manner of keeping any records, statements or accounts which have to be kept in that department, due regard being paid on the one hand to the provision of prompt, reliable and complete information for the preparation and verification of accounts, and on the other hand to the avoidance of unnecessary delay or increase of cost in the execution of work.'[1]

[1] *Memorandum to accompany the Accounts (Boroughs and Metropolitan Boroughs) Regulations, 1930*, pp. 8 and 9.

In short, the position in England is that, whilst the Ministry subscribed to the idea of integrated financial arrangements, they did not feel able to prescribe that the financial arrangements must be under the supervision of a single officer. The Ministry confirmed their attitude in 1959 when Circular No. 4/59 was issued. (See Appendix F.)

(7)

The chief financial officers of Scottish local authorities are in a happier position, for their existence is statutorily recognized; not only must a treasurer or chamberlain be appointed in all types of authority, but he must, under the Local Government (Scotland) Act, 1947, also be the chief financial officer. He cannot be the same person as the Clerk unless the Secretary of State agrees—a loophole provided on the advice of the Jeffrey committee for those authorities too small to warrant the appointment of a qualified officer.[1] Scottish law, greatly in advance of English in this respect, provides that the chief financial officer must in counties and large burghs be qualified by examination for membership of at least one of the accountancy bodies specified. In small burghs and in the counties of Kinross and Nairn the requirements are not so strict.[2]

Furthermore there is more security of tenure in Scotland, for the treasurer or chamberlain, together with a number of other officers, cannot be removed except by a two-thirds majority of the council present at a meeting at which notice of the proposed dismissal has been given.

The Scottish Act is also important in that it prescribes some of the duties of the chief financial officer, notably: the keeping of accounts on lines broadly set out in the Act itself, the duty of ensuring that sums receivable are credited to the local authority's account, the making of payments, the control of receipts and payments of the Common Good and the making of returns.

(8)

In the absence in England of statutory regulations, any formal prescription of the chief financial officer's duties has to be made by standing order, regulation, or minute of appointment. In many

[1] See *Local Government and Public Health Consolidation (Scotland) Committee First Report.* Cmnd. 6476, 1943, p. 38.

[2] This is governed by Regulations—The Local Government (Qualifications of County Treasurer and Town Chamberlain) Scotland Regulations, 1948, as amended by further regulations: No. 1913 of 1950.

cases there will be no written provisions at all, the position of the chief financial officer being governed by tradition and accident: or the written provision will be incomplete and little guide to the real position. Such written regulations as do exist fall into two categories: those where a single all-embracing clause makes the chief financial officer generally responsible for finance and financial administration and those where some attempt is made to define duties in detail.

A typical standing order of the first type reads as follows: 'The City Treasurer is required under the Town Council acting through the Finance Committee and in pursuance of the Report of the Treasurer dated April 30, 1896, and adopted by the Council on the 6th day of May, 1896, to take entire responsibility of the whole of the Accounts and Finances of the City in all respects and with respect to every Department of the Corporation.'

This standing order seems to be sufficiently comprehensive to cover the duties of the chief financial officer as they are conceived in these pages. Many authorities however prefer a detailed list of duties, presumably to avoid doubts about the exact nature of the chief financial officer's obligations. The single comprehensive provision is the more flexible method: the detailed list of duties is perhaps the safer; it may help to avoid disputes either between the council and the chief financial officer, or between the chief financial officer and the other chief officers. A detailed list also serves to show a candidate seeking an appointment precisely what would be expected of him.

Local circumstances—size and nature of the authority, structure of the administration and the like—will dictate the exact provisions, but the following list, compiled in the light of the principles set forth in this book and after examination of the conditions of appointment of a number of chief financial officers, is believed by the author to cover the principal points in general terms. Its inclusion in the text instead of in an appendix has the advantage of providing within the chapter itself a summary of the work of the chief financial officer.

A chief financial officer carrying the full responsibilities of the position might well expect to be required:

General
to hold office as treasurer, accountant and financial adviser to the council, carrying out all duties imposed upon his office or offices by statute or by direction of the council;
to attend all meetings of the finance committee of the council and

other committees where business with financial implications may be transacted;

to report annually to the council on the financial organization, with suggestions for future developments;

to be responsible for the control of the finance department;

to be responsible for the training of staff engaged in financial work in other departments, and, in conjunction with the heads of departments, for their deployment;

Accounting

to be responsible to the council for the maintenance of a centralized accounting system, the supervision of all financial records wherever kept, and the preparation of the accounting manuals;

to prepare and submit to the committee, the council and the auditors, the accounts relating to all of the authority's activities;

to be responsible for printing the annual abstract of accounts;

to prepare and submit all financial returns required by government departments;

promptly to supply, in conjunction with other officers where necessary, the council, committees and all departments with the financial data they need for the management of the council's business;

Audit

to maintain an internal audit of the financial records of all departments in order to ascertain that they are duly kept in the form approved and entered up promptly, efficiently and completely;

to report annually to the committees on the work of the internal audit and the state of the financial records and organization in each department;

promptly to report to the committees irregularities discovered in the course of audit;

Payments

to make, in accordance with the instructions of the council under the Local Government Act of 1958, arrangements for the verification of accounts for payment;

to make all payments, including salaries, wages and pensions;

to prepare, sign and dispatch all cheques and similar documents;

to pay, from an imprest account to be kept under conditions laid down by the council, all urgent accounts;

to obtain from any chief officer concerned all the information needed for a proper examination of claims made for payment under any contract with the corporation.

Income

to make, in accordance with the instructions of the council under the Local Government Act, 1958, arrangements for the collection and recovery of monies due to the council and handling, custody, security and banking of cash;

to have custody of stocks of receipts, tickets and similar documents;

Annual Budget

to compile, in conjunction with the departments, the council's budget, submitting estimates to the operating committees and summaries and reports to the finance committee;

to call the attention of the committees to overspending or unauthorized expenditure;

Management of Funds

to manage, subject to the instructions of the finance committee and the council, all funds of the council;

to see that monies not required for the time being are suitably invested;

to advise the finance committee on the raising of capital monies;

Miscellaneous

to act as rating officer;

to carry out the functions of the council in connexion with the valuation of property for rating, and valuations in respect of acquisition and disposal of property;[1]

to act as registrar of stocks and bonds;

to direct and supervise the financial transactions of the council with their bankers;

to carry out financial negotiations on behalf of the council and assist in other negotiations when financial aspects are involved;

to give such financial evidence as may be required on behalf of the council;

to effect insurances for all departments of the council;

to make claims on insurance companies and recommend settlements;

to settle the income tax liabilities of the council.

---

[1] If the council has an estate or valuation department these duties will not usually fall to the chief financial officer.

(9)

So far we have considered the chief financial officer as carrying out the full range of financial duties. In fact there are some local authorities whose financial arrangements fall notably short of those described in the preceding paragraphs. Many of the smaller local authorities have no separate finance department, the financial work being done by the Clerk who probably holds the designation 'clerk and chief financial officer'. This combination of duties is to be avoided except in the smallest authorities not able to afford two salaries, though the practice of appointing a deputy clerk—sometimes a qualified accountant—to take charge of finance does something to mitigate the disadvantage of having the Clerk as the chief financial officer.[1] Though many new finance departments have been set up during the last few years, the position is still far from satisfactory, despite the general condemnation of the practice of combining the work of the Clerk and the chief financial officer and the criticisms of district auditors who observe at close quarters the consequences of finance and accounting being treated as a side issue of other work. The case for a separate finance department hardly needs emphasis, and it is interesting to recall that, as has been noted earlier in the chapter, in Scotland the Jeffrey Committee[2] gave weighty support to the need for the chief financial officer to be independent, and their recommendations were accepted by the legislature.

But this is only the beginning of the matter, for the existence of a separate finance department does not guarantee that it carries out the duties of financial branches of the administration as they are understood in the central government, the boards, and progressive commercial concerns. In local government the head of the finance department may not be responsible even for all the final accounts. It is not unknown for a local authority to employ a staff of qualified accountants in the finance department and yet allow final accounts to be prepared by unqualified staff of other departments, any attempt by the chief financial officer to control the form or content of the accounts being resisted. With the subsidiary book-keeping the position is much the same. It is sometimes the practice of the local author-

[1] The alternative of two or more small authorities sharing a chief financial officer seems to be almost unknown.
[2] *Local Government and Public Health Consolidation (Scotland) Committee First Report*. Cmnd. 6476, 1943.

ity to leave the chief financial officer with little or no control—except indirectly through audit—over the subsidiary accounting, even when he is responsible for the final accounts. Both the form in which he is supplied with the details he needs for the final accounts, and the time of their arrival, may be dictated by the whim of the departments, who will also indulge their particular fancies about the pattern of book-keeping and financial records.

Similarly a chief financial officer may be prevented from playing his proper part in the formation of policy and the carrying out of financial transactions. He may not even be welcome at meetings of operating committees, and may first learn of matters of financial importance from the minutes of the council or, in the case of business needing confirmation of the finance committee, at the meeting of that committee.

In short there are still some authorities who have little or nothing in the way of standing orders to control their financial business, who have yet to adopt the basic financial safeguards to see that committees keep within their estimates, who have no means of ensuring that at the inception of new projects the council are apprised of all the financial implications, whose chief financial officers are in control of only a part of the accounting arrangements and whose committees and officers treat other committees and departments at arm's length.

Happily, as was indicated earlier in the chapter, authorities who fail to make proper use of their chief financial officer are now a small minority. The good example of the better conducted local authorities, the pressure of auditors, the expressed views of the Ministry of Housing and Local Government,[1] the realization of the opportunities which modern mechanization offers to authorities with centralized financial arrangements, all combine to induce local authorities to fall into line with the best practice.

There are in Great Britain about two thousand local authorities, excluding parish councils, each with autonomy in its internal affairs. Inevitably they vary in their willingness and ability to adopt the most up-to-date procedures. It is therefore not surprising that some years should elapse before good habits in financial administration become general.

---

[1] The Ministry's circular 4/59, though primarily concerned with the arrangements for handling receipts and payments, makes specific reference to the desirability of appointing a professionally qualified chief financial officer and to the need to invest him with adequate authority. (See Appendix F.)

CHAPTER V

THE CHIEF FINANCIAL OFFICER'S DEPARTMENT: GENERAL CONSIDERATIONS

(1)

WHAT is the effect on departmental organization of the pivotal position occupied by committees, of the answerability of members for administration as well as policy, or of the ever-present possibility that the least important act of the humblest employee may become the subject of public discussion? How should the official organize the task of advising committees—one or more of which are usually sitting—and, at the same time, supervising the operations of twenty-four hour services? What modifications in normal administrative practice are needed to cope with the slow rate of reaching decisions, the effects of political compromise, the lack of tangible measures of success or departmentalism?

These questions have received even less attention from writers than the broader aspects of local government discussed in the opening chapter. Though it would be out of place to attempt to explore them fully in a book concerned with only a single aspect of the work of the authority, these special features of local government must not be overlooked in considering the organization of the finance department. In addition there are some general points to be observed, some springing from the nature of the chief financial officer's work, whilst others are merely special applications of well-known principles of administration. Accordingly, the description in the next chapter of the pattern of organization of the finance department is prefaced in this chapter by a discussion of the more important factors to be borne in mind in deciding what form the organization shall take.

(2)

Of the many features of the local government structure affecting departmental administration, three are of special significance to the chief financial officer seeking the appropriate organization for his department.

First there is the need for a deputy. Having his masters corporately in frequent session, and in urban areas on the door step, the head of a local government department must accept the need for a different pattern of senior staff arrangements from that needed by a board of directors who meet fortnightly or monthly, and leave their staff largely free at other times to attend to administration. At all times he must be ready to provide a representative for committees considering matters of concern to his department, and be ready to discuss policy with individual councillors. In between times he must supervise his department. These considerations apply with especial force to the financial officer because, like the Clerk, he is concerned with all the committees and activities of the council. Therefore to ensure that their chief financial officers can fulfil these demands, all but the smallest English local authorities provide for a deputy chief financial officer, even though they may not have deputies to all their chief officers.

In the largest offices, especially in urban areas, the work of local government has become so complex, and committee work has increased so much, that in addition to deputy chiefs, one finds 'assistant' chiefs. Their position and functions are discussed in the next chapter. In the meantime, this growth in the number of senior posts should be noted as an interesting illustration of the effect of the committee system on the administration.

Secondly local authorities need to exploit to the full the unique contribution the finance department can make towards counteracting departmentalism and providing an object lesson in smooth inter-departmental relationships. The finance department should, therefore, be organized with as much regard to the convenience of the other departments who use its services as for the convenience of the chief financial officer and his staff. Operating departments should, for the sake of simplicity, have to deal with as few individuals as possible in the finance department. They should know who is responsible for each class of work, they should have immediate access to persons in authority and they should be provided with business-like methods for the passing of documents between departments. If co-operation is to be intelligent, finance staffs of the departments should have opportunities to understand the aims and organization of the chief financial officer's department, a topic taken up in a later chapter.

Thirdly, there is a need to guard against the danger of the leisurely consideration of policy at committee being reflected in the office, probably in the form of *ad nauseam* study of minor matters. English local government is a somewhat extreme example of government by discussion. But though deferment, adjournment, reference back and reconsideration may be justified at committee level for determining policy, they bring paralysis if imported into administration. The danger of over-much discussion of administrative matters is increased by the organization of each department's work into a separate discipline regulated by a professional association, an excellent feature of English local government, but one liable to encourage the practitioner to ascribe too much importance to small points of administration. Discussions about the form of a time sheet can easily proceed with all the formality of a medieval disputation and the office be converted from a place of business into a Senior Common Room, delightfully stimulating, but administratively ineffective. Every chief financial officer has, therefore, to be on the alert against the appearance of too many discussion groups in his office.

(3)

The organization of the finance department has to be studied not only in the light of the distinctive administrative arrangements of local authorities but also with regard to such features as the nature of the chief financial officer's work, the methods of staffing his department, and his place in the administration. A few of the more important of these features are shortly considered in this section.

Subject to the qualification that questions of policy are settled by the members in committee, the chief financial officer is in effect a 'director of finance', responsible for a number of duties of different kinds—financial advice, accounting, auditing, cash collection, cash payment, and the management of funds. Under some systems of local government—e.g. in many cities of Europe and the United States—more than one finance officer is employed; for instance, the handling of receipts and payments is often separated from the work of financial control or from that of accounting, the underlying idea being that there is greater security if the financial work is spread over a number of chief financial officers.

Modern practice in large-scale concerns follows that of English local authorities in having at the top one financial officer, e.g. the National Coal Board has a Director General of Finance, and the British Transport Commission a Chief Accountant and Financial Adviser, the separation of duties for the purpose of internal check being made at the next stage lower down. A chief financial officer of a local authority must remember, when organizing his department, that there are certain of his functions which must be kept separate from the others for the purpose of internal security, e.g. his audit must be an independent unit and his cashier must not be responsible for accounting work. The principles of financial security must be applied right down the scale. Thus the setting up of debits and the receipt of cash must be in different hands, the checking of accounts for payment must be divorced from the issue of cheques, duties must be arranged to make fraud difficult without collusion, staff should be transferred periodically to other jobs, and so forth. However small the department, these basic safeguards must be observed, though the smaller the office the harder they are to achieve.

Next there are the problems brought about by the existence of so much routine work. It is significant that the chief financial officer has —except in counties—normally the largest clerical staff of any department. In a county borough of only average size there will be many thousands of employees to be paid, accounts to be settled, and properties for which rates—and in many cases rents too—have to be collected. The chief financial officer simply must pay attention to office routine and organization. This is why, long before 'Organization and Methods' came into prominence as a distinct activity, every sizeable local authority finance department carried out an almost continuous survey of clerical procedures, and why the more progressive local authorities have always been in the forefront in the use of office machinery. Organization and methods teams are particularly to be encouraged in any office where routine work looms large. But they are of special importance to a public authority, because so much of its work affects the rights or lives of the citizens, and because even the junior officer can set in motion coercive powers not possessed by commercial concerns: a lapse in posting the cash to a rate book may involve distraint upon the goods of a ratepayer whose rates have in fact been paid. The routine work is therefore of immense importance. Local authorities should be prepared to pay for such checks as are necessary to ensure that the work is accurate, e.g. that ratepayers do not receive incorrect accounts. Every board of directors can settle for itself how far it pays to check accounting work. A local authority has not such a free choice, for being the custodian of public funds it cannot afford even to appear to the ratepayers to be negligent; it may have to institute checks which a board of directors would regard as not worth while.

Another feature affecting the organization of a finance department is the system of in-breeding under which a chief financial officer will but rarely be able to recruit an accountant from another field of activity. Local government finance is almost a closed profession in the sense that to reach the top, one must normally enter at an early age and spend a lifetime in the service of local authorities. This is in the main a good thing for it has made possible a highly specialized discipline. But in-breeding has its disadvantages, and a chief financial officer in organizing his office should aim at counteracting them by taking as much advantage as he can of outside techniques and skill, and by encouraging as free a movement of staff as the rigidities of local government organization permit.

(4)

When a chief financial officer comes to the task of applying the general principles of office organization—the need for a properly defined chain of command, the allotment of responsibility according to ability, age, status and experience, the maintenance of good staff relations, the establishment of good office routines and so forth— he will find that two of them are of peculiar importance in his department: the need for precise definition of responsibility and the place of delegation. Therefore, though the general principles of organization do not call for treatment in a specialized treatise, these two points are considered briefly.

Clear definition of responsibility is specially important because work which is concerned with handling the finances and monies of public authorities includes an element of trusteeship, as significant for the humble task as for the more exalted. The chief financial officer must lay as firmly on individuals the responsibility for putting cheques into the right envelopes as he does the responsibility for protecting the council's interests in claiming grants, settling income tax liabilities or advising committees. This principle is not always easy to apply to those operations for which corporate responsibility can hardly be avoided, e.g. the making up and payment of wages. All that can be done is to lay down how far the corporate responsibility extends.

The second need—that for adequate delegation of all appropriate matters—is not peculiar to local government but is of special importance, partly because the chief financial officer will spend so much of his time in session with the policy makers, and partly because there are so many departments and services. No one person can keep the detailed financial features of all the services in mind or carry out all the important functions himself. If a chief has only one other person in the office besides himself, there is delegation: if he has several score—or several hundred—he has to be content for many minor decisions to be taken by others. Very little will be done exactly as the chief would do it himself. Sometimes it will be done better: sometimes not so well. But rarely will he be able to revise or interfere, though he must accept complete responsibility, since, in accordance with the traditions of local government, everything will be done in his name. Elaborate pains will be taken by subordinate officers to guard against the suggestion that they are putting forward their own point of view. The chief financial officer of a large authority must cheerfully accept the consequences, sign letters couched in language that he would not himself use, and be prepared, on occasion, on some question of which he is in complete ignorance, to support a subordinate who has told a committee or department what the chief financial officer 'thought' about some particular question.

(5)

One other general aspect of management remains to be considered before the pattern of organization in a finance department can be described—the need for a constant review of organization and procedures.

Staffed by permanent officers, subject to the direction of a chief with a lifetime's experience of local government finance, most finance departments operate in an orderly and punctilious manner. But the very factors which bring stability, if coupled with nervousness in launching forth in new administrative methods, can produce a static, conservative administration. The hesitancy may be that of the council, the chief financial officer or his staff. All too often one hears of newly appointed chief financial officers having to contend with obsolete offices where the very thought of change is anathema to council and staff alike; and there must be instances—though officers naturally talk less of these among themselves!—where the local authority senses need for radical re-organization but the chief officer is too set in his ways to respond.

Such unfortunate situations can be avoided by keeping both the pattern of organization and the clerical procedures under continuous review. The office will then be kept almost automatically up to date, and the council, chief financial officer, and staff will welcome change instead of resisting it: all but that minority of born conservatives to be found in every walk of life will become so accustomed to periodical advances in office techniques that they will be disappointed with long periods without modifications of organization or office methods. Nothing has a more bracing influence on local administration, nor does more to counteract the natural tendency of public bodies to become stereotyped in their habits, than a staff always on the watch for improvements.

There is singularly little excuse for any department failing to keep abreast of the times; for the English habit of making the work of every department a separate profession results among other things in the chief officer having access to a wealth of information about the best current practice. This is achieved through the medium of vocational associations In this respect the chief financial officer is exceptionally fortunate, for his association—the Institute of Municipal Treasurers and Accountants—has been conspicuously successful among the associations of local government officers. Conferring a coveted diploma recognized as the hall-mark of competence in local government finance, providing a forum for discussion, offering facilities for research, tendering advice to government departments on the technical aspects of local government finance, the Institute is established alike in the world of accountancy and in that of local government. The chief financial officer who fails to read its literature, or take part in its deliberations will hardly be able to keep abreast of developments in local government finance.

A further spur to efficiency is the attention given in recent years to the study of organization and methods, to which reference has been made earlier in this chapter. The more progressive local authorities have become conscious of the need for periodical overhauls of their clerical processes and administrative machinery, e.g. the distribution of duties between and within departments. Many 'O. & M.' units have now been established, the method of operation depending on the size of the local authority, the attitude of the council, and the views of the chief officers. A chief financial officer would naturally make the most use of such a unit, if only because it can approach problems with a dispassionate view impossible for those who work with the problems day to day. But an O. & M. unit, though a valuable ally, can never be a substitute for critical examination within the department. Able to visit any particular department only occasionally and at irregular intervals, organization and methods officers can be expected to cope only with general clerical procedures and not with the technical accounting procedures which form so large a part of the work of a finance department; and being external to the department, they have not the intimate knowledge of those in daily contact with the work. The impetus for reform must come from within: a methods officer can show a man who is willing to work how to set about his job; but he cannot give a man the will to work, nor even the desire to use the best methods: his role is purely passive.

Even in a small department, where the initiative for good organization will tend to be that of the chief and his deputy, the staff should be encouraged to think critically about office methods. In a large department much of the thinking on this subject will be done by more subordinate staff. But whether the authority is large or small, staff at all levels should be given opportunity to see other offices and other methods, and to participate in discussions, enquiries and research projects initiated by the various branches of the Institute of Municipal Treasurers and Accountants and other bodies. The dividends reaped over the years will be incalculable.

The technique of determining new routines is a subject in itself and outside the scope of this book. But it may be pertinent to remind the reader in a chapter devoted to the general principles of organization of a finance department, that a most valuable organizational aid to surveys of routines is to commit them to paper. The mere knowledge that they are to be written down will guarantee that they are looked at critically, and the existence of an intelligible account of what is being done makes it easy to appraise the routine at any time. Manuals of instruction are in any case likely to be more common as the mechanization of offices develops, and so much more of the work of the individual becomes a link in a chain of operations instead of a self-contained job. At the same time the tasks themselves, thanks to the growing complexities of the public services, become more involved. An additional justification for written instructions is the decline in quality of the clerical staff, a present day phenomenon more pronounced in some areas than others, but general throughout local government. It is referred to in several other places in this book. From the point of view of our present purpose its significance is that the first-class clerks whom local authorities were formerly able to recruit, rapidly acquired the appropriate techniques, sensed the role they were expected to fulfil, and tended to stay with the authority for a number of years. To write down the operations on paper was largely superfluous. Their successors, drawn from a different educational stratum, and less likely to settle in local government, need more guidance.

Not all local authorities will be able to justify an officer whose whole time is devoted to the examination of finance department procedures, and review—at least of the simpler processes—may have to be carried out *ambulando* with such help as is available from an organization and methods unit. This is perhaps as well because it drives home the lesson that it is part of the duty of every member of the staff to find the best methods of work. But the man doing a job and his immediate supervisor have not always a sufficiently detached view to make suggestions for improvement, though they must both be associated with investigations. Most chief financial officers therefore find it necessary to put the responsibility for reviewing office methods upon some senior officer of the department who stands aside from the day-to-day work. Often the chief auditor plays an important part in the organization of the financial records within the finance department as he does in other departments, though the deputy or assistant treasurers (if they exist) may be charged with the main responsibility. The important point is for the task to be specifically assigned, so that the work does not go by default.

CHAPTER VI

THE CHIEF FINANCIAL OFFICER'S DEPARTMENT:
PATTERN OF ORGANIZATION

(1)

IN the services of the central government, local branches are organized on identical lines: an official transferred from one employment exchange to another finds forms, procedures, staff gradings, and even furniture familiar. The world of local government presents a marked contrast. An officer moving between authorities soon realizes that finance departments are fashioned, not on a general pattern, but according to the size of the local authority, its range of work, the distribution of duties between departments, and the ideas of the chief financial officer.

There can, therefore, be no blueprint to show how the general principles discussed in the last chapter crystallize into office organization. But there are certain points to be observed and alternative patterns to be studied. In the following paragraphs an attempt is made to examine these general considerations and to describe the organization of the chief financial officer's department. Staff recruiting, staff training and cognate matters are treated in a later chapter.

Of the importance of the subject, there can hardly be two opinions. The pattern of organization determines the conditions under which the staff spend the greater part of their active life; it settles the way they set about their work; and it is the criterion by which the members of the authority, staff in other departments, and the public judge the efficiency of the department. A well organized office enables the best to be made of individual ability and energy; a bad organization inevitably spells inefficiency, waste and frustration. Moreover, because the work of the finance department is so closely interwoven with other departments, an ineffectual finance department may well impair the whole of the services of the authority.

(2)

Subject to any directions which the council or its committees may give, the chief financial officer himself determines the organization of the department. But hardly less important than the organization is the precise nature of the work he assigns to himself and the manner in which he discharges it. In local government—perhaps to an exceptional extent because of the absence of a central chief executive —a department takes its tone from the head of the department. The texture of life in the department and the quality of the department's relationships with other departments are largely conditioned by the chief financial officer's action and attitudes. Accordingly any study of the organization must begin by considering his personal role.

No general rules can be laid down about his day-to-day work. It will be determined by the scale of the local authority's operations, the nature of the organization of the local authority as a whole and the expectations of the members. If there is a major difficulty in a committee, or serious trouble with a ratepayer or a councillor, or if a reluctant department is to be induced to accept an unpalatable policy, then the chief of the department should take a hand himself.

In the smaller authorities he may be present at the meetings of all the major committees. Even in the largest authorities he will personally attend and advise the finance committee and will, in most authorities, attend some other committee meetings. For the most part, however, the committees, especially those of county boroughs, will be so numerous that he will have to be content to be represented by a senior officer. Some chief officers make a point of being personally present at committees which they do not normally attend if a matter of first-rate importance is to be discussed. There are occasions when this is warranted—indeed when it is the duty of the chief financial officer to attend personally; but if he does this too frequently he will weaken the influence of his regular representative who will come to be regarded by the committee as only capable of discussing minor matters.

Some other tasks fall naturally to the chief financial officer himself—in small authorities major government returns, preparation of statistics and abstracts of accounts, and in nearly all authorities money market transactions, presentation of evidence at enquiries, handling the final stages of the budget, and drafting reports on new or major policy. In any sizeable office he will not deal with details except to the extent that he will satisfy himself by occasional enquiry and, if necessary, examination, that the work is being properly done, but will keep in touch with the work of all sections. Some chief officers maintain a direct relationship with their internal audit sec-

81

tion, insisting on regular reports from the chief auditor. All wise officers take as close a personal interest in their staffs and their welfare as time allows, and keep an open door for any member of the staff who is in trouble or who feels strongly enough about some official matter to wish to see the head of the department personally. A good tradition in the office will guard against abuse of the privilege. The far-seeing chief financial officer spares no pains in welding his staff into a team. If his staff is large he must accept the fact that his direct contacts with the more junior staff will inevitably be limited. But the lack of close personal association makes it all the more necessary for him to make sure that the posts in the office are correctly graded and remunerated, and that the office is free from petty tyranny, favouritism and incompetent supervision.

Most chief financial officers of counties also keep in close personal touch with their colleagues in boroughs and district councils within the county, bringing them together at regular intervals to discuss common problems. The emergence of 'County Financial Officers' Associations' for such purposes has indeed been a praiseworthy development in local government finance in recent years. Chief financial officers of counties can also help individual officers with advice and support, even though there are occasions when officers of counties and districts may have opposing interests. Many of the contacts between county finance departments and those of the lower tier authorities will be in connexion with such routine matters as reimbursement of funds. These questions will be handled by the staff, but there is a great deal to be said in favour of chief financial officers of counties taking as active a personal part as possible in all transactions of magnitude or of difficulty with district councils.

Finally, a chief financial officer should be discreet in the production of bright ideas. He is the leader, and the principal driving force, but to be compelled continually to alter the organization of the office to conform with his passing notions is a frustrating task for a subordinate. He must root out what is radically wrong as rapidly as possible, but that is a very different matter from capricious disturbance of the office organization.

(3)

The deputy, to whom brief allusion was made in the previous chapter, is the chief financial officer's *alter ego*, a junior partner rather than a subordinate. If both the chief and his deputy carry out the partnership agreement properly, the members of the council, both individually and in committee, should be equally happy to accept the advice of either. The relationship is intimate, and for that reason must be on the right basis. Each partner has something of the disadvantages; if the deputy has the detailed cares, the chief is left with the stickiest problems; if the deputy acts as the buffer between the world and the chief, it is nevertheless the latter who takes the final kick; and if the deputy receives too little of the credit and much of the work, the chief on the other hand has to bear the whole of the opprobrium. There is nothing difficult about the relationship provided it has the proper foundation. If the chief treats the deputy as a partner, keeps him acquainted with all matters of importance, sees that no member of the staff side-tracks him, if he always consults him on major matters, or when he has to make an important decision in his absence takes particular care to tell him personally later, if he supports the deputy, if he sees that the deputy has a proper share of privileges, then it is easier for the deputy to do his part, which is to be loyal, both in and out of the office, to keep the office running briskly but smoothly, to acquaint the chief with anything he hears that is important, amusing, or even scandalous, and quietly to fill in any gaps left by his chief.

One interesting feature of the deputy system is that it works better if the chief has no high level personal assistant or staff officer. If he does, the intimacy of the relation between him and his deputy will be destroyed, confidences and comments which would automatically be made to the deputy will be made to the staff officer, members and staff will tend to learn the chief's views from the staff officer. In short, the deputy will not stand as near to his chief as the local authority organization makes desirable. Therefore, any chief financial officer who finds a personal assistant necessary should have a relatively junior officer and keep him in the background.

In a moderate-sized authority, the deputy will be present at those committees not attended by his chief; in the larger authorities he will look after the committees of intermediate importance, leaving the top level to his chief and the smaller committees to other members of the staff. As with the chief financial officer, the actual duties of the deputy will depend largely on the size of the authority. In an authority of moderate size he may well handle some of the most important technical work—income tax, settlement of grant claims and the like, whilst in most authorities he will be specially charged with the responsibility of looking after the staff. Though he will filter many matters put forward for consideration by the chief, he must avoid becoming a bottleneck. To make a rule that everything should pass through the deputy would be unsound, for the chief will naturally from time to time deal directly with other senior officers. Both chief and deputy should make it their business to see that no work is held up for want of decision by themselves, or for that matter by anyone else in whom power to make decisions has been vested. Few administrative matters are so grave that they need to be thought over for a lengthy period.

(4)

Expansion of local government services and the increased complexity of administration have combined in many of the larger authorities to swell the volume of top level work beyond the capacity of two people, especially where committee meetings are becoming more numerous and more prolonged—a very common occurrence. In these circumstances additional officers have to share the committee work. It follows from earlier comments about the committee system and its relation to the administration that senior officers must attend, because members of the council expect always to deal with persons of authority.

One way of meeting this increase in committee work is to send to committees the heads of the various sections of the office or some of their most senior men. This has the advantage of bringing the sections into closer touch with the committees; on the other hand it makes harder the task of insulating the office work from the fluctuations of committee work. There is much to be said for the view that heads of sections should be always in the office to supervise their sections and able to plan their days and those of their subordinates in the knowledge that their plans will not be upset by unexpected calls to attend committees, conferences or inspections. In other words the 'outside' contacts of the sections should be the consultations in the ordinary course of business with colleagues in other departments or attendance at a committee for a routine purpose, e.g. to present accounts for payment, but not attendance at lengthy sessions.

The increasing volume of the work of the finance department is another reason why the chief and the deputy may in a large authority find themselves overburdened to the point of inefficiency. This growth in the amount of office work is due to two interesting factors.

84

First, the more elaborate nature of the services rendered by local authorities and of the legislation controlling their work. Secondly the greater volume and complexity of the financial data now produced for management purposes, a feature which local government shares with other public authorities and with commerce.

Many authorities, therefore, now try to solve both problems—more committee work and more administrative work—by making an extra appointment at the top of the office, of what is in effect an 'assistant' chief financial officer, though he may be called a variety of titles, e.g. assistant chief financial officer, chief assistant, principal assistant. In the largest or very active authorities two such officers may be appointed. What has then happened is that the general direction of the office is shared by three (or perhaps even four) people instead of two, and though there must be flexibility, the chief financial officer has to make a clear division of duties between them. Powerful arguments can be adduced for giving the assistant chief financial officers specific responsibility for the supervision of a group of sections of the office, so that the deputy need attend only to major questions affecting those sections. They then occupy a clear position in the hierarchy and feel a sharper sense of responsibility. If officers at this level are not given responsibility for the work of others they cannot show their full potential. They may suffer a sense of frustration, and they will in any case tend to operate as spare wheels unconnected with the rest of the machinery. A final advantage of making the assistant chief financial officers responsible for supervision of specified sections of the work is that this is the most effective way of making use of their professional skill in bolstering up weaker sections. In practice the distribution of supervisory work between the deputy and assistant chief financial officer will be made as much with an eye on the calibre of the staff and that of the section heads as on theoretical considerations. Offices have to be made to work with the staff actually there, not with those that the chief financial officer hopes to have some day.

Some chief financial officers also attach to the assistant chief financial officer *direct* responsibility for some part of the work, making him in effect a section head. Usually it is the statistical or financial control section which is attached. In any case the volume of routine work for which assistant chief officers are made directly responsible should be limited, or one of the main purposes of having them, i.e. to allow the routine work to be directed by persons undisturbed by the vagaries of committee meetings, will be defeated.

85

(5)

Most of the tasks of the finance department of a local authority can be classified in two ways, either according to the particular department of the local authority to which the service is rendered, or according to the nature of the service provided—e.g. audit, accountancy, control of cash. This two-way classification gives the clue to the alternative ways of organizing a finance department, which may (at least theoretically) be divided into 'service' sections, one for education and one for health, and so forth, or it may be divided functionally having an accountants' section, a cashiers' section, etc.

In practice the distinction cannot be clear-cut. The necessity for a division of responsibility to give the local authority internal security, which was put forward as one of the principal points to be observed in the organization of the finance department, of itself makes a purely service division of duties less acceptable. If, for instance an education finance section does all the work on the payment of bills, receipt of cash, compilation of accounts, internal audit, and financial control, there is some loss of security, unless the authority is of sufficient size to warrant the allocation of each class of work to a separate senior officer. Also there are financial operations which must be conducted centrally, e.g. the raising of capital monies, handling of insurances, etc. Finally there are, even in a large authority, departments too small to warrant an individual service section: their affairs must be dealt with in a 'miscellaneous' services section, or else the local authority must apply the functional principle and create an accountancy section, a cashiers section, etc. to serve the small departments. Thus the 'service' pattern of organization is inevitably a hybrid. In any case it can only apply to the larger authorities for in the case of both moderate-sized and smaller authorities, the activities of no individual service would be sufficiently extensive to warrant a service section. One could also argue that the functional method too is not pure in that it has an element of the service organization within the sections. For instance, in an accountancy or audit section the work will be shared out partly on a service basis, each accountant or auditor having charge of the accountancy or audit work of a department or group of departments.

But however blurred the distinction, it is none the less real, and therefore the relative merits of two methods of organization fall to be discussed. The principal advantage of the service method of organization is its greater convenience to departments who find most of their contacts with the finance department in one section, which may be housed in the operating department, though forming part of the finance department. The staff of the section become knowledgeable about the work of the department, sympathetic to its aims, and closely acquainted with the departmental officers. This form of organization is attractive in that it places automatically in the forefront the chief financial officer's obligation to serve the departments. The head of the department comes to know the staff of the service section well and may feel much more at home with them than with a head of an accountancy or cashiers' section with whom he comes into only occasional contact, and who has on his mind the business of many committees. Similarly the service form of organization has special merits in counties from the point of view of divisional executives and of 'lower-tier' authorities to whom functions have been delegated and who find their business with the county finance department simplified. The chief financial officers of some counties have 'Area' financial officers for health or education, thus providing examples of a decentralized service basis.

The merits of the functional form of organization are briefly as follows. It gives more internal security, being founded on a division of duties specifically designed to afford the maximum amount of internal check. It also makes more use of specialization. Take the recovery of debts for example: the head of a service section can scarcely hope to rival the knowledge, skill and expert records of a section whose sole business it is to recover money. It brings economies by bulking work such as collection or payment of wages. Further, it facilitates the use of office machinery: often machines can only be used to advantage if all work of the same type is centralized. Again, it avoids the problems of co-ordination which a service organization brings. Thus, for example, in a finance department organized on a service basis, changes in the form of presentation of accounts or accountancy methods have to be the subject of conferences, internal memoranda and the like, whereas under the functional method only one section is concerned both to make decisions and to carry them out. Also under functional organization there is no danger of inconsistency in such matters as grant claims, presentation of data to committees, etc. Moreover, the staff in service sections may identify themselves too completely with the departments to the detriment of financial control and integration of financial work. Finally, functional sections are more interesting because they cover many services and are less likely to get technically out of date. Service sections, having something of the characteristics of a jack-of-all-trades, tend to become pockets of conservatism, a feature which, coupled with their limitation to a single service, makes the keen young municipal accountant wish to avoid them.

In the main there is little doubt that, except perhaps in the very largest authorities of all, the balance is in favour of functional organization, and the trend is markedly in that direction, sometimes by deliberate policy and sometimes because sections such as salaries and wages—a functional section—appear, and gradually undermine the service organization. A fillip will be given towards functional organization by current developments in mechanical accounting which presupposes functional organization to an even greater extent than previously. In any case—sad to relate—some of the service organizations which remain are relics of the failure of local authorities to assimilate the education administration into that of the local authority at the passing of the school boards in 1902, rather than the products of deliberate policy.

(6)

The most important functions of a chief financial officer fall into a few obvious categories—financial control, accountancy, audit, receipt and payment of cash—so that there is a natural division of work which forms the basis of the organization of most finance departments. Allowing for a miscellaneous section into which are put the chief financial officer's ancillary duties and perhaps functions not entirely financial, there will normally be about half a dozen main sections—a number which by common consent is about right for supervision; for it is said by experts on office organization that no man can deal satisfactorily at first hand with more than about six senior executives. Division into a relatively small number of sections has the additional advantage of ensuring that each is under an officer of seniority and prestige. Moreover, though the sections will vary in importance, the work can usually be so arranged that there is not too great a difference in the status of the heads of sections. It is of interest to compare this division of duties in the finance departments of local authorities with that adopted by the nationalized industries. Thus, for example, the work of the headquarters staff of the National Coal Board is organized under four headings: Accounts (cash and banking, financial accounts), Management Accounting (cost accounts, official cost investigations and standard cost installation), General Finance (control of income and expenditure on revenue account, control of capital expenditure, taxation and special financial problems) and Internal Audit. The finance department of the British Transport Commission is under a Chief Accountant and Financial Adviser, to whom report the Chief General Accountant, the Chief Railway Accountant, the Director of Budgets and the Director of Funds and General Division. The Director of Accounts and Statistics, the Director of Costings and the Director of Audit report to the Chief General Accountant.

The size of the authority, the range of its activities, and the degree of centralization of financial work, are the factors determining the volume of work. The more the work, the more comprehensive will be the organization; no one would expect a borough of 50,000 to have so complete an organization as one of the large counties. But the nature of the chief financial officer's work is such that much the same problems of organization present themselves in both cases. It is indeed significant that the finance departments of local authorities, irrespective of size, exhibit a basic similarity of organization, notwithstanding the outward differences referred to in the opening paragraph of this chapter. We can, therefore, proceed to a discussion about the distribution of work within the sections of a finance department in the knowledge that the variations are not sufficiently wide to rob a general survey of its value. Financial control is dealt with first, followed by accountancy, audit, collecting income, making payments and finally miscellaneous functions.

(7)

Some of the larger offices have a 'financial control' or 'technical' section. Drafting reports for committees, preparing data for negotiations, enquiries and court proceedings, looking after financial relations with other authorities, settling income tax and government grants, considering financial legislation, control of funds both capital and revenue, management of investments, scrutinizing departmental costs, comparing the performance of departments with the budget or other yardsticks, advising on charges to be made for services rendered—these are the principal duties the section would carry out. It may also be responsible for the production of financial statistics and booklets. There can be no dogma about the exact duties: for instance, some chief financial officers regard the handling of grant claims as the business of the accountancy section even where there is a financial control unit.

The practice of separating, within the finance department, financial control from accountancy is common in large-scale concerns, e.g. the nationalized industries, and it has much to commend it. The two tasks are different in many respects. In particular, accountancy is essentially a service rendered by the finance department to a customer, whilst a financial control section, though it may spend the bulk of its time co-operating with departments in common tasks, not only has some watchdog functions but exercises as its name suggests a certain amount of restraint. The financial control section does not exist mainly to please the customer, and needs a somewhat different outlook; though in the end both financial control and accountancy sections stand or fall by their success or failure in carrying departments with them. The creation of a separate financial control section helps a chief financial officer to make clear to outside departments the distinction between his role as a servant of the departments—supplying them with data, paying their bills, and collecting money on their behalf—and that of acting as the independent adviser of the council on financial matters. There is, too, a difference of kind in the work of the sections: an accountancy section is concerned to achieve a regular output according to a pre-arranged timetable; a financial control section, on the other hand, deals with more irregular work.

The case in favour of segregating the control work is thus strong. But it is by no means conclusive. There are many arguments for combining the work with that of accounting. Foremost among these is the growing recognition that accountancy is a dynamic subject, an accountant being as much concerned with the interpretation of his figures as he is in compiling them. An accountant certainly has more time to devote to the interpretation of his figures now that mechanically prepared ledgers have relieved him of so much of the routine work. He will be a less efficient accountant, and certainly a less interested one, if his responsibility stops at the production of statements. To make accountants responsible for using the products of their work may well be the best way of keeping the purpose of accounting before them. Allied to this argument is the contention that if the accountants' section deals also with financial control and related duties, the accountancy system can be more expeditiously adapted to the needs of the authority and the task of co-ordinating the two sections within the finance department avoided.

Combination is certainly likely to be more economical, because departments will deal with a smaller number of officials, and questions of accountancy procedure and financial control can be settled at the same time. Also avoided is the uneconomic operation of one section within the finance department explaining to another the details of the accounts, so that the explanations may be passed on to outside departments at second hand. Further, so much of financial control relates to matters of detail that the accountant who has kept the books and has a knowledge of the build-up of figures can probably be most helpful. Finally—a most important practical point—the number of first-class officers in a finance department is inevitably limited and may not be sufficient to provide adequate staff for both sections, and the tendency will be for the control section to attract the better men because of the more spectacular nature of the work, much to the detriment of the accountancy section and hence to the quality of the service rendered to the departments.

In short a separate financial control section may be something of a luxury unless the local authority is one of the very largest. In the smaller authorities the creation of such a section would in any case be unjustifiable for the work can be shared between the accountancy section and the deputy chief financial officer. Whatever may be the local solution to the problem, the chief financial officer should remember that what has been alluded to in this section as the financial control work is, if the financial system is well-developed, considerable in volume but irregular in its incidence. He must organize his office to cope promptly with these fluctuations without prejudice to the more regular duties.

(8)

Possibly the two most obvious sections are those for accountancy (with or without financial control) and audit, and it is not surprising to find that such sections exist in all but the smallest offices. The audit section has duties demanding an independent outlook and status and should not be combined with another section. It suffers if extraneous work of any kind is introduced, and to make it a link in the day-to-day operations is to distract the audit staff from their true mission: the exercise of a roving commission. Given a knowledge of the general approach of a chief financial officer to office organization, one can predict—at least in general terms—what the scope of his audit section is likely to be. With the accountancy

91

section it is otherwise. In addition to the accountancy work in the narrow sense, it may be responsible for costing (very often), financial control (frequently), and one or more of such duties as loan registration, superannuation or machine accounting. Already we are approaching the difficulty of discussing intelligibly the details of so many variations in forms of organization.

The organization of accountancy work will be considered in the chapter devoted to the chief financial officer as accountant and in its relation to financial control it has been considered in the preceding section. These aspects of the chief financial officer's work do not, therefore, need further treatment. Nor is there need to discuss the organization of a machine section (where the volume of machinery warrants a separate section) or of audit work, because these subjects are dealt with in the chapters on the chief financial officer as machine accountant and as internal auditor respectively.

(9)

We now pass to a group of duties which can be organized in many alternative ways—the work of making payments and collecting income. Perhaps the most logical approach is to have three sections: (a) an income section to keep the debtors' accounts and follow up outstanding accounts (see chapter on control of income); (b) a payments section to establish the correctness of all proposed payments including salaries and wages (see chapter on payment of accounts); and (c) a cashiers' section to handle the money, including outside and inside collection, banking, and the payment of all accounts and salaries (also referred to in the chapters on collection of income and payment of accounts). But many variations are to be found, e.g. checking bills for payment may be given to the internal audit, a practice which often works well, though it cuts across the view taken in these pages that the internal audit should be concerned with tests imposed on work to which the regular checks have already applied. Again many authorities make a four-fold division by separating the calculation of wages and salaries from the checking of bills and the preparation of payment schedules, often combining payroll preparation with the establishment work in cases where the chief financial officer is the establishment officer. Authorities with such separate sections find little difficulty in justifying them on the grounds of the extent and complexity of the work, and of the specialized skills demanded. Often a salaries and wages section also undertakes the administration of the superannuation acts, work discussed later in the chapter. Other authorities have a payments cashier and a receiving cashier.

However the work of making payments and collecting income is arranged, there are well-known principles of internal check which should be applied to the assignment of duties between and within sections. For example, the person responsible for computing wages should not pay them: nor should the officer responsible for the debtors' accounts handle the money. These principles are of cardinal importance, but provided the local authority observes them—they are always easier to apply in a large authority than in a small one— distribution of the work associated with collection and payments can be settled on grounds of expediency, though there is a great deal to be said for the threefold division described above.

(10)

Those aspects of the chief financial officer's work considered so far are major tasks involving considerable blocks of work. The remaining duties are of the 'miscellaneous' kind, many of them too small in volume to warrant sections of their own, and at the same time not lending themselves theoretically to grouping with other work; though in order to avoid too many sections they must in practice be combined with other duties.

There would be little point in attempting to refer to all these different tasks: many of them, though supremely important, raise no problems of organization. The work which does warrant mention because of its volume can be classified as follows: managing loans and investments, supervising insurances, administration of superannuation and the typing, registration and filing services. The management of the machine room also falls into this miscellaneous group in the smaller offices. Reference is made to the ways of grouping these duties in the next section, and the more important of them are discussed individually in the chapter on the miscellaneous duties of the chief financial officer.

In addition to these sundry financial duties, many chief financial officers have tasks, referred to in an earlier chapter, which are not exclusively, or even largely, financial and which do not form part of the subject of financial administration. They must, however, be borne in mind because they influence the organization of a department. In the main, they are either important enough to be allotted to a separate self-contained section—for instance this is often the case with housing management—or alternatively they may be treated in the same way as a miscellaneous financial task. Though these extraneous duties will not be mentioned again, the reader should remember that in practice finance departments often include, if not extra sections, at least additional administrative 'pockets' to cope with work of this nature.

(11)

How are these miscellaneous functions—the loans and insurance work, typing pools, central filing units, postal sections and other adjuncts of a finance department—to be allotted? Even authorities of the same size distribute the work differently. Some of the miscellaneous duties may be incorporated into the main sections, two examples already mentioned being those of loans registration work given to the chief accountant, and superannuation allied to that of salaries and wages. Similarly, insurance work is often attached to accountancy or to payments, though it does not fall naturally to either. But all the miscellaneous tasks do not lend themselves to attachment to the major sections, and in the moderate sized and larger offices there is a great deal to be said for grouping these sundry tasks under an office manager who would have a status not much inferior to the heads of the major sections, and who might therefore be responsible for such work as machine accounting (where there is no machine accountant and the work is not given to the accountancy section), typing, correspondence, central filing, loans registration and insurance. This grouping avoids the existence of minor section heads and also limits the number of sections. There are, however, no vital principles at stake, once the sections have been sufficiently differentiated to satisfy the requirements of internal security. Accommodation, staff available, and traditional association of duties in the office, are as likely to be the determining factors as theoretical ideas of administration. Appendix C shows in tabular form one common pattern of organization.

(12)

This chapter concludes with a note about office accommodation. A finance department tends to be distinguished from other departments by the large volume of routine work, and in boroughs and district councils by the existence of one office, the rates office, where nearly all the citizens regularly resort. Suitable office accommodation is therefore particularly to be desired and inadequate or dull accommodation specially to be condemned, first because it accentuates any depressing effect which the routine nature of the work may have and secondly because of the bad effects on the ratepayers. Bright and attractive offices tend to compensate for humdrum work, much of which will persist, for, whilst the development of office machinery is taking away the most monotonous and tiring arithmetical work, some operations are likely to remain manual for many years, if only those of preparing data for the machines.

The small offices often found in town and county halls are not suitable for much of the work of a large finance department. Commodious offices where supervision is facilitated, where work can pass from desk to desk in logical sequence and where partitions can be moved to adjust the layout of the office to correspond with changes in clerical procedures are the best for most of the work of the department. A roomy centralized collection office, with ample accommodation for the public and opportunity for quick access to all the records concerned with debtors, is also desirable, It should be well signposted and should allow for the public to flow through, separate entrances and exits being the ideal. On the other hand, small self-contained sections will probably work better in a separate office than in a room where work of a dissimilar nature is being conducted. Whatever the layout of the offices, there should be provision for members of the public to discuss their business in privacy.

In the main, the quality of office accommodation provided for local government staffs compares unfavourably with that of business concerns of comparable size. In many local authorities the pattern of organization within the finance department is unsatisfactory and illogical because it is dictated by unsuitable accommodation, and often not a little of the difficulty of securing co-operation between departments in local government is due to physical separation of departments. These matters are outside the control of officers who may have to wait for many years to make elementary reforms in organization; for there are inevitably demands on the public purse thought by local authorities to be more pressing than the provision of new office accommodation.

CHAPTER VII

THE CHIEF FINANCIAL OFFICER'S DEPARTMENT:
RECRUITMENT AND TRAINING OF STAFF

(1)

THE staff of a chief financial officer's department is recruited from three main sources. First there are the local school-leavers, i.e. those who leave the local grammar and secondary schools at ages between fifteen and eighteen. These boys and girls, the bulk of the intake, are normally required to hold an educational certificate at least equivalent to a General Certificate of Education at ordinary level in three subjects including English and Mathematics. Many of them will remain in the service in subordinate positions; others, more ambitious, will qualify as local government accountants by passing the examinations of the Institute of Municipal Treasurers and Accountants and join the professional stream; a few will take alternative qualifications, e.g. degrees or diplomas in administration, in which case they may attain a fairly high status in the service of the authority, but can only in exceptional circumstances reach the top posts in the finance or any other major department because, for the highest offices, persons professionally qualified in the work of the particular department are required. Secondly, the local authority may recruit mature clerks with outside experience, but not on a large scale, because the conditions of local government—salaries, superannuation, promotion, etc.—are in favour of life-long service. Thirdly, many local authorities engage professionally qualified local government accountants who, with very few exceptions, entered the service of other local authorities as school-leavers and attained to professional status elsewhere by passing the appropriate examinations. A few local authorities have now a fourth stream: university graduates, in whom local authorities are becoming interested, if only because most of the better scholars now pass to universities.

There is no division corresponding to the administrative, executive and clerical classes of the civil service. A school-leaver and a university graduate start with the same prospects, though the graduate receives a higher initial salary. All entrants have a chance of qualifying, and hence of attaining the highest positions, a democratic feature of which those engaged in the financial branch of local government are justly proud. In practice only a small portion of the entrants qualify. Most of the entrants (many of whom are girls) remain in routine posts. The larger finance departments may have posts in the middle grades for which other qualifications, e.g. an administrative qualification, would be suitable. But these are inevitably posts with limited prospects.

Thus a chief financial officer engaging a bright boy is recruiting a potential senior officer for his own or some other local authority. When he engages an applicant of less promise, he is bringing into the service a clerk or minor administrator who is likely to stay in the same local authority throughout his career (though there is now a tendency for more entrants to leave in their twenties). The clerk may move from one department to another within the local authority, but there are in local authorities many officers whose whole working life has been with one department.

Such a staff structure is inflexible in many ways. It provides no scope for the pure administrator, it assumes in practice that the professional training for the chief posts can be obtained only in local government, and it allows, at the minor administrative levels, for little movement between authorities, and not a great deal between departments. At the same time there are the rigid salary scales and conditions of service usually to be found in large-scale organizations, particularly those concerned with government, which make it difficult to recognize individual merit or to stimulate the promising individual. Further, the national salary scales and conditions of service apply to large and small authorities alike and are apt to make the difficulties of recognizing individual merit particularly pronounced where the scale of operations is limited.

Before the Second World War, local government finance was a relatively attractive occupation to those seeking clerical employment. The posts were permanent, they were remunerated as well as comparable jobs elsewhere, and conditions of service—pension arrangements, holidays, working conditions, etc.—were on the whole superior. Counting themselves fortunate to be admitted, most of those who entered intended to make local government finance their life's work. They were conscious of the advantages they had over clerical employees in many other kinds of concern, and were anxious for promotion for which competition was keen. The ambitious youth knew that he could qualify himself as a local government accountant, and could become eligible in due course not just for modest promotion in his own office but for the highest posts in the service. Perhaps most important of all, there were plenty of good entrants—intelligent, capable young men and women possessing integrity, drive and the other qualities needed to make satisfactory public servants. In a local government finance office one therefore expected to see a mixture of people of different ages with a permanent interest in local government, knowledgeable about their own local authority and priding themselves on the quality of their work.

A good deal of this has changed. Those bright sixth-formers whose ambition it was to secure an appointment in the Town Hall, now go to the university, and their local authority is deprived of their services, unless it is one of the few—though they increase in number —who recruit at graduate level. Further, the relative advantages of local government as an occupation have declined : there are so many new attractive openings and alternative employments. Potential employees are hard to find, their calibre deteriorates and the personnel change more rapidly now that the attractions of local government as a lifetime occupation are less. The proportion of married women employed also increases and use is now sometimes made of part-time employees. Local government has become merely one of a number of employers of clerical labour and, particularly in industrial areas, local authorities suffer from the competition of commercial and factory offices.

(2)

What are the outstanding features from the point of view of recruitment of a staff so constituted? The most obvious perhaps is the importance of attracting the right type of school-leavers, for they constitute the bulk of the entrants and are likely to remain in local government for life. Competition for entrance to the local government service being less keen than it was, local authorities must make positive and energetic efforts to attract applicants instead of relying on applications coming in automatically. At least a sprinkling of better types of entrant is essential for the finance department, because, unlike departments such as health and education which recruit their senior officers as professional men, finance departments are, with negligible exceptions, directed, as well as staffed, by persons recruited to the local government service as clerks. Vacancies should be made known in every likely quarter. The interest of Youth

Employment Bureaux and headmasters of schools must be sought, and use made of appropriate propaganda, e.g. pamphlets setting out in an attractive way the prospects in local government financial administration.

In addition, some of the promising youths who eluded the local authorities at eighteen must be attracted into the service when they leave the universities. If this is not done, local authorities will in the future have to appoint their chief and senior officers either from outside the service or from school-leavers who do not reach university entrance standard. A study of the methods of attracting graduate trainees would be outside the scope of this book, but their recruitment brings management implications which can properly be mentioned. University graduates do not constitute a separate cadre of administrative assistants. They are, as was explained earlier in the chapter, on the same footing as any other entrant, though the national conditions of service allow them a higher starting salary. The only additional privilege they are likely to enjoy is a shorter period on the duller routine jobs, coupled with more rapid transfers between sections in the first few years of their service.

(3)

The other feature of staff recruitment meriting specific reference here is that of the actual process of selection from among the candidates for a vacancy. Discriminating selection is of importance in every kind of administration, but is surely particularly so in a sphere where the possibilities of the person appointed remaining in the service of the authority for life are so great.

Local authorities differ in their methods of engaging junior staff. Some have centralized machinery: others allow departments to select; and many have arrangements which are a compromise between the two, e.g. a central register and interviewing panel, but final selection at departmental level.

In recruiting staff, chief financial officers look first for the ordinary attributes of a good public servant—common sense, ability, industry, integrity, loyalty, a sense of humour and so forth. Generalized ability is in the main what is wanted, for even those who will eventually qualify as local government accountants do not need to have shown a marked flair in some particular direction. Accountancy is not a subject like the arts or advanced science which demands some highly specialized aptitude. But it does demand certain traits; the power of clear logical thinking, ability to feel at home with figures, capacity to understand the classification of data (not higher mathematics), the knack of setting out in simple terms the inferences to be drawn from accounts and statistics. A candidate who is to rise to one of the higher positions must also possess the qualities of the administrator.

In local government, vacancies, whether for junior or senior staff, are filled mainly on the strength of a competitive interview. It therefore pays every chief financial officer to give attention to the technique and art of assessing suitability by interview, remembering that a series of bad choices can in a short space of time seriously impair the harmony and efficiency of the department. Fortunately there is considerable literature on the subject so that every officer should at least be able to avoid the worst faults.[1] Whilst it would be outside the scope of the present book to deal with the process of interviewing in detail, some brief remarks may be useful. Both the interviewer and the candidate should come to the interview briefed, the interviewer knowing exactly what type of applicant he is looking for, and the applicant having been told at least sufficient of the post to enable him to decide that he is potentially interested. The interviewer should be business-like but friendly, every effort being made to make the applicant feel at home, and pains must be taken to explain the nature of the post, the remuneration, conditions of service and prospects. The author has long made a practice, when interviewing applicants, of seeing all the candidates together in the first place, and discussing these details with them. This practice saves time, ensures that they all have the same information, and gives them an opportunity to make acquaintance with the interviewer and the room in which they are later to be seen individually.

Whilst so much depends upon imponderables, it is none the less useful to have some kind of mark sheet, however informal, on which to record comments and assessments on specific points. A brief estimate of the candidate's energy, general ability and potentialities, his capacity to work with others, is often worth making, even if the interviewer relies largely on his general assessment. There is also much to be said for small panels of interviewers instead of interview by a single individual, whilst two successive interviews of the same candidates by different interviewers also have their advantages. Every chief financial officer must evolve his own methods, and even learn by his mistakes. But the chances of errors of judgment can be

---

[1] A lucid straightforward treatment of the subject can be found in *Interviewing for the Selection of Staff*, by E. Anstey and E. O. Mercer (Allen and Unwin, 1957).

reduced by common-sense application of the established techniques of interviewing.

(4)

The second aspect of staff with which this chapter is concerned is that of training. Training has two meanings to the staff of the finance department: first, the tuition given to intending examinees; and second, practical training in the office. With the first we are concerned only in so far as it impinges on the duties of the chief financial officer and the organization of his office. A chief financial officer must give every encouragement to his staff to qualify, for this is the only way they can attain to the higher ranks, and only through a constant flow of successful examinees can the finance departments of local authorities be provided with a supply of senior officers. In every office someone should be charged with the duty of watching the careers of the junior staff, and of guiding, advising and where necessary stimulating. If the office is small, the chief financial officer will do this himself for it is an excellent way of keeping in touch with his more junior staff. But in the larger office there is a danger that the task will go by default unless it is specifically given to some very senior officer—often the deputy—and systematically carried out, adequate records being kept of the progress of all juniors in their studies.

But this is by no means all. The examinations of the Institute of Municipal Treasurers and Accountants are so designed that they cannot be passed by candidates without adequate office experience. The chief financial officer must make sure, by giving his prospective examinees a variety of work, that they are not handicapped by insufficient practical knowledge, if necessary at some inconvenience to the office arrangements, provided that the work of the local authority is not jeopardized or the rights of other members of the the staff prejudiced.

The profession of municipal accountancy is passing from an era in which all theoretical study is done in the candidate's own home, under the guidance of a correspondence college, to one when part-time day release and oral instruction are also available, at least in the large urban centres of population—a development long overdue. Upon the chief financial officers of larger authorities, especially those in regional centres, lies the responsibility of inducing local technical colleges to institute appropriate classes and of encouraging their own and adjacent authorities to give the staff facilities for attendance. What are the obligations of a chief financial officer in respect of the theoretical training of those who show no inclination to become professional financial officers or to take a degree or diploma in administration? The most obvious requirement seems to be that they should have some instruction in local government. Many local authorities in England and Wales provide for this by giving day release to all young recruits to enable them to prepare for the clerical examination of the Local Government Examinations Board, the simplest of the specialized local government examinations. Almost equally important is a grounding in book-keeping. Modern mechanical accounting, by making the fundamentals of book-keeping less obvious to the beginner, has made it more, rather than less, necessary for those responsible even for simple accounts such as those with debtors, to understand the principles of that interesting and invaluable concept—double entry book-keeping. Anyone without this basic theoretical knowledge is a menace in a finance department and unlikely to progress far.

The training facilities offered by local authorities to their staffs have greatly improved in recent years. Financial assistance towards tuition and examination costs, part-time day release, payment of expenses to meetings of students' societies, the provision of office libraries, and the encouragement of office study circles—all these are now to be found in local government. It therefore behoves both chief officers and staff to do their utmost to make sure that full advantage is taken of the opportunities provided. Chief financial officers and their qualified staffs can contribute, not only by interesting themselves in the studies of their junior colleagues, but also by participation in the work of students' societies and weekend schools. Organizers of these activities are dependent for their lecturers and tutors upon volunteers from the qualified ranks of the local government service.

(5)

Theoretical training, whether that voluntarily undertaken by the aspirant for a professional diploma, or the *quasi* compulsory kind advocated in the preceding paragraphs for all recruits, is not given by the chief financial officer, though he may arrange it. Office training is, however, entirely a matter for him, and he will be the first to reap the reward if the training is good. It pays him, therefore, to make the practical training of the staff a specific task, and not a by-product of office work. New juniors should be instructed in the nature of the financial work of the local authority, its distribution between the departments, and the organization of the department. They should be shown how each section is staffed and where it is housed. If there are no general courses for juniors covering the work of the local authority, the chief financial officer should additionally see that his staff at least understand the scope of the work of each department. In their early years juniors should be given experience of several sections of the finance department, the chief financial officer insisting that they are properly taught the work of every post they hold. Records of the experience of all the members of the staff are a *sine qua non* of a good office (unless it is very small), and are especially necessary in a service where changes in the directing personnel are frequent. Anyone who has taken over a deputy's post in an office with records showing the history of all the members of the staff can testify to the value of such data.

Rules and regulations about conditions of service—some national and some local—are many and elaborate. The dice are loaded against initiative in staff management for grading systems can so easily take away flexibility, and make periodical changes of duties—so essential if the staff are not to become stale—difficult to achieve. Local authorities have, therefore, to be on their guard lest their grading schemes become their masters and not their servants, and chief financial officers have continually to combat any unwarranted desire on the part of the staff to be allowed indefinitely to do the same work in the same way. A pattern of organization which never changes is the first step towards a second-rate department, and the beginning of a belief in the infallibility of existing methods. A dislike of change on the part of subordinate staff is often fortified by the hostility of section heads to a disturbance in their arrangements, the task of training an officer in some fresh but humble task assuming in their imaginations heroic proportions. What a contrast is the atmosphere of an office accustomed to the continuous adjustment of the routines to meet changed circumstances or to take advantage of improved techniques of administration : here the staff not only welcome change, but expect it, and a chief financial officer who did not make periodical improvements in the organization would soon lose caste!

103

(6)

Transfers of staff, whether the result of rearrangement of routines or not, should take place regularly. The temptation to leave an individual undisturbed in a post for a long time is strong. He comes to know the duties thoroughly, performs them easily and rapidly, and acquires a valuable fund of knowledge and of the finer points of the work. None the less, the temptation should be resisted, for periodical transfers stimulate individuals, increase the total stock of knowledge in the office, make for mobility, encourage the critical examination of routines, and assist management in assessing the posts and the aptitudes they call for. Once a person has been left too long in a post, he may be as resistant to transfer as many officers are to changes in office procedures, and there is the danger that his transfer will become difficult. The fewer posts carrying imposing titles, the more naturally can transfers be made, for not only do individuals become attached to them, but unnecessary titles encourage the growth of traditions— often ill-founded—about the relative importance of the different posts in the office.

Allied to the circulation of staff generally, is the question of promotion : indeed many staff movements involve promotion of one kind or another. That promotion should go by seniority, other things being equal, is a well recognized tenet in the local government service. Promotion automatically by seniority is another matter. The temptation to take this easy course is strong if only because the chief officer may be called upon to justify to a committee the passing over of a colleague, and may well shrink from the invidious task of calling attention to his shortcomings. He may easily forget the frustration of those compelled to work under a senior known to be inferior, or the damage a wrong appointment may do to the authority's interests and the reputation of its officers. It is in accordance with the spirit of English local government that such justifications must be made by chief officers to committees, but the safeguard will only work for good if officers are completely fair and fearless in their comments, and if committees, upon whom the ultimate decision depends, are understanding, impartial and thorough in sifting the evidence.

CHAPTER VIII

THE CHIEF FINANCIAL OFFICER AS FINANCIAL ADVISER

(1)

WE have already noted that the two essential agents of a good financial system are an effective finance committee, and a chief financial officer responsible for the whole of the finances and accounting arrangements of the authority. So far we have considered the finance committee, the scope of the work of the chief financial officer, and the organization of his department. We can now proceed to a more detailed study of the chief financial officer and shall begin with his duties as financial adviser, usually regarded by chief financial officers themselves as their most responsible and exacting role.

This chapter opens with a description of the chief financial officer proffering financial advice, sometimes on his own, and sometimes in collaboration with other officers, and continues with a study of the techniques of interdepartmental co-operation, and of the principles upon which reports and joint reports should be constructed. Later chapters illustrate the application of the principles enunciated here to such incidents of financial administration as budget making and the management of contracts.

(2)

The smaller the authority, the more will it rely on the chief financial officer himself for advice, the closer will be his relationship with the heads of the departments, and the more intimate his knowledge of the council's affairs. On the other hand, the larger the authority, the more must the chief financial officer rely on the financial 'system' and upon subordinates for the first-hand contacts with committees and departments, who will look not so much for the chief financial officer's personal view as that of the finance 'department', just as the central government departments think of the 'Treasury', and not of an individual. In the small authority the chief financial officer has continuous personal contact with the members, and, as he gives the bulk of the top level financial advice himself, has no·problem of instructing subordinates in his point of view. Nor has he to encourage committees and officers to accept advice from his subordinates. On the other hand, the larger the finance department, the less is an operating department seeking advice dependent upon the personality of a particular individual. But however large or small the authority, the attitude of the chief is supremely important, for even the best system for giving departmental financial advice will not long survive the arrival of an indifferent chief officer. Thus, whatever the scale of operations, the personal influence of the chief financial officer counts for a good deal. If the advisory work is to be shared with subordinates, his influence needs to be backed by sound departmental practices and loyal, intelligent and informed officers. The chief financial officer has to take care that by regular conferences, and by himself pursuing a consistent, predictable course, the task of giving advice on his behalf is made as straightforward as possible.

The same fundamental points have to be covered in all authorities, and though the administrative procedure discussed may need to be more elaborate in some authorities than others, the distinction is one of degree and not of principle. To bring out all the relevant points, it will be convenient in this chapter to assume the circumstances of a large authority.

(3)

Our study can best start with those cases on which the chief financial officer is advising individually and not as one of a team of officers. The most onerous of these are finance committee matters, and they fall into two classes. There are first of all purely financial matters on which the chief financial officer has to proffer advice—management and investment of funds, raising capital monies, collection of rates and other income, management of insurance and so forth. Secondly, there is the chief financial officer's function in those instances where the finance committee is considering recommendations and proposals put forward by other committees.

Advising on purely financial matters is perhaps the chief financial officer's most specialized task, the committee being largely dependent on the zeal, perspicacity and care he brings to the task. No attempt will be made to enumerate, let alone describe, this kind of financial business: to do so would be to survey the whole of local government finance. It will be sufficient to illustrate the nature of the chief financial officer's obligations by studying his duties with regard to the

106

establishment and maintenance of reserve and renewals funds. The theory that English local authorities can raise in any year only such sums as they need to meet the expenditure of the year is relaxed by statute to allow of the accumulation of monies for certain purposes: reserve funds for trading undertakings, funds for meeting minor capital expenditure, repairs funds for houses, renewals funds for plant, insurance funds and so forth. Power to establish such funds is conferred or regulated partly by general statutes and partly by private acts or provisional orders. The chief financial officer must first see that his local authority has all the available powers, for the initiative to establish such funds will not normally come from members or other officers. Next, he must advise his committee on the nature and scale of contributions to the funds, the conditions under which they should be used, and investment policy. He may have to caution the committee against the use of the funds for purposes other than those for which they were established, or the temptation to build up funds unnecessarily.

This sketch of the obligations of the chief financial officer in the establishment and management of funds, though intended only as an illustration, brings out an important feature of his responsibilities as financial adviser: the obligation upon him to keep the long-term view before the council. This applies equally to the exclusively financial matters discussed in this section and to the others considered later. Only the chief financial officer can put before the council forecasts of their future financial position, whether it be in connexion with rate levies, capital expenditure, borrowing position, renewals funds or otherwise. The members themselves are naturally preoccupied with immediate problems and cannot be expected unaided to appreciate the cumulative financial effects of current policies. It is the chief financial officer's task to supply this data.

(4)

The second aspect of the finance committee's work on which the members will look to the chief financial officer is that of reviewing the proposals of other committees. When engaged on such reviews the finance committee must have the same information about particular projects as the operating committees have had, because they will resent the supply of additional information to the finance committee. But the finance committee must also be told the over-all

107

effect on the council's finances. For instance, if the proposals are for supplementary estimates, the chief financial officer must show the finance committee the aggregate effect of such estimates from the beginning of the year up to the date of the committee. The finance committee will also want to know about precedents for decisions they are about to make, and will expect to be advised when they are creating a precedent likely to embarrass them on a future occasion. The closer the knowledge the chief financial officer has of the work of the operating committees, the greater his power to help the finance committee to avoid unreal decisions. All finance committees know that one of the worst pitfalls is that of making, in all good faith, decisions—especially those disapproving expenditure or imposing extra charges—which are not practicable, or which are not likely to prove acceptable. It is, of course, primarily the business of the elected members of the finance committee to keep in touch with current trends of thought in the council and outside. This is one reason why in an earlier chapter attendance of chairmen of operating committees was advocated. But a chief financial officer who knows each committee's work, who is acquainted with the background of proposals, and who knows the prevailing temper and mood of committees, can be invaluable and a wise finance committee will not disdain his help.

(5)

The next step towards understanding the role of the chief financial officer as financial adviser is to watch him at work as a member of a team of chief officers, each offering specialized advice to the council and its committees.

What conditions have to be fulfilled before the chief financial officer can make his full contribution to such a team? The most obvious are that inter-departmental relations must be such that all proposals having financial implications become automatically known to the staff of the finance department at the earliest possible time, that consultations begin at once at the appropriate level with all interested departments, that all points of view are put forward whilst proposals are in a malleable form, that differences are as far as possible resolved before schemes are put to committees, and that any remaining divergencies of opinion—and they will normally be found to be few—are put concisely and clearly to the committee, concurrently with the initial presentation of the scheme.

If departments are in each other's confidence, it follows that no department will spring surprises upon another at committees or conferences with members present. In particular the head of a department will not, either behind the scenes or otherwise, advocate a course of action upon which other officers have a right to express an opinion without first consulting them; nor will the chief financial officer criticize a department's finances, financial procedure or proposals in front of a member or committee without prior notice and discussion with the department.

Another feature of a good team is that if one of the officers is in default, or has made a mistake or miscalculation important enough to be reported to a committee, he should himself report it. This is of special importance to the chief financial officer, for the nature of his function as a financial watchdog and as the officer with the responsibility for ensuring the regularity and propriety of financial transactions, means that from time to time he will unearth shortcomings, irregularities, or errors of judgment which the members have a right to know about. How much more pleasant the position, and how much happier the eventual result, if the departmental head joins in explaining the circumstances to the committee, or better still reports them himself!

The aim of the chief financial officer should be to encourage departments themselves to think out the financial implications of everything they do, calling upon him to supply specialist information and advice and to certify that nothing of financial significance has been omitted. There is a great deal to be said for the notion that the test of a chief financial officer is the extent to which he has succeeded in inculcating a feeling for finance in the departments. If he finds that he has to work out most of the financial implications himself, write most of the reports and constantly intervene at committees to make sure that financial considerations are fairly put, he has not succeeded. If he has on the other hand only to underline the salient points of his colleagues' comments, then the presumption is that the authority is enjoying an administration in which finance has its proper place.

Parallel to the chief financial officer's right to insist upon compliance with financial regulations, there should be a right of the departmental head, backed by standing orders of the council, to have all the information and advice he wants. A departmental head will expect a chief financial officer to show expenditure in the most significant way, to suggest appropriate units for expressing the cost of services, to help in devising scales of charges and principles of assessment which fit in with the aims of his department. He will not expect the chief financial officer deliberately to show expenditure or present financial information in a way that will provoke petti-fogging enquiry or misunderstanding. He will remember that the chief financial officer can become remote from the services them-selves. The building of schools or the layout of parks tends to be a paper operation to the chief financial officer, so the keen depart-mental head will regard it as part of his mission in life to make sure, so far as he is able, that the chief financial officer knows what he is talking about, e.g. a local authority architect might well make a practice of giving the chief financial officer an opportunity of seeing all the major schemes in progress at least once a year. Though the departmental officer may encourage his financial colleagues in this way, the principal obligation must be upon the chief financial officer himself: he must ever guard against the danger of thinking only in terms of files and procedures.

Translated into terms of practical administration all this means that the chief financial officer or his representative should be required to attend all committees where financial matters, or important matters with financial aspects, are to be discussed. The chief financial officer should have the agenda in advance, and standing orders should provide for him to have adequate notice of impending financial business. Where several chief officers are concerned with a project, they should come before the committee as a team, all the aspects of the proposal being presented at the same time. Only by cross fertilization of ideas at the outset can a balanced scheme be prepared. It should never be possible for an officer to say to a committee: 'If only I had heard about this proposal at an earlier stage.'

(6)

Having considered the chief financial officer both in his capacity as an individual adviser and as one of a team, we must now study in more detail the nature of his distinctive contribution. Like the Clerk to the authority, and unlike his other colleagues, he is concerned with all committees and nearly all transactions, for there are few incidents of local government, and very few matters of major policy, without financial implications.

The extent to which officers suggest policy depends on the nature of the matter under consideration, the size of the authority, the local traditions, the working of the local party machine, the calibre of the officers, the open-mindedness of the members and many other

110

features. But in the field of finance, the council will look to its chief financial officer, not only for guidance, but for some at least of the initiative. Members, committees, and political parties are more likely to have spontaneous ideas about the building of clinics, the siting of markets, or the merits of comprehensive schools than about provision for replacement of assets or the ways of charging for services. As has been mentioned earlier in the chapter, members are rarely able to take a long-term view of over-all financial policy without the help of the chief financial officer. They must, therefore, rely upon him to bring forward data forecasting the future trends of the council's activities, and to suggest long-term policy. For example, most housing authorities expect their chief financial officer to produce schemes for rent policies designed to avoid undue fluctuation either in rents or in the charge to rates. Many of the matters he has to broach will be delicate, for no committee relishes being reminded of charges needing to be increased or of services not justified by current demand.

Then again, recommendations by teams of officers, or joint reports, do not imply anonymous contributions or corporate responsibility, so that when officers act as a team, committees are not absolved from their obligation to ask for individual opinions. The chief financial officer will, therefore, frequently be asked at committee meetings to give assurances or explanations from the financial standpoint.

Finally there are those occasions when the chief financial officer has in the course of discussion, or perhaps in a written report, to put forward advice that differs from that of his brother officers; and at times he may have to raise matters contrary to the wishes of another officer, for he has a duty not to compromise financial principles and not to allow the council's interest, as he sees it, to be prejudiced. He should be allowed to express his view without hindrance or discouragement from members or officers.

A chief financial officer has thus to blend with the duty of co-operation that of exercising an independent judgment, and must not let the habit of compromise, so essential to successful administration, blunt his determination to secure proper attention to financial considerations.

(7)

Only in the finance committee is the chief financial officer the officer most intimately concerned with the work of the committee. Elsewhere his interest in the proceedings, being limited to one aspect of the committee's work, is secondary to that of the head of the operating department, and therefore he needs a somewhat different technique from that of the officer whose interest is concentrated on the running of a single service.

The committees of the council must expect to hear their financial officer on the financial aspects of all their activities. But he must confine himself to finance, though the temptation to offer opinions on matters that do not concern him is strong; for very much passes through his hands, and his knowledge of current local affairs is wide. As the financial conscience of the council, it will often fall upon him to start heart-searchings about projects, but though he must not shrink from putting financial implications plainly, he must avoid speaking against schemes. Indeed he must not express opinions about the advisability of schemes unless he is specifically asked to do so; and a committee which knows its business will *not* ask him.

No financial officer will carry conviction with a committee unless he finds a way of associating himself with the work of the committee without encroaching on the preserves of other officers or sacrificing his independent financial view-point. If the chief financial officer or his representatives attend operating committees only occasionally, it will be hard for the finance department to keep in touch with the work of the committees. When representatives of the chief financial officer appear—and it will usually be over a matter of some difficulty—they will then come as strangers at a loss for the best approach, for every committee evolves over the years its own distinctive atmosphere, and has to be treated accordingly.

Regular attendance at committee meetings fulfils other functions besides ensuring that the committee has financial advice on appropriate occasions or bringing to bear the chief financial officer's knowledge of the financial practices of other committees. It serves as a gradual education of the members in financial matters, not an easy objective to achieve because the financial aspects of a committee's work are apt to be intricate and dull. Few members will have any special interest in finance and none will have much time to spend on the subject. Elected members can be expected to master financial principles only gradually as projects come up for discussion and decision. The presence at committees of the chief financial officer or his representative will serve as an automatic reminder that there are financial aspects to almost every matter of importance, and will help the members to appreciate that the chief financial officer is the servant of all committees.

The benefits are not wholly to the members. It is by attendance at committees that the chief financial officer and his staff keep abreast of the trend of opinion in the council, find out about impending projects, become acquainted with the views and personal characteristics of individual members and learn to identify themselves with the aims and policies of the council. A chief financial officer without acquaintance with the committees, and without appreciation of their distinctive casts of mind, can make but a meagre contribution to the deliberations of his authority. If he has such a knowledge he will over the years come to understand the activities of the committees and departments and appreciate their difficulties.

The chief financial officer's relations with the chairman of the finance committee have been dealt with in an earlier chapter. His relations with the chairmen of other committees fall for mention here. The chief financial officer must aim at keeping in touch with them, though not behind the backs of the other chief officers. The chairmen must regard him as available for consultation, and he must see that they are informed about the current financial problems of the services they control. At least once a year—at budget time—consultations with all the chairmen will be necessary, consultations which are likely to be much more fruitful if the chief financial officer or his senior representative has been in close touch with the committees and their chairmen throughout the year.

If the chief financial officer regards as desirable some action likely to prove unpalatable to a committee, e.g. an increase in charges, he should have preliminary consultations with the chairman, in conjunction with the officers concerned. Again, if the chief financial officer believes a committee is acting detrimentally to the financial interests of the council, he should only as a last resort bring in the finance committee, or even the finance committee chairman, for the seeds of inter-committee antagonism, so easily sown, take root all too quickly. At the stage when the chief financial officer feels that some failing of a committee is sufficiently grave or persistent to be reported to the finance committee he will normally first mention the business informally to the chairman of the finance committee, hoping that persuasion (or even pressure) can be applied behind the scenes. Avoidable disagreements between committees or departments are specially to be shunned in local government because, in the absence of centralized management, they must be settled in open council, to the detriment of the council's reputation and the bewilderment of the public.

(8)

Two practical aspects of giving advice need to be considered. First the technique of inter-departmental co-operation, which is dealt with below, and secondly the principles upon which reports, both individual and joint, should be constructed; these are dealt with in the remaining sections of the chapter.

An efficient finance department will become aware of new projects immediately they are mooted, normally through their regular contacts with the officers of the department. As soon as proposals for schemes begin to mature the financial details will be worked out by the staffs of the two departments, the extent to which the departments rely on the finance department depending upon the distribution of duties and the nature of the particular project; but the finance officer of the operating department would in any case play a prominent part. The concern of the finance department is not so much to do the financial calculations as to ensure that correct financial assumptions are made. The proposal may raise awkward financial issues, or there may be alternatives with varying financial implications. Discussion between the chief officers themselves may be necessary, the departmental head wanting advice on such aspects as the possible reactions of the finance committee to the proposal. Or the project may affect a sufficient number of heads of departments to warrant an inter-departmental conference. Or the scheme may be a by-product of a policy already adopted by the council and now in the hands of the officers for the purpose of working out the details. From the chief financial officer's point of view, the essential thing is to have a representative present as soon as financial points emerge.

So far we have considered new projects. Most of the financial points coming before committees relate, however, to continuing activities. For these there must be regular consultation, usually most conveniently done by the financial control or accountancy staff visiting the departments when financial negotiations are afoot or agenda for committees or reports on such questions as variations in charges are in course of compilation, more senior officers of the finance department being drawn in—if necessary the chief financial officer himself—as the occasion demands. A wise chief financial officer will encourage heads of other departments to use the finance staff freely at all times: one of his aims should be to have senior assistants who are as much at home in the room of the chief officers of the operating departments as in that of the chief financial officer himself.

Not all the business with financial implications will be sufficiently important to justify a specific joint report of the kind discussed in the following sections. Much of it will relate to minor or routine matters. These can be dealt with either orally at the committee, or by the head of the department including in his monthly or quarterly report a note agreed by the finance department's staff.

(9)

Written reports, as is explained in the chapter on the chief financial officer as accountant, are needed for a variety of purposes—new building schemes, purchase of properties, potential overspendings, charges for use of property or services rendered and routine reports and accounting statements of many kinds.

Among the reports presented, some are prepared in accordance with local tradition; others will be required by standing orders: it is for example a common practice for standing orders to prohibit the consideration by the council of proposals involving new liabilities, either on capital or revenue account, without a report from the officers setting out the full financial implications. Whether prepared in accordance with standing orders or otherwise, reports are most effective if they are presented jointly by all the officers concerned. Once established for this major purpose, the habit of joint reporting will spread to other matters, even to the submission of accountancy statements and accompanying comment. For though at first sight accounts and conclusions to be drawn from them might be thought to be matters exclusively for the chief financial officer, this is not the case. The chief financial officer is himself unable to take advantage of the lessons to be learned from the accounts: he is merely the purveyor of information, and the tenderer of advice. At officer level, the person to translate the lessons into action is the head of the department. He needs the chief financial officer to compile the accounts and to interpret them. But having realized their significance, the head of the operating department should be associated with their presentation to the committee and with any conclusions to be drawn. He will then be much more interested in the accounts themselves, the position they disclose, and the action to be taken. For this reason the author some years ago abandoned the practice of reporting independently on the annual accounts of the trading undertakings. Instead, the accounts

115

and their implications are now discussed with the departments and a report is prepared either jointly or by the head of the department alone. In the latter case a paragraph is included either stating that the City Treasurer agrees and has nothing to add, or else incorporating his comments. In this way the committees are presented with one document instead of two, close consultations between the departments are ensured, the head of the department is given an additional incentive to take notice of his accounts, and support is given to the idea that the accounts are an instrument of management, and not an external document inflicted on the committee by an officer who stands outside the working of the department.

The arguments put forward above in favour of supplying committees with managerial comments concurrently with the presentation of accounting data, apply with special force to documents submitted to a committee to enable it to supervise the administration. Thus, for instance, figures submitted by the chief financial officer showing the idle time of plant should have beside them the comments of the head of the department on variations from the norm or on any unusual features. Some committees ask for reports of this kind only if expectations are not being reached, e.g. if idle time diverges from the approved margin sufficiently to warrant enquiry, or if expenditure shows significant variations from budget figures.

(10)

The principles underlying the preparation of financial statements and reports for committees will now be considered. Possibly the most important is always to remember that the members, whatever their vocations, serve as laymen. Technicalities must therefore be avoided, though to reduce them to general terms will often be the most difficult part of the preparation of a report, and certainly the task calling for the highest intelligence and imagination. In the case of financial reports and statements, the layman's lack of training in the specialized art of comprehending and interpreting figures is an added difficulty. Many laymen do not understand—and indeed do not like—the intricacies of finance. It follows that, paradoxical though it appears, the fewer figures a financial statement contains the better, a conclusion possibly not much to the liking of accountants. Further, a financial statement or account, other than one submitted regularly and fully understood by the committee, should be accompanied by a brief note explaining the significance of the figures.

A chief officer must always remember that the committee is concerned with the policy and with the supervision of the administration, not with the administration itself. A report extending beyond two sheets of foolscap is likely to be looked at askance by the busy committee member who tends to read short reports and ignore, or only glance through, the others. Even when an intricate matter is under consideration, there is much to be said for a short report with supporting data in appendices. R. W. Bell puts the matter thus:

'If you have a lot of material which must be put in the report but is secondary to the main thread of argument, use the device of setting it out in appendices. By this means you comply with the requirement of keeping your report brief and crisp, yet nothing essential for full study of the problem need be left out. This is especially desirable if much of this material takes the form of figures or tabulated information.'[1]

Every officer seeking to present facts or views to a committee has to decide whether to circulate a report before the meeting or to rely on oral exposition. Often the choice is not easy. K. C. Wheare says on this topic:

'No hard and fast rules can be laid down. So much depends upon the personalities and capacities of officials and committees. But it may be suggested that it is perhaps easier to err by choosing the side of circulating written matter in some detail beforehand. There are at least two difficulties. One is that a concise statement of an issue is extremely difficult to set down in writing; the other is that, as indicated already, councillors, though usually able to read, are usually also unwilling to do so. A great many points may be more effectively grasped by a committee if expounded orally in committee by an official. Obviously some matters require treatment at length and in advance in a written document; some decisions must be based on information; appointments can be made only after perusing particulars of the candidates' qualifications and experience. But it seems certain that the amount of paper circulated to members of a committee should be kept to a minimum. Administration by committees is administration after discussion, and the oral method of presentation is more effective in provoking and guiding discussion than the written.'[2]

[1] R. W. Bell, *Write What You Mean* (Allen and Unwin, 1954), p. 74.
[2] K. C. Wheare, *Government by Committee* (Oxford University Press, 1955), pp. 187–8.

The chief financial officer has one advantage in this connexion: he knows that accounting information of all kinds must be in writing and be circulated in advance if it is to be of value. Few members will be able to take in figures given orally at a meeting and they should not be expected to do so. It follows from this that though occasionally the chief financial officer will have a choice between a written and an oral report, for the most part the matter is settled in favour of written reports by the very nature of the subject matter: sometimes they will be required by standing orders. His department, has, therefore, to be organized to produce lucid documents promptly. Having settled the form of a regular statement he should not alter it capriciously, for changes in the form of statement can easily disconcert the layman. On the other hand a judicious and well-timed change may attract attention to a statement and prevent it from being a mere routine paper disregarded by members.

(11)

Finally we have to note the special features of joint reports. For the purpose of illustration let us assume that the officers are reporting upon a proposal to build a new swimming bath. The purpose of a joint report is to give the operating committee a brief but comprehensive view of the project, together with the views of all the appropriate officers. It would begin by describing the work very briefly, leaving the architect to supply the details—probably by submission of draft plans supplemented by oral explanations. A short justification of the proposal might follow, e.g. the obsolescence or inadequacy of the existing establishment. The committee would be reminded of the stage the proposal had reached; for instance, the report might be the initial document merely asking for consideration in principle, or it might be a firm report on the strength of which the council is expected to go forward for loan sanction. If the projects were part of a larger scheme, it would be necessary to remind the committee of the circumstances.

A short statement of the estimated capital cost would follow showing separately the cost of land, buildings, engineering works and professional services, and the probable phasing of the work over financial years. Next would come estimates of running costs including loan charges, and income, together with notes about the bases used, periods assumed for loans, numbers of bathers allowed for, etc. These notes might pose problems of principle for the committee to determine. The committee should also be told what the next stage would be, e.g. submission to the finance committee, and to what extent the cost of the project has been allowed for in the current estimates.

Any minor differences of opinion could be noted in the course of the report, e.g. if the chief financial officer and the baths superintendent held differing views about the probable income. But major differences of opinion—and, as was noted earlier in this chapter, it is encouraging to find how rare they are—would be the subject of a separate dissenting note. The right to differ must be carefully guarded, for if joint reports operated to stifle opinion they would soon fall into disrepute.

An example of a joint report appears in Appendix D.

(12)

There are, alas, no formulae to guarantee success to the chief financial officer as financial adviser. So much depends upon the factors beyond his control such as the receptiveness of the committees, the tradition of the authority, the efficiency of the departments, the personalities of the officers and their willingness to work as a team. Cordial personal relations are perhaps the most valuable single aid, but these are beyond the power of a single officer to establish, though the Clerk and the chief financial officer, having duties relating to all departments, are in the best position to set a good example. But even the most unanimous band of officers cannot make sure that their views will receive adequate consideration at committees. Officers can, however, see that every encouragement is given to early consideration of projects at departmental level by a good system of inter-departmental collaboration: and they can further help themselves by adopting sound techniques of committee reporting.

CHAPTER IX

THE CHIEF FINANCIAL OFFICER AS ACCOUNTANT

(1)

THE duties of the chief financial officer as accountant are:

(a) to prepare, publish and submit to audit, final accounts, and to produce the data needed for such purposes as the assessment of tax and the calculation of grants;

(b) to supply the council, the committees and the departments with financial and costing data;

(c) to control all the accountancy and financial records whether they are kept in the operating departments or in the finance department.

Each of these duties is discussed below, together with the organization of the accountancy work done in the chief financial officer's department.

(2)

Published final accounts will be considered first. In English provincial boroughs, the 'treasurer' must print an abstract of the accounts not subject to district audit. In Scotland not only must accounts, including a balance sheet, be prepared, but they must give certain information set out in the Local Government (Scotland) Act, 1947. The accounts must be prepared by a prescribed date and laid before the council together with the auditors' report and deposited for inspection by the ratepayers.

In practice nearly all authorities publish final accounts. These 'abstracts of accounts', as they are called, are notorious for their bulk. Covering a wide variety of activities and often including such *minutiae* as a record of each loan raised, the printed volume may run to two, three or even four hundred pages, and may cost as many hundred pounds to produce. Latterly there has been some attempt to reduce the number of pages by omission of historical matter (particularly that relating to loans) and by condensing headings, whilst the cost has been reduced by cheaper methods of reproduction, e.g. stencilling. A few English authorities now publish their accounts in the same volume as the budget for the next year but one—an economical practice, but one involving a delay in the issue of the accounts.

That final accounts have a place in management cannot be denied. In the case of trading concerns, the accounts for the year give the verdict on the year's working: they are the chief means by which the trading committee 'accounts' to the council; and they form the basis for computing transfers to or from the rate fund. They should, therefore be prepared in an informative way and be accompanied by a succinct report by the chief officer of the department and the chief financial officer. The earlier they are prepared after the end of the financial year the more use they are to the committee and the council as an instrument of control.

The bulk of a local authority's work is, however, concerned with non-trading activities. Although the final accounts are also important here they are less important than the budget, for it is on the strength of the budget that the local authority makes its most far-reaching decision of the year—the determination of the rate. Further, its preparation automatically involves a review of the position for the current year as well as a forecast for the following year. The presentation of the budget is, therefore, the time when most notice is likely to be taken of current trends. The figures eventually shown in the final accounts must then be closely compared with the revised estimates for the year in question, which were based on data gathered three or four months before the end of the financial year, and any important divergencies reported, with explanations, to committees. This use of the final accounts as the means of disclosing divergencies from the revised estimates is important: without it a vital link in the financial chain is missing. Unfortunately the following up of the revised estimates in this way is by no means universal. The final accounts of non-trading concerns are also valuable aids to management inasmuch as they give clues to efficiency, e.g. unit costs, trends, etc. can be computed from them.

Publication of accounts is often a tardy process with local authorities. Even where an abstract of accounts is printed as a separate volume it may appear any time within the next twelve months after the close of the financial year, though some large volumes are produced in three or four months. Where the chief financial officer has complete charge of all book-keeping and accounting arrangements there seems to be little excuse for late issue. Early publication of an abstract of modest size is far more likely to interest members and ratepayers than late publication of a thick tome.

Up-to-date information about other towns is useful when new projects are mooted, or when some aspect of the work of the authority is under criticism or examination. If the accounts of other authorities only suggest where further enquiry would be fruitful, they are worth while. Comparisons between authorities are at present hindered by diversity of presentation and differences in principles of allocation of expenditure; but the general adoption of the standard form of accounts put forward by the Institute of Municipal Treasurers and Accountants in May 1955[1] will make comparisons easier.

(3)

There are in local government two main levels of management, the committee and the operating department. Our next task is to consider how the chief financial officer can best set about supplying both organs of the local authority with appropriate financial and costing data, bearing in mind the limited use for management purposes of the annual final accounts discussed in the preceding paragraph. The supply of accountancy information to committees is dealt with first.

Committees must have information to help them to reach decisions, to appraise results, to keep in touch with the trends during the year, to gauge the efficiency of the departments and to decide upon instructions to officials. Among the statements which the chief financial officer must provide are: comparison of revenue expenditure and income with the budget; information showing the progress of capital schemes, however financed; particulars of the exercise of loan sanctions; costs of individual jobs, processes, vehicles, plant, etc. in sufficient detail to enable the committee to judge the efficiency of the departments; interim results of trading undertakings showing trends and variations from standards or other yardsticks; periodical comparisons of local results with those of other similar authorities; details of reserve, renewal and other funds which are liable to escape

---

[1] See *The Form of Published Accounts of Local Authorities* (Institute of Municipal Treasurers and Accountants, 1955). In Chapter I the uses of published accounts are discussed with particular reference to standardization between authorities.

regular scrutiny; specialized statements such as those needed by the finance committee for controlling the loans and cash position, the management of the council's funds, the collection of revenue, etc.; and *ad hoc* information for special purposes, e.g. fixing charges or making long-term forecasts.

Of these types of data, that relating to capital expenditure and loan sanctions needs to be specially noted, for capital works are important from so many points of view. They need the most careful consideration before they are undertaken; they call for the utmost wisdom in the selection of the contractors and in the settlement of the terms of the contract; and they demand close supervision. The subject of capital expenditure will therefore recur throughout these pages. The point of importance at this stage is that the chief financial officer must acquaint the operating committees at significant intervals with the financial position, i.e. the expenditure against estimates and loan sanctions. He has also to prevent unauthorized payments and see that applications for supplementary loan sanctions are made, control over these matters being secured partly by use of accounting statements and partly by the control over contracts described in a later chapter. A routine to ensure that small overspent balances on loan sanctions are not left outstanding indefinitely is essential. Supplementary sanctions should be applied for expeditiously, or alternatively the over-expenditure should be met from revenue or other appropriate sources. If the council is carrying out work by direct labour, statements showing the progress of expenditure, and comparing at each stage performance with estimates, are of outstanding importance. Ideally they should be submitted concurrently with reports by the officer responsible for the work.

(4)

To pass from the supply of accounting data for committee use to the task of giving the departments the information they need, is to pass from the committee room with its periodical meetings and broad view, to the rough and tumble of everyday administration. Departments want—or should want—not the general statements suitable for committees, but the dynamic kind of data given to production managers in industry. They are more interested in the immediate future than in the distant scene: and past results are significant mainly from the point of view of their influence on current working, e.g. if the rate of spending of a controllable item has been greater than the budget permits, the department is interested in finding ways of balancing this by an underspending in the next period. Moreover, departments need different kinds of statement for different levels of management. The Director of Education may want to know how his estimate for heating and lighting is working out and what are the relative costs of different methods of heating, but the caretaker in the school needs to know his weekly fuel consumption, and how it compares with his standard. In between, the administrative officer must watch the expenditure school by school, but by intervals longer than a week and in less detail than the caretaker who is concerned with the separate pieces of apparatus, individual meter readings and so forth.

Departments are entitled to expect that the chief financial officer will apply the best and most up-to-date accounting and costing practices to the production of the statements. This applies alike to the refinements of cost accountancy—use of standards, variance accounts, etc. and to modern devices such as charging for stores consumed at standard or estimated prices, or the use of automatic means of indicating to the department when each item of stores stands below its minimum or above its maximum level. Departments are also entitled to expect the accountancy system to be the handmaid of their operations. For instance, it should yield all the information required for fixing charges for work done or estimating prices, a very important point for a direct labour organization preparing estimates of cost.

The regular financial documents, if properly presented, will give pointers to the formulation of policy, and should, over the years, help the departments in their task of advising committees, as well as in the administration of their departments. But at times the departments, when searching for the solution to a problem, will need *ad hoc* financial information. The accounting organization must be such that the information can be supplied helpfully and readily.

The staff of the department must be made to feel at home with the forms used. With manual records this is relatively easy, but mechanical accounting systems, however capacious and flexible, can produce information only in certain forms, and the statements produced are rarely immediately intelligible to the layman. A rigidity in the layout, the printing of information in an apparently illogical order, the appearance of disconcerting abbreviations, the use of continuous stationery—all these features are apt to puzzle the layman using the statements. Those who produce them are not conscious of the limitations and drawbacks: living with the machines they naturally think in terms of machine techniques. The chief financial officer has not completely succeeded in his task until he has made outside departments as familiar as his own staff with the statements. Officers who use the figures must not feel they are remote or less informative than figures they might themselves prepare. A discussion of the position or trends disclosed by the figures is often valuable, especially for statements prepared for technical officers, foremen, and workmen not trained in the interpretation of statements. There is, therefore, much to be said for personal delivery of accounting statements by relatively senior staff.

The necessity to take infinite care in settling the forms of statement in order to avoid frequent sweeping changes, must not operate to prevent a regular examination of the procedures and forms. Small adjustments or additions, the institution of new forms, the discontinuance of unwanted statements or changes in the frequency of submission must be made as they are wanted: and major overhauls, even though they may involve root and branch changes, should not be shirked when they are due. Once every year or so all those who use the data should have a chance of discussing their usefulness and the desirability of modifications. All organizations suffer from the tendency to produce more information than is justified or to continue to produce figures no longer needed. When the statements are supplied by one department for use of another the tendency is particularly strong, unless there is very close liaison between the two. It is sometimes said that the way to establish the necessity or otherwise of a return is without notice to stop producing it. This is no doubt an effective way, but to have resort to it is surely to admit that inter-departmental understanding is defective. Accounting and cost statements are expensive to produce. Finance committees may therefore reasonably insist on assurances that they are actually being used. The best way to satisfy them is for the annual examination of the form of the statements to be accompanied by enquiries into the uses to which they are being put.

(5)

The third duty of the chief financial officer as accountant is to devise and control the whole of the financial accounts. In this task the statutes give him little help, except for the provisions about publication of final accounts referred to earlier in the chapter.

The meagre provisions of the statutes themselves are, however, slightly supplemented by the Rate Accounts (Borough and Urban District Councils) Order, 1926, and the corresponding orders relating to rural authorities and metropolitan boroughs, and by the Accounts (Boroughs and Metropolitan Boroughs) Regulations, 1930, which lay down general rules for the keeping of accounts. The Rate Accounts orders apply only to rate collection accounts, whilst the 1930 regulations, though of general application, apply only to boroughs and metropolitan boroughs and are restricted to such of their accounts as are subject to district audit. They therefore cover only a small proportion of the account-keeping of local authorities. In addition, as has been noted in an earlier chapter, the regulations allow the work of account-keeping to be dispersed over a theoretically unlimited number of officers and do not provide even for central supervision, though in the memorandum accompanying them the Ministry expressed the hope that the control of accountancy operations would be in the hands of one chief financial officer. In Scotland the statutory prescriptions about the final accounts strengthen the position of the chief financial officer even though there may be departmental accountants. Moreover, in Scotland the honorary treasurer (i.e. the chairman of the finance commitee) has a responsibility to 'exercise general superintendence over the finances of the council', and in practice will use the chief financial officer to assist him in this duty. None of these provisions in either England or Scotland touch any aspect but the preparation of final accounts and the basic accounting data supporting them. They are concerned with securing regularity of transactions and with the stewardship of public monies. Vitally important though these aspects are, they form but a small part of the duties of a modern accountant.

(6)

It is never possible for the whole of the financial records and duties of a local authority to be centralized in the chief financial officer's department. Ordering of goods, the initial steps in the verification of accounts for payment, the recording of workmen's time, the keeping of stores bin-cards are random examples of work which must be done in the departments. On the other hand, the preparation of final accounts, submission of grant claims, preparation of the budget and similar work must be done centrally. In between there are classes of work which are sometimes done centrally and sometimes done in the departments; even within a single authority the distribution of the work between the finance department and the other departments may vary. Decisions about this distribution of work have therefore to be taken in every local authority and are of the utmost importance. Where the chief financial officer is not in complete charge of the accounts, these decisions cannot be made in any logical fashion. They will be the result of inter-departmental struggles, with the chief financial officer advocating centralization because he is unable to exercise a proper control in any other way. Where, however, the chief financial officer has control of the accounting system throughout the whole of the authority, the decision can be made on merit. No rules applicable to all authorities can be made, for every local authority has its own internal organization. All that can be done is to indicate broadly the considerations to be borne in mind, on the assumption—and it is a vital assumption—that there is unified control and that the location of records is to be determined dispassionately.

An initial difficulty is the variation in size and function of local authorities. At the extremes there are authorities with departments large enough to have qualified accountants working in the individual departments, and authorities too small even to warrant a separate finance department, the Clerk doubling the role of Clerk and chief financial officer.

Authorities large enough to justify qualified departmental accountants are very few in number, and even in the largest of all, the tendency will be towards centralization of such of the routine work as can be done mechanically, a point which is developed later. For the purpose of this discussion these 'outsize' authorities will be ignored, though many of the points made can be applied to them. In any case the doctrine that there should be one chief financial officer ultimately responsible for the organization of the financial work and the final drawing together of the threads applies irrespective of size.

The influences which work towards centralization even of much of the subsidiary work can be briefly summarized as follows:

(a) Only the chief financial officer's department will normally have a reservoir of skilled accountants, and accounting done elsewhere may be amateurish. A sensible local authority will normally insist on the professional knowledge of the qualified staff being fully used, which means centralization of all the higher work.

(b) There is a good deal to be said for divorcing the responsibility for carrying out work from that of computing the cost. The advan-

127

tage of the independence of a centralized accounting system should not be forgotten or lightly cast aside. A wise authority will not expose its officers to the inevitable temptation to suppress inconvenient or unfavourable results.

(c) Whilst accounts have to be fashioned primarily for the particular department, there are many matters in which uniformity is desirable, e.g. it helps members of the authority greatly if common headings of expenditure are in use, where appropriate. A measure of uniformity can be achieved by the issue of directions to dispersed points but is most easily and effectively obtained by a centralized unit.

(d) The preparation of accounts is one of the main tasks of the chief financial officer. To the head of a department it is only an incidental task, and may well be irksome. Better results are likely to be obtained if the chief financial officer carries out as much as possible of the work, leaving the departmental officer to do his main work undistracted by duties more properly falling within the province of the chief financial officer.

(e) Modern mechanization and above all the application of electronics will virtually compel local authorities to a deal of centralization if full advantage is to be taken of available appliances.

There are also some tendencies commonly supposed to work towards decentralization of the subsidiary work, if not of the final accounts:

(a) The departmental staffs may take greater interest in the accounts if they are prepared in their department. They may even understand them better. The object of most financial statements being to stimulate departments to action of some sort, this is not an advantage lightly to be discounted.

(b) It may sometimes be more convenient for costs to be computed in the department. The transmission of documents to the centre, however well organized, must involve some delay if only slight.

(c) Departmental officers will have a closer knowledge of the working of the department and may therefore be able to prepare more useful and intelligible statements.

(7)

In practice the issue cannot be settled by a mechanical weighing of these or any other factors: a nice judgment is needed which takes into account all the relevant points. Close consultation between the departments is imperative, and the chief financial officer should endeavour to carry the departments with him in the distribution of duties. If the chief financial officer always bears in mind that the purpose of the records is to serve departmental needs, and the heads of departments are prepared to accept the desirability of as much standardization in procedure between departments as possible, disagreements are likely to be infrequent. If they occur, the council must settle them. Disagreements in the past have usually stemmed from the unwillingness of a local authority to place upon the chief financial officer the job of integration, rather than from differences about the distribution of work under an integrated system.

It cannot be gainsaid that in the near future most of the routine work will be done centrally in order to take advantage of mechanization. But the same considerations do not apply to such work as the coding of bills for payment. As a local authority grows in size there is much to be said for decentralization of any clerical work which can be done as well in the departments as in the finance department; it prevents the piling up of routine work in one place and it helps to foster a sense of financial responsibility in the departments. The prerequisites are that the work is properly done and that all the necessary safeguards are applied. The chief financial officer must lay down the procedure to be followed, and must have some means of making sure that the routines are conscientiously carried out. A rough and ready generalization on the subject of decentralization might be that, given an integrated system and proper control, whilst the higher accountancy work and the work which can be done most readily on machines should be centralized, other clerical work can often be done in the departments. In no case should a record be centralized if it reduces its value to the department, e.g. a record of gas and electricity consumptions over a period is of most value in the place where the consumption can be controlled. A rider might be that the chief financial officer should aim at satisfying the departments, and must, therefore, sometimes be prepared to compromise and should never press a rule to an absurd conclusion. For instance, though the cost accounts based on labour costs, stores issued and bills paid may be centralized, it may sometimes pay to provide the engineer with a simple means of making a 'memorandum' addition to the figures prepared in the costing department in respect of liabilities incurred but for which bills have not been received or passed forward.

A few authorities make use of a half-way house arrangement between complete centralization and completely independent departmental accounts, posting into outside departments officers who are attached to the chief financial officer's department. Sometimes they form part of the staff of the outside department but take technical instructions from the chief financial officer. In other places they may be complete enclaves of the finance department, merely housed in the outside department for the sake of convenience. This compromise has the material advantage of keeping the finance staff in close touch with the work of the departments and encouraging the heads of those departments to make full use of the financial organization. Such an arrangement, however, needs very careful handling if confusion of responsibility is to be avoided. Its principal disadvantage is that it prevents the organization of the finance work on a functional basis and thus makes uniformity and the economies of functional organization, already discussed in an earlier chapter, difficult to obtain.

Whatever the distribution of duties, no duplication of records should be permitted. Unfortunately local authorities have acquired bad habits in this respect because of the failure in many places to integrate financial arrangements. The setting up of unofficial records outside the system should be categorically prohibited and the chief financial officer should, through his audit, watch that no duplication does in fact take place. But to condemn duplication is not to argue in favour of either centralization or decentralization. It is merely to recognize that no sensible régime can condone two records for one purpose. But the chief financial officer must not condemn out of hand suggestions that a department needs some additional information which can be better accumulated on the spot. Sometimes these requests can be justified, and a chief financial officer should arrive at a decision only after most careful enquiry. If he is to err it should be on the side of placating the department.

(8)

How should the chief financial officer organize the accountancy which is done in his own department? Usually it will be segregated in a separate section which is normally also responsible for the budget and, as has been explained in an earlier chapter, may be called upon to do some or all of the work for which the description 'financial control' has been used.

In most accountancy sections of the larger authorities, there are sub-accountants subject to the control of the chief accountant or chief accountancy assistant. Some chief financial officers prefer the latter title in the belief that the term chief accountant might suggest that the occupant of the post is of chief officer status. These sub-accountants are responsible for one or more of the services of the authority, and are officers of importance, especially where their duties also embrace financial control, for they are the day-to-day link with the departments on a wide range of matters. In a smaller authority, instead of sub-accountants, the chief accountant and his deputy may themselves take immediate charge of the accounts with qualified or partly qualified assistants to help them. In assessing the contribution of an accountant in the modern organization, one has to remember that mechanization, whilst it has relieved him of dull and detailed book-keeping, has added to his responsibilities, in that the number of accounts and operations for which one officer can now be made responsible has increased. He has to use intelligence to understand the content of his accounts, for so much of the data arrives in totals from a machine accounting section with whose operations he must be familiar. Intelligence of a high order is therefore needed to make a successful accountant, and modern techniques and increased pressures of work have certainly advanced his status. The accountancy section needs, therefore, to be staffed with first-class officers, conversant both with the affairs of the departments and with accounting techniques.

In addition to accounts relating to the services of the authority there are accounts and other duties which relate to the authority as a whole—loans accounts, accounts for common services, over-all cash control and so forth, and returns to government departments for audit and other purposes, but these offer no particular organizational problems.

131

CHAPTER X

THE CHIEF FINANCIAL OFFICER AS MACHINE
ACCOUNTANT

(1)

DURING the past thirty years, office machinery has developed from the status of an adjunct to clerical work to that of a separate tool of administration. Originally imitative of hand-written methods, accounting machinery now arrives at its results by its own very different routes. Only a small proportion of accounting machinery is standard; most of it has to be adapted to the particular purpose it is to serve. Every chief financial officer has to decide what machines to have and precisely how they are to be used. With the technical content of such decisions we have no concern here. But there are organizational problems which fall to be discussed. What arrangements does a chief financial officer need for studying the potential of machines in his office or for deciding upon an installation? How should he set about installing machinery? How should accounting machinery be housed and administered? What special problems does accounting machinery present to the internal auditor? What is the significance of the present trend in machinery from the point of view of office organization? How is the development of office machinery likely to affect the integration of finance and the position of the chief financial officer? These are the questions to which an answer will be attempted in this chapter.

Three preliminary comments are necessary. First, we are not concerned with advocacy of mechanized accounting. It will be assumed that it is the duty of every chief financial officer to examine the work of his office from time to time, and to recommend his council to install mechanical accounting for every operation for which it would be more efficient.

Secondly, there are difficulties in writing for local authorities of such varying size. The author has had to be content with dealing with the general principles. If some of the more detailed comments appear to relate to the larger offices that is because only in this way can all the significant points be brought out. Obviously a small office has too few machines to warrant a machine accountant, or often even a

132

machine section, but it may none the less make extensive use of machines.

Thirdly, this chapter is not concerned with the simpler kinds of machinery—addressing machines, receipting machines, key-driven calculators, desk calculators. Indispensable though these aids are in a modern office, they can hardly be said to bring organizational problems of sufficient magnitude to warrant discussion here. Our purpose is to consider the administration of the more elaborate machine installations of which there is a great variety—keyboard accounting machines, punched card machines, electronic calculaters and computers. Most of what follows applies to all these various types. Such comments as refer more particularly to punched card, calculator and computor installations, rather than to keyboard accounting machines, should be readily identified by the reader.

(2)

The first step is for the officers to investigate the task needing to be done, bearing in mind that the installation of machinery affords an opportunity to examine critically the form of existing statements and the possibilities of improvements. Each task, in each department, needs separate investigation and must be treated as an individual problem.

After the investigation of the work comes the selection of machinery. New office machinery must be selected with the utmost care for three reasons. First, the changes in supporting clerical procedures involved in the installation of new accounting machines are too radical to be undertaken frequently. Secondly, because the existence of so many alternative types of machinery and their great capacity implies a bewildering choice of applications. Wisdom of a high order is needed to make sure that the best is selected. Thirdly, the chief financial officer can easily be mistaken about the potentialities of the particular machines he proposes to recommend. He must foresee how the machine is to set about solving his particular problems. Examination of the performance of similar machines in operation, critical analysis of the outputs claimed by the sellers, determination of the nature and magnitude of the alterations needed in clerical procedures, computation of staff costs and careful scrutiny of the relative merits of hiring and purchasing (where the alternative is available) are all essential features. Every machine has its own characteristics and sets about its task in a different way. Often a machine which is good for one application is not good for another. All these considerations have to be weighed against price and dates of delivery. The more complicated accounting machinery becomes, the greater will be the difficulty of visualizing exactly how any particular piece of machinery can be harnessed to the work of the department.

(3)

The task of installing equipment is twofold: first the revision of the clerical procedures outside the machine room so that the machine can be fed with accurate data in a form acceptable to it, and secondly the organization of the machine processes and procedures, the latter term covering both the technical programming of the machine by a specialist, and the programming of the work in the machine section, including the flow of clerical work directly associated with machine operation, e.g. control records.

The first task, that of the revision of clerical procedures, will involve a thorough review of the methods of accumulating data, from the making of the initial record—often by workmen—to its transfer to the machines. It is a separate task requiring an analytical approach and the application of the best O. & M. techniques. The procedures must be intelligently and conscientiously carried out, for the smallest loophole in the arrangements may have disastrous consequences. Even assuming the chief financial officer has full powers to determine the form of accounting records, he will find that intensive, patient missionary work in the departments is needed if the system is to work smoothly, for departmental staffs have to be shown not only what is needed but why it is needed. They must also understand broadly what happens to the information after it leaves them, and hence what are the consequences of mistakes or failure to produce the information in accordance with the programme. (Incidentally, if the departments understand the reasons for feeding the machines with data in a particular way, they are much more likely to feel at home when the information comes back to them in the form of cost and expenditure statements.)

Much of the second task—that of deciding how the machines shall be used and of planning the flow of the work—is technical and outside the scope of this chapter. Some organizational features applicable to electronic installations and the arrangements for programming the work of the machine section are dealt with in later sections. (One technical aspect of planning an installation has important administrative implications: that of computing work loads. Makers of office machinery are naturally optimistic about the amount of work their machines will do and new installations are apt to bring requests for additional information as soon as their potentialities are fully realized. Every chief financial officer has to make allowance for these two features in the knowledge that it has been a common experience for new equipment soon to become overloaded.)

(4)

Applied to limited specialized tasks and functioning as adjuncts to written records, accounting machines were for many years attached to the section which happened to make use of them. The advent of general purpose machines, capable of doing much of the routine work of the department, has combined with their increasing complexity to bring into existence machine sections and the existence of a machine section or subsection can be taken for granted in the larger local authorities. Little has been written on the organization of such sections, and it is therefore worth while to discuss the organization in some detail. The remarks which follow apply in principle, irrespective of the size or type of the installation, though the method of application will vary widely.

A machine section has to be organized to fit in with the requirements of its 'customers', whether these are other departments of the local authority, or other sections of the finance department. It must be organized as far as possible on mass-production lines, each task being governed by a comprehensive programme covering every stage from the arrival of the prime documents until the dispatch of processed work, allowance being made for late arrival of documents and for breakdowns. Because of a tendency to underestimate the time required to plan new systems, or variations and improvements to existing systems, the over-all plan and its flow charts and instructions can easily become out of date—a danger to be avoided at all costs. Divergencies between planned time and actual time should be systematically examined, for they give the clue to necessary adjustments and improvements in the routines, and are invaluable when machine loadings and performance of operators and machines are under consideration.

A large and intricate installation, without a margin of staff and machine time, cannot guarantee a continuously satisfactory service, and the staff complement must therefore be such that sickness or holidays do not impair the service. Ideally all operators should be interchangeable and the more intense the training in the broader aspects of the machine work, as well as in the machine processes, the greater the possibilities of intelligent operation. But even so it is likely that some of the more junior machine operators will not appreciate the full significance of their work, however thorough the staff training may be, and there may be only a small proportion of the staff who understand the whole of the procedure and the full consequences of errors. There must be vigorous supervision to ensure that routines are carried out, including prescribed precautions for testing the accuracy of the machines. The supervisor must know the exact position of every job which has to be processed, so that by careful selection of the sequence of operations, not only will work be completed on time, but machines will be kept continuously occupied, and bottlenecks eliminated. Discipline will be greatly helped if desks are kept cleared, interruptions reduced to a minimum and unauthorized visitors forbidden.

In the best-run installations infinite care is taken to avoid mistakes. This involves arrangements to see that the data supplied to the machines are accurate and intelligible: for instance, operators should not have to struggle with illegible time sheets. Full use should also be made of such devices as stage-by-stage verification in the machine room, together with control by predetermined totals. But however complete the system, even the best operators cannot work without occasional errors, and it is worth while to go to almost any length to filter them out at the earliest possible stage. A cast-iron procedure has to be established to make sure that any corrections and alterations are verified and initialled by a responsible member of the staff at each step of the adjustments, for alterations not properly carried out make for confusion and soon undo the advantages of mechanization.

Every chief financial officer with a centralized machine installation of any magnitude has to decide whether—apart from the checks, such as the verification of punching, which must take place within the machine room itself—controls shall be applied within or without the machine section. Are the machine room staff to be responsible for the scrutiny of their own work—agreement with predetermined totals for instance—or is the control to be with the 'customer' department or section? The former course is preferable. It increases the sense of responsibility of the machine room staff and it improves their relations with other sections and departments who receive work guaranteed to be as accurate as the machine room can make it. Moreover, mistakes are then merely domestic matters for the machine section, and not a potential cause of recrimination between sections and departments.

Checks on machine operations should as far as possible be an integral part of the machine system. Hand-written records in the machine section should be kept to a minimum, full use being made of such devices as feeding balancing totals at the end of a job as part of the normal machine output to make the final total of a correct run zero, or of control accounts in the form of punched cards.

In a large installation a small clerical control team can be justified, to which senior operators are attached on a rota basis, thus extending operators' understanding of the system. In smaller installations the control may be kept by the machine supervisor, who needs to have full knowledge both of the machines and of the clerical procedures.

Within the machine room, errors, though domestic matters, should be treated seriously, a record being kept to obtain an indication of proneness to error on the part of individual operators and machines. Action is not complete until the error has been corrected and, most important of all, the cause of the error discovered and removed.

Adequate office accommodation, in which equipment can be laid out to avoid unnecessary movement of documents is essential, and, since the work of a machine section tends to include a large number of small operations, adequate storage facilities are required, so that only documents about to be processed are around the machines. Queries should be dealt with, as far as possible, by those who are not operating machines, for machine time is expensive and lost time can rarely be recovered.

A qualified machine accountant will be almost indispensable if the machinery is extensive and elaborate, but all installations need skilled direction because they are so vital a link in the chain of operations. It is a great mistake to underestimate the calibre and training of the man needed to take charge of a modern machine room. There is a world of difference between the task of supervising a battery of keyboard machines and that of looking after a large punched card or electronic installation. All but the simplest machines also need intelligent operation. The calibre of staff required in a machine room can also be underrated, and as machines and machine systems grow in complexity, better-educated and more highly trained staff will be needed. Female staff take more readily to machine room work than men. A chief financial officer able to recruit and train intelligent girls will, therefore, normally find that, with the exception of the machine accountant, all his machine room staff are females, unless he has a computer, when his programmer may well operate the machine upon occasion.

(5)

So far, only incidental mention has been made of particular types of accounting machinery because the matters considered have been, in the main, common to all. The recent application of 'automation' to office work in the form of electronically operated machines does, however, call for separate and extended comment. Opinions may differ whether this change is one of degree or kind, but no one would deny that electronic machines herald a minor revolution in office techniques. The prodigious speed made possible because calculation is by electrical impulses instead of by revolutions of a gear-wheel, and the ability of the machine to 'think', i.e. to take an intermediate result and decide what the next step in the calculation shall be, are perhaps the most significant features of electronic calculation from the point of view of the accountant. Machines can now be constructed which take calculations in their stride; involved tasks such as the preparation of payrolls can be done as one unbroken operation, instead of a series of separate operations, some manual and some mechanical; intractable masses of data can be easily handled; the production of statistics and costs, which hitherto could only be taken out at disproportionate expense, can be justified; additional information can be prepared as a by-product of other operations; and new kinds of information, e.g. data for controlling the ordering of stores, can be produced. Machines which can read the original data—already available in a rudimentary form—are expected to develop apace.

At the moment no one can foresee whether the future is with the relatively small units which local authorities are now beginning to operate, or with large installations to which we shall take our bundles of work for processing, as the modern housewife takes her washing to the launderette. Two things are, however, clear. The first is that electronic calculation, and manipulation of the routine data, will supplant other methods in the near future. In so far as the bulk of the routine work of local authorities is financial, most of the applications will be to tasks which are, or should be, the business of the chief financial officer, though there are many other potential uses: public health statistics, transport traffic analysis, register of electors and so forth. The virtual abolition of ready reckoners except for casual calculations, the saving of manpower, the lowering of cost, the additional information which can be prepared, the flexibility and speed of the machines—these are only some of the factors which, taken together, make it plain that electronic accounting machinery will be widely used in local government offices in the years to come. The monetary savings alone will virtually force local authorities to adopt it, a feature which will be envied by chief financial officers of a past generation who have so often had the task of persuading local authorities to use mechanical appliances, highly desirable for many reasons, but showing only a modest financial saving.

Not only those offices able to justify installations of their own will do their routine work electronically. Other offices—except perhaps the very smallest—will take their work to a computing unit. Electronic accounting, therefore, cannot be brushed aside by the smaller authorities as a device applicable only to their larger neighbours. The chief financial officers of authorities too small to justify a unit of their own will need to keep abreast of developments, and to be ready to seize the opportunity to use an electronic service unit as soon as one is available. Neighbouring local authorities may be induced to forget their suspicions of one another sufficiently to set up joint installations. A new kind of local government enterprise—an electronic unit which could do work for adjoining authorities, and use spare capacity for taking in work from other kinds of concerns, is already on the horizon.

(6)

What are the special features of electronic machinery from the point of view of office organization?

First, electronic machines, with their exciting possibilities, will involve radical reconsideration of accounting operations. Techniques of management new to local government, e.g. shift-work in offices, may become necessary because of the high cost of the machines. If, therefore, the potential of electronics is to be fully realized, local authorities must be willing to spend time and money on preliminary enquiries and investigations much more elaborate than any they will have authorized before. They must also be prepared to acquiesce in transitional periods when the full savings of the changes will not be enjoyed, upon occasion going to the length of allowing the new equipment to run side by side with existing methods for a limited period.

Next, the traditional methods of organizing the work of accounting and book-keeping staffs must be revised and room made for new types of employees. Accounting units will need new organizations for the changing times, and accounting techniques and mathematical skill must be blended with the knowledge of the electronic engineer. Machine accountants, computer programmers and specialists in electronics will have to be secured, retained and used to the best advantage. The accountancy profession will have to devote attention to the general training of accountants in electronic processes and to the more intensive instruction of those who intend to specialize in machine accountancy. The programming of the machines and of the flow of work brings to the chief financial officer a fascinating job involving the employment of a new kind of specialist, the computer programmer, and the co-ordination of the knowledge of this specialist with that of his accounting staff. Whether he has an accountant trained as a programmer, or whether he engages a programmer as such, he will need somewhere in his organization a person with sufficient knowledge, both of the potentialities of the machines and of the accounting system, to enable the utmost use to be made of the equipment.

Finally, the mere determination of the best type of equipment will of itself become more and more difficult as the number of types of computers—each setting about accountancy work in its own way—increases. The power of decision, and courage of one's convictions always necessary for important administrative decisions will be specially needed, for one feature of electronics, already abundantly clear, is that, at least for some time ahead, advances and improvements will be continuous. No sooner will an installation be decided upon than it will become out of date. The temptation, therefore, will be either to sit indefinitely on the fence, letting the benefits of the new world go unrealized, or else, having made a choice, to make premature changes in the hope of keeping up with developments. To get the most efficient system, a local authority may well be constrained to install equipment too large for its own purposes, with the intention of 'selling' the spare machine capacity to other local authorities or commercial users. This possibility adds greatly to the preliminary work of deciding upon and installing the equipment, and is another reason warranting a distinction between the installation of machinery in pre-electronic days and a present-day mechanization scheme.

(7)

The next aspect of machine accounting to be considered is that of its effect on the work of the internal auditor. This subject is dealt with here, instead of in the chapter on the chief financial officer as auditor, because of the light it sheds on the nature of accounting machinery from the point of view of organization.

With manually kept records, the entries can be followed through stage by stage as they have been performed, records being largely designed to make transactions easy to trace. Auditing is straightforward. Mechanization has brought a different state of affairs. Machines are made to produce the correct final result in the most economical way, and they may or may not keep a clear track of each step in the process. The records are on loose sheets with items arranged to suit the working of the machines and not the convenience of the auditor. Documents may be sorted and re-sorted as the exigencies of machine processes dictate, and few of those engaged in keeping the records or working the machines will have a clear idea of the whole operation. The auditor, coming in at the tail end, will be short of intermediate figures and links, for all he sees is the prime data at one end and the finished product at the other.

The more highly developed machines become, the greater will be the divergence from mental and manual processes and procedures, and the less will they enable the auditor—or anyone else—to follow operations step by step. Indeed it is conceivable that accountants will eventually cease to record the references—numbers of stores requisition notes, etc.—altogether. To check manually what the machine has done automatically would be a long, though in some cases interesting, task. In fact what the auditor does is to test aspects of the work, varying the feature selected on each audit visit, e.g. in a payroll he may test the amendments made to the standing information one week, the temporary variations for sickness another, the correctness of the standard information in a third week, and so forth.

Much unnecessary mental confusion is brought about by haphazard nomenclature in machine rooms. A clear distinction should be made between (a) accounting statements proper, (b) management data, and (c) tabulations prepared for the internal purposes of the machine room—balancing tabulations, 'disagreement' state-

141

ments, tabulations of adjusting entries, e.g. transfers in between cost accounts, and so forth. The auditor must understand the purpose of each statement, clearly remembering that even the tabulations prepared for internal machine room purposes have some audit value in so far as they call attention to what is not straightforward and may need investigation. He can also put statements of other kinds to audit uses. Thus a list of the divergencies between the standard prices of stores and those actually being paid, compiled primarily for the purpose of keeping the standard price under review, may throw up an occasional bad purchase at too high a price. The auditor may also have tabulations prepared especially for his own use, e.g. a list of stock items on which there has been no movement for a period, or intermediate job costs which he wishes to investigate. Mechanical accounting techniques can be as useful to the intelligent auditor as they are bewildering to his unimaginative colleague.

There are many other manifest advantages to the auditor in these changes : for instance, the wider distribution of duties offers additional security against fraud : the clerk of other days who had everything under his control was a potential menace, mine of information though he was. But the most significant feature of the institution of mechanical accounting is that it gives further impetus to the movement towards reliance upon the system and the machine discipline rather than on detailed verification. Basically the auditor has to satisfy himself that the machine is giving accurate results. To do this with an electronic machine he must be sure that the machine programme is right, and that all the tests laid down to ensure that at any particular time the machine is working correctly have been carried out. He has no longer to fear, as with manuscript systems, the accidental omission of a vital link in the chain of operations. Records of the routine tests are of prime importance and must be strictly kept. If the machine is one which stores information on magnetic tape or some similar device, the auditor is even more dependent upon satisfying himself that all the necessary checks, e.g. cross-balancing or agreement with predetermined totals, have been carried out.

If it is not necessary for the auditor to be versed in the subtleties of programming an electronic computer, he must understand the principles and establish that the programmes settled upon give the right results. But he need not take fright because he has no special gift for higher mathematics. There is no more need for him to worry because he does not understand the internal processes of the machines than there is for the accountant consulting a sinking fund table to be alarmed because he does not know, or has forgotten, the formula upon which the table is constructed. Clearly everything points to an approach to auditing vastly different from the wholesale, pedestrian ticking of items so long associated with auditors, both external and internal.

(8)

The intensification of the development of accounting machinery and its effect on the organization of the finance department itself have already been explained. It remains to add some observations of the wider repercussions on the financial administration of the authority as a whole.

All the data to be used in an advanced mechanical installation has eventually to be expressed in common form for the machines. All the records must therefore be designed with this in mind. The routing, timing and supervision of work must be conducted in accordance with one central plan, for the preliminary clerical work and the ultimate machine processes are part of one operation, taking place partly in the departments and partly in the finance department. The work must therefore be planned as a whole.

Only to a limited extent can the chief financial officer solve his troubles by taking work into his own office. He must have some means of controlling, co-ordinating and integrating the whole of the financial work, wherever it is done. The advances in machine accounting have thus not only fortified an already overwhelming case for integration of financial administration; they have imported an element of urgency, for full use cannot be made of modern accounting equipment unless financial arrangements have been unified.

It may be appropriate to conclude by remarking that, though the toils of a changeover from manual to mechanical methods have been dealt with as problems of the chief financial officer's department, heads of other departments and their staffs have also an important contribution to make towards the successful planning and running of an installation. This is so, not only because the records must be conceived and worked as part of one plan, but also because, as the users of so much of the data produced, they can, if they are sympathetic, greatly help both in the initial period and later in ensuring that the machinery is used to its best advantage. An intelligent head of a de-

143

partment will readily see that a properly run installation, using the comprehensive equipment justified by the concentration of all financial work, will be a boon to departments, enabling them to take advantage of techniques otherwise denied to them, and offering facilities for the production of statistical as well as financial information.

CHAPTER XI

THE CHIEF FINANCIAL OFFICER AS INTERNAL AUDITOR

(1)

IN this chapter we consider the scope of internal audit, its relation to external audit, collaboration between internal auditors and methods officers, and the management, staffing and control of internal audit sections. The auditing of machine installations is discussed in the chapter on the chief financial officer as machine accountant.

Memorandum 150/Accounts quoted in an earlier chapter assumed that internal audit was indissolubly linked with the supervision of accounts and that both tasks would fall to 'one chief financial officer'. Those officers designated 'Treasurer' in a borough or county, as has already been explained, have, according to some lawyers, a duty to carry out an internal audit. In any case, the Local Government Act, 1958, having put a responsibility upon the treasurer to supervise the arrangements for making payments and controlling receipts, he will be compelled in future, for this reason alone, to have some kind of audit by whatsoever name he may call it. We can, therefore, take it for granted that—as is now almost the universal practice—internal audit will be part of the work of the chief financial officer and proceed to a consideration of the nature of this most important function.

(2)

In 1950 a report on management accounting quoted the following extract from the 'Charter' of the internal audit department of an American company:

'Internal auditing is the independent appraisal activity within an organization for the review of the accounting, financial, and other operations as a basis for protective and constructive service to management. It is a type of control whose functions are the measuring and evaluating of the effectiveness of other types of control, the installation of corrective action, and improvements. It deals with accounting and financial matters, but it may also properly deal with any operating, management or other corporate matters.'[1]

The traditional outlook on internal auditing in English local government was at one time just as narrow as the view quoted above is wide. An internal audit of this restricted kind follows up the receipt of income and sometimes verifies payments, though the latter function is often performed in other sections of the chief financial officer's department, since in many authorities it involves detailed verification and partakes more of the nature of a routine check rather than of internal audit. The aim of such an audit is security, though naturally audit staffs, however restricted in their formal mandate, encourage departments to install adequate records and institute safeguards against fraud. Also, where the chief financial officer has incomplete control over the form of accounting records he often has to use his internal audit section to collect information which under happier circumstances he would receive automatically. Of recent years a wider view has been taken of the scope of internal audit in local government, though it falls short of the definition in the quotation above, in that internal audit in local government could never concern itself with the appraisal of policies or with investigations involving qualitative judgments. These are matters for members. Nor does an internal audit section normally undertake anything in the nature of an efficiency audit. Local authorities have therefore to find other means of evaluating the effect of the local authority's policies and the efficiency of the departments. With these exceptions, the substance of the passage can now be applied to internal auditing in local government: the modern view is that it should review the accounting and financial operations not only to secure regularity but 'as a basis for protective and constructive service to management'.

Rectitude is, of course, of special importance to a public authority, for the monies, stocks, materials and plant which are at stake are public property financed by compulsory levies on the citizens. Public confidence is quickly shaken by irregularities or financial laxity on the part of public servants, the inevitable impression being that the elected representatives who are responsible for the administration, and who can be fairly assumed to keep in close touch with day-to-day affairs, have failed in their duty. Hence, incidentally, the power of surcharge possessed by district auditors and the Secretary of State for Scotland, a distinctive feature of English and Scottish local

[1] *Productivity Report*, 'Management Accounting' (Anglo-American Council on Productivity, 1950), pp. 55–6.

government. Safeguards designed to prevent misappropriation of funds, rigid rules about public tendering for contracts, and the insistence on such features as meagre subsistence allowances, are therefore regarded as pivotal points in the local government organization. Notwithstanding the increasing importance of the other work of audit, the prevention and detection of fraud and misappropriation will remain its central task. Every chief financial officer has to decide for himself the point where checks must stop and risks should be taken. Often, knowing that lapses in honesty may well become magnified by public discussion out of all proportion to their real importance, he will carry verification further than if he were accountable to a board of directors. One could hardly expect public opinion to exercise a sense of proportion in such matters, which is perhaps as well, for there are few opportunities for objective tests of efficiency in local government. No spur to good behaviour can be lightly discarded, even if the price to be paid is some excess of caution on the part of officials.

A modern internal audit staff will, however, go far beyond security: they will be charged with the duty of seeing that the system of internal check is properly worked; they will watch that the council's regulations about purchases and contracts are observed; they will ensure that subsistence payments and car allowances are uniformly applied throughout the local authority; they will be called upon to make, or assist with, special investigations into financial administration; they will be a means by which the chief financial officer keeps in touch with the financial personnel in the outside departments, especially with the departmental finance officers; and they may devise the course of training for staffs engaged on subsidiary accounting throughout the authority. Unless the chief financial officer takes the view that it is unsound for an audit department to have anything to do with the institution of the systems they are to audit, they will also play a large part in shaping departmental records. The internal audit staff will, if they are successful, make themselves useful to the heads of departments as well as to the chief financial officer.

(3)

Two postwar features of local government financial administration, different in kind, but all important, have reinforced the tendency towards a wider view of internal audit work: first the growth in the volume and complexity of documentation; secondly the difficulty

147

of securing competent staff in all grades and the consequent deterioration in the quality of office work. A third feature—the recent strides made by mechanical accounting—has already been dealt with in the chapter on the chief financial officer as machine accountant.

The first feature is well known to those with a long experience of office work. Practically every operation has become more involved. The compilation of payroll for instance now involves a complex tax calculation, many more deductions from pay, and even the computation of bonuses. Again, much more analysis is now done for management purposes. The workman has not only to charge his time over a large number of heads of account, but often he is required to cope with a coding system instead of simply describing his work as 'paving' or 'trench digging'.

The significance of the second of these factors—the falling off in the standards of clerical work is discussed generally in the chapter on the organization of the finance department. To the auditor it brings added anxieties. Few offices have now a solid cadre of experienced clerks, conservative perhaps, but reliable and able to make almost any system work. Errors on documents put out by finance departments were once a rarity, each one being the subject of an inquest, often with uncomfortable consequences to the perpetrator. Nowadays a sprinkling of errors may be regarded less seriously. The auditor has difficulty in finding reliable, knowledgeable people to answer his questions about either current or past operations and may be tempted to indulge in detailed checking in circumstances when he should give more attention to the system, the allocation of duties, the institution of internal check, the process of committing to paper the routines and procedures, and the training of newcomers. It is when the staff are poor that the system becomes of most importance.

(4)

The accounts of local authorities are subject to external as well as to internal audit.[1] There is of course much that is common to the

---

[1] All the accounts of counties, metropolitan boroughs, urban districts, rural districts and parishes and some of the accounts of boroughs are subject to the district auditor appointed by the Ministry of Housing and Local Government. The remaining accounts of boroughs—and they constitute the bulk—are audited at the option of the council by (*a*) three borough auditors—an obsolete system of amateur audit now very little used (*b*) professional accountants or (*c*) the district auditor. The accounts of Scottish authorities are audited by professional accountants appointed by the Secretary of State for Scotland.

two classes of auditors. Both are concerned with the accuracy of the accounts, the soundness of the supporting records, the diligent collection of income, the correctness of payments, the proper custody of stores, and precautions against fraud. Both have to understand accounting and know the law in so far as it affects the financial aspects of local administration. The purpose of the two kinds of audit is none the less different. External audit, as its name implies, is an outside check on the local authority and its servants, imposed or adopted primarily to protect the interests of the public. The external audit has a mandate independent of the council, for even professional auditors, whose duties are agreed between the parties, are primarily concerned with the accuracy of the final accounts of the council as stewards for the ratepayers. External audit also acts as an assurance to the central government that the law relating to finance has been complied with and that the accounts of the local authority can be fairly used as a basis for the payment of grants. It is for the most part an annual 'completed' audit taking place after the close of the financial year.

Internal audit is, on the other hand, a tool of management, and its scope is decided upon by the council. It exists to protect the members against lax officers, to help the chief financial officer to carry out his supervision of the local financial arrangements and the other chief officers to look after their departmental finances. Continuous operation, prompt following up of all record keeping, anticipating and preventing trouble rather than curing it afterwards, close relations with departments as guide and helper as well as inspector and verifier, are the distinctive ingredients of internal as compared with external audit. One would, therefore, expect their methods to be different, and each to lay emphasis on particular aspects. Whilst the outside auditor is concerned with documents drawn up after the close of an accounting period for the information of outsiders, the internal audit is concerned with the live daily data used within the authority for administrative and management purposes.

Both forms of audit combined can check only a small percentage of the work of those engaged on financial records. To obtain the maximum benefit from their joint efforts external and internal auditors need a clear working arrangement, for their duties should be complementary to one another rather than merely supplementary. Each needs the help of the other: the external auditor can make good use of the detailed knowledge of the internal auditor whilst the internal auditor can benefit by drawing upon the outside auditor's wide knowledge of other concerns and authorities.[1] They will in effect—though both may deny it—agree on something like a division of labour, the internal auditor beginning by explaining exactly what he does in each department. The external auditor needs the information because he must take the operations of the internal auditor into consideration when he is conducting his audit, and he must appraise its prestige and efficiency just as he appraises the quality of the accounting arrangements. He is entitled to comment on the efficiency of the internal audit and to suggest ways of strengthening or modifying it. A wise chief financial officer will take careful note of such comments, though he has to watch that the outside auditor is not unreasonable in his requirements.

An astute internal auditor will go much further. He will note the phases of the work which the external auditor examines in detail and those which he treats more cursorily. If the latter are in his view important aspects, he will quietly cover the deficiency. Again, remembering that audits by district auditors are completed (i.e. year-end) audits, and that other kinds of external audits, if not completed, are rarely really continuous, he will lay special stress on those matters—cash control, correctness of payments, follow up of income, etc. for which a year-end or periodical audit is of much less value. Further, if he serves an authority whose accounts are audited partly by district auditors and partly by professional auditors, he will remember that these two types of auditors are prone to lay stress on different aspects of the work, and will vary his audit accordingly. Above all he will remember that the most humiliating occurrence for an internal auditor is for an external auditor to detect something that he has missed.

The better the internal audit records are, the closer can the co-operation be, and the more frank the audit staffs are with one another the greater are the chances of their work being complementary. All the internal audit files for instance should be freely available to the external auditor.

[1] The general relationship between the two types of audit was concisely described by the Institute of Chartered Accountants in England and Wales in *Notes on the relation of the Internal Audit to the Statutory Audit*. They are reproduced in *Internal Audit in Local Authorities and Hospitals* by W. L. Abernethy (Shaw and Sons, 1957), pp. 16–20. The notes also draw a clear distinction between internal audit and internal check.

(5)

Also worthy of examination are the relations and connexion between internal audit and the 'organization and methods' units now to be found in the larger local authorities, attached sometimes to the Clerk and sometimes to the chief financial officer, and sometimes operating as an independent team.

The job of the methods officer is to examine office methods and organization and make recommendations to heads of departments. He comes into a department as an outsider able to take a detached view, and, having no executive responsibility, he is able to concentrate on the task of examining and considering the methods of work of the department. The employment of a specialized officer thus makes possible not only impartial, critical and at the same time constructive appraisals, but also investigations which would otherwise go by default, departments having their hands full with pressing tasks of administration.

In accordance with the practice in other comparable organizations, the methods officer in local government normally withdraws after making and discussing his recommendations, leaving to the head of the department the responsibility for carrying them out, and also the decision whether or not they are to be accepted. In other words the methods officer's responsibility ceases when he has made his suggestions: strictly he has no continuing interest in any of his 'cases'. Nor does he concern himself with technical processes; he does not tell the lawyer how to draw up a conveyance, the accountant how to keep accounts or the architect how to prepare plans; but he is concerned with the distribution of duties between technical officers, their relation to other officers and the organization of ancillary technical processes.

How does this compare with the work of the internal auditor? The auditor also comes into a department from outside, and gathers strength from the fact that he can take a detached view. He too is concerned with organization, and with methods of work, but only in so far as they concern the financial aspects of the council's activities. Like the methods officer he is able to bring experience of one department to bear upon the problems of another.

But there are also differences. The methods officer has a wider mandate: he can deal with the whole organization of a department and with its general efficiency, whilst the internal auditor has to keep to financial aspects and records. The internal auditor is a professional man exercising his *expertise* in his particular sphere: the methods officer is a general administrator applying experience, common sense and the technique of investigations to office problems. The methods officer goes to departments intermittently on the invitation of the head of the department: years may elapse between his visits. The internal auditor on the other hand must have a right to examine the records at any time; he must make frequent visits and keep in constant touch with the work of the departments. Further, the methods officer is normally concerned with making recommendations about improvements in methods, desirable but rarely imperative, a task also familiar to the internal auditor who has the additional responsibility of insisting upon some safeguard he regards as indispensable. Finally there is the continuous responsibility of the internal auditor to see that the council's financial system is being operated all the time; he thus has a task of inspection, absent from the work of the methods officer. An internal auditor cannot close a case; he has to be vigilant in all places at all times.

These are differences substantial enough to dispose of the idea that internal audit work should be amalgamated with methods work. But the two officers must co-operate, whether the methods officer is attached to the Clerk or to the chief financial officer, or whether he is an independent officer. The methods officer must make sure that his proposals are sound from the point of view of financial control whilst the auditor must never proceed as if the financial transactions were carried out *in vacuo*. There are many records which are partly financial and partly general; and often, with a little thought, many others could be made to serve a dual purpose, examples being registers of residents at homes, works orders and plant records. Financial records divorced from others are frequently the least efficient.

Again, incidents of departmental organization such as methods of arranging holidays, ways of ordering stationery which at first sight would appear to have no interest for the audit staff, all may have some significance from the point of view of security. Finally mutual help can be given in the conduct of investigations: the audit staff may find the financial organization suffering from some weakness with roots in the general set-up of the department: the methods officer may find himself handicapped in an investigation because of his lack of regular contacts with the department and its officers. In short, working together sensibly and helpfully, the internal auditor and the methods officer can be a great power for good in a local authority.

This relationship emphasizes the outstanding potential of the internal audit of a local authority as an influence helping integration. The audit staff spend most of their time in other departments. They should be the spearhead at staff level of the movement for financial co-ordination and integration. They should so blend their roles of inspector and adviser that the humblest officer engaged on financial work feels that he has the backing of the whole administrative organization of the authority.

(6)

The clue to the organization of a good internal audit section is detachment from general financial work. Even in the smallest authorities it is better to give all the audit work to one individual rather than to spread it over officers having other duties. Audit staff, however large or small the section may be, can acquire the right approach only if they are undistracted by other work. For this reason, incidental extraneous work should not be lightly introduced into an audit section. Allied to the need for detached outlook is the necessity for independence. The chief internal auditor and his staff must have a general measure of independence not accorded to other members of the staff. They should, for instance, be given a right of direct access to the chief financial officer on any matter they feel to be of prime importance.

This independence should be used with restraint. On all but the exceptional occasion the chief auditor should function as an ordinary section head, freely exchanging views about current problems with his colleagues in other sections. Similar moderation should govern his conduct with operating departments and, though he will possess power to conduct a surprise audit and to examine financial records at any time, normally he will visit departments by arrangement, taking pains to interrupt the work of the department as little as possible. His aim should be to serve the departments, and to establish a spirit of co-operation, notwithstanding his duty always to be on the look-out for errors, slackness and fraud, a duty which will not endear him to the staff of the departments. The test of an internal auditor's relations with departments comes when some difficult or delicate investigations are in progress, or when fraud or irregularity is suspected. If relations are right, the internal auditor will get every assistance. Indeed one way of ascertaining whether a department genuinely regards the internal auditor as existing as much for their protection as for that of the authority is to enquire whether the departmental staff freely pass to him all the information which might throw light on any enquiry he is making. All too often valuable information is held back because the internal auditor is not in the complete confidence of the departments.

(7)

Of the various sections of the finance department none offers to the chief financial officer more problems of organization than the audit section. He has to decide the scope of the audit and the scale of its check; he has to find staff with that distinctive and much maligned outlook known as the 'audit mind'; and he has to make sure that whilst all the financial work of the departments comes systematically under audit review, the methods of the section are flexible. He has also to face two special dangers: first that of an audit department which appears to be effective and busy with verifications and checking, yet is accomplishing little but the making of arithmetical corrections; and secondly that of an audit section, highly efficient, but not in the confidence of the departments because it relentlessly pursues small errors, or follows up the more important ones with arrogance and lack of understanding.

The chief financial officer needs as his chief internal auditor an officer thoroughly versed in local government finance, energetic, imaginative, tactful, resourceful and persistent, for an auditor must pursue his investigations to the end. An internal auditor must also be able to discriminate between what is important and what is unimportant, what is true and what is false. He must not be unduly exacting in his expectations, too impatient of persons of lesser ability and must be ever aware that, though finance is the sole preoccupation of the finance department, to others it is but an incidental aspect of a more absorbing task. He must not be disconcerted by the apparently negative nature of so much of his work, or worried by the fact that he can examine only one aspect at a time. He must be prepared patiently to explain simple points of organization which to him are monotonously familiar and even self-evident, e.g. that petty cash payments must not be made out of sundry cash income. Above all, an internal auditor needs to be conscientious, for his work cannot be checked or supervised except in a general way, and in any case much of it is carried out at dispersed points throughout the area of the local authority. All the departments of the authority will soon become aware if the chief accountant allows his work to get into arrear. But an internal auditor can go through the mere motions of audit without exposing his deficiencies until some monumental fraud or irregularity brings a rude awakening.

The other key personnel in the section should have the same qualities as those needed by the chief internal auditor. To guard against the great danger of audit work—that of its becoming stereotyped—chief financial officers have long advocated periodical changes in the staff, and constant alteration of duties within the section. Freshness of approach is of greater importance than in other branches of the finance department's work, and knowledge of past history is of less. Given a good system of records, a new auditor becomes effective much more quickly than an accountancy assistant who has so many threads to pick up. Eighteen months is thought by some observers to be a long enough period for a man to be in charge of an audit, for even the best auditor tends to begin to take some things for granted after a few visits to a department.

Transfers, especially of junior staff, can, however, be too rapid, and indeed are likely to be so if the local authority is afflicted with compulsory changes in both clerical and professional staff due to constant resignations. To counteract the effect of the lack of a stable staff, audit records need to be complete. The day-to-day work of the staff must be controlled and a careful account of the scope of the financial transactions of all departments prepared, lest some precaution be dropped because of staff changes either in the outside department or in the audit section.

In smaller authorities rotation of staff may be difficult. The audit staff may consist of one or two persons who are not qualified, the section being under close supervision of the chief and his deputy. The latter may well have to do a certain amount of the audit work himself. All that can be done in such cases is for the chief financial officer not to let slip any opportunities to make changes which do occur even if they are infrequent, and for the rest always to bear in mind the need for extra vigilance because of the static staff position.

(8)

The staff of an audit section must concern themselves as much with seeing that clerical procedures are sound and are properly observed as with the verification of entries, though the two aspects are not unrelated. Is the system in use the best and most economical available? Is it suited to the calibre of staff? Is it clearly defined? Is everyone fully acquainted with his responsibilities? Are newcomers instructed in their duties? Are the principles of internal check—proper division of duties, etc.—being observed? Is there effective supervision? These are the kinds of questions the auditor must continually ask and, still more important, he must not rest until they are answered satisfactorily.

The auditor has to bear in mind two guiding considerations. First, that the bulk of the subsidiary financial work of a department is of a routine nature and capable of being broken down into a series of simple tasks often self checking, but needing to be carefully organized if the data for the finance department are to arrive in correct form and on time. Organization of this kind may be alien to the other tasks of an operating department. The auditor may well need all his persuasive power to convince the department that the financial work needs to be treated as a link in the chain of the authority's financial administration and not as an isolated task. Secondly, the auditor has to remember that the vast majority of cases of fraud in local government have been made possible because some elementary precaution has not been taken, or some standing instruction has been ignored: goods have been supplied without official orders, vehicle records are neglected, unauthorized persons are allowed access to stores, plant or cost returns have not been scrutinized, monies have not been banked promptly, vital returns have been submitted late.

The lesson is clear: the internal auditor must not come to believe that, because he has to concern himself with the larger questions of organization, he is absolved from the necessity of watching the smaller points. Every internal auditor has to determine his own priorities according to the circumstances of his authority and the staff he has available. Possibly the only rule of general application would be that an audit section of one or two persons will, unless the authority is very small, normally be best employed on testing systems and trying to influence departments rather than on detailed checks which could cover so small a part of the ground. Some chief officers think that there are certain exceptional kinds of work such as loans transactions and loans registration or property transactions which always warrant detailed check. They will usually be transactions involving large sums or far-reaching consequences if not properly carried out.

Internal auditors of local authorities always have placed, and probably always will place, special emphasis on the verification of income, partly because income collection offers so many opportunities for irregularity, and partly because the work of supervision cannot be centralized so easily as can the control of expenditure. Departments therefore tend to neglect it. The internal auditor will, however, do well to remind himself from time to time that the major frauds in local government have been concerned with expenditure.

(9)

Though this is not a treatise on the technique of auditing, some comments will be offered on the merits and de-merits of audit 'programmes' because of the light the controversy throws on the nature of internal audit and its place in financial administration. Should an auditor be supplied with a detailed programme for each step in every audit for which he is responsible, or should he be allowed to use his initiative and ingenuity? If the former view prevails, there will be detailed programmes for every audit and the audit will always proceed on much the same lines. If audit programmes are not in existence, procedure will vary between different auditors, and, if the officer is imaginative, between the same auditor on different visits. The truth surely lies somewhere between the two extremes. An auditor must have some guidance when he comes to undertake a fresh audit. Information about the scope of the department's work, its organization, its books and records, instructions about dates for submission of documents, regulations about cash control, notes of past queries, difficulties or infringements— all these must be available to the auditor. He should also have categorical instructions about any checks thought to be obligatory exercises whatever form the audit takes. What he does *not* want, is to have his discretion tied by a mandatory detailed procedure, if only because this is the way to stultify initiative in the very officers in whom it is most needed. In practice, senior assistants will be allowed more latitude than junior officers.

More important than a code of detailed instructions is an audit staff well versed in the principles of audit and trained in the application to varying circumstances of general tests and methods of verification. Just as most frauds occur because some elementary check, known to every auditor to be necessary, has lapsed, so the *form* they take is usually a variation on a few equally well-known themes—

157

failure to bank monies collected, use of dummy invoices, over-issue of stores to jobs, entries on receipts which differ from those in the books, incorrect entries in vehicle logs, and so forth. An auditor must be up to date in his techniques. Take, for example, the selection of items for test checking, which in the past has mainly been done on hit-and-miss methods. Nowadays, thanks largely to the advance made in factories during the Second World War, a great deal is known about the application of the science of sampling to test checking, and no auditor should ignore this new, though as yet tentative, body of knowledge.[1]

In short, the quality of audit depends not on the thoroughness of the auditor's instructions but on his grasp of principles and on his conscientiousness, care and power of persistence. In any case a programme is useless when the auditor is confronted with the tasks of appraising systems, devising new records and discussing organization and personnel.

(10)

Audit sections, like accountancy sections, can be organized on a service basis, i.e. the work can be allotted according to the services, some staff taking charge of all matters pertaining to the education audit, others of the highways audit and so forth. Or the work may, within limits, be given out according to its nature, some staff looking after payments, others after receipts, some specializing on contracts or some on salaries or wages. Much the same considerations apply as to accountancy sections. An additional reason for a functional division in the case of audit is that the movement from department to department keeps the auditor fresher. If he is always auditing in the same department he may become too stereotyped in his methods and may become part of the mechanism of internal check rather than of internal audit. But, again as in the case of accountancy work, neither method can be pressed to its logical conclusion. No chief auditor would send two men to an outlying school, one to check receipts and the other petty cash payments. Some counties organize their work regionally rather than on either a functional or service basis.

[1] See Laurence L. Vance, *Scientific Method for Auditing* (University of California Press, 1950); also Laurence L. Vance and John Neter, *Statistical Sampling for Auditors and Accountants* (John Wiley, 1956).

(11)

The chief internal auditor will control the output and operations of his assistants by means of programmes of work, control charts, etc., for he must see that audit visits are made to every place where financial work is done and where financial records are, or ought to be kept. Where departments have themselves a comprehensive system of internal check, e.g. an education finance section paying regular visits to schools, he will arrange his audits to avoid overlapping or the irritation to departments of too many visits. He will also make his audit complementary to the internal check, e.g. if the checks made by departments are regular, he will make his visits irregular, to provide the element of surprise. He must also see that a correct balance is struck between the frequent audit of short duration and limited scope, and the more exhaustive audit which can take place only at longer intervals.

Surprisingly little has been written about the mechanics of control of work within an audit section. Yet the subject is of special importance for the very features which make control difficult, such as the intangible nature of the work or the need for flexibility, are those which make it so easy for audit work to go by default, or to be badly done without the chief financial officer being aware of the position. The audit work is not part of a series of operations which if not performed, or if not performed in accordance with instructions, causes immediate dislocation. By its very definition it comes in at the end when the work is completed. If it is not done, there is no obvious inconvenience or disruption. Moreover, because hardly any audit is exhaustive, the auditor selects what is to be checked, so that it is exceedingly difficult to measure the work load objectively.

But at least a measure of control can be exercised, through a work allocation system based on a job card for each audit, the card showing the particulars of the audit and, in the light of past experience, the time allowed. The card can be used as the basis for dividing the work over the staff, and as a record of the visits, summary sheets being kept to show that each team, and within each team each individual, has a fair share of the work. Another simple summary suffices to show how the frequency of each audit compares with the standard laid down. The summaries are also useful in determining audit policy and in working out staff requirements. The same system can be

159

applied to the running jobs in an audit office, e.g. control and issue of receipt books.

Such a system is not a precision instrument, and it yields no information about the quality of audit work. It will, for instance, not reveal whether an auditor genuinely makes enquiries or whether he only claims to have made them, nor will it find out whether the auditor passes mistakes. But it does give some notion of the volume of audit work and its distribution, and, equally important, shows what ground the staff have at least purported to cover, and what has been left untouched.

(12)

The chief financial officer will keep in close touch with his chief auditor by frequent conferences and by reports. Some chief financial officers prefer a periodical report at stated intervals summarizing the work done and the state of the audits: others deal only with reports of difficulties. Whichever method is used there should be some automatic means by which the chief financial officer knows if audit work is in arrear.

Most of the errors and weaknesses found by the audit staff will be put right at once by co-operation with the departments, but major deficiencies will be discussed and adjusted at chief officer level, reports being made to the appropriate committees if the head of the department and the chief financial officer disagree, or if matters of administrative principle or irregularities are involved. Committees may reasonably want, in addition to an *ad hoc* report when some outstanding difficulty or difference of opinion has occurred, a periodical report on the state of the financial records in the departments for which they are responsible. When the Organization and Methods team of H.M. Treasury made their investigations into the administration of Coventry City Council they suggested that an annual audit report should be submitted to every committee explaining broadly the work that had been done during the year, and calling the attention of the committee to weaknesses still needing to be rectified. These reports have proved to be a valuable part of the financial procedure of the council. They help to make the committee conscious of the importance of financial records; they give an independent appraisal of the quality of the departmental work; they provide a stimulus to the departmental staffs, for finance officers take pride in a clear report; and they give the committee a reminder of persistent weaknesses due to such factors as inadequate accommodation, imperfect administration, insufficient or mediocre staff. They have also been found useful to the heads of large departments who are provided with a convenient annual opportunity to survey their financial arrangements.

CHAPTER XII

THE CHIEF FINANCIAL OFFICER: COSTING AND MISCELLANEOUS DUTIES

(1)

EACH of the duties of the chief financial officer examined so far—those of giving financial advice, acting as accountant, internal auditor and machine accountant—presents organizational issues numerous enough to warrant a separate chapter. There are, however, other kinds of work which, though they do not raise so many administrative problems, must receive attention. They are: costing, management of debt, management of investments, arranging insurances, administration of the superannuation acts, correspondence, mailing and registration of documents. These functions are dealt with in the sections which follow.

(2)

Our examination of the first of these miscellaneous duties—that of the chief financial officer's responsibilities for cost accounting—can best begin by considering in some detail the extent to which the financial accounts of local authorities and the data associated with them yield the information essential for management purposes, a subject already touched upon in the chapter on the chief financial officer as accountant.

Chief financial officers of local authorities have ever been at pains to make their final accounts informative. Income and expenditure—not receipts and payments as in the accounts of the central government—have been set out in significant detail, and accounts, complete with balance sheets, have been presented as nearly on commercial lines as the circumstances of local government permit. Judged by the completeness of their accounts, or by the lively attention paid to the subject over the last sixty years, English local authorities show up well by comparison with the central government or their continental counterparts. Recently further advances have been made: the Institute of Municipal Treasurers and Accountants has issued standard accounts incorporating new and carefully thought-out classifications of income and expenditure which can be generally applied throughout the country but at the same time allow for the incorporation of additional local features. The new forms of account, especially those of the balance sheet and capital expenditure account have been devised in the light of the most up-to-date practices of commercial undertakings and the nationalized industries.

A local authority can, therefore, fairly expect from its accountant a high standard of presentation. Similarly no accountant to a local authority has any excuse for old-fashioned techniques in the production of his data. Most local authorities employ an adequate qualified accountancy staff (local authorities usually have at least as many qualified accountants in their employment as other concerns of comparable size), and their chief financial officers have access through the literature of the Institute of Municipal Treasurers and Accountants and otherwise to all the technical information they need. In general, local authority accounting methods are second to none and many a local authority opens its accountancy system with justifiable pride to inspections by local directors, secretaries and accountants.

Chief financial officers have in the main also been alive to limitations of the traditional budget as a means of controlling some items of expenditure and have for many years developed cost accounts— usually of the historical type—for many services. Indeed most sizeable local authorities have a costing section in the chief financial officer's department.

Further there is in the local government service a sound tradition of treating the final accounts as something more than a means of ensuring that money has been expended on authorized purposes. Costs are expressed in units (per child maintained in a home, per meal supplied, etc.) as well as in the aggregate, and there is a wealth of comparative information available to enable an authority to compare local costs with those of other places. There are very few local government services for which comparative figures of some kind are not issued by government departments, the Institute of Municipal Treasurers and Accountants, or the Society of County Treasurers. Relations between authorities are such that enquiries to other authorities for further details will be readily answered.

But attention to these aspects of accountancy does not exhaust the chief financial officer's obligations as accountant. He has also to ask himself how far, in the light of the stable nature of most of the services of the local authority, the more dynamic conceptions of cost accounting can be applied to local government. What place is there for 'costing before the event', for flexible budgets, for standard costs and variance accounts? Do the costing techniques of local authorities enable them to decide whether divergencies between their costs and those of other authorities are due to different principles of allocation of expenditure, differences in the nature or quality of the service rendered, differences in physical conditions, or to varying efficiency? Do local authority accountants make as effective a distinction as their commercial counterparts between variations within the control of the authority and those beyond their control? Do the cost accounts bring home responsibility sharply to the individuals responsible, or vaguely to a department? Is the accounting such that every individual who spends money or uses goods must meet a day of reckoning when the quality of his stewardship will be judged? Have recent developments in costing affected the truth of the present author's statement in 'Internal Financial Control' (1936), that 'it would be folly to entertain any but the most modest expectations of the future of costing in English local government'?

(3)

For the answers one has to look first at the nature of the services provided by local government, and in particular at the comparisons between productive enterprise, for which modern costing is primarily designed, and the rendering of a public service. There is a world of difference between the two kinds of activity. Local authorities are not making a product of measurable weight and quality: they are for the most part rendering intangible services—the housing of an old person in a home, the education of a child, protection from fire, regulation of weights used by a shopkeeper. Whilst it is possible, and indeed desirable, to express costs over units, the results cannot possibly have the same precision as in industry. The library service of one authority might cost more per 1,000 of the population or even per book issued than that of another, but this does not show whether the ratepayers are getting better or worse value for money. Even with the engineering services, e.g. road construction or repairs, there is still a vital difference, for no two jobs are identical. There are also contrasts between the conditions under which local authority services are rendered. Some have to be carried out to meet a need in a particular place, e.g. home nursing has to be done as required in the home of the person. In other cases physical conditions such as varying weather exert an influence, examples being road repairs and refuse collection.

Mention has been made elsewhere in this book of the effects of the absence of the profits criterion of success, another distinguishing feature of most public services. In no respect is it more important than in the consideration of the practicability of costing. The fact that the local services are judged on their quality and extent and not on a profits test, raises an unfortunate presumption that the more that is spent on a service the better. Whatever truths may lie embedded in this conception it is certainly the exact opposite of that brought to the examination of costs in productive industry. As the present author said in 1950:

'In industry the *raison d'être* of a factory manager is a product of given quality at the cheapest possible figure. His cost statements are his touchstone. If he disregards them his future is imperilled. Indeed, costing largely developed because the factory manager and overseer felt the need for an up-to-date financial appraisal of each stage of manufacture. Now, in the case of Local Government, the circumstances are different. Criteria and standards vary, so that the head of a service, especially of a cultural, health or social service, cannot measure his success by a low unit cost. He may assume that the more he spends per unit of service, the more successful is his work. Further, if he is a good official, he will be an idealist, and he may even despise money and its implications as an irrelevancy—or worse, as a sacrilegious intrusion. Fortunately, most public officers have a sense of their responsibility for the spending of public funds.

'But we have by no means finished with the peculiar circumstances of Local Government from the view-point of the cost accountant. There is, too, the different attitude of the governing body—the Council. Who would deny that an elected body will place much more emphasis on the expansion of a service than on an examination of detailed cost statements, any disturbing features of which can be so easily explained away as due to the peculiar "local circumstances" or the superiority of the service rendered? An employee in business regards himself as primarily accountable to his Board in terms of his financial results: the official of a Local Authority in terms of the elaborateness of service. With most Local Government services, no one can prove, unless there is flagrant mismanagement, whether or not the same result could have been obtained at less cost.'[1]

[1] *Studies in Costing*, a collection of papers edited by David Solomons (Sweet and Maxwell, 1952), pp. 614-15.

Most chief financial officers have had the experience of submitting to committees figures comparing local costs with those of other authorities, only to find the members ignoring those items which showed the committee's expenditure to be above the average and concentrating on those which were below, in the belief that the latter indicated an inferior service.

The authors of the Productivity Report on Management Accounting said of American Industry:

'A new generation of managers has risen, many of whom have had training in management at the business schools attached to many of the universities, or at such institutes as the famous Massachusetts Institute of Technology. They have learned the value and utility of figure statements and what can be reasonably inferred from them. At the same time many accountants have realized that service to management is their main objective.'[1]

There is no parallel to this in English local government. Much will depend on the zeal and enthusiasm of the chief financial officer, and his ability to persuade committees and officers to use the costs and statements which he produces. However, notwithstanding all the influences working to the contrary, many local authorities are cost conscious.

(4)

Clearly it would not be sensible to advocate the wholesale adoption of commercial costing for local government services. The chief financial officer of a local authority must take the activities of his authority not in total, for they vary in their nature, but individually, and decide to what extent the conceptions of cost accountancy can be usefully applied to them. This is largely a technical matter, but the availability of costing data is so highly germane to a study of financial administration that this book would be incomplete without a general survey of the possibilities of the development of cost accounting in local government.

It is important to remember that because the operating committees and departments will not be clamouring for costs, as would the works manager of a factory, a conscious effort will always be needed on the part of the chief financial officer if use is to be made of costing. There may be inertia and indifference to be overcome, and all the dis-

[1] Extract from *Productivity Report*, 'Management Accounting' (Anglo-American Council on Productivity, 1950), p. 8.

abilities of costing in local government described in the preceding paragraphs will be put forward as reasons for taking no action. The chief financial officer will find that he has two extra tasks: that of supplying the driving force for the costing and, at least in the initial stages, that of persuading his colleagues and perhaps his masters to take an interest in the figures. As we have seen in this and in earlier chapters, he must watch that the records he produces are used. In short, the chief financial officer of a local authority has to shoulder the task of rousing an interest in costing as well as that of producing the costs. Should he be inclined to resent this, he can at least fortify himself with the thought that costing is vitally important in local government, for the deep-seated reluctance to accept costing, springing from the nature of local government and local government administration rather than from defects of individuals, makes it all the more necessary that costing should not go by default. Dislike of costing is closely related to an indifference to cost: and it is one of the main duties of the chief financial officer to try to combat any tendency towards the latter.

The corollary of this is that the chief financial officer must keep constant watch to see that his production of costing information is not in advance of the will and capacity to consume it. In no field of accountancy is it so easy to produce superfluous information as in costing; and in no field of activity is the temptation greater than in local government, because, added to the infinite variety of figures that could be devised for the multiplicity of services provided, is the fact that the desire for it is less. Constant review of the use made of the information is therefore imperative if wasted effort is to be avoided.

Bearing in mind all these limiting factors, how far can a chief financial officer expect to go in costing? There are, first of all, many operations in local government, identical with or closely akin to those of commercial concerns. The maintenance of plant and vehicles, the erection and maintenance of buildings, the provision of meals, printing work, are obvious examples. For these operations local authorities should keep the same kind of cost accounts as their commercial counterparts. Thus, for example, the officer in charge of a department using a number of vehicles should have access not only to information of the cost of running and maintaining each type of vehicle, but also to comparisons of costs of different types for different periods, statistics of idle time and information about dead mileage. He should expect to see plant accounts which show in significant detail in what directions the actual cost over a period has varied from the estimate, so that he can quickly establish the reasons for the variations.

In the second place the chief financial officer has to make full use of the device of expressing cost in relation to an appropriate unit. For he will often find that the unit cost is the only measure available, especially in the social services. Local authorities have given a good deal of attention to working out the significant units, and they should not rest until the subject has been exhausted. Unit costs can be immensely useful in budgeting, in day-to-day control, and in the final appraisal of the services. In some services, e.g. school meals, they are the foundation of the financial relationships between the central government and the local authority, as well as the obvious method of controlling expenditure. They can be arrived at by simple division of the cost shown in the financial accounts by the total units or they may be derived from subsidiary data, e.g. more detailed analysis; they may also be associated with the more advanced types of costing discussed below.

Thirdly, there is the question of applying to local government the modern conceptions of cost accounting—costing before the event, standard costs, variance accounts and so forth. This is a vast subject, only considered here from the point of view of management. Some aspects of the detailed commercial technique are in any case inapplicable to local authorities, being designed to deal with the production problems of a varying (often unpredictable) volume of sales. In local government there are no factory conditions and no production for sale; output is at an even level. But this disposes of some aspects only of costing, and local authorities have to ask themselves, for example, to what extent standard costing can be applied to local government.

Standard costs can take the form of memorandum records used for statistical or control purposes—not entered into the books of account—or they may be used as the basis for entering the accounts. In the latter case, as the books must eventually record the actual charges, the standard costs are supplemented with 'variance' accounts which adjust the standard costs to the 'actual' costs. The 'actual' costs are then in two parts: that which is standard and that which represents the variation from standard. It is the variance account which focuses the differences, enables responsibility for them to be assigned, and discloses to management the reasons—variations in output, alteration in prices or wage rates, inefficiency of plant or labour, etc. The technique and significance of the variance account are matters of dispute,[1] but the basic idea is clear and very important. Standard costs are computed for operations or processes and regarded *pro tem.* as the actual costs. When the true costs become available they are in such form that a detailed analysis of the variances from the standard can be made and appropriate action taken. Is there any scope for this idea in local government? (The question of whether standard costs should actually be entered into the books of account is left aside as an accounting matter.) The idea is not new: for instance, plant accounts already common in local government show periodically to what extent the cost per hour tallies with the figure used when the charge was fixed, and what elements of cost are responsible for the variations.

Another illustration which comes perhaps nearer to true standard costing is the use in local government of predetermined labour 'targets' in conjunction with bonus schemes for house building maintenance, e.g. painting. The essence of these arrangements is that there is a record which discloses the differences between the actual and a standard. For instance, the mere fact that bonuses are being earned on any operation is of itself an indication that costs for that operation are coming out on the right side of the standard. Conversely, the absence of bonus earnings on an operation would be prima facie evidence of the need to make enquiries into the correctness of the target and the circumstances of the job upon which it had not been attained.

A further example is that of costing for meals in residential establishments. If the catering superintendent prices out his menus for the week on standard prices, he can, knowing the number of his residents, compare the estimated average unit cost of the meals he proposes for the week with his allowance. Subsequently the actual costs can be compared with his calculations and the differences investigated in accordance with costing techniques. In the case of provisions, the principal factors to be examined will be quantities used, purchase price, wastage and theft. Experience of such a system has shown that its introduction brought a fall in provisions costs and greater satisfaction to the residents because of the steadier quality of the diet. When the costs were kept on the historical principle without a pre-established standard, periods of relative extravagance were followed by periods of relative austerity which were the cause of dissatisfac-

[1] See *A Re-examination of Standard Costs*, an N.A.C.A. bulletin reprinted in *Studies in Costing* (Sweet and Maxwell, 1952).

tion. This method does not involve a standard diet: endless permutations and combinations are possible within a week (or whatever period is taken), so long as the average cost of the meals is within the allowance for the particular season of the year. This technique is equally applicable to school meals, civic restaurants and indeed catering of all kinds.

The possibilities exist and it remains for local authorities to explore the application of similar techniques to other services, of which the most likely to yield results appear to be the engineering services—road construction and maintenance, street cleaning, refuse collection, etc. Little progress will be made by discussing the application of modern costing methods to local government as a whole: local government services must be examined individually.

(5)

There remains the organization of the costing work, a specialist branch of accounting with its own techniques. When cost accounts were divorced from financial accounts, an independent section for costing was perhaps inevitable. Such a section would make detailed dissections of expenses, which might or might not be made the basis of the posting of the financial accounts. These dissections, together with many detailed apportionments not employed in the financial accounts, would be posted to a separate cost ledger, cost statements from the ledgers being prepared as needed. At the year end the cost ledger accounts would be grouped and compared with the financial accounts, an exact balance not always being achieved.

Nowadays all the accounts are part of one ledger system. Such data as are imported into the accounts for costing purposes, e.g. costs built up on standards rather than on actual costs, are finally adjusted to the actual figures by the use of variance accounts and similar devices. The automatic case for a separate costing staff has thus largely disappeared. But costing has still its own contribution to make and as we have seen in the preceding sections of this chapter, has made rapid advances in recent years. Chief financial officers of the larger authorities have a duty to make use of its potentialities. Occasionally there is still an independent costing section, but often the costing staff either form a subsection of their own in the accountancy section, or else are attached to one of the other subsections where there is the greatest call for costing techniques, e.g. that dealing with the engineering services.

170

The trend is undoubtedly towards integration of the two kinds of work, if only because modern cost accounts are not now an independent set of books as they once were. Now that so much of the detailed dissection is done mechanically—often in a machine section—and the accountant is not himself faced with the labour of hand analysis, the need for a separate costing section is not so obvious, and an increasing number of chief financial officers regard costing as a specialized aspect of accountancy rather than a separate subject, even though they may employ costing specialists. Amalgamation of costing work with that of accountancy has several advantages. It ensures that close contact is maintained between costing and general accountancy. This is essential if costing is to be accorded its proper place in the financial system. Moreover, amalgamation is probably less confusing to the operating departments who are unlikely to appreciate the fine distinction between costing and other accounting statements; they merely look for the most significant data. A disadvantage is that the possibilities of costing may be overlooked, or not fully used, because of the preoccupation of the accountancy section with capital and revenue estimates, final accounts, grant claims and other more general aspects of accounting work. Also, costing being concerned with a mass of documents may be thought to be a disturbing influence in the accountancy section which normally deals with broader analyses and more summarized information. No general rule about the location of costing work can be laid down. The essential point is to make sure that full use is made of the possibilities of this very important aspect of accountancy.

When the pattern of organization of the costing section is being determined, the need to work continuously and harmoniously with the departments must ever be kept in the forefront. The planning of costing schemes, the interpretation of results, and the drafting of costing reports must all be joint products of the finance and operating departments.

(6)

The next of the miscellaneous functions falling for discussion in this chapter is that of organizing the work of raising loans and managing the authority's debt. As local authorities at the time of writing raise about £500,000,000 of new loan monies every year, this task forms no inconsiderable part of a chief financial officer's responsibilities, though it does not involve a large staff. The work varies in volume from time to time according to money-market conditions, the borrowing policy of the authority and current legislation. For instance, from 1945 to 1952 local authorities had no direct access to the market. Monies came through a government agency and the work entailed was at a minimum.

Finance committees take a close interest in loans management, and the chief financial officer has to keep his committee informed of the total needs, the methods of borrowing, and the advantages and disadvantages of the various methods under current conditions. The chief financial officer and his deputy have to keep in close touch with the day-to-day operations in the raising of capital, for though the council, on the advice of the finance committee, will lay down the general borrowing policy, the chief financial officer must clinch the bargains. He must watch the money market and be acquainted with the policy and experience of other local authorities. In the larger authorities an assistant will gather information and may negotiate individual deals, subject to the concurrence of the chief financial officer or his deputy and, if the deals are of magnitude, the chairman of the finance committee. The chief financial officer and his deputy must so organize their affairs that one of them is available to give decisions, and a subordinate officer must be on hand to collect market information and to receive proposals from lenders or their agents.

In contrast to the money market operations referred to above, money loaned by small investors through the post or over the counter, at rates of interest fixed in advertisements, involves no high level decisions, receipt of these monies being merely a matter of routine. At the other end of the scale are stock issues, the most impressive of the money market operations of a local authority. Shrouded in secrecy in the early stages, with private consultations between the issuing houses and the chairman of the finance committee, stock issues become suddenly public, involving special meetings of committees and of the council at short notice, the local authority being forced to make an immediate decision, a somewhat unusual thing in local government. The management of a stock issue is a subject in itself. From the point of view of office organization, the important point is that the local authority's borrowing arrangements must be business-like and prompt or the reputation of the authority as a borrower—and indeed that of other local authorities—will be affected. There are also a number of security arrangements concerned with the receipt of monies and the issue of documents of title which must be strictly adhered to.

If the local authority's borrowing directly from the public or through the money market is extensive, the loans registration work may become sizeable enough to warrant the creation of a section, or more commonly, a subsection, exclusively for this purpose. This is a section where the staff must be thoroughly acquainted with the law relating to the issue and transmission of securities and the standard of accuracy impeccable. Mistakes are serious; they may affect the finances of the local authority and those of private individuals; and worst of all they may lie undiscovered for many years with shattering consequences. The staff in this section must be senior in status and in no circumstances should they work under pressure. This applies as much to the initial task of registering a stock issue as to the day-to-day jobs of paying interest, registering changes of ownership and receiving money from the public. If the loans staff has to be temporarily augmented from other sections for the purpose of stock issues, only staff of first-class calibre should be selected. The work of a loans section is confidential and the staff must establish good relations with the money market and with lenders. Individual lenders, to whom the investment of money in the council is an important occasion, must not be made to feel that the transaction is to the loans office one of many other similar routine transactions.

Promptness is also essential. Loans interest has to be paid on time, and changes in registration of title should also be made without delay to avoid embarrassment to loan holders. An indication of the importance traditionally attached to loans records is that they were the last stronghold of copperplate writing in local authority finance offices! But even they have now succumbed to mechanical means of preparation.

Closely related to the raising of capital monies is the management of investments, another function of the chief financial officer, the importance of which cannot be gauged by the amount of time it takes. Again, as with loans transactions, the financial techniques, which are outside the scope of this book, are of more importance than matters of organization, but there are a few organizational points to be made. The volume of work depends as much on the policy of the local authority as on the amount of the investments, some authorities holding their investments and others pursuing a policy of constant change; though whatever the policy of the authority, there must be regular attention to make sure that the most profitable outlets are found and that investments are 'matched' with the obligations of the funds. New fields of investment for superannuation fund monies have now been opened up in those authorities where under a local Act, a proportion of the superannuation fund may be invested in industrial securities. The staffs of such authorities must in future keep in close touch with the trends of industrial securities as well as those of the gilt edged market. The need for the chief financial officer to arrange his office to keep a watch on investment trends is not affected by the employment of brokers or panels of advisers because, although the specialists may advise, the final decisions will be those of the authority who will always expect also to hear the views of their chief financial officer.

(7)

Another task falling to the chief financial officer, that of arranging insurance, is similar to that of loans management in that it bristles with technicalities, but has at the same time interesting and important organizational problems. They are not, however, problems of volume, for only in the largest authorities will the insurance work occupy the time of more than one official. They are rather those associated with diversity. Loss of or damage to buildings, machinery, vehicles; legal liabilities to third parties, employees, passengers in vehicles; claims by persons prejudiced by the errors or negligence of officials in the registration of land charges, or in looking after scholars —these are examples of scores of risks against which the authority must insure. Only the insurance specialist will be aware of the existence of some of the more obscure risks.

The management of insurance has to be centralized, to secure the financial economies of the aggregation of the authority's insurance business, and the benefits of specialized management. Usually the work is given to the chief financial officer, the finance committee being responsible for insurance and insurance funds.

Though the management may be centralized, success hangs on co-operation between the Clerk to the authority, the chief financial officer and the departments. Upon departments must be placed the responsibility of informing the chief financial officer of the risks to be covered. Departments know what plant and property they have, and what departmental operations involve danger or risk. There may, however, be chances of claims by third parties, and other potential liabilities which only the insurance expert with his special training will think of. Departments have also a general idea of the amounts for which most of their property should be insured, but

174

they will be less knowledgeable about the more intangible kinds of insurance. Here again, the specialized insurance officer must assist, for he knows the current trend of judges' awards of damages and the prevailing attitude of insurers towards the computation of loss. The Clerk must decide all points of legal difficulty, close liaison between the Clerk's department and the insurance officer being imperative, for nice legal points, outside the experience of the insurance practitioner, will occur. Similarly with claims and potential claims, whilst the majority come within ordinary insurance practice, there are others involving new questions of law, often of a highly controversial nature.

The chief financial officer must take all the precautions he can to ensure that risks are covered, even though the primary responsibility has been placed upon the departments. He must scrutinize minutes and current transactions, and he must consider the possible claims to which new or occasional activities may give rise—knowing that it is the risks for which no normal 'routine' exists that are always liable to be overlooked. An agricultural or flower show or a gala can so easily discredit the chief financial officer and his insurance officer. The chief financial officer must also watch the effect of changing value of money on the council's insurance cover.

The work of effecting insurances and making claims must be done promptly and efficiently for insurance work cannot be allowed to fall into arrear. Cover must be obtained as soon as the risk appears and claims must not be delayed, or the interests of the council and its insurers will be prejudiced. If any class of claims is to be made directly by a department, e.g. routine claims for damages to passenger transport vehicles, the responsibility of the department should be clearly defined.

The chief financial officer's insurance officer should be fully acquainted with insurance practice, expert in the devising and construction of policies, conversant with current trends in the insurance world, and familiar with the council's activities. He needs firmness for dealing with the insurers, and keenness to prevent under-insurance, over-insurance or indeed insurance at all in any directions in which the local authority could better carry its own risk. He should be expected to advise the chief financial officer on the latest techniques of insurance, and, like the officer in charge of loans registration, he should not be so placed that he can plead pressure of work as an excuse for some major oversight: and oversights can occur more easily, and have more disastrous consequences, in insurance work than in almost any other branch of the work of the finance department.

Finally, as the legal textbooks remind students, insurance contracts are contracts of the utmost good faith. Insurance companies have shown commendable trust in the administration of local authorities, accepting values, costs, estimates of expenditure and the like with the minimum of enquiry, dispensing with detailed schedules and relying on the work and judgment of employees of the authority. In addition, local authorities have enjoyed generous treatment on claims. The inescapable corollary is that the authority should conduct its insurance business in faultless fashion.

(8)

The other miscellaneous tasks can be dealt with more shortly. The administration of the superannuation acts will not need a large staff, important and complex though the work may be. It is important because appreciable sums are at stake in the computation of lump sum payments, pensions, transfer values and so forth, and complex because local authorities have now to cope with several superannuation codes and often local act variations in addition. Formerly chief financial officers could be expected themselves to have a close knowledge of superannuation matters. It is now a specialist's subject. The day-to-day administration needs to be under the control of an officer with an intimate knowledge of the Acts and regulations, for apparently small mistakes may prejudice individual rights and they may also, as with errors in loans registration, remain undiscovered for long periods.

The chief financial officer has to make sure that both the routine tasks of making deductions from pay, calculating pensions, and the higher work of elucidating difficult points and watching for pitfalls are properly done. Some continuity of personnel in the superannuation section or subsection is therefore desirable. The practice, already mentioned, of attaching these duties to those of the payment of salaries and wages is very common, but they can be equally well fitted into other sections.

Typing, registration of documents and filing services also need careful organization, and of particular importance in a finance department are the arrangements for opening and recording the mail, so much of which is in the form of remittances. There is sufficient similarity in the work of the various sections of a finance department to make a central typing, registration and filing service practicable. These sections, like the machine section, are service sections, established to help other sections, and they have to be organized accordingly, but their problems are relatively simple and do not justify elaboration here.

CHAPTER XIII

THE ROLE OF THE CLERK IN FINANCIAL ADMINISTRATION

(1)

THE Clerk and his department come into contact with the financial administration at many points. As the secretary of the council and its committees, the Clerk drafts the agenda and minutes, sees that committees receive all the necessary documents and information, whether issued from his own department or otherwise, and makes sure that all the appropriate officers are consulted before decisions are taken.

Usually the Clerk is also the council's legal adviser. He is responsible for drawing up, and securing the observance of, the internal rules regulating the conduct of the council's financial business, a feature of his financial work discussed later in this chapter, and also in the special chapter on this subject. Though the chief financial officer, like other heads of departments, will have a working knowledge of the law relating to the operations of his own department, he will look to the Clerk to advise him in unusual cases. In particular, he will be careful to inform the Clerk of any happenings—especially cases of suspected irregularity—likely to involve the council in legal proceedings. Similarly, though the officers of the finance department may conduct day-to-day proceedings in the courts for recovery of debts, the assistance of the Clerk would at once be enlisted if points of law had to be determined.

The chief financial officer is entitled to expect the Clerk to advise him whether proposed expenditure is legal (later the Clerk may have to satisfy the district auditor of its correctness), and to call upon him to interpret the law governing such aspects of local government finance as superannuation, grants, income tax or rating.

Again, the Clerk is responsible for formal acts affecting the finance department such as the promotion of bills in Parliament, application for loan sanctions, conduct of enquiries, issue of notice of audit, custody of statutory registers, and registration of mortgages (and sometimes stock). The chief financial officer will be dependent upon the Clerk to inform him of periodical receipts or payments to be made under agreements and leases, and of operative dates of agreements and other similar documents. He must also rely on the Clerk for the renewal or cancellation of agreements. Sometimes the Clerk is the Local Taxation Officer, and there are a few other aspects of the local authority's work which sometimes fall to the Clerk and sometimes to the chief financial officer, e.g. management of insurances.

Finally there is financial work in the Clerk's department akin to that in the operating departments. Thus, the Clerk will have invoices to pass for his departmental expenditure, petty cash to handle, and money to receive for the issue of licences. Most of these transactions are on a relatively small scale, but very important are the Clerk's duties in certifying for payment accounts in respect of property transactions, both purchases and sales. The same pattern of organization will be needed for the financial operations of the Clerk's department as for those of the operating departments, whose arrangements are considered in the next chapter. Internal audit will also be applied in the same way.

The contacts of the Clerk with the financial administration, briefly set out above, are, in the main, those normally associated with the position of secretary and legal adviser in most large-scale or multipurpose organizations. But the more intangible and elusive aspects of the role of the Clerk in financial matters are the result of the distinctive nature of the administration of local authorities. It is with these less straightforward aspects that this chapter is mainly concerned.

(2)

Chief financial officers must, under their conditions of appointment laid down by the Joint Negotiating Committee for Chief Officers of Local Authorities in England and Wales, bear a direct responsibility to their authorities for the advice they give and for the conduct of their departments. No other officer can bear any of this responsibility on their behalf and no other officer can give them instructions.[1] But this independent and direct responsibility has to be reconciled

---

[1] 'A chief officer shall be the executive and administrative head of the department of which he is the chief officer. He shall be responsible therefor to the Council through the appropriate committees.' Conditions of service laid down by Joint Negotiating Committee for Chief Officers of Local Authorities. September 1950.

with the duty of the Clerk to act as the council's chief administrative officer[1] which is normally interpreted to mean that he will co-ordinate the work of the departments, advise the council on the distribution of duties between departments, and on such matters as the use to be made of common services. He is also expected to hold a watching brief, at least to the extent that he would call the attention of the heads of departments, and if necessary the council, to gross inefficiency or malpractice likely to prejudice the work of the authority.

Clerks to local authorities differ greatly in their interpretation of their duties as 'chief administrative officer', but even those who place the narrowest possible meaning on the expression, would admit to some responsibility for advising the council on the allocation of work to departments. One might look to the Clerk not to accept with equanimity a failure by his local authority to observe the canons of financial administration as accepted by other kinds of comparable concerns. In other words the Clerk may fairly be expected to interest himself in the establishment of an integrated system of finance, the value of which as a co-ordinating influence has been discussed in an earlier chapter. The Clerk is, of course, the officer to reap most benefit from the adoption of practices which educate departments in each other's work, which compel them to consult one another before approaching committees on matters not the sole province of a single department, which lay emphasis on joint reports and which stress the need for the chief financial officer to regard himself as much the servant of the departments as the financial watchdog of the council. So many of the major matters coming before local authorities have financial implications, that if the Clerk is assured of adequate inter-departmental consultation on these, he has made a most important advance towards securing co-ordination generally. Moreover, financial co-ordination, apart from its direct value to the local authority, is likely to bring in its train other benefits; for example, it is not accidental that those authorities with good financial arrangements are usually those with adequate personnel management and common purchasing facilities.

To encourage his local authority to put the financial administration upon a firm basis would therefore appear the first financial obligation of the Clerk. A satisfactory financial system means ade-

---

[1] 'The Clerk shall be the chief executive and administrative officer of the council. He shall be responsible for co-ordinating the whole of the work of the council.' Conditions of service laid down by the Joint Negotiating committee for Town Clerks and District Council Clerks. September 1949.

quate, dynamic, co-ordinated financial and accounting arrangements together with a means of ensuring that the system is carried out. The chief financial officer must have his methods of enforcing compliance with the prescribed procedures, and the heads of operating departments must have means of holding the chief financial officer to his obligation to provide them with a financial and accounting service. From the Clerk's point of view the first step towards securing this will be to have proper internal rules and prescription of duties. The financial standing orders and any regulations or instructions—excepting those dealing with technical matters of accounting —will be matters of concern to the Clerk. Though the chief financial officer may suggest their content and wording, the Clerk must satisfy himself not only that they are in proper form, but that they are reasonable and workable. Having satisfied himself that they are desirable, he will have to pilot them through the council with the aid of the chief financial officer. It is also the Clerk who must see that the council's standing orders and regulations are observed. In practice immediate watch is kept by the chief financial officer, and, given good relations between departments, occasions for drawing the Clerk's attention to breaches should be rare. But they may occur, and there may be cases where the chief financial officer defaults in rendering the prescribed services to departments. Failures to comply with correct committee procedures are more easily dealt with than defaults at a lower level because they will come automatically to the notice of the Clerk and indeed to that of the members. The fact that the Clerk, not being a general manager or chief executive in the ordinary sense of the term, cannot issue directions to departments on domestic matters, but must rely in the last—unpleasant—resort on laying the facts before the council, does not affect his duty to secure co-ordination and observances of rules : it merely makes the job more delicate.

(3)

Day-to-day relations between the Clerk's and chief financial officer's departments are inevitably close, and if they are not cordial the local authority is indeed in an unhappy state. The chief financial officer and his staff have some interest in many of the items on the agenda of committees. Both he and the Clerk are concerned to see that the proper procedures are carried out; the Clerk generally, the chief financial officer in matters with financial implications. Much of the information gathered by staff of the two departments in the course of inter-departmental discussions is of mutual interest, an observation which applies as much to the small matters of detail gleaned from juniors as to ideas for new policy tentatively talked about between senior officers. Official documents, committee data, and correspondence on major matters pass through the Clerk's hands in any case. The chief financial officer must keep him in touch with any current financial matters with legal implications and with anything he learns in the course of his duties which affects the work of the authority as a whole. Conversely the Clerk must give the finance department the opportunity of scrutinizing at the appropriate stage all documents with financial bearings; for instance, the chief financial officer should see papers relating to proposed contracts. It is not always easy in local government to establish the idea that documents should pass freely between departments and that the files are the authority's files and not those of individual departments. The Clerk and the chief financial officer are in an excellent position to set a good example.

Where the Clerk is the establishment officer there must be a clear distinction at committee level between the establishment and financial aspects of personnel matters and at the same time a close co-ordination between the departments, for there is a very intimate relation between the work of the departments on such questions. There is, for instance, a danger of duplication of records between the establishment officer and the chief financial officer, if understanding is not complete. The relation between organization and methods work and internal audit, another point of prime importance and great interest, has been considered in the chapter on 'The Chief Financial Officer as Internal Auditor'.

There is in fact a unique community of interest between the Clerk and the chief financial officer. Both of them have a vested interest in good inter-departmental relations. Both are concerned with certain aspects of departmental activities, though neither of them has any direct responsibility for the actions of departmental officers. Both of them exist partly to oil the wheels of machines set up by other officers. If there were no departments carrying out the more positive task of education, highway construction and the like, there would be no Clerk and no chief financial officer. Notwithstanding the element of control in their work, and despite any influence they may have on the policy of the council, the functions of the Clerk and the chief financial officer—though sometimes they do not like to be reminded of it—are largely those of helping the departments. When they retire they leave no roads, bridges, or schools as monuments to their enterprise. Should they regard their work as an end in itself; should they set greater store on their powers of control and influence in their respective spheres, than on their main task of assisting others, then whatever virtues they may have, they most certainly will have failed in one important respect.

(4)

In an earlier chapter we saw that only in the smallest authorities may the posts of Clerk and chief financial officer be justifiably combined. We must now consider the special problems, so far as they relate to finance, of the Clerks of such authorities and of those larger authorities who have yet to separate the duties.

A Clerk holding both offices may or may not have a professional qualification. If he is an accountant he will have the necessary financial knowledge, but will suffer from two disabilities. First his work as Clerk may prevent him from giving the financial aspect due attention. Secondly, he cannot, because of his responsibilities as the council's general adviser, put forward a purely independent financial view. There is no complete way of compensating for these disabilities, though if the authority is large enough to warrant the appointment of a deputy, it helps if he is specifically charged with financial affairs. Some Clerks wisely encourage the deputy to express opinions on finance directly to committees.

Where the Clerk is not an accountant there is the additional risk of the financial work not being well conducted. The first safeguard is staff able to keep and balance double-entry accounts. Simple but comprehensive internal rules are also needed. The collection of income, the making of payments and the calculation of wages must be properly done. Moreover, though internal audit may be out of the question, there must be checks to ensure compliance with the rules.

In short, the Clerk will take pains to ascertain and install the fundamental precautions upon which an accountant would insist.

CHAPTER XIV

THE FINANCIAL ORGANIZATION OF OPERATING DEPARTMENTS

(1)

THE financial work of a local authority is carried out not only in the offices of the finance department, but also in other offices, in workshops, trenches, buses and schools. That part falling to the finance department comes under the direct control of the chief financial officer; the rest is primarily the responsibility of other chief officers. This outside work is the raw material used by the finance staff, whose specialized skill will be wasted if it is not well done. Similarly with financial control; vigilance on the part of the council, the committees and the financial staff will be of little avail if departments are not so organized that everyone who spends money, or controls the use of goods, is imbued with a sense of financial responsibility. Departmental financial organization is therefore of immense importance, and a student of the financial administration of local government must consider not only the chief financial officer's department, but also how other departments set about their very substantial share of the work.

There is an inevitable contrast between the attitude of the finance department and that of others. Finance is the *raison d'être* of the former; it provides all the normal work; there are no individuals to whom it is a side-issue. Elsewhere it is, or may be, incidental; it occupies the complete attention of but a few individuals, and only in a large department are they numerous enough to form a separate section, so that much of the work is done by persons with other preoccupations. They range from professional and office staff to the workman who makes out a stores requisition as a part—a very small part—of his daily duties. Moreover, in the finance department the work is directed by a chief officer who has made this discipline his life's work, whilst outside it is a subsidiary part of the responsibilities of chief officers belonging to other callings and professions, who may regard finance as a distraction from their principal tasks, or even as a distasteful aspect of their work. This difference of attitude has to be borne in mind in all the dealings the chief financial officer and his staff have with their outside colleagues. Another significant factor is that finance looms larger in some services than in others. It would be foolish to expect it to play as large a part in the mind of a weights and measures inspector as in that of a transport manager, or to count upon the same approach in a children's department as in a public works department.

This chapter is devoted to an examination of the financial duties of operating departments and to the organization of the work. The subject cannot be dealt with in a comprehensive categorical fashion because of variations in the nature and range of duties, scale of operations, outlook and organization, both between individual departments in the same authority and between different local authorities. All that can be done is to set out a few general principles in the knowledge that the mode of application will take many forms.

(2)

To guard against the primary danger, that of failing to give finance its due share of attention, the Organization and Methods team of H.M. Treasury, reporting on the organization of the Coventry City Council, recommended that every department, large and small, should have a 'finance officer'. New appointments were not contemplated: an existing officer was to be designated, and where the department was too small to have a subordinate officer of sufficient standing, the head of the department was to be appointed. By 'finance officer', the Treasury team meant something very different from an officer in charge of a section in which the bulk of the financial work of the department has been segregated, a practice already common in local government. They had in mind the creation of a corps of officers of considerable status, trained in financial procedures, in continuous touch with the finance department, who would act as the financial conscience of the department and seek to foster a sense of responsibility in all their colleagues who deal with money or money's worth. These officers would feel a loyalty to the council's financial system as well as to their departments. They would maintain the financial work at a high pitch of efficiency and would ensure for finance its due weight in all departmental activities. In short they would reflect in a single department the activities which the chief financial officer endeavours to carry out for the local authority as a whole. They would be the standard bearers of integrated financial arrangements.

185

This conception, new to local government, has now been crystallized in Coventry by the designation in every department of a finance officer who carries out the functions visualized by the Treasury team. These officers regard themselves not merely as departmental officers to whom financial duties are given, but also as a body of officers kept in close touch with the finance department by means of training schemes, regular meetings, accounting manuals and so forth.

(3)

To turn from the general position of a departmental finance officer to his actual duties is to meet at once the difficulties of the varying sizes of local authorities and of departments within a single local authority, together with the differing nature of their activities. The following account of the work is offered in the knowledge that it could not be applied to any particular set of circumstances without modification. The mere fact that in most of the departments of a small authority and in some departments in a large authority the head of the department will himself be designated as the departmental finance officer is sufficient to make a categorical description of the scope of the work impossible. With this qualification in mind we can, however, proceed to consider the principal tasks of a departmental finance officer, some of which are developed in more detail in other chapters.

One of the most important aspects of his work is that of acting as the chief link between his department and that of the chief financial officer. Day-to-day relations between the two departments form a two way traffic: each day primary documents such as bills for payment, time sheets, stores issue notes and the like are passed *to* the chief financial officer, whilst management data—cost accounts, stores lists, expenditure tabulations and so forth—will be received *from* the chief financial officer; other kinds of data, e.g. that for reports, will be passing both ways.

Upon the maintenance of efficient and friendly contacts depends the smooth working of the financial system. Documents should flow as easily between the two departments as they do between the officers within the departments. The chief financial officer must none the less be wary of using the departmental finance officer as the sole day-to-day link. Many other officers will have regular contacts with the finance department's staff, though on most matters of importance, the departmental finance officer will also be involved. He should act as a co-ordinating and liaison officer in inter-departmental affairs rather than as a counter at which all financial enquiries are answered.

The link with the finance department serves another purpose besides that of facilitating the work. It is the means by which the departmental finance officers are made to feel part of the integrated system of finance, and it helps to foster in them the realization that they are carrying out duties with a professional flavour. The means of forging this link are the title, the official prescription of duties, the backing of the finance department in operating the financial system, the accounting manuals and the training courses, described below.

The specific tasks of a departmental finance officer can be classified as follows:

(a) Advising the head of the department on the financial aspects of the department's work and assisting in the drafting of reports.

(b) Playing a part of cardinal importance in making the budget and in the formulation of departmental schemes, whether financed from capital or revenue.

(c) Forming the main link with the finance department including the internal audit.

(d) Controlling day-to-day expenditure in accordance with budgetary provisions, loan sanctions or other standards. This includes supervision of the systems for issuing orders, control of petty cash payments, authorizing use of departmental transport, etc. The larger the department, the more will the departmental finance officer's function be that of seeing that the system is worked rather than that of actually ordering goods or controlling transport. The departmental finance officer must also make sure that all officers who can control costs, from the engineer or other officer in charge of major works to a school caretaker regulating fuel consumption, are encouraged to use appropriate cost statements. Departmental finance officers should be invaluable in the control of expenditure for they are exercising control at the vital time—before the expenditure is incurred, and their intimate knowledge of the department, coupled with the fact that they are part of the department's organization, enables them to exert an influence which no 'outside' person could ever hope to equal.

(e) Controlling income. A departmental finance officer should see that cash is properly handled, acknowledged, recorded, banked or paid to the chief financial officer's department, and that the chief financial officer is promptly and correctly informed of all credit income to be collected. He should also review scales of charges and watch that no potential source of income is overlooked. Departmental stocks of tickets and receipt books should be in his care.

(*f*) Controlling stores and stores records. Whether or not the stores themselves are directly under the control of the departmental finance officers will depend on circumstances. But in any case they should be responsible for the stores records, including the allocation to expenditure heads of the stores used, the ordering of stores, continuous stocktaking and the oversight of the arrangements in the stores. In particular they should watch that purchases are not excessive and that obsolete stock is not accumulated.

(*g*) Maintenance of records of employees. A departmental finance officer must see that due authority (including financial provision) exists for all appointments. Save in the very largest departments where there is a departmental establishment officer, the departmental finance officer must be responsible for all clerical procedures relating to establishment, including preparation of personal records and the examination of time sheets. Even where there is a departmental establishment officer the departmental finance officer must satisfy himself that the personal records are a sound basis for the compilation of the payroll.

(*h*) Ensuring that all departmental income and expenditure is allocated to the proper heads of account.

(*i*) Supervision of the process of verification of accounts for payment, whether on capital or revenue account, including certification of all accounts passed to the chief financial officer for payment, and supervision of contract documents and records.

(*j*) Maintenance of plant and vehicles records and inventories, and the exercise of oversight over vehicle operating costs, idle time, etc.

(*k*) Ensuring that timetables for the completion of all financial work are adhered to, and that all registers containing financial matters are promptly and correctly written up and reconciled.

(4)

In discharging his duties the departmental finance officer may have to contend with those factors which tend to make finance the Cinderella of local government departments. To combat them he needs all the influence and prestige he can acquire. He will be helped in this by his high departmental status, by his intimate knowledge of finance and the financial regulations, by his control of expenditure, by his ability to help his colleagues in the interpretation of financial data and by making his own section an object lesson in smooth administration.

The relationship between technical officers and departmental finance officers is most important. Primarily the task of the latter is to help the technical officers in the financial aspects of their work and to see that such financial work as is carried out by them is done in the approved way. But there are technical officers such as engineers and quantity surveyors, who do financial work which will not normally come under the oversight of the departmental finance officer. For example, he cannot be expected to control the issue of a variation order, or the making of a final settlement with a contractor as he can the purchase of day-to-day equipment. But he has some responsibilities, amongst them that of ensuring that proper records are kept. One of his most useful functions is to encourage technical officers to make the utmost use of the financial data provided. Indeed, if essential data were being consistently ignored, it would be his responsibility to report to the head of department. The technical officer for his part is entitled to expect the departmental finance officer to provide information promptly and in a form that is intelligible and will expect the departmental finance officer to take up at once with the chief financial officer any deficiencies in information supplied from a central accounting or costing organization.

The dual allegiance of the departmental finance officer also falls to be mentioned, though in practice it is not found to present much difficulty. A finance officer is subordinate to the head of his department. To give him any independent responsibility would be to cut across the principles of administration adopted by English local authorities. But he should have a distinctive point of view and he should feel a sense of responsibility to the council's financial system as a whole. There is of course nothing in this which is incompatible with subordination to his departmental chief, except in the circumstances where the latter gives instructions for some irregular financial procedure. One chief officer on the introduction of the finance officer system gave his finance officer written instructions that 'he should regard himself as completely free to deal correctly with any certification of accounts or finance . . . and if necessary to disregard any wishes that I may have in this respect'.

189

(5)

The chief financial officer has a number of specific responsibilities towards departmental finance officers. He must supply them with the technical instructions and guidance they need, partly through written regulations, accounting manuals, inter-departmental memoranda and the like, and partly by less formal means. He must keep in close touch with them, holding consultations to discuss problems, difficulties, proposed amendments to the accounting system and new instructions of the council. But they are not under his control and he must not be tempted, because of his special relations with the departmental finance officers, into forgetting inter-departmental proprieties such as the passing of correspondence through the heads of departments. Nor must consultations with finance officers ever be allowed to become a substitute for inter-departmental consultations between officers, including those of chief officers. The aim must be to use the finance officers to bring departments closer together. There is nothing unusual in the relationship between the chief financial officer and the departmental finance officers. In many large-scale organizations there are departmental officers responsible to the head of a branch but looking to some officer at a regional or head office for technical guidance, e.g. the chief clerks of groups and districts in a Gas Board may have a dual responsibility to the divisional accountant and the manager of the undertaking or group of undertakings. Departmental finance officers will of course make demands upon the chief financial officer: one of their functions is to use their unique combination of knowledge of their department's work and of the financial system to look critically at the services which the chief financial officer gives the departments. At times they will press for additional information, e.g. more detailed costing, or they may ask for support in upholding the regulations. The chief financial officer must not regard them as a passive tool—or indeed a tool of any kind.

The chief financial officer should be required—possibly by formal standing order—to see that departmental finance officers and their staffs are properly trained in financial work, for departments will not be adequately equipped for such instruction. Courses at different levels describing the council's financial system, and more intensive courses in the technique of specific operations should be regularly held. The comments made in other chapters on the increasing need under present conditions of recruitment, for simplification of routine work, precise definitions of responsibility and intelligent supervision, apply as much to the routine financial work of the operating departments as to that of the finance department.

(6)

What should be the attributes of a departmental finance officer? He needs to be a man with an aptitude for handling and classifying figures, capable of establishing cordial relationships with officers of many types including technical officers who may be impatient with, or even contemptuous of, financial considerations. As a member of the operating department his prime duty is to be zealous in furthering the interests of that department, but as the finance officer he must be careful to see that the council's financial system is carried out and that the cost is counted. Though wholly under the control of his departmental chief, he must have something of a split personality, for whilst taking all his instructions from one officer, the head of his department, he looks to another, the chief financial officer, for information and help.

It is immensely important to the chief financial officer that the posts of departmental finance officers be properly filled, and that they should be provided with staff as adequate and competent as can be obtained. It was for this reason that the Treasury team suggested in Coventry that the chief financial officer should be consulted in the appointment and deployment of departmental finance officers and their staffs, a recommendation which has been carried out by providing, by agreement with the departments, that a representative of the chief financial officer's department should sit as an adviser on panels appointing departmental finance staffs. This ensures that departments, whilst retaining full responsibility for the appointments, have the benefit of specialist views about the candidates, their abilities and experience. The appointments of departmental finance officers themselves would be made by committees, after hearing the views of the heads of departments and the chief financial officer.

It is not always easy to determine the place in the official hierarchy to be occupied by the departmental finance officer, and no rules of universal application could be laid down. Clearly he must have power, prestige and influence: and he must be in a position to take an independent line with senior colleagues. Moreover, as he will represent the department on many matters and may well appear regularly before committees, e.g. in connexion with the passing of bills for payment, he must be of sufficient status to be accepted by committees and other departments. In the smaller departments the head of the department must himself assume the additional responsibilities of departmental finance officer. But this is to be avoided wherever there is another officer sufficiently senior, for it may be difficult for the head of department to attend to the details. An officer of the right standing is needed, but one who will not become a mere figurehead, e.g. a deputy already overburdened with other work, for whoever is given the post must have time to keep in close touch with the department's financial arrangements and must be personally accessible.

(7)

Departmental finance staff cannot normally become heads or deputy heads of their own departments because all departments are professionally directed. In one sense, therefore, it is true that their prospects of promotion are limited. If, however, an officer aspires to the full professional status which can lead to a chief officer's post, he can transfer to the finance department.[1]

On the other hand the departmental finance officer, especially in a large department, acquires a kind of professional status of his own, as an expert in financial procedures if not in the higher flight of accountancy, and as an officer with a wide experience in co-operating with the finance department. This status is of inestimable value to him, both in discharging his duties and in helping him towards such higher posts as may be open to him, either as finance officer in an even larger department, or in some other branch of the authority's administration.[2] Departmental finance officers and their staffs may

[1] Officers of other departments engaged on financial work who wish to qualify as accountants are now allowed to count service on such work in an operating department as qualifying service for determining their eligibility to sit for the intermediate examination of the Institute of Municipal Treasurers and Accountants, provided the local authority 'will so far as possible give facilities for the transfer of the candidate if successful to the finance department to enable him to qualify for admission to the Final examination'. (See Institute Examination Regulations and Syllabus, May 1959, Regulations for all examinations No. 6.)

[2] A few of the very large authorities may have sufficient work in their major departments to justify the employment of a qualified accountant, such posts being often filled by transfer from the finance department of an accountant who is willing to leave the main stream of local government accountancy. At present this might be detrimental to the career of an officer whose objective is a chief

improve their status by passing the Diploma in Municipal Administration, but if they are to have breadth of practical experience to match their theoretical qualifications, local authorities must move them between departments. It should be easy, as well as valuable, to transfer finance staffs, for much of the basic financial technique is common to all departments. What differs is the work of the departments, not the financial duties: the *raison d'être* of the fire service for instance is sharply contrasted with that of the welfare department but they both have to order goods, prepare time sheets, control expenditure and so forth. It is by serving departments with such diverse functions that an officer obtains the essential breadth of view. Experience on non-financial duties is also invaluable.

It is also desirable that departmental finance officers and their staffs should work for short spells in the various sections of the chief financial officer's department. Here they see the use to which the departmental prime records are put, learn to appreciate the reasons for the precautions upon which the chief financial officer insists, realize the dire results on subsequent accounting operations of inaccurate primary records and come to understand why a certain amount of departmental convenience has to be sacrificed for the sake of attaining some common objective in financial practice or record keeping. Perhaps most important of all, such officers return to their departments with a more vivid appreciation of their own departmental duties as one link in a long chain, no longer conceiving the finance department as performing remote mysterious operations, but merely as finishing the work begun in the departments.

The effect on the chief financial officer's staff of a flow of officers on short transfer from other departments is equally salutary. They learn the point of view and problems of their colleagues, find out how they can best help them, and establish personal relationships of great value to the administration as a whole. But the greatest benefit of mobility comes when they themselves serve in other departments, gaining first-hand knowledge of the services of the authority. It is all too easy for the staff of the finance department to think of departmental operations as entries in a budget or ledger. Local authorities could do much to encourage mobility if, when making appointments of professional accountants, they did not look askance at outside experience.

---

financial officer's post, but one hopes that with the spread of the idea of integration of financial arrangements such experience will come to be accepted as beneficial rather than otherwise.

(8)

A local authority laying down detailed conditions of appointment for the chief financial officer will usually do the same for other chief officers. If so, the council should at the very least prescribe that heads of operating departments should (*a*) conform with the council's internal rules and the chief financial officer's requirements in accounting and financial matters; (*b*) supply the chief financial officer with all the data he requires to carry out his duties; and (*c*) collaborate with him in submitting reports on the financial implications of business coming before committees.

An authority which has adopted the principle of integrated financial arrangements may well wish to go further, for the essence of such a financial system is that the chief financial officer exists as much to encourage others to exercise financial control as to exercise it himself. A judge in a celebrated case laid down the dictum that the auditor is a watchdog and not a bloodhound. In the case of the chief financial officer of a local authority one might say that additionally he must be a breeder of watchdogs. He should not be satisfied until everyone concerned with the spending of money or use of goods and property has become alive to finance. He is much more likely to attain this aim if the council has made it abundantly plain that the prime responsibility for control of departmental income and expenditure is that of the operating department itself.

This being so, it may well be that local authorities whose custom it is to prescribe the duties of chief officers in detail, should introduce a more positive note into the descriptions of financial duties, instead of merely requiring heads of departments to comply with the financial regulations.

Earlier in this chapter the part played by departmental finance officers has been considered in some detail. The responsibility for their actions is however that of the heads of department, so that any list of the duties of the latter would comprehend those of their finance officers.

The duties of all chief officers might cover the following:

(1) Control of departmental income, expenditure and costs within the amounts allowed by the council.

(2) Verification and certification of all accounts for payment.

(3) Prompt collection and payment over to the chief financial

194

officer of monies due to be collected in the department; prompt furnishing of details of sums due for collection by the chief financial officer.

(4) Arranging for purchase and proper custody and use of stores, vehicles, plant and equipment; carrying out a continuous stock-taking; notification to the chief financial officer of discrepancies.

(5) Prompt supply to the chief financial officer of the information needed for accounting purposes for advising committees or for supervision of the financial arrangements.

(6) Co-operation with other officers in the preparation of joint reports.

(7) Conforming with the council's accounting and financial rules and the requirements of the chief financial officer in financial matters.

(8) Prompt notification to chief financial officer of any case, or suspected case, of financial irregularity.

(9) Collaboration in the preparation of the annual budget and other financial forecasts.

(10) Passing to the chief financial officer all the information necessary to effect insurances and to make claims.

CHAPTER XV

THE PAYMENT OF ACCOUNTS

(1)

MANY of the more elaborate features of financial administration are to be found only in the larger authorities. Training courses for finance officers, separate financial control sections, machine accountants or special committees for applying scales of assessment, for instance, would hardly make sense applied to the affairs of a small authority. Other devices—joint reports, supplementary estimates, inter-departmental conferences—are needed regularly in large authorities but less frequently as the size of the authority diminishes.

We now come to work—the payment of accounts—which is a continuous feature in all local authorities. No local authority, however small, can escape its problems. Indeed the smaller the authority the more difficult it is to achieve the distribution of duties which is the basis of a proper system of control. Verification of accounts for payment, entering purchases in subsidiary books of account, guarding against illegal or irregular payments, making arrangements for prompt discharge of liabilities—these are the unexciting but vital duties with which this chapter is concerned. They are tasks for which members, operating departments and the finance department all have responsibilities. Our examination of the subject must therefore include a discussion of the role of each of these branches of the local authority.

In approaching the subject the dispersed nature of the operations of local authorities has once again to be remembered. Goods will be ordered, received and checked, and invoices passed forward for payment, in scores—often hundreds—of points throughout the area of the authority, so that watertight methods of checking are difficult to achieve and uniformity is out of the question. Many of the goods are highly specialized and units of administration are often tiny: sometimes one office carries out several of the functions concerned with the ordering and receiving of goods and passing invoices forward for payment, thus violating the principles of internal check. It is not surprising that frauds by persons ordering and controlling goods in isolated departments have occurred from time to time. Moreover, the great number of creditors and delivery points also brings book-keeping complications unknown when goods come to a central factory from a limited number of suppliers.

Another important factor is that the payments made by a local authority are subject to a much more rigorous *post mortem* examination than those of commercial enterprises. The strict application of the doctrine of *ultra vires* to the activities of local authorities, together with the district auditor's power of surcharge and the personal liability of the treasurer as laid down in the case of *A. G.* v *de Winton,* may have specially unpleasant consequences for individuals. Both members and officers must have in mind the results of illegal, as well as of excessive or irregular, payments. For these reasons the routines adopted by local authorities for the certification and payment of accounts will be more complicated than those of other kinds of organization.

Finally members, being responsible in their corporate capacity for administration, must be kept in touch with day-to-day business. Whatever the office routine for making payments may be, committees will rightly insist on access to particulars of payments, and on means of satisfying themselves that vigilance and care are being exercised in contracting and discharging liabilities. A local authority, unlike a commercial concern, cannot delegate the control of payments entirely to the administration: a way must be found of combining business-like office routines with some oversight by members.

Therefore, humdrum though the subject of payments routines may appear to be, it is not only of immense importance to the local authority; it also brings problems of a distinctive kind. No local authority can afford to treat either the organization or the supervision of its payments routines lightly. It is incidentally for this reason that local authorities are required by law to make rules laying down the arrangements for making payments.

We shall consider first the effect of the changes made in 1958 in the law governing the making of the payments; and then the principles upon which a payments routine should be founded. Next there will be sections devoted to the distribution of duties between the operating departments, the chief financial officer and the members. Two final sections deal with the payment of salaries and wages, and the organization of the payments section of the finance department.

197

(2)

Until the passing of the Local Government Act, 1958, English local authorities had to organize the payment of accounts under statutory provisions long out of date. Broadly, the old legislation provided that payments could be made only upon an 'order on treasurer' signed by three members of the council and countersigned by the Clerk. Those provisions, stemming from days when transactions were so few that members could be expected to have personal cognisance of them, were useless for the complex and voluminous transactions of modern local government. They brought in their train two evils: widespread evasion, and a false sense of security.[1]

These provisions, which incidentally differed for different classes of authority, have been repealed. The new law, set out in detail in the appendix, provides that local authorities shall make safe and efficient arrangements for the receipt of monies paid to them and the issue of monies paid by them, and that the arrangements must be supervised by the treasurer. Subject to these two provisos, local authorities are now free to devise their own methods. It is to be hoped that, stimulated by the new provisions, local authorities will reconsider their payments routines critically, for it would be unfortunate if, in the future, payments procedures were cluttered up with useless survivals of the days of 'orders on treasurer'.

(3)

But though the traditional payments routines need revision they will not need to be entirely discarded. Indeed the experience of the more progressive authorities under the old law is invaluable in devising the new arrangements. It is, therefore, desirable briefly to set out at this stage the practice prior to April 1, 1959.

Counties excepted, the common method of payment of accounts in local government prior to the passing of the Act had been for schedules of accounts to be submitted to monthly meetings of the

---

[1] It is curious that similar statutory provisions were made when the National Health Service was set up. Not only do payments, subject to certain exceptions, need sanction by a board or committee, but cheques must be countersigned by a member (See *National Health Service (Hospital Accounts and Financial Provisions) Regulations, 1948*). Some modifications have, however, been introduced by the Minister of Health, by both general circular and individual consent. But the general principles of the original circular remain in operation.

committees. Sometimes the bills were then paid, but more often payment had to await the confirmation of the council. In the meantime a consolidating process took place to ensure that only one cheque was sent to a supplier who had dealings with more than one committee. A creditor waited at least a month for payment, and often considerably longer, especially if he submitted his accounts soon after the date of a committee meeting. County councils whose meetings were quarterly could hardly keep creditors waiting three months. They, therefore, either had more frequent meetings —possibly of sub-committees—specifically to pass bills, or else allowed their chief financial officer to pay, subject to subsequent report, thus providing for the discharge of liabilities to be practically a continuous process. Much the same result was obtained by some other types of authorities, who delegated to a weekly meeting— usually to a sub-committee of the finance committee—authority to make payments. In addition, most sizeable authorities had some kind of imprest account for making immediate payments—wages, payments to earn cash discount, interim payments to contractors, and so forth. Another method of making urgent payments is that of the Local Government (Payment of Accounts) (Scotland) Regulations, 1948 under which payments of a recurring or routine nature or incurred in circumstances of emergency can be made without prior sanction of a committee.[1]

The date of committee meetings was however the principal controlling factor throughout, and local authorities were on the whole tardy payers, for accounts inevitably accumulated during the intervals between meetings. There were no doubt times when the prospect of having to wait for their money deterred suppliers from quoting the keenest prices. In addition, the basic analysis of 'expenditure' being done on a cash basis, the monthly scheduling system held up the accounting, for it was usual for the scheduling and analysis to be part of the same process.

(4)

Unhampered by the necessity to wait for 'orders on treasurer', local authorities can now adopt and develop methods of continuous pay-

[1] The various devices in use for making payments of all types—many of them of doubtful legality under the old law—were described in *Methods of Scheduling Accounts and Expenditure Analysis* by John Drury, an Institute of Municipal Treasurers and Accountants research publication, 1951.

ment. As with other aspects of local government, the routines will differ according to the size of authority, its pattern of organization and the view taken by the members of their responsibilities for scrutinizing payments, but there are some useful principles of general application worth noting.

The machinery for placing orders and incurring liabilities is dealt with in later chapters. Consideration of the practical arrangements for payments can therefore begin with the procedure in the department responsible for the expenditure, including the central supplies department for goods supplied to a central store.

The correctness of the bill must be established by those who know the facts: the person who received the goods can vouch the quantity and quality, the buyer can check the price, and so forth. Similarly, the person who knows for what purpose the goods were used should code the bill to the appropriate head of expenditure. Finally, having made sure that the account is arithmetically correct, that it has not been paid before, that it represents properly authorized expenditure, and that all the checks laid down have been applied, the certifying officer passes it forward to the chief financial officer for payment.

The detailed technique of the verification of bills, e.g. the ways of guarding against accidental duplicate payments in the absence of creditors' accounts which are not kept in local government, is not a matter for discussion here, but there are some overriding points of principle which should govern procedure in the operating departments. The first is that, even in the smaller authorities, more than one person should be concerned with the process leading to the certification of accounts. Failure to observe this precaution has probably made possible more expenditure frauds in local government than any other single feature, for 'one man' administrative units abound. But even if departments are compelled to tolerate them for general administration, they are not satisfactory for the purpose of financial administration. It is not sound practice for the man who is to use the goods to order them, have custody of them, and pass forward the bills for payment without the active participation at some stage of another official.

Then there is the desirability of a written code of instructions about the payments of accounts, applicable, with any appropriate modifications, to all departments. Such codes would deal in detail with the various classes of accounts and would aim not only at ensuring that all safeguards are taken, but that there is uniformity of treatment throughout the departments in such matters as deduction of cash discount or the application of the council's rules for payments of travelling and subsistence allowances. The code could be embodied either in regulations or, if greater detail is required, in manuals of instruction. The differences between the two methods are described in the chapter on internal rules.

There must also be a clear understanding about the person whose final certification shall be accepted and the nature of his responsibility. In small departments the head of the department can reasonably be expected to certify accounts personally, and to take a close interest in their content and correctness. Even in a larger department he may be well advised to adopt the practice of scrutinizing the accounts. It is an excellent way for him to keep in touch with events, it stimulates keen buying and wise ordering, and it is a powerful deterrent to a potential wrongdoer. But if the department is large enough to justify a finance officer, other than the chief officer, he should be the person immediately responsible for the correctness of all accounts passed to the chief financial officer for payment, though the ultimate responsibility will rest on the head of the department. Whether the head of the department allows the chief financial officer to pay on the certification of the finance officer, or insists on countersigning personally, will be a matter for local arrangement, but, whatever the precise procedure, the chief financial officer should encourage the head of the department to take an interest in the bills.

Finally the process of certification of bills and forwarding to the chief financial officer must proceed according to a rigid timetable. Creditors must be paid promptly or the council's relations with its suppliers may be prejudiced, terms of purchase may be worsened and discount for prompt payments lost. Moreover, the chief financial officer, who has to cope with bills from many departments, must be able to programme his work to avoid peak loads. An even flow of work, highly desirable in a manual system, will be essential under a mechanized system if the machinery is to be economically used.

(5)

Assuming that the checking of bills within the departments is soundly organized along lines discussed above, is it necessary for the chief financial officer to scrutinize the bills in detail? Or can he devolve to departments the whole business of account checking, merely carrying out test checks to make sure that the departments are observing the prescribed routine, and that the quality of their work is satisfactory? If he does, are there any special categories of accounts which in any event he should verify in detail?

The answers to these questions depend mainly on the size of the authority, the nature of the financial organization and the quality of departmental staffs. They will also be coloured by the views of the chief financial officer about the extent to which he can delegate the work of verification in view of his personal responsibility for the correctness of payments. The chief financial officer, particularly if he holds the designation of treasurer, would be conscious of the need to carry out a final check to make sure that accounts submitted would not involve irregular payments for which he would under the *de Winton* judgment be personally responsible. Similarly, and irrespective of the designation of the chief financial officer, there hangs over his head—and his council—the possibility of surcharge by the district auditor.

Naturally the chief financial officer strives to prevent irregular liabilities being *incurred* in the first instance and in this sense his most effective safeguards must be carried out at an earlier stage. But the final sieve is the payments routine. No two chief financial officers will take exactly the same views about the extent to which it is safe to rely upon checks in other departments. There can therefore be no categorical answer to the questions posed above, but whatever the attitude of the chief financial officer, the bulk of the checking work must be done in the departments. Only the departments can certify that the goods have been received, and that quantities, prices, etc. are correct. In practice they must also make sure that they have authority for the expenditure and that the bill has not been previously paid. If, therefore, the chief financial officer takes it upon himself to check any of these features of a bill there will be some duplication. For this reason, there is prima facie a good case for placing the prime responsibility for checking bills on the departments, subject to the chief financial officer satisfying himself that the necessary safeguards are being properly applied. But before a chief financial officer can pay upon the certification of a department he must (*a*) have formal authority from his council for leaving the checking of bills to departments; (*b*) be satisfied that there is in every department a division of duties sufficient to guarantee at least the minimum amount of internal check; (*c*) lay down, preferably in writing in conjunction with the departments, a precise routine for the work; (*d*) have means of ensuring that the staff is adequate and properly trained for the work; and (*e*) have established an audit sufficiently elaborate and comprehensive for him to know automatically, and at once, if a department becomes lax.

It is relatively easy to arrange a payment routine for a large department where duties can be subdivided and staff can concentrate on different aspects of the work. In the case of the bills of small departments, the chief financial officer may have to carry out some of the detailed work in his own department in order to provide the necessary safeguards, e.g. to provide the minimum spread of duties between individuals. In any case, common sense must be allowed to mitigate the rigorous application of rules about the allocation of work between departments. For instance, even though the departments may be responsible for the arithmetical accuracy of the bills, there is no reason why they should not make use of the chief financial officer's calculating equipment to avoid mental arithmetic.

Another and more far-reaching argument in favour of decentralizing to departments the verification of payments is that it is in keeping with one of the principal aims of a good financial system, i.e. to bolster up the sense of financial responsibility in the departments. A department knowing that accounts certified for payment are not subject to further routine check will feel that the job is entirely theirs and take pride in doing it properly. There are also important administrative advantages of decentralization, e.g. avoidance of concentration of routine work in the finance department with the attendant staff difficulties.

(6)

Whatever the general distribution of duties, the chief financial officer will find that in practice some categories of accounts need special treatment. Payments to contractors, for instance, will pass through a different routine in his office if he maintains specialist staff for dealing with contractors' accounts. Again, there will be classes of payments likely to cause trouble if they are not treated uniformly throughout the local authority, e.g. payments to members and officers for subsistence allowances, officers' telephone accounts, or payments where no invoice is received. Uniformity can be achieved either by a code of detailed regulations, supplemented by a test check applied to a few accounts, or by the chief financial officer handling such accounts in his department. In the smaller authorities the latter may well be preferable: but in a larger authority there is much to be said for decentralizing the task. It is an excellent way of underlining the departments' responsibility. Payments of which other chief officers have no knowledge, such as loans, interest payments, and a few miscellaneous kinds of accounts, like members' 'financial loss' claims, will in all cases be dealt with by the chief financial officer.

It is important that a local authority should find an expeditious way of dealing with inter-departmental transactions—charges to departments for work done by engineering departments, use of pooled transport, supplies from central stores, etc. Chief financial officers of local authorities often handle these transactions in a way incomprehensible to commercial accountants, by rendering accounts and treating them in the supplying departments as if they were owed by outside debtors, and in the paying department in the same way as tradesmen's accounts, i.e. including them in schedules of accounts for payment and drawing cheques in settlement. A good deal of unnecessary administrative machinery is thus set in motion.

The simple way to deal with these transactions is for the chief financial officer to treat them as book-keeping transfers in the council's accounts, at the same time informing the department which is being charged, giving sufficient particulars to enable the departments to satisfy themselves that the charges are fair and correct. Disputed accounts must be settled by agreement between the departments concerned, any adjusting entries being made by transfers in the accounts. The number of these adjustments will be found to be negligible for, though departments habitually grumble about charges made by others, they are rarely able to disturb the basis of calculation.

(7)

Save for petty cash and other small imprest accounts, the actual payment of accounts will be done by the chief financial officer in his capacity as paymaster. Much ingenuity has been expended on methods, mechanical and otherwise, of scheduling accounts for payment in order to produce at the same time, or at least as part of the same process, the schedule of accounts paid, an advice note for the creditor and an analysis of payments for accounting purposes. These methods are extensively discussed by Mr Drury in the study already mentioned and are outside the scope of this book. From the point of view of organization within the finance department the important factors in handling payments are (a) to have a routine which enables the accounts coming from the departments to be rapidly and smoothly dealt with and (*b*) to make sure that the principles of internal check are rigorously applied, e.g. even in the smallest office an officer concerned with the checking of the accounts should not be responsible for the issue of the cheques. Proper arrangements for the custody and issue of cheques are of immense importance, especially if the cheques are pre-printed with the signature of the chief financial officer; duties must be divided between two or more persons, at least one of the most senior officers must be involved, and the independent scrutiny of paid cheques must be a daily process.

(8)

Of the many aspects of local government finance discussed in these pages, none focuses more sharply than the payment of accounts the problems brought to members by their obligation to keep in touch with administration. Here is a mass of varied transactions, the only common thread running through them being that they represent a financial liability contracted on behalf of the local authority. Here is the work of many clerks skilled in the intricacies of financial checks and in the exercise of traditional financial safeguards. How can the members in committee and council discharge their constitutional liability? What scope is there for the committee to exercise effective checks? Or, to put the problem in more concrete terms, assuming that accounts have been certified by the operating departments and accepted by the chief financial officer, should they be submitted to a committee before he pays them? If the chief financial officer is allowed to pay accounts without presentation to a committee, should the paid accounts be subsequently submitted to the committee? If so, how should the members of the committee proceed with their examination?

Clearly, members can bring under their personal supervision only a fraction of the operations and documents; and their task is to exercise a layman's judgment and technique for they cannot be expected to know the routines of financial control and check. Their supervision needs to be highly intelligent, and it must not prevent the adoption of a business-like office routine for the payment of accounts. If members are to be found week by week carrying out a full check of the same stage in the process, e.g. patiently 'calling over' the amounts of individual bills to a schedule of accounts for payment, then one may infer that the real check exercised by the members in that authority is small indeed.

Modern practice therefore provides for members to select at random for detailed scrutiny bills from the schedules of accounts paid or to be paid. In some authorities the accounts are selected by the chairman beforehand: in others the committee selects the accounts. Many of the questions asked can be answered at the time the account is selected, whilst others call for a detailed report at a subsequent meeting. The members may ask, for example, for the production of all the documents relating to an account, beginning with the authority for the placing of the goods, and ending with the entries in inventories and stores accounts. The utmost use should be made of the chief financial officer and he should be required to state whether all the regulations have been complied with prior to the submission of the account. This not only gives the members an independent assessment of the quality of the work of the departments, but at the same time enables the effectiveness of the chief financial officer's supervision to be gauged. In the main the committee should be left to select both the individual accounts and the nature of the examination themselves, but it is the duty of the chief financial officer as the financial adviser to remind the members from time to time of any aspects of the payments process they may be neglecting. Committees, like individuals, develop habits, and the probability is that, if the members are not guided, they will tend to concentrate on one kind of enquiry or check. For instance, they may become obsessed with watching the prices paid for goods.

(9)

Having examined the nature of the members' function in the bill-checking process, we must now consider what kind of committee is most appropriate for the purpose. The traditional method of committee scrutiny in English local government was for all committees to have at every meeting a list of bills for payment, the signed list becoming the 'order on treasurer'. Counties, with their quarterly meetings, had as has already been mentioned to make other arrangements. Often they placed block sums at the disposal of the chief financial officer who made payments which he reported later for confirmation, usually to the individual committees.

In most authorities therefore, each committee is accustomed to having its bills, paid or unpaid, laid upon the table. Routines which will supersede the examination of payments by individual committees are made possible by the new statutory provisions. The abolition of orders on treasurer will enable local authorities to pay their bills continuously, either by adopting the county system of giving the chief financial officer authority to pay subject to report later, or by a small sub-committee meeting weekly to pass bills for all departments. Such a committee can carry out the test checks described in the previous section, and will soon acquire special skill in the supervision of payments. Scrutiny of accounts for payment will be the committee's *raison d'être* and they will therefore not treat it in the casual fashion which has made the examination of accounts by committee ineffective in so many local authorities. Even if the chief financial officer is allowed to pay the accounts in the first instance, there is much to be said for submission to a single committee for confirmation.

A more fundamental reason can however be adduced for taking the primary responsibility for scrutiny of payments away from committees operating the services. Control by individual committees over the incurring of liabilities, if it is to be effective, must take place at a much earlier stage than that of the presentation of bills for payment. When a bill, duly verified for arithmetical accuracy, etc. is presented for payment, it represents a liability which must be discharged. Any checks open to members at this stage are mainly for the purpose of bringing to light weaknesses in procedures or in the quality of the clerical work. Real control of expenditure must take place before the liability is incurred. If committees examine their own bills for payment, they are apt wrongly to regard this scrutiny as control of expenditure, and may then fail to exercise control over the *incurring* of liabilities. If, on the other hand, a special committee examines invoices, the committees operating services are encouraged to concentrate on expenditure control, allocation of contracts, the giving out of orders and other controls which can be imposed before the event.

In those local authorities where all bills are passed by a single committee or sub-committee there is sometimes a requirement that the chairman of the operating committee should attend when accounts relating to his committee are to be examined. This avoids the operating committee becoming isolated from the scrutiny of accounts. The chairman's presence would in any case be essential if any major investigations were afoot. This linking of the chairman with the work of the bill-passing committee is also one way of reinforcing any lessons to be learned from the accounts submitted for payment, e.g. the need for improvements in the departmental procedure for issuing orders. Some authorities who do not go to the length of having the chairman of a committee present at meetings of a bill-passing committee, require the chief financial officer to lay on the table at each meeting of operating committees the bills passed since the committee last met, thus giving the members an opportunity to keep in touch with the payments made by the departments under their control.

Finally, and perhaps most important of all, a committee which specializes in the examination of accounts, and scrutinizes the payments of all committees is in a strong position to draw general inferences and in particular to appreciate the wider implications of deficiencies revealed in the course of the examination of bills. In particular, weaknesses in the buying arrangements of the authority should be quickly sensed by a committee which regularly sees the bills of all committees and can compare the purchases of one committee with those of another. An alert committee can hardly fail to note any discrepancies in prices or methods of purchasing, or to detect further opportunities for central buying or standardization of goods purchased.

The question whether the sub-committee which examines the bills is an *ad hoc* committee or a sub-committee of the finance committee, as described in an earlier chapter, must be settled in the light of local circumstances. Some local authorities take the view that the work of examining the accounts for payment is of sufficient importance to warrant the undivided attention of a committee or sub-committee, and think it a disadvantage if the task is assigned to a general finance sub-committee which has other work.

(10)

Among the payments made by local authorities, two classes call for separate treatment: (a) payments to contractors for building and civil engineering works, dealt with in a separate chapter later in the book; and (b) salaries, wages and pensions, briefly considered in this section.

The employees of a local authority vary from members of various learned professions to unskilled labourers. The control of their numbers and levels of remuneration are therefore matters of supreme importance to members, as well as to chief officers. So far from saving administrative time, the national scales of remuneration and conditions of service now governing most local government employees have become so complex that the task of applying them to local conditions is often more onerous than that of devising local scales. Decisions about the numbers of employees are partly matters of financial control and partly establishment questions: they are dealt with, in so far as they affect financial administration in the chapters on budgets. The regulation of levels of remuneration and application of national conditions, though primarily establishment questions, concern financial administration in two ways. First, so many matters coming before the establishment branch have financial aspects, e.g. a proposal to regrade staff involves, as well as a consideration of the merits of the proposal, an estimate of the cost; secondly, there are occasional matters, such as incentive bonuses, in which finance and establishment aspects are so intertwined that they almost become one. Neither of these classes calls for separate treatment, because financial considerations should play the same role in establishment matters as they would for other kinds of business, i.e. they should be given their due as one factor among others, and this role must be the same whether the chief financial officer happens to be the establishment officer or not.

In addition to determining the numbers and rates of remuneration of employees there is also the purely financial work of paying them: It is this which calls for consideration here. Employees may be paid weekly, fortnightly or monthly, and they may be paid by cash, cheque or bank credit. The employees are of so many different kinds and work under such a variety of conditions, that local authorities have, in effect, not one payroll but many, even though the routines for different kinds of pay may eventually have to be reduced to a common form for processing in machines. Because of the existence of independent departments and the dispersed and dissimilar nature of their activities there can be no 'personnel' department in a local authority. Every department will engage and control its own labour and keep its own records. The chief financial officer has therefore to gather his information from many separate points; indeed from practically every depot, school, institution, store and office maintained by his authority.

As with so much of the work of the finance department, that of computing and paying salaries and wages is not a self-contained easily-defined process. On the contrary, it is the last step in a series of operations which differ from department to department, and which defy easy definition. It brings a number of problems, the first being that of deciding upon the division of duties between the finance department and the other departments. At one extreme, the finance department may delegate the whole task to an outside department, merely supplying a cheque for the total amount needed and relying on the internal audit's supervision of the departmental procedure. For very large authorities, and for large departments of moderate sized authorities, this is a common, and indeed in many cases the inevitable method. At the other end of the scale are those departments for whom the finance department does practically the whole of the work, only deriving from outside the information—time worked, sickness, etc.—which it cannot itself accumulate. This is the common method in small authorities, small departments and local authorities who have adopted a policy of centralization. It is also generally used for the salaries of monthly paid employees. In between these extremes there are many ways of sharing the work. Often the chief financial officer pays the wages, though he leaves the departments to prepare the payroll. Another widespread practice is for departments to work out gross wages, but for the finance department to make the deductions to arrive at the net sum payable.

There can be no method for general adoption, and often no best method within a single authority, the chief financial officer having to curb his natural inclinations to impose uniformity. There are, however, guiding principles which can be summarized as follows:

(a) The chief financial officer must, under the provisions of the Local Government Act, 1958, supervise the arrangements for the payment of salaries and wages, irrespective of the location of the records.

(b) He must satisfy himself that all necessary safeguards by way of internal check (especially division of duties) are continuously operated.

(c) The arrangements must be smooth-running and strictly regulated by timetable. Payment of wages is one of those imperative tasks which must be done to time, but must not be allowed to disrupt the other work of the office. Information supplied to the chief financial officer for payroll purposes must arrive every week according to schedule, if confusion is to be avoided.

(d) Calculations which can be done as efficiently and expeditiously in the operating departments as in the finance department may well be allowed to remain there, thus avoiding unnecessary accumulations of dull routine work.

(e) Mechanical methods and specialized skill should be used as fully as the size and circumstances of the authority allow. Without doubt the arrival of machines which, as has been explained elsewhere, can calculate gross wages and handle the computation of tax deductions so expeditiously, means that the tendency will be to centralize and mechanize the routine work on payrolls.

(*f*) A special watch must be kept against duplication. Unnecessary and unjustifiable wages records tend to appear in most organizations. They must be prohibited.

(*g*) In deciding the form of payroll and other wages records the chief financial officer should bear in mind the researches of a group set up by the Institute of Municipal Treasurers and Accountants. Their warning against the use of machinery merely as an elaborate writing machine still holds good.[1]

(*h*) The computation and payment of officers' salaries can usually best be dealt with centrally.

(*i*) Peak loads should be reduced by such practices as the systematic planning of the flow of documents, the staggering of pay days, or sensible delegation to departments, e.g. allowing them, subject to proper safeguards, themselves to pay their employees in outlying districts.

(*j*) In handling wages and salaries, as in other matters, the 'service' aspects of the work of the chief financial officer should be kept to the fore and information which departments or employees need should be readily available.

(*k*) The case for written instructions, already referred to in connexion with payments generally, is especially strong for salaries and wages because of the inevitable division of duties, and the impossibility of applying simple uniform procedures to the whole of the departments of a local authority.

(*l*) Even if much of the work of preparing the payrolls is done in the departments, there will still be a need for specialist advice from the finance department. Though a large department may have clerks skilled in elaborate wage rates, national insurance law, rules about income tax deductions, computation of bonuses, etc. the smaller departments will tend more and more to rely upon a central service.

---

[1] See *Wages Records of Local Authorities and Public Boards*. Institute of Municipal Treasurers and Accountants, 1952.

(11)

As was explained in an earlier chapter, chief financial officers do not regard it as self-evident that the task of making payments automatically warrants a separate section of the office. In some cases the work of verifying accounts is given to a section with other duties, but a separate section is created for salaries and wages. There are many other ways of distributing the work. Because the work is so often combined with other duties, the main principles to be borne in mind by the chief financial officer in settling the office organization for making payments have been considered in the chapter on the pattern of organization of the finance department rather than in this specialized chapter. It may, however, be useful to add here a brief note of the scope of the work of a comprehensive payments section where such exists.

In accordance with the principles of internal check, the section would be concerned with the verification of payments, both salaries and wages, and accounts for payment, but not with the actual payment. They would be responsible for the payroll—even though it may be produced in a machine section—and for the checking and scheduling of accounts for payment. The staff would become expert in the national wage and salary scales and local rules associated with them. They would also interpret the council's regulations about payments generally, including rules about subsistence claims, travelling expenses and other payments to members and officers, the extent of their participation in the verification process depending on the degree to which the work has been delegated to the departments. The administration of the superannuation acts, a duty of constantly increasing complexity, can, as has been explained in an earlier chapter, be given to the payments section because it is so closely connected with payroll work.

Wages and salaries will not be paid by those who have compiled or verified the payroll. The task of payment is so heavy that in most offices the staff of many sections will be drawn upon each week, with some inevitable disturbance of the routines. The more wages payments can be spread over the week, and thus made a task for regular staff, the less will be the disruption of the office. It is in fact in the actual payment of wages that the greatest advantages accrue from the avoidance of peak loads.

In a payments office the main division of work will almost always

212

be on a functional basis, in so far as the preparation of payrolls will be separated from the verification of accounts for payment. But within the two main sections—payroll and verification of accounts —the work may, at least to some extent, be further divided either on a functional basis or on a service basis.

Thus, as soon as the volume of payroll work reaches a certain point one officer or team may deal with the calculation of wages, another with the compilation of salaries, and a third with the income tax deductions for all payrolls. Alternatively, work may be allotted according to the departments, each officer or team looking after the payroll for a department or group of departments. Both methods have advantages though the service basis is in general preferred because it makes the work of the staff more interesting, an important point for the preparation of payrolls tends to be a dull task.

In the case of the payment of accounts the basic organization is almost bound to be service or departmental. But here again a functional element can, and often is, introduced. One member of the staff may specialize on some class of payments, e.g. subsistence and travelling allowances or, above all, contract accounts, the complications of which are described in a later chapter. That chapter brings out the nature of the chief financial officer's function as a final sieve for payments, for though contract accounts pass through the hands of other professional advisers, the chief financial officer has responsibilities. The chapter also shows the chief financial officer as a member of a team of officers responsible for the form and administration of contracts. If the chief financial officer assigns all the work to one officer or team—whether the work is carried out in the payments section or elsewhere—consistency is much easier to attain, and specialized knowledge much easier to accumulate, than if the work is treated as a by-product of other duties. In practice, an officer who has had some years of experience in passing final accounts for contracts becomes a useful centre of reference for all the departments concerned with the council's contracts. Some chief financial officers regard the verification of contract accounts as mainly audit work and others as mainly a payments function. But wherever the duties are located, they call for a measure of specialization, and hence support the case for functional organization.

The most important point to remember when settling the distribution of duties in a payments section is the need to guard against the concentration of all the processes of payment in one pair of hands. This point has already emerged several times in the course of the chapter. This means (*a*) the actual payment (whether of wages or accounts) should be done by a section other than the payments section—normally that of the cashier; (*b*) duties should be arranged so that no one officer does all stages of the work of checking of accounts for payment or preparation of payrolls. The larger the organization, the easier it is to apply these precepts, but the small organization must find a solution if necessary at the cost of some inconvenience to the department as a whole.

CHAPTER XVI

THE COLLECTION OF INCOME

(1)

THIS chapter describes how local authorities decide what charges they will make, and how the amounts due are recorded, collected and recovered. But it is only concerned with administration, for technical aspects—legal requirements, methods of book-keeping, the form and content of scales of assessment, procedures for recovery and the like —are outside the scope of the present work. The subject will be considered in three stages: the making of decisions of policy about income; the ascertainment of the amounts due from individuals in accordance with that policy and the collection of the sums due.

Because of the multiplicity of dispersed activities within a local authority, the dangers of overlooking potential sources of income, of inadequate scales of charges, of incorrect recoveries, of neglect to recoup in individual cases, and of failure to account for cash collected, are considerable. As has been explained in the chapters on audit, these features are responsible for the special attention traditionally given to income by the internal audit sections of local authorities, and they account for the obligation laid upon all local authorities by the Local Government Act of 1958, to make safe and efficient arrangements for the receipt of monies.

The income of a local authority is varied. It includes classes where the aim is to recoup the whole cost of the services, e.g. water, passenger transport, catering and markets; cases where the income covers not the whole but a substantial part of the cost of the service, such as housing, baths, games in parks; and finally, income which is merely incidental.

(2)

Control of income begins with the decision of the council or a committee to make charges. Where the council reserves to itself the right to make the decision, it will none the less be made on the strength of the recommendation of a committee. A specific injunction in standing orders to have an annual review of all charges is a useful way of encouraging committees to adopt a proper attitude, but many committees automatically reconsider scales of charges at budget

215

time in the belief that, by making increases, they may induce the finance committee to agree to additional expenditure which might otherwise not be allowed. In times of rising prices, recoupments made by local authorities tend to fall behind, for the natural instinct of elected bodies will be to limit increases in order to provoke as little opposition as possible. This tendency is especially marked when the charges are incidental or cover only a part of the cost of a service.

Thus it is much easier to overlook the need for increased tariffs for games in parks than it would be those for water or passenger transport, for in the latter cases, the deficiencies shown in the accounts would focus attention on the need for action. Moreover, because the tariffs of transport, and often those of water undertakings, can normally be increased only after public enquiry by some outside authority, the local authority will be required to produce long-range forecasts of income and expenditure, analyses of the trend of different classes of demand, estimates of possible consumer resistance, e.g. in the case of transport, and statements showing the need for reserves, renewals or other provisions. But whatever the nature of the service, local authorities should watch for high costs or other circumstances which might warrant adjustments of the rates of charge. They should also use all available financial techniques: for instance, in some undertakings—catering is an example—the flexible budgeting on industrial lines described elsewhere in this book will prove a good guide to price policy.

In the main, it is the business of the operating committees to settle the charges. But the finance committee will have an overriding duty to see that unnecessary costs do not fall upon the rates: this applies to trading undertakings as much as to other departments, for the rates are the source from which losses must ultimately be met. Theoretically the finance committee could review in detail the decisions of operating committees about charges, but in practice most local authorities think it sufficient if the finance committee is kept in touch with the proposals, and if the chief financial officer is specifically enjoined to report matters of moment relating to the council's income.

It is the duty of the head of the department and the chief financial officer, jointly to suggest to operating committees what services or commodities should be charged for, and what the tariffs might be. In the presentation of reports, the techniques of inter-departmental co-operation and joint reports of officers would be employed, but the chief financial officer has the special task of watching that the need

216

for adjustments is not overlooked. It is easier to keep scales of charges up to date if the committees lay down principles rather than scales. Thus some authorities have a rule that charges for games in parks shall cover the working expenses but not the service of debt, or that the amount to fall on the rate for specified services shall be limited to a fixed rate poundage. Charges are then automatically (though with formal confirmation) adjusted to meet changing circumstances. For instance, some authorities have during recent years decided to abolish rate subsidies for housing, or to limit the subsidy to a prescribed sum or rate poundage. The housing committees of such authorities are thus compelled to keep their rents under regular review. Some charges, e.g. rents of commercial properties, are fixed by the higgling of the market rather than by the local authority.

(3)

Having considered the machinery a local authority needs for settling the principles upon which charges shall be demanded, we must now turn to the determination of the sums due in individual cases.

Departments have often to make the first move. They know that a service has been rendered or goods supplied to an individual; sometimes only they can supply the figure to be charged, e.g. for the sale of goods; at other times they must provide the data for the calculation of the charge, for instance hours for which a home help has worked for a particular householder. Even in cases when the charge is made by the chief financial officer from figures revealed by costing statements prepared by his department, he is often dependent on the operating department's coding of the expenditure in the first instance. In short, however the work is organized, 'central' collection implies for most items of income that the collection is centralized only from the later stages: some preliminary work will be done by the departments. They must, therefore, retain a close interest in the process, watching for new sources of income, and supplying the chief financial officer promptly with all the information he needs to render accounts. This is why the duties of heads of departments should include the responsibility for the initiation of credit income, and why continuous co-operation between departments is essential if income is not to be lost.

217

(4)

At this stage it will be convenient to consider the procedure for the assessment of charges to be made where a means test is to be employed. Several services, including education, health and welfare, will be concerned with such recoupments. A clear distinction must be made between the tasks of fixing the full or standard rate, and of devising the scales of assessment. The means test is designed to ensure that no one will pay more than he can afford. In fixing the standard charge there is therefore no need to have regard to the straitened circumstances of debtors; the application of the assessment scales will look after that aspect.

Should scales of assessment be applied departmentally or centrally? The advantages are in favour of the latter, for many families are concerned with more than one service. The system of separate assessment for each service is uneconomical in so far as there are several sets of machinery and records to do the same kind of work. Assessments determined departmentally also lack uniformity, however close inter-departmental co-operation may be, a feature soon noticed and criticized by those liable to pay.

The chief danger of centralized assessment is clearly that of isolation from the services, the assessment process becoming an end in itself. This has to be guarded against by close co-operation with departments, by sufficient flexibility in working and by making the central assessment machinery fit into that of the departments. For assessment is but one of a series of events in the rendering of a personal service, often of a long drawn out and complicated nature. Though the assessment of the amount to be paid and its subsequent collection are themselves business transactions, they are part of a social service and have to be conducted with this in mind. Whoever does the central assessment must work in close collaboration with the staff of the departments in the collection of information and must make full use of the departments' knowledge and contacts with the National Assistance Board, personnel officers in local factories and local social workers. Conversely, the departments must do all they can to assist the process of assessment and collection, e.g. a children's department must be willing to apply without delay for any necessary court orders.

The chief officer responsible for central assessment would advise the responsible committee about scales of assessment, the scales being based on the same principles for all services. His main work, however, would be the application of the scales to individuals, special cases being referred to the committee for determination. He must act promptly, for, until his work is done, collection cannot begin. Regular collection being important socially as well as financially, there are many reasons why assessment should be made immediately to avoid the accumulation of arrears.

The allocation of the work of assessment within the department responsible—often the finance department—will depend on the size of the authority. A large authority may have a separate assessment section. A smaller authority will not be able to warrant a separate section, and will allocate the work of assessment to one of the other sections of the responsible department.

Some of the larger authorities have created an assessment committee to match the specialized sections; others give the work to one of the social service committees. Both courses have advantages. A separate committee with no other functions encourages specialization, is more impartial, more thorough, and more willing to see that the scales of assessment are kept up to date with changing legislation and social conditions. Allocation of the work to an existing committee is, however, a more economical arrangement and is less likely to encourage the inflation of the work beyond its true importance.

(5)

We now pass to the arrangements for collection. Some income will be collected by the chief financial officer from a central office: rates, water charges, and rents are examples. Other kinds of income may be collected either by the chief financial officer or by the departments; for example, social service income or receipts from sales of materials. Finally, there are many sources of income which must always be collected at the time the service is rendered, e.g. bus fares, fees for admission to baths, or café sales.

The tendency in recent years has been for collections of credit income, i.e. money paid on an account rendered, to be taken over by a centralized collection organization. Under an integrated system of finance which is assumed throughout this book to be the ideal, collections would certainly be centralized. Centralized collection has the advantage of specialization. The collection staff are expert in debt recovery law and procedures, including distraint, bankruptcy and liquidation and they accumulate information about debtors,

219

especially bad payers. From the point of view of the public, centralization is much more convenient inasmuch as payments of all kinds can be made in one place. Further, the bulking of the work, as in other branches of finance, enables the economies of mechanization and expert personnel to be realized. A section whose sole task it is to collect the money due to the council, will follow up collection more vigorously than one to whom it is an incidental matter. Uniformity of policy in dealing with debtors, which should be the aim of all local authorities, can also be achieved only by centralization. Similarly, control from above, whether the oversight of the chief financial officer or the final supervision of the committee, is much more easily achieved.

But this principle of centralized collection must not be raised to the status of a dogma. In most authorities, especially counties and very large urban authorities, there will be exceptions on grounds of expediency. Moreover there is room for difference of opinion whether in the case of services provided in the home (e.g. home helps), the employee who has attended should collect the sum due, or whether collection should be a separate task. Properly done, collection by the officer who has rendered the service has obvious economies and even psychological advantages. On the other hand, it involves in the processes of calculation and handling of cash, officers who are trained for other work, who may not take kindly to cash collection duties or may believe that the collection of cash goes ill with social work. Both systems are, and are likely to remain, in operation.

(6)

The next aspect of income to be considered is that of office organization. How should the central collection office of the chief financial officer be organized and how should the central records of credit income and the following up of outstanding accounts be arranged?

In accordance with the principles of internal check, the duties of cash collection will not be vested in the same person as those of the keeping of debtors accounts and the follow up of arrears. The cash receiving aspect can be dealt with simply here. There may be within the finance department a cashier who handles both receipts and payments or a separate income cashier whose duties would be to receive the money, issue receipts where they are required, and lodge the cash and cheques in the council's account at the bank. A cashier must be a man of unquestioned integrity, a quick worker but careful. In many of the smaller offices the cashier, because of his many contacts with the departments and his relatively senior status, acquires considerable prestige, often becoming a general enquiry officer. Aside from the technical precautions, the one essential is that he and his staff shall be not unduly hurried in their work. Pressure of work is inevitable on the public counters, but at the rear, where the money is handled in bulk, there should be no possibility of errors because of lack of time.

The more extensive organizational problems are those of recording and following up debtors. In the debtors' section there will be accounts for every ratepayer for rates and water, rent accounts, accounts for engineering services, accounts for social services and many miscellaneous accounts for goods sold on credit, premises hired, privileges granted and so forth. The large number of regularly recurring routine transactions offers opportunities to the organizer. Mechanical accounting of some kind will therefore be found in all progressive collection offices. It is also easier to use statistics to regulate work loads and staff activities than in some branches of the chief financial officer's department: thus the output of the clerks can be controlled by assigning to their care a prescribed number of debtors accounts, while that of outside collectors can be regulated by the number of 'calls' they are required to make, and so forth. Statistical tables are also invaluable for watching the progress of collections.

Some of the qualities needed for the head of the debtors' section are obvious: energy, vigilance and firmness. He must also have the knack of co-operation, for so much of his data comes from other departments, and so much of his work affects the services. Moreover, with the exception of the collection of the local rates, few collections are entirely the business of the chief financial officer. The exact point at which he should take over from departments must be decided individually for each source of income. For some kinds of account it may be advantageous for the department to prepare the bill for dispatch: periodical collections, rents and some other services may not lend themselves to this treatment, for there may be data to be used, or calculations to be made, of a kind that can be most readily done in the finance department.

All but the smallest debtors subsections will need officers to follow up bad payers by letter and personal visits, to initiate action in the courts, and to carry out distraint on goods in the case of debts for rates. In fixing staff quotas allowance should be made for the heavy demands on staff time made by obstinate debtors, receivership proceedings and the like. The staff must also have adequate time to keep proper records. Often a good deal of their work will be the 'outside' collection of money from difficult payers who cannot be induced to pay otherwise, but care has to be taken that the authority does not in this way unwittingly set up an expensive system of outside instalment collection of debts which could, with a better handling and more firmness, be paid into a central office.

The staff of a central collection office must keep departments in touch with the progress of collections generally and closely informed of debtors who are unsatisfactory. In some cases, e.g. sale of waste paper, supplies to such customers can be stopped; for others payment in advance can be required. In the children's, health or social services, persistent bad payers raise questions which call for close discussion—and sometimes joint action—between the departments, and often also involve decisions by committees and sub-committees. The social worker rightly expects to be informed if proceedings are contemplated against one of his 'cases', for at the very least he will regard the information that the person is a bad payer as part of his essential data. The collection of income, in fact, provides one of the best illustrations of the need to regard the financial arrangements of local authorities as one seamless garment.

(7)

In terms of total collected, the money received centrally by the chief financial officer will usually constitute the greater part of the income of the authority. But it is by no means the whole, for, as we have already seen, monies will be received in offices, depots, schools and clinics. Teachers, nurses, policemen, home helps, attendants of many kinds, indeed most classes of employees, at some time or other receive money on behalf of the local authority. Even some of the credit income will be paid to outlying departments, and in counties there may be divisional offices where an appreciable proportion of the credit income may be received. The arrangements for the receipt of cash, sprawling over all departments, and over the whole area covered by the authority, are difficult to organize because so much of the work is done by officers with other duties to perform.

The resulting problems of the cash collections of operating departments are not so much those of administration as those of the application of elementary techniques of accountancy and audit. Clear definition of responsibility, detailed prescription of procedures, internal check, internal audit, statistical control—all these, and other well-known precautions, have to be applied. Prompt banking of monies, the best possible arrangements for the safe custody of cash, and rigorous observance of the regulations, are imperative. Internal check is also of special importance, for neither the best designed set of records nor the most efficient system of internal audit can compensate for the absence of a proper division of duties, adequate departmental control of the quality of work, and check of the entries in records by independent persons. The chief financial officer should assist those who handle cash in outlying areas by making arrangements for the use of branch banks, night safes and area offices. Above all, the departments must take as seriously their responsibilities for the handling of cash as they should their duties relating to the initiation of those charges which are to be collected centrally. However small the authority, however centralized its arrangements or efficient the internal audit, the arrangements for receiving cash will work smoothly only if the departments themselves instil into their employees the importance of the task, and supervise the work as keenly as if it were one of the major duties of the department.

(8)

Four classes of income—government grants, rate income, housing rents and motor licence duties—warrant separate mention.

As to government grants, it is the chief financial officer's business to know the regulations about grants for all services and to claim the monies to which his authority is entitled. Administrative processes so apparently dissimilar as the procedure for authorizing expenditure, the form of records and accounts, the methods of charging for common services and the way of apportioning administrative expenses, must all be shaped with an eye on the grant regulations. The chief financial officer must take care to ensure that his accounting system will at once disclose any failure to keep within limits approved by central departments. Appropriate action may then be taken to avoid loss of grant, e.g. it may be desirable to curtail expenditure, or necessary to seek supplementary approvals from the sanctioning authority. At the policy forming level too, considerations of grant should not be ignored. The chief financial officer must see that the possibility of earning grant is not overlooked and should dissuade departments and committees from pursuing policies which may prejudice the grant position of the authority, e.g. to condone a marginal infringement of grant regulations which may jeopardize the grant for an entire service. Serious shortcomings may, of course, involve loss of grant under the 'default' section of the Local Government Acts, 1958.[1] Though the responsibility of the chief financial officer to see that his authority receives all the grant monies to which it may be entitled may be onerous, it does not call for specific administrative arrangements; the possibility of loss of grant is rather a contingency to be borne in mind in fashioning *all* the financial procedures.

(9)

The rate income of a local authority is not only the most important source of local income; it is the only local tax collected by local authorities. Though it is a relatively simple tax to collect it brings a number of interesting problems of organization because of the large number of transactions involved, the drastic powers of recovery possessed by the local authority and the necessity not only to observe the legal code governing collection but also to carry out the work of collection with the minimum of irritation to the ratepayers.

The local authority in addition to fixing each year the amount of the rate in the £, a subject to which three later chapters of this book are devoted, has also to decide the period of collection, the amount of any allowances to owners, or of any discounts to be allowed. Other decisions of principle which must be taken by the local authority itself relate to the extent to which instalment payments are to be accepted or encouraged and in large areas the opening of branch collection offices.

The chief financial officer's duties include those of ensuring that all relevant data in the possession of the local authorities are given to the Inland Revenue authorities who make the assessments, and that all properties eligible for rating are in fact rated. To carry out these functions he will need an outside inspection system which will also deal with the verifying of claims for void properties: often these duties are combined with those of outside collection.

The chief financial officer has also to keep the accounts of the ratepayer and follow up payment in the same way as for other debts, though in this case he has special powers of recovery. Advancing techniques of mechanization are rapidly making the traditional rate

[1] *Local Government Act, 1958*, Section 3, and *Local Government and Miscellaneous Financial Provisions (Scotland) Act, 1958*, Section 3.

book obsolete and the accounts with ratepayers tend to become more and more like those with other debtors.

It was at one time the custom to treat rate collection separately from other collections, a special staff of rate collectors being maintained. Nowadays rate collection is assimilated with the other income work; rates and water charges are jointly demanded and collected;[1] unpaid accounts are followed up by the same staff who deal with the outstanding accounts; and instead of 'rates offices' one finds 'central collection' halls.

(10)

Housing rents are sometimes collected by the chief financial officer and sometimes by a housing manager. There are two principal ways of organizing the collections. Either there is a rent collector who does little else except collect rent, or there are housing 'assistants' or housing officers who, in addition to collecting the rent, keep an eye on the property, deal with requests for repairs, and look after difficult tenants. The first system focuses attention on collection, and economizes the time of more skilled officers by relieving them of the humdrum collection work. The second method has the advantage of being more intelligible to the tenant, and of making sure that all the operations of housing management are considered parts of one operation. Whichever method is employed, the techniques must be adapted to the changing times. Local authority tenants are no longer exclusively or even mainly drawn from that stratum of the community which can think only in terms of discharging its obligations weekly, or which needs more attention from public authorities than any normal cross-section of the community.

(11)

The collection of the income from vehicle and driving licences is one of the very few functions carried out by local authorities as agents for the central government. No local policy decisions have to be made: the chief financial officer has merely to collect the monies in

[1] In Scotland there is statutory encouragement for this. Section 237 (4) *Local Government (Scotland) Act, 1947*, reads: 'So far as practicable every rating authority shall include in one demand note all the rates levied by the authority in respect of the same lands and heritages and payable by the person named in the demand note.'

accordance with the detailed instructions issued by the Ministry of Transport.

There are, however, interesting organizational problems brought about mainly by the necessity to issue most of the licences during the first few days of January, April, July and October. The problems are therefore largely those of managing peak loads. A large volume of routine transactions and a mass of documents have to be handled within short periods. The routine to be followed therefore warrants the most exhaustive examination. A half-minute reduction in the time of issue of each licence represents a considerable aggregate saving. Visits to other authorities to compare methods and assistance from O. & M. officers are both to be welcomed.

Security arrangements—distribution of duties, efficient internal check, arrangements for dealing with post, etc.—are also important. Many authorities find it advantageous to combine the collection of motor tax licences with that of the council's own revenue, using one central collection hall and one set of arrangements for handling and banking of cash. Assuming there is interchangeability of staff and flexibility of management, this practice is of immense advantage in helping to cope with peak loads.

CHAPTER XVII

PURCHASING AND CONTRACTING: I—GENERAL

(1)

WHO is to be allowed to order goods or services? From whom are they to be purchased? What formalities are to govern the transaction? Who is to be given authority to enter into contracts for building and civil engineering work? This chapter sets out broad answers to these questions. In the next chapter the detailed procedure for regulating contracts for building and civil engineering work is considered. Neither chapter is concerned with the authorization or control of expenditure, but with the mechanics of spending sums already authorized.

To all large concerns, except those personally managed by the owners, the organization of the buying function is an anxiety. The democratic control, the ease with which disappointed tenderers can create doubts about the procedure, the high standard expected of a public authority, the diffusion of purchasing throughout a multitude of departments with widely varying requirements, make the task of finding a satisfactory procedure especially difficult in the case of a local authority. They also make it incumbent upon a local authority to insist on a standard of conduct stricter than that which is customary in some other spheres. It is hard to avoid formal machinery, elaborate arrangements to guard against irregularity and such precautions as a rule that contracts must be allotted—save in exceptional circumstances—to the lowest tenderers. All of these features, essential in the interests of purity, will occasionally involve the local authority in expense. There will also be some loss of efficiency because of the cumbersome nature of the machinery needed to meet the varying requirements of departments and because of the difficulty—sometimes a virtual impossibility—of fashioning arrangements to enable the local authority to take advantage of changes in the market, bargain lots, special discounts, and so forth. For instance in times of shortage of materials the inevitable inflexibility of purchasing arrangements may hamper the local authority and delay the execution of contracts.

So difficult is it to legislate for all circumstances and occasions, that the standing orders of a local authority referring to purchasing and contracting, can never give a complete guide to practice, and must recognize the exceptional instances for which the normal procedure is unsuitable. Only by a detailed examination of actual transactions can a complete picture of the practice of an authority be obtained. Chief officers, when asked for copies of standing orders relating to purchasing and contracting, are apt to observe that they are in need of revision, which can only mean that they do not fully—perhaps even correctly—reflect local practice, a state of affairs easy to condemn but hard to rectify. In other words regulations must be construed with common sense and must contain an element of flexibility. The difficulty of finding watertight standing orders is reflected in any discussion on the subject and it is hard to write on the matter without making the arrangements of local authorities sound simpler and more logical than they are. The same common-sense qualifications must therefore be read into the statements made in this chapter.

None the less, there are rules so important that they should always be observed. Local authorities have to discriminate between those which should be inviolate, and those which can be interpreted in more elastic fashion. Failure to make the dividing line correctly is the most frequent cause of trouble in their purchasing and contracting arrangements. Fortunately, considering the magnitude and diversity of their operations, and the many influences to which they are subject, the record of local authorities is highly commendable.

In the following paragraphs the underlying principles which should govern purchasing and contracting arrangements are first considered, whilst the latter part of the chapter is devoted to the written regulations a local authority needs, whether by standing orders or otherwise.

Throughout this chapter the expression 'purchasing and contracting' has been used in discussions of the general principles, in order to make it clear that they apply to the whole of the commitments into which a local authority enters for the supply of materials and the execution of work, from the purchase of a piece of soap to the construction of a major road or building. All such transactions are strictly speaking 'contracts', but local authorities tend to use the term 'contract' in more restricted ways, to indicate only transactions where a formal document is executed, or merely contracts for civil engineering and building work. Hence the need to use, in a chapter referring to all transactions in which the local authority buys goods or enters into liabilities for work to be done on its behalf, whether a formal contract is entered into or not, the somewhat cumbersome expression 'purchasing and contracting'.

(2)

The general principles underlying good buying arrangements, the respective roles of committees and officers, and the peculiar needs of managers of central buying departments and heads of direct labour departments and similar officers—these matters call for some consideration before we proceed to consider the form of a local authority's regulations.

In working out the purchasing and contracting arrangements of local authorities, the guiding principle, already hinted at in the introductory section, is that the local authority must be able to demonstrate at any time that all reasonable measures have been taken (a) to buy competitively at the keenest price and (b) to avoid even a suspicion of irregularity.

The local authority's sheet anchor in securing both economy and purity is the open competitive tender or quotation. Local authorities should therefore lay this down as a general principle. The construction of rules about purchasing and contracting is largely the art of working out this principle and in particular of defining the kind of instance in which departures are to be permitted. Whilst it may not be possible to make rules to cover every contingency, it is essential to have rules sufficiently practical to cover all but the most exceptional instance; otherwise they will be quickly ignored or circumvented. Competitive tendering can be considered in several stages:

(a) Fully open tendering where tenders are invited at large.
(b) Tendering which is open but which is only advertised in a restricted way, e.g. in local papers or technical journals.
(c) Tendering from selected firms of suppliers (often from lists compiled after public advertisement), either in the form of an annual list or one drawn up for a particular purchase or series of purchases.
(d) Informal requests for a quotation, as opposed to formal invitations to tender, from firms selected for their ability to supply the particular service required.

Methods (a)–(c) are alike in that they assume formal tenders for sums of considerable size. Such transactions are regulated by the standing orders and they normally need the approval of council or committee. Class (d)—the day to day transactions—have to be considered separately. Many of them must be carried out by officials, and they raise the question of the division of duties between officers and committees. The local authority must decide the limits of the officer's power. For example, in a medium-sized authority, the officers may be allowed to purchase at discretion (but always with the competitive principle in mind) if the expenditure is below £100. Items estimated to cost between £100 and £200 may also be purchased by the officers, but subject to a specific requirement to obtain estimates. Articles estimated to cost over £200, but less than the amount for which a formal contract would be required, would then be dealt with by the committees, who would consider tenders from a few selected firms unless the transaction came within the limits for which the standing orders lay down a more formal procedure, thus taking them out of class (d). There would be exceptions to provide for the purchase of proprietary goods at standard prices, other goods the prices of which are controlled by trade organizations or statutory regulations, goods bought at public auctions, and emergency supplies. The authority's regulations should also make it impossible for committees or officers to purchase continuing supplies without frequently testing the market. The tendency to resort automatically to the previous supplier is strong and it has to be resisted. The competitive principle must be observed, and the normal procedure must be the soliciting of quotations, records of quotations being kept as carefully as the records of formal tenders.

Some local authorities do not subscribe to the view that an officer should be allowed to make even humble purchases. Through a system of 'Requisition Books' they require officers, at least theoretically, to get authority from the committee for all purchases before they are made. Views differ about the value of requisition books. Sound in principle because they impose a check before expenditure is incurred, they are certainly apt in practice to receive scant attention at committees and they inevitably include many items which have already been ordered. Some regard them as exercising a moral restraint. Their greatest failing is that they violate another principle subscribed to in these pages, i.e. that the business of committees is not to attempt to control the small incidents of administration, but to carry out tests to see that the system is being adhered to. It may therefore well be that the members will be better employed in selecting purchases at random for detailed enquiry, than in a perfunctory examination of a mass of detail to which they could not in any case do justice. Whatever the system, the committee or sub-committee responsible for scrutinizing payments, described in another chapter, should systematically enquire into the purchasing procedure which has been followed in the transactions they select for enquiry. They will be assisted in their task if all bills are marked to show whether the purchase has been made from a central contract or a departmental contract and, if not, whether competitive quotations have been received. The committee should call for full particulars of the quotations relating to the bills they select. In the author's opinion it is by intelligent scrutiny of selected bills that the members can best judge the quality of the buying arrangements.

(3)

Purchasing operations can be greatly simplified by taking full advantage of the fact that many supplies are on a continuing basis and can therefore be dealt with on a system of annual contracts. The task then becomes one of sufficient magnitude to warrant the preparation of detailed schedules, annual advertisement for tenders and selection by committees or sub-committees. Some authorities even have a special committee or sub-committee to handle the tenders. Annual tenders for individual departments lead naturally to the bulking of the business of the local authority. Many commodities are common to more than one department and the savings which can be made by central contracts are considerable. A local authority which is not exploiting to the full the possibilities of central purchasing is certainly remiss. The process of amalgamating the requirements of departments brings incidental savings in the shape of standardization between departments. It also makes for keener buying, because the purchasing officer is critically watched by his colleagues, and the buying committee finds that its actions are carefully scrutinized by the committee using the goods.

Whether bulk buying is to be accomplished by the setting up of a supplies department, or by spreading the task over the various departments, is a question for local decision and is outside the ambit of a book on financial administration. Whether there is a central supplies officer or not, there is much to be said for avoiding central depots, because they add overhead costs which may offset the savings. The danger of centralized arrangements is that they may become an end in themselves, instead of a tool to be used by the services. Centralized supplies departments are possibly more prone to sin in this respect than heads of operating departments who find

231

themselves buying a range of commodities for other departments, for the latter are in a better position to keep the view-point of a departmental officer in mind.

The task of the financial branch of the administration is to provide the committees, and hence the council, with the means of judging whether purchases are being made in the most favourable way. A chief financial officer may upon occasion have to suggest improvements but his efforts will be of little avail if his council lacks the will to act.

(4)

There remains the question of purchasing arrangements for direct labour departments, supplies departments and others who have to make purchases in the course of fulfilling their customers' orders. Should they be allowed more latitude than the ordinary non-trading department? Clearly the competitive principle must be adhered to: quotations must be sought and recorded, though there may be some case for arguing that heads of these departments should be allowed a higher limit for purchasing without committee authority. In general, the principles of control by committee must be applied, but there must be some elasticity, e.g. the committee controlling the officer may well be content with more *post mortem* control than with other kinds of purchasing. Arrangements will also have to be made for special kinds of supplies. For instance, a local authority may find it preferable to allow a central buyer of foodstuffs to buy vegetables daily on the market rather than let a sub-committee buy them weekly on tender. One authority has retained the principles of competitive quotation but allowed reasonable latitude to its building department by a standing order which provides that the building department may purchase outside the standing orders if all the following are fulfilled:

(*i*) a more favourable purchase could be made;
(*ii*) the item is reported to committee;
(*iii*) it is included in the requisition book (requisition books are in general use in this authority).

(5)

We now pass to a consideration of the internal rules needed to ensure that the principles already discussed are adhered to. So important is the making of contracts that it is one of the few matters of internal administration regulated by statute, and the only one for which local authorities are compelled to have standing orders. Our consideration of internal rules will begin with a discussion of the statute and the circular issued by the Ministry of Housing and Local Government. The manner in which local authorities have adopted and applied the advice of the Ministry, the extent to which they have found additional safeguards to be necessary, and ways of handling minor rules too detailed to warrant inclusion in standing orders, will also be considered. To obtain an idea of the practices of local authorities the current standing orders of nine local authorities selected at random have been examined. They disclosed in general the same outlook on the part of local authorities as was revealed by the much larger sample taken in 1933 for the author's previous book 'Local Authorities: Internal Financial Control'.

(6)

The Local Government Act, 1933, provides that all contracts made by English provincial local authorities must be made in accordance with standing orders.[1] Except as provided in the standing orders of the authority, notice of intention to enter into all contracts for the supply of goods and materials must be published, and tenders must be invited. The standing orders must regulate the manner in which such notices are to be published. These provisions were applied to London by the London Government Act, 1939, and there are corresponding provisions for Scotland.

To assist authorities in the formulation of orders to comply with this statutory requirement the Ministry of Housing and Local Government have issued model standing orders which were last revised in 1957. The following is a broad summary of the Ministry's suggestions:

(1) Every contract is to comply with the standing orders except as otherwise provided by the council; alternative methods of procedure for exceptional cases are suggested. Exceptions made by a committee are to be reported to the council or an express note made in the minutes of the committee.

(2) Before entering into a contract for the execution of any work the council must obtain an estimate in writing of the probable initial cost and the annual cost of maintenance.

---

[1] The statutory provisions relating to Contracts are set out in Appendix B.

233

(3) No contract for the supply of goods or the execution of works which exceeds (£500) in value is to be made unless at least (10) days' public notice inviting tenders has been given in local newspapers.

Where the contract exceeds (£5,000) in value, notice must also be given in trade journals.

(4) Contracts which exceed (£100) in value must be in writing. All such contracts must specify the price to be paid, and the time to be allowed for performance.

(5) Pecuniary penalties for default must be specified in all contracts exceeding (£250) in value.

(6) All written contracts must provide for cancellation in the case of bribery and for recovery of any loss from the contractor.

(7) Tenders must be forwarded to the Clerk in plain envelopes. He must retain them until the time appointed for opening, which must take place at one time only, in the presence of the appropriate members of the council at an office specially designated by the Clerk.

(8) A tender other than the lowest shall not be accepted except upon a written report from the appropriate officer.

The figures in brackets would vary according to the range of the activities of the authority and should be reviewed from time to time. Other suggestions, dealing with fair wages clauses and the like present no special problems from the point of view of financial administration. They are, however, included in the outline of internal rules in Appendix E. It may also be pertinent to remark that prescriptions in standing orders about fair wages and similar matters need to be practical. Often they are found to be ineffective in practice because large contractors cannot depart from the conditions and agreements ruling in their trade or industry. The standing orders of local authorities should provide for such situations.

(7)

In this section the principal standing orders suggested by the Ministry are briefly discussed in the order in which they are set out in the previous section. Other desirable standing orders, not included in the Ministry's recommendations, are considered in later sections.

Most authorities recognize the need to provide for exceptions. Usually committees are allowed to make exceptions, subject to report to the council. The report would be made simultaneously with the recommendation to enter into the contract if the committee had no delegated power. In cases where the committee has power to execute the contract, deviations may be reported to the council individually, in batches periodically, or they may be referred to a general purposes or similar committee, either for confirmation or merely for information. But the use of general purposes committees on such occasions is not a common practice, notwithstanding the recommendations of the Ministry. Local authorities always need persuasion to adopt any procedure involving review of the actions of the committees by some central or functional committee. It is interesting to note that in Edinburgh, where the writ of the Ministry's circular does not run, deviations from standing orders about contracts require a three quarters majority of the members present at the council meeting. The general principle to be observed is that, however powers to enter into contracts are distributed between the council and its committees, exceptions should be specifically reported and noted, otherwise the way may be open to deals which might cast doubt upon the integrity of the authority.

The second suggested standing order—that requiring from the officers an estimate in writing of the initial and maintenance costs before a contract is entered into—is widely but not universally adopted by local authorities, a common limit being £500, below which no written estimate is required. Some authorities exclude from their standing order the requirements to report on maintenance costs. This suggested standing order is an excellent example of the difficulties of laying down categorical requirements about contracts. A clear distinction must be made between the initial adoption of a scheme on the one hand and the subsequent allotment of a contract or contracts to enable the scheme to be carried out. When the scheme is approved an estimate must be given, a point which has been emphasized in several places in preceding chapters. This estimate, though not given specifically for the purpose of complying with the contract procedure and no doubt made under other standing orders, will in practice serve the dual purpose. For example, an authority considering whether to construct a new market would call, under other standing orders, for full estimates of cost both capital and revenue before a decision were taken. Having taken the decision the local authority, when it comes to the subsequent task of giving out the work, would be concerned to compare the tenders with the original estimate of the officers for that particular piece of work. But no new estimates are required at the time of entering into the contract. On the other hand there are transactions for which no specific estimates will have been submitted on a previous occasion. This standing order then comes into full operation. An example would be minor engineering work forming part of a general estimate head.

The next standing order lays down a general principle of local advertisement for small contracts, and wider advertisements for the larger contracts. Authorities have adopted differing limits for these two classes, some taking the view that advertisements—even local—should apply to larger purchases only (e.g. those of £1,500 or even £3,000), others that advertisement is appropriate for all except small transactions—below say £250. But many authorities list exceptions, such as proprietary goods, specialist goods, urgent purchases, machinery or plant parts, goods purchased at auctions, and prices controlled by trade organizations. Some authorities, in lieu of inviting tenders for defined types of contract, maintain lists of contractors or suppliers who are invited to tender. Often these lists have themselves been compiled after the local authority has advertised for the names of those who wish to be included in the list: alternatively a list may be prepared (after advertisement) for a specific contract. The lists are kept up to date in ways prescribed in the standing orders. Lists have the advantage of avoiding the submission of tenders by contractors or suppliers thought by the local authority to be unsuitable. A judicious blend of the two methods—open tenders and a list—is probably the ideal, the most important point being that the local authority should not in fact rely upon lists while purporting to proceed by open tenders.

The fourth model standing order—that contracts over a specified sum should be in writing—has not been generally adopted. Some local authorities regard it as impracticable, others as being fulfilled in effect by the requirement common in local government that official orders must be issued for goods, leaving the Clerk to the authority to determine the classes of case for which a more formal document is needed. A number of authorities, however, have adopted the model standing order, some having limits as low as £50.

The fifth standing order—that providing for a penalty on default—is notoriously difficult to enforce, but is important as a deterrent. The sixth which protects the authority in the case of bribery is self evident.

The seventh of the model standing orders—that relating to the opening of tenders—also needs comment, for this is an aspect needing strict regulation. Some authorities require tenders to be addressed to the chairman. Many amplify the Ministry's model in various ways, such as by requiring the chairman to initial all tenders on opening. Some vary their procedure for different classes of tender, e.g. over and under £750 in value. At least one authority has a special box into which tenders should be deposited. Other officers besides the Clerk are allowed to have custody of tenders in some authorities. Care needs to be taken to ensure that the arrangements are effective practically as well as theoretically. For example, initialling of a tender by a chairman or other member on opening, is a useless precaution unless accompanied by safeguards to ensure that any subsequent alteration of the tender would be revealed. For this reason some standing orders require the chairman to initial, on opening, any figures which the tenderer has himself altered. Nor is it sensible to treat tenders for annual supplies in the same way as tenders for the major engineering and building works considered in the next chapter, for the latter will require detailed examination before final acceptance, checking of calculations, and technical as well as arithmetical checks upon supporting documents such as bills of quantities. Similarly, annual contracts for supplies may involve testing of samples for quality and must be dealt with differently from tenders for small supplies which can probably be settled at once, the opening of tenders and the allotment of the contract being done at a single sitting. This standing order has been extended by some authorities to provide that a late tender must be reported to committee who decide whether it is to be considered or not. Other authorities automatically rule out late tenders from consideration.

The eighth model standing order deals with one of the most troublesome aspects—the occasion when the local authority is recommended to accept a tender other than the lowest. The power to do so may be vested in a committee if it has delegated power to enter into the contract; or it may need confirmation of the general purposes committee, or even the council itself; but all deviations should be reported to the council, even those made by a committee under delegated powers. There may be a number of reasons for such deviations: the officers may think the tenderer incapable of doing satisfactory work, they may regard his experience as insufficient, or enquiries may show his financial resources to be inadequate. Should an officer be required to make a written report as the Ministry suggest? Many—indeed most—local authorities think not, and therefore exclude the word 'written'. Obviously cases must occur where an officer would be willing to advise orally against the acceptance of a tender but would not be prepared to put his views in writing. Unless an oral report is permitted, the officer may feel that he must allow his committee to enter into a contract which, in his opinion, is not the most advantageous, a state of affairs destructive of the morale of officials as well as inimical to the financial interests of the authority. The question is difficult, because oral reports have many defects; in particular, they open the door to the allotment of contracts on sentimental rather than business considerations. The occasions for considering tenders other than the lowest are likely to be very few if the local authority has adopted the method of compiling lists of tenderers, either general lists or lists for specific works, for by definition the lists will include only the names of tenderers acceptable to the local authority.

The prime necessity is to compel the acceptance of the lowest tender except where the official on technical grounds recommends otherwise. To ignore the difficulty, i.e. to omit from the standing orders any provision for accepting tenders other than the lowest, does not appear to be wise. These exceptions to the rule of acceptance of the lowest tender must occur and they should be specifically provided for. This is not one of those matters where latitude in interpretation should be permitted.

However wisely the standing orders are drawn, and however complete the understanding between officers and members, there will be times when an officer will have to stand back and see his authority enter into contracts with concerns with which he would not himself do business. This will happen on those occasions when the officer knows he cannot produce sufficient facts and evidence to back his judgment, though he feels sure that his opinion—partly intuitive though it may be—is right. The board of a commercial firm allotting a contract has unfettered discretion in deciding when to accept the judgment of its employees. A public authority is in a different position. It may be called upon to 'account' to the public. It must, therefore, have chapter and verse for its actions, an inevitable feature of a democracy but one not always productive of the most economical or efficient results.

(8)

There are also a number of incidents of formal contracts, not alluded to in the Ministry's model, but regarded by many authorities as worthy of inclusion in standing orders. They include arrangements for making sure that contractors are informed of the conditions of contracts, rules about withdrawal of tenders (e.g. anyone withdrawing a tender may be disqualified from tendering for a period of three years), the procedure for compiling lists of tenderers, and the disqualification from tendering for a period of years of anyone convicted of a criminal offence in connexion with a transaction in which the authority was interested. Standing orders have also to make clear the extent of the delegation of purchasing and contracting power to committees; if a loan is involved the council must itself pass a resolution. Local authorities vary in their attitudes, though many of the larger authorities delegate to committees the power to make contracts the value of which does not exceed a stipulated figure, for example £500 or £1,000. Occasionally the figure varies from committee to committee within the same authority—a sensible example of flexibility which one would expect to be more common. Some local authorities allow committees to fix maintenance, stationery and similar contracts without limit.

(9)

So far we have discussed those rules about purchasing and contracting sufficiently important to be included in standing orders. We must now consider to what extent these standing orders need to be supplemented by other kinds of internal rule or regulation, less formal, and more easily altered to meet changing circumstances. These include the inter-departmental procedure for common supplies, the office arrangements for handling tenders for annual supplies, and the form of records in connexion with purchasing and contracting (some specialized aspects of these are considered in the next chapter on civil engineering and building contracts). Some authorities deal with these matters by incorporating them in their internal financial rules. Many allow them to go unregulated, relying on the fact that the standing orders governing purchases and contracts are so much more complete than for most other administrative matters.

In the writer's opinion there is a great deal to be said in favour of a written code or manual of administrative practice in all moderate sized and larger authorities. Strictly there would be no need for regulations in addition, though if any of the points which would otherwise be included in the manual were thought in any authority to be of particular importance, they could be included in the financial regulations or laid down in one of the other ways adopted by local authorities for matters regarded as important but not warranting the status of a standing order.

A purchasing manual would cover such matters as the following:

(a) Division of responsibility for purchasing between committees and officers—persons authorized to requisition supplies—officers authorized to issue official orders—budgetary control of purchases.

(b) Central contract arrangements—items included—committee responsible—contracting organization—relationship between user department and contracting department—procedure for collating requirements from the user departments; inviting, opening and selecting tenders; informing user departments of accepted suppliers' terms—procedure for ordering from supplier—approved exceptions from central contract arrangements.

(c) Central stores—committee responsible—stores organization—items stored—procedure for requisitioning and ordering stores—issues to user department including procedure for ordering, issuing and charging for issues—transport arrangements.

(d) Other centralized arrangements—building, plant and vehicle maintenance, printing, photography, laundry, dry cleaning, etc.—relationship between service and user departments—procedure for ordering, carrying out the service and charging.

(e) Purchases negotiated and made direct by user department—competitive tenders and quotations—prescribed lists of suppliers approved by committees—testing the market for routine purchases of small value—advertising—purchases during cut price periods—'bargain' lot purchases.

(f) Quality and quantity control—extent of standardization—definition of standards—use of British Standard specifications—check on quantities delivered—test checks by analyst and weights and measures inspector—reporting defective purchases—submission of samples.

(g) Special terms available—trade discounts—quantity discounts—rebate schemes.

(h) Purchasing contracts—advice on the form of requisitions, orders, quotations, or tenders—transactions justifying a formal contract—price variations—delivery terms—payment on account—retention money—security.

(i) Trade restrictions—information—action to be taken on restrictive practices and price rings.

(j) Incidental operations—disposal of surplus or obsolete equipment, plant, vehicles or stores—insurance of purchases—inventories.

(k) Purchasing officers—exchange of information.

Such a code would, in conjunction with the standing orders, cover the subject of purchasing completely. It would focus attention on the importance of a strict buying procedure, it would assist the staff of the departments, especially those newly appointed, and it would generally help to secure that the principles adopted by the council in the standing orders were translated into action. Moreover, as is always the case with codifications, the mere fact of having to commit the procedure to writing would encourage critical examination.

CHAPTER XVIII

PURCHASING AND CONTRACTING:
II—ENGINEERING AND BUILDING WORKS

(1)

IN the last chapter no distinction was made between (*a*) purchases of goods and (*b*) contracts for building and engineering works (called in this chapter 'contracts') though in fact the latter have so many distinguishing features that they almost constitute a subject in themselves. The present chapter explores such of these characteristics as are relevant to our subject[1] and concludes with some notes about 'direct labour' from the point of view of financial administration.

(2)

First of all, the distinctive features of contracts, using the term in the restricted sense described above, must be mentioned. Contracts relate to individually designed projects, and are often large-scale operations, so that the task of defining the works is of itself of some complexity involving at the tender stage specifications, bills of quantities, drawings, and other documents, with additional data at the constructional stage. Then there is the variety of skills needed: architects, engineers, quantity surveyors, building workers, various kinds of technical specialists, lawyers and accountants all have something to contribute. Contracts therefore bring a problem of co-ordination as well as of complexity. Next, because the works take place mostly in conditions—climatic, geological and the like—which can never be exactly foretold, a contract for building and civil engineering work is not definite and conclusive in the sense that a contract for the purchase of a piece of machinery would be: modifications during the course of the work are almost inevitable. Moreover, in addition to unavoidable alterations due to unpredictable circumstances, contracts are often of such an elaborate nature,

---

[1] The subject is considered generally in *Building Contracts of Local Authorities*, a study prepared for the corporate members of the Royal Institute of Public Administration, 1958. Another relevant R.I.P.A. study which will probably be called *Organization of Building Construction and Maintenance in Local Authorities* is shortly to be issued.

and are spread over so long a period, that there is every possibility of minor variations in design during the progress of the work, for the long period offers an opportunity for changes of mind on the part of the committee, the department and the designer. Decisions have, therefore, to be made as the work proceeds. Someone has to be invested with power to make these decisions and care has to be taken that the power is not exercised in a way which nullifies the control of the council over operations. Whether these decisions are major or minor depends largely on the extent of the pre-planning. Finally, because of the complexity of the operations, the task of making a final settlement with the contractor is inevitably involved and may be long drawn out, particularly if lack of pre-planning has produced the need for a multitude of variations.

(3)

Clearly there are a whole host of problems here, technical, legal, administrative and financial. Our task is to select for comment such of them as are of direct significance to the financial administration. We begin with some essential points to be covered if the financial interests of the local authority are not to be prejudiced. The first is the need for careful pre-planning. Projects must be considered in good time, and the architect given clear instructions about the nature of the building needed, and an idea of the amount of money the council is prepared to spend. Plenty of time must be allowed for consideration and settlement of the plans and later for the contractor to plan the building or other work.

Secondly there should be as few variations as possible. They are a prime cause of overspending of original estimates, they disrupt the contractor's planning, forcing him to uneconomical working, they are a potential source of disputes, and they are prone to make other unforeseen modifications necessary. In any case, variations are liable to involve extra administrative costs and professional fees.

Thirdly there is the control of sub-contracts. The inclusion in the total amount of the main contract of the sub-contract figures encourages committees wrongly to think that in approving the main contract they have disposed of the whole question of allocation of the work. This is not so. From the administrator's point of view, though not from the lawyer's, a large contract is not really a single contract but several, for there are usually sub-contractors and suppliers as well as the main contractor. Enquiries made by the author in 1957 of a number of towns in the Midlands showed that the value of work done by nominated sub-contractors on schools and other buildings involving specialist construction and selected finishes could be as much as 50 per cent of the contract. The main contractor will select most suppliers and with permission may appoint some sub-contractors to do work which he has priced in the bill of quantities. With these we have no concern, except to remark that the contract should secure as far as possible that the position of the local authority will not be prejudiced by the bankruptcy of either the main or the sub-contractors. The authority may reserve the right to nominate certain sub-contractors and suppliers for specialized work by including prime cost items in the bill of quantity. Although there is no privity of contract between the local authority and these nominated sub-contractors and suppliers, their selection is as much the business of the local authority as the selection of the main contractor, and there is even more need for responsibility to be defined because open market tendering is rarely applicable.

(4)

We now proceed to look at contracting from the point of view of the committees of the local authority.

Bearing in mind both the constitutional responsibility of members of committees to keep in touch with day to day affairs, and the complications of contracts as set forth earlier in the chapter above, the reader will readily see that it is not easy to determine or explain the precise lines of demarcation between the duties of committees and those of the various officers, technical and administrative, in the regulation of contracts.

The first stage to be dealt with in this section is the giving out of the contract by the appropriate committee on behalf of the council. The council will have approved the project in the round, and not in detail, though if the scheme is of magnitude (e.g. the building of a new town hall), the siting and general design will have been debated and approved in the council chamber. It will be for the appropriate committee to take the responsibility for the details of the design, though points of fine detail will be left to the architect. The committee must pay special attention to the 'economics' of the contract, satisfying themselves that the materials are durable, the design is serviceable and that the savings in capital cost have not been made at the cost of disproportionate expense for maintenance later on.

It is within the province of the committee to consider the use of alternative materials and layout of buildings and grounds. Before settling the contract, the committee is entitled to be assured that all the officers concerned—the department which is to use the building, the technical officers who are to build it, the Clerk and the chief financial officer—are, from their different points of view, satisfied with the arrangements.

The next stage is the selection of sub-contractors, for as was explained in the preceding section, the giving out of the main contract does not end the task of selection. Most contracts of any magnitude provide for some sub-contracts in the form of prime cost items. Sub-contracting work should be at a minimum if the contract has been properly pre-planned. On this topic the Royal Institute of Public Administration team commented:

'The details of some specialist work do not have to be settled before construction begins, and architects sometimes misuse the system of prime-cost items to postpone their planning of work on these parts of the building until the building contract has been entered into. The so-called prime-cost item is then really a provisional sum, with all the disadvantages of that device which have been described. The similar practice of planning the specialist work but not seeking tenders for it until after the main contract has been settled —provisional sums being inserted in the contract meantime—is also to be deprecated.'[1]

The committee must retain the ultimate responsibility for this task and they must as far as possible preserve the principle of competitive tendering. Some committees allow a good deal of latitude to their technical officers in selecting sub-contractors; others supervise the allocation of the work themselves. Whatever their attitude, they must be made aware of the sums included in the main contract for sub-contracts and they must lay down the procedure to be followed, in so far as this is not governed by standing orders.

A common procedure is for the technical officer to report at tender stage of the main contract, the details and amounts of the prime cost sums included together with recommendations about the way of selecting the sub-contractors. For some items he may suggest competitive tender, for others selection from a list, and there will be a minority of cases where he recommends outright the name of the supplier on the grounds that there is no alternative. If selection is to

[1] *Op. cit.*, paragraph 34, p. 16–17.

245

be made from a list the committee must decide how, e.g. from a general list or a specially compiled list.

If the tenders are to be dealt with by a committee, the normal tendering procedure should be followed. If the allocation is to be made by an officer, a procedure for receiving and opening tenders and quotations must be laid down and a complete list of tenders must be kept. Administrative staff as well as technical staff should play a part in the arrangements which should be of the kind able to bear the strictest scrutiny. Tenders accepted by officers should be reported to committees.

Having settled the design and nature of the contract and selected the contractor and sub-contractors, the committee must itself approve subsequent variations in design, and be kept informed of inescapable variations due to technical considerations, e.g. unforeseeable bad site conditions. If the contract has been properly pre-planned, variations of the first kind will be few. When they occur they will normally come from the officers, the technique of joint reports being used where appropriate. Variations of substance should be confirmed by resolution. There are, however, in every sizeable contract minor variations, representing obvious improvements, too small to warrant submission to committees. These must be handled by the technical officer—normally the architect—but always, unless they are purely technical, in conjunction with the chief officer of the operating department.

One of the prime duties of a committee is therefore to see that plans are brought forward in ample time and are fully discussed before approval. Once the design is settled, the committee should turn its face against afterthoughts on the part of either the committee, individual members of the committee, or its officers, unless there are irresistible reasons to support them.

Committees should take an interest in the progress of the work, the technical officer making periodical reports indicating what work has been done and what remains to be done. The periodical data needed include statements showing the cumulative value of work to date, total value of orders given for prime cost work to date compared with the amounts allowed in the contract, the number and aggregate effect of variations agreed to date, a note of the possible effect of interim decisions of all kinds on the final cost and of wages settlements and price changes of materials. Summaries of this information will be submitted to committees at appropriate intervals. Eventually the committee will receive a statement comparing the original estimate with the final result, accompanied by full explanations from all the officers concerned. Often, because of tardy submission by contractors of particulars needed for drawing up the account, these final statements are submitted long after the contract has been completed.

(5)

Before describing the function of the chief financial officer in relation to contracts, we must make clear the distinction between those contracts for which the authority employs outside architects, engineers and other specialists and those for which the local authority's own professional staff are used. In the first case the relation of the professional specialist to the local authority is that of professional man and client, and the conventional relationship will apply. In the latter case the specialists are the servants of the authority, paid to give their professional skill and to play the part allotted to them by the authority. Though they must keep unsullied their professional integrity and judgment, they must also function as members of a team of officers each contributing their part to the common pool. To speak therefore, as is sometimes done, of a committee as a 'client' of an architect's department is as meaningless as regarding a committee as a 'client' of the Clerk because he tenders them legal advice in the ordinary course of his duties. In dealing with his brother officers on matters relating to contracts, the chief financial officer (and, incidentally, also the Clerk) has therefore to observe and expect the ordinary inter-departmental courtesies, whilst his relations with outside architects and the like are governed by the traditional relationship between a professional man in practice and a representative of the client. Thus in the matter of obtaining information, though the chief financial officer's records and those of an architect or other professional employee of the local authority should be freely open to one another, the chief financial officer must not expect the records of professional men in private practice to be so readily available.

In the main, however, the chief financial officer's duty is the same whether outside or inside specialists are employed, and unless the context otherwise indicates, the comments made in this chapter apply irrespective of whether the chief financial officer is dealing with his colleagues or with an outside specialist.

247

(6)

The chief financial officer's duties in connexion with contracts can be divided into three categories: those relating to the form of the contract, those he has to undertake during the course of the contract, and those pertaining to the final settlement. The first two are dealt with below and the last—his work on final settlements—is discussed in the next section.

The chief financial officer's first responsibility is to satisfy himself that the financial provisions of the contract are not likely to be difficult to interpret and that they afford the local authority adequate security. He should be consulted on the general form of the contract, e.g. the decision whether a local form be used in preference to the R.I.B.A. form. If the council decides to use a form of contract in national use, the chief financial officer may suggest local amendments bearing in mind that the fewer amendments which are made to a form of contract in general use, the better. Needless to say, chief financial officers will in time of stable prices favour firm price contracts with their relative freedom from detailed claims in respect of fluctuating costs and their incentive to the contractor to reduce costs. If there are price fluctuation clauses, they must be anchored to specific dates and methods of ascertaining prices; if there are basic price lists, the items must be clearly defined; if a price index formula is used, it must be equitable. The chief financial officer will see that provisions governing interim and final payments are unambiguous and fair.

The council will look to the chief financial officer for advice about the general security of the contract and will expect him to safeguard their interests without making procedures irksome. The chief financial officer will be asked to report on the financial standing of the prospective contractor and he will also be concerned about the nature and amount of security required. Sometimes the security will take the form of a bond, in which case he will have to examine the financial standing of the guarantors. A few local authorities themselves negotiate insurance cover against default and make the terms available to contractors. There are, of course, other methods of giving security, e.g. deposit of money in a joint account. Whatever the method, the chief financial officer must be satisfied that the contractor has complied with the terms of the contract. He must use his own judgment in advising the council to dispense with security either for all contracts or for a number of specified contractors. The chief financial officer will see that works and other contingencies arising from the contract are covered by insurance, that there is no overlapping or gap between the contractor's insurance and the local authority's own cover on completion of the works, and that insurance does not lapse during the contract period. He will check that retention moneys provide adequate security for the completion of the works in accordance with the contract. The chief financial officer must also make sure that any penalty clause is fair and workable. Whilst the paramount object of these security clauses, namely completion of the contract without loss to the council, must never be overlooked, the chief financial officer must guard against unnecessarily high security, for the cost of all forms of security is reflected in contract price.

Provisions in the contract which are of particular interest to the chief financial officer are those relating to variations and nominated sub-contractors and suppliers. The chief financial officer will see that the method of authorizing variations and of making financial adjustments is clear, practical and fair. He will check that the contract precisely defines the relationship between the council, main contractor and nominated sub-contractor or supplier on such points as the method of appointment, interim and final payments, variations, price fluctuation, discounts and payments to main contractor, and liability on default.

We now pass to the second group of the chief financial officer's responsibilities: those he has to undertake during the course of the contract. He must ensure that interim payments are in accordance with the contract, but he will rely upon the technical officer's certificate that work has been done to the value stated. He will check that financial provision has been made for the contract payments and that contract formalities have been completed. Special care is needed to maintain the interest of operating departments in contracts: they must not be regarded as purely the business of the technical officers. All contract payments should therefore be endorsed by the operating department's finance officer and operating departments should join in financial reports concerning the contract. The chief financial officer must pay certificates without delay, not only to comply with the contract but to create good relations with contractors who often have to operate with relatively low working capital. He must be careful to observe to the letter the provisions of the contract about payment. A case is known in local government of a day's delay in making an interim payment being successfully used by the contractor as an excuse for determining the contract.

The chief financial officer will also hold a watching brief to ensure that all routine procedures which have financial implications, such as issue of variation orders or appointment of nominated sub-contractors and suppliers, have been carried out in accordance with the council's instructions. He will see that variations issued in accordance with the contract are precise, and show the basis for the calculation of their cost and that the council's instructions on the selection of nominated sub-contractors and suppliers are rigidly followed.

Finally he has some responsibility to make sure that an account is kept of the estimated cost of decisions taken during the course of the contract and of the cumulative effect of all such decisions. This information is needed for the reports to committees whilst the work is in progress as well as for administrative uses and for the final settlement.

(7)

Experience has proved that whatever the nature of the examination by technical officers, proposed contract settlements should be reviewed by the chief financial officer before the technical officer gives his final certificate. Local authorities who have adopted this practice testify to its fruitfulness, and it is no secret that the district auditors every year report instances where an examination of a final account by an accountant would have revealed errors. On this subject the First Report of the Local Government Manpower Committee commented as follows:

'The view expressed by the departmental representatives . . . that the chief financial officer should as a regular practice be given an opportunity to review contract settlements either before the technical officer (or professional adviser) gives his final certificate or retrospectively, raises a question which is solely the responsibility of each local authority. Nevertheless we commend to local authorities generally the procedure suggested in this paragraph, which we understand is already followed by many authorities. Whether the review takes place before or after the contract settlement, it is intended that it should be concerned not with the technical aspects of the contract but with the accuracy of the accounts. We feel in particular that it is undesirable that a local authority should take formal steps which would deny its chief financial officer the opportunity to comment on contract settlements at some stage.'[1]

This pre-settlement examination by the finance department has been a feature of the examination of contracts in the most progressive local authorities for many years. It gives satisfaction to the officers and safeguards ratepayer and contractor. An increasing number of authorities are now inserting in their contracts a clause which prescribes this pre-settlement examination. Here is an example selected at random, of a standing order providing for the council's chief financial officer to review proposed contract settlements:

'Where under the provisions of any contract entered into by the Council for the execution of works, payment for such works is made dependent upon the issue of Certificates by an Officer of the Council, before issuing the final Certificate for payment under any such Contract, the Officer concerned shall consult with the City Treasurer so as to give him an opportunity of reviewing the contract settlement before the issue of such final Certificate, from the point of view of the accuracy of the accounts upon which such final Certificate is based and not from the technical aspects of the contract.

'In appointments of Professional Advisers in connection with the erection of works for the Council, the Town Clerk shall include a clause providing for similar consultations between such Professional Adviser and the City Treasurer.'

Where the council's own officers are concerned, and where the integration of financial arrangements advocated in this book prevails, this requirement is hardly necessary, as the procedure visualized in the standing order would take place automatically in the ordinary course of business. But this does not cover contracts where outside professional advisers are employed. Such a clause is thus to be recommended for general adoption. The nature of the pre-settlement audit (before the technical officer gives his certificate) will vary according to the circumstances of the contract and the agreed distribution of duties between the technical officer and the financial officer. Among the items to which financial officers can usefully devote attention are: the adjustment of variations, settlement of prime cost items, build up and calculation of day work charges, computation of discounts or other percentage adjustments, e.g. on day work rates. Contract settlements are inevitably complex affairs, and whatever the division

[1] *First Report of the Local Government Manpower Committee.* Cmnd. 7870, 1950, p. 20.

251

of duties, there must be the closest co-operation between the chief financial officer and his technical colleagues.

Settlements should be made as expeditiously as possible, and to facilitate the examination of the final account as much checking as possible should be carried out in stages before the account is submitted. For example, day work claims can be examined as they arrive, and claims in respect of fluctuations in cost can be cleared periodically during the term of the contract. Prompt settlements are also facilitated by a clear understanding at the outset about the vouchers and data to be produced in support of the final account. Late settlements have nothing to commend them. They take longer to prepare because changes in personnel and fading memories make the facts harder to establish, and they are apt to be based on compromises which would have been avoided had settlement been prompt.

The responsibilities of the chief financial officer for final settlements have been discussed in some detail, partly because of their importance and partly because insistence on the pre-settlement examination can be misunderstood. It can be considered not only a cause of unnecessary delay, but also a slight on the professional competence of technical advisers, instead of being appreciated as a common-sense method of making use of the accountant's special experience in this field. The author would add that he has never failed to come to amicable working arrangements with technical officers and advisers, both internal and external, on the subject of accounting reviews of proposed contract settlements and that his assistance is welcomed in the interests of accuracy when his objects and responsibilities are understood. He has further found that working arrangements with outside professional advisers are facilitated when the council's own technical officers act as the chief liaison between the outside practitioner and the local authority, e.g. if the local authority has its own architect, it is helpful if he acts as the link with any private architect the local authority may employ.

(8)

It will be convenient to discuss, as an appendage to the consideration of contracts, the special problems of direct labour, a direct labour department being regarded for the purpose of the discussion as a department of a local authority which undertakes, on a considerable scale, works of building construction and maintenance which could alternatively be put out to contract. Closely allied to direct labour work in this sense are the tasks of road maintenance, sewer maintenance, etc., which have traditionally been done by the local authority's own employees, and also the incidental building and plant maintenance done in many departments of local authorities. Therefore, though this section is concerned only with direct labour departments proper, many of the points apply in some measure to the road, sewer and incidental building maintenance carried out by employees of the authority.

(9)

Direct labour is not only important: it operates under peculiar difficulties and is much misrepresented. It is indeed ironical that direct labour, an activity of a local authority which should be considered and judged on a business basis, has become in so many places a matter of ideology. But before studying the safeguards necessary to keep direct labour on the right lines from the view-point of financial administration, we must consider some of its special features. First of all one must remember that the tasks assigned to direct labour are usually those which do not lend themselves to easy supervision—outside building work in dispersed places, jobbing repairs, school painting and so forth. However efficient the organization, it is therefore not easy to ensure that the local authority receives value for money. Secondly the fact that lapses are likely to be construed by hostile critics as evidence of the supposed unsoundness of the principle of direct labour, fosters a desire to hide discrepancies and difficulties; even upon occasions to the extent of deliberate misallocation of expenses. A third difficulty of direct labour departments is that there is no absolute measure of success or failure; whatever the works cost, the local authority has to pay. The only sense in which the competitive element can be introduced is in the initial tendering stage in those instances where the direct labour organization submits a price in competition with outside tenderers; the competitive process cannot be taken further.

The direct labour department cannot be regarded as a contractor; it is merely a part of the local authority's machinery, the cost of which has to be spread over the various jobs on which the department is employed. A check on some of the activities of a direct labour department can be obtained by the preparation by pro-

253

fessional staff of a notional 'final' account on the same lines as those adopted for outside contracts, and a comparison of this account with the actual cost. This is particularly relevant if the direct labour organization has secured a 'contract' by open competitive tender upon the basis of normal tendering procedure. Another type of check is the preparation of memorandum accounts showing the aggregate difference between estimates of cost and the actual costs for a period, but these are of limited significance, and can be actually misleading in so far as they are merely comparisons with the department's own estimates. For several reasons, therefore, direct labour departments tend to be surrounded by obscurity and prejudice. On the other hand, many direct labour departments have surmounted all the obstacles and have been operating for many years, not a little of their effectiveness being due to a sound financial framework. Indeed there is no branch in which financial administration can make a greater contribution to efficiency than that of direct labour.

(10)

There are a number of conditions to be fulfilled if direct labour departments are to be kept on the right lines and judged on their merits. The local authority should have arrangements which will stand the test of unlimited investigation and enquiry. The methods and the results must not only be sound, but must be demonstrably so. It is for this reason that direct labour works need to be closely regulated by standing orders and independently costed. Also, the direct labour organization should be judiciously used. It is not good policy to employ a direct labour department on specialist work for which it has neither suitable plant nor employees. Nor is it wise to expand the organization to cope with a peak load, with consequent embarrassment when the volume of work falls off. Moreover, the department must be carefully integrated with the arrangements of the local authority. Departments should be co-operative in helping direct labour departments to spread their work over the year. On the other hand, they must be able to rely on the work being done as it is needed: for instance, there should be no danger of a department 'losing' a budget provision because the direct labour department failed to do the work during the year. Also the total budget allocation allowed to departments for work to be done by direct labour should tally with the amount that the department is capable of doing during the period.

An additional point is that a direct labour department must not operate to destroy the sense of responsibility of other officers. Departmental heads should be responsible for spending their own estimates and for seeing that their committees get value for the money spent. The local authority should be particularly anxious to guard against a situation in which the heads of departments cynically accept standards of work from direct labour departments which would not be tolerated from a private contractor. Nor should they be made to feel that protests against inferior work are likely to be interpreted as hostility to the principle of direct labour. Further, there must be common sense in appraising the reasonableness of the costs of direct labour work, for the tendency will be for difficult work not likely to interest contractors, or work which has to be done at awkward times, to be given to direct labour. Moreover, the restricted number of 'customers' for which a department works makes planning harder for it than for an outside contractor of comparable size. Then again, the local authority should explore all possible incentives to good work and efficiency, including the payment of bonuses wherever a reasonable basis can be devised. In addition, all those concerned with the running of a direct labour department should remember that it is in one respect like all other service departments of a local authority such as establishment, finance, or central purchasing: it must be efficient and helpful, otherwise the departments might well be better off making their own independent arrangements. Finally, a local authority must bear in mind that the financial administration, however effective, cannot compensate for inadequate technical supervision of work.

(11)

If a local authority accepts the principles laid down in the previous section, how should it regulate direct labour work?

In the first place a limit must be set to the classes of work which should be allowed automatically to be done by direct labour. Before direct labour can be employed on works chargeable to loan, government departments normally insist on the submission of a tender in competition with outside tenderers. Many authorities adopt this method for other works not chargeable to loan. Those taking a restricted view, fix low limits beyond which the direct labour department has to compete with outside contractors; those taking a more liberal view fix a higher limit. Regulations should also provide that estimates shall be submitted for work for which a competitive tender is not insisted upon, exceptions being provided for the small jobs. The obligation to submit estimates is important. It assists outside departments in controlling their expenditure and it ensures that the direct labour department systematically estimates the cost of work before it is embarked upon. Works having been completed, independently prepared final costs, including an appropriate share of overhead expenses and showing variations from the estimate, must be submitted to committees together with the explanations of the variations by the officer in charge of direct labour. These reports of costs should be presented both to the department controlling direct labour and to the department for whom the work was done. There are numerous small jobs such as replacement of tiles, repairs to taps, which are too small to be individually costed. Although only strict supervision on the site can ensure that the local authority gets value for money for these small repairs, financial administration can help by providing for specimen jobs to be costed, and for the average cost of jobs of the same type to be extracted and studied. The committee in control of direct labour should have an annual report showing the volume of operations, the overheads of the departments and the extent to which they have been absorbed during the year. Some committees also call for a 'memorandum' account on the lines mentioned earlier, which shows the aggregate difference for the period between the estimated cost of the jobs and the actual cost. The committee in control should have regular statements showing the work on hand and the work for which orders have been received but which have not yet been executed.

Direct labour presents the chief financial officer with an opportunity to prove how valuable accounting and costing techniques can be as a tool of day-to-day administration. For the information described above as necessary for top management needs considerable amplification for the purposes of those in immediate charge of direct labour operations. Job costs and costs of operations must be supplied as they are needed: in the case of labour costs on selected jobs this may be as frequently as daily. Charges for plant and equipment must be made on a more flexible basis than that used for the more straightforward operations of a local authority. Charging-out prices for stores must be fixed in a way that absorbs the cost but does not hamper the direct labour department when it is competing with outside tenderers. A satisfactory way has to be found of spreading overhead costs, whether those of the direct labour department itself or of central establishments. These are examples only of the technical problems to be solved. They illustrate the truth of the contention made in an earlier chapter that costing systems have to be devised individually for departments and not for the authority as a whole. They also provide absorbing exercises in the application of the principles of cost accountancy.

CHAPTER XIX

THE PRINCIPLES AND FORM OF THE BUDGET[1]

(1)

THE budget has long been the focal point of the financial procedure of public authorities, and would in any case call for extended treatment in the present work. It happens, however, that because the budget goes to the roots of financial administration, it affords the best practical illustration of the working of the machinery described in earlier chapters. The council, its committees, heads of departments, departmental finance officers, the chief financial officer and the staffs of departments, all have to co-operate in budgeting. The subject is therefore of outstanding importance both to the practitioner and to students of financial administration.

In this chapter are considered: the nature and significance of the budget, the relevant statutory provisions, the two main types of budget—capital and revenue; the relation of both these kinds of budget to policy making; and the form of the revenue and capital budgets. Subsequent chapters deal with budgetary procedure and the administration of the budget.

(2)

Public authorities, the pioneers in budgeting, traditionally regarded budgets primarily as plans of expenditure. Industry, which came to the use of budgetary control later than public authorities, has developed budgeting as a tool of management, and our study can best begin by explaining the part which local authority budgets should be expected to play in the light of the best practice in other kinds of public authority and in industry.

[1] Whilst writing this book the author was a member of a study group sponsored by the Royal Institute of Public Administration whose report *Budgeting in Public Authorities* has recently been published (Allen and Unwin, 1959). The two books being in the press at the same time, detailed reference here to the Royal Institute's publication has not been practicable. The author would however commend it to readers as valuable background reading. At the same time he would acknowledge the stimulus he received from the group's deliberations, which have greatly enriched this chapter and the two following.

The main functions and features of a local budget are as follows:

(a) It fixes the rate of the local tax, and the purpose to which the produce of the taxation shall be applied. Competing claims being many and resources limited, budget making presents a local authority with its most difficult recurring problem. The intangible benefits of one service have to be compared with those of another, and weighed against the 'burden' of taxation. Current national policy, the pressure of public opinion, the predilections of local politicians—and indirectly of officers—all play their part in the process. It would be idle to expect a neat conclusion based on the scientific measurement of pros and cons, or even to expect a budgetary procedure as ordered as the meticulously-minded officer might desire. Compromise will be inevitable.

(b) The budget is the handmaid of policy making, both short-term and long-term, and one of the means by which it is implemented. It brings the various activities of the authority into focus, it helps the council to take a forward look, it enables them to keep policy under review, and it provides a means of avoiding either neglect or lopsided development of the services.

(c) The budget is a plan of action. Section 86 of the Education (Scotland) Act, 1946, relating to the budgets of Scottish education authorities, provides as follows:

' . . . authorization of the expenditure included therein shall be sufficient authority to the education committee to incur on purposes falling within the description of any head in the prescribed form, expenditure not exceeding in amount the total under that head in the estimates so provided . . .'

Whether in English counties and metropolitan boroughs, prior to the coming into operation of the Local Government Act, 1958, approval of the budget gave authority to spend without the submission of further estimates was always a matter of doubt. The repeal of the relevant provisions has now left all English authorities free to determine how the budget is to operate as the plan of action for the period it covers.

(d) The budget is the medium for ensuring that the monies of the local authority are ultimately laid out in the way the local authority has decided, and for making during the year modifications dictated by unforeseen circumstances.

(e) A budget does more than ensure that money is spent in the way the local authority has decided: by providing suitable yardsticks it helps to secure efficient and economical administration.

259

Accordingly, the budget should be related wherever possible to physical units of output. It should set standards of efficiency for each part of the administration and provide means of gauging the extent of their achievement.

(3)

The statutory provisions relating to budgeting can be briefly disposed of. Although only county councils are specifically enjoined by statute to make estimates, the law makes each year's or half-year's finances self-contained. Under the Rating and Valuation Act, 1925, a rate must be levied to cover the estimated needs of the period, the liquidation of deficiences on previous rates and sums required for contingencies or for a working balance. General reserves are forbidden, and extra-budgetary funds such as those for the equalization of expenditure on renewals of buildings and plant are limited and strictly regulated by law. To comply with these legal provisions accurate estimates are essential, and for this reason alone budgeting in local authorities, in so far as it relates to raising the correct sums to accomplish the declared purpose of the authority, is well done. Divergencies between plan and performance are generally modest, whilst the manipulation of budgets for electoral purposes, if not unknown, is not a noticeable or even a significant feature of English local government. As with other aspects of administration, internal budgetary arrangements are left for each local authority to determine.

The legal code in Scotland is more elaborate, for the Local Government (Scotland) Act, 1947, in addition to laying upon authorities the duty to make a rate, provides that separate estimates for capital and revenue expenditure for trading and non-trading services must be presented to the council with a report from the finance committee. The finance committee's recommendations may be either adopted or revised and the Act specifically allows provisional estimates to be submitted to the council and later amended. Except in emergencies, and under appropriate safeguards, no expenditure outside the budget can be incurred without approval of the council.

Both English and Scottish provisions are set out in Appendix B. Though the Scottish provisions are more detailed, and indeed even cover some aspects of internal procedure, the position in both countries is broadly that the law makes only certain minimum demands, designed to ensure that the budget fulfils its traditional functions.

Each local authority must decide for itself to what extent its budget is to become the more ambitious tool of management described in the preceding section.

(4)

In addition to the legal requirements there are also some special features of local government to be borne in mind in studying budgetary arrangements. There are, in the first place, the variety and dispersion of activities, so often mentioned in this study, which make the budget voluminous, and the process of its compilation laborious: for instance, in counties, divisional executives and excepted districts may have to begin to prepare the budget for the following year before the first half of the current year has expired. Again, the contrast between a local authority, able to settle the level of activities a year ahead, and the commercial undertaking, constantly called upon to adjust its budget to a fluctuating demand, and subject to upheavals such as re-tooling a factory, suggests a second distinguishing feature —the relative rigidity of budgetary systems in local government. A further point is the existence of so many services which do not lend themselves to the establishment of standards of efficiency, including many of the social, health and education services and the whole of the 'regulative' services. It would, for example, be ridiculous to judge the efficiency of the police by the cost 'per person apprehended' or the weights and measures department by the cost 'per prosecution'. Control must take the form of a scrutiny of individual items of expenditure. Finally, English local authorities use their budgets as one of the means by which the members discharge their duty of controlling administration. Accordingly budgets will tend to show the heads of expenditure in considerable detail.

The broad effect of these features is that, however the budgets of local authorities are developed and refined, their prime functions will be to plan, authorize, and control, expenditure. They will, in the circumstances of local government, serve other purposes, such as the encouragement of economy, only if the financial arm of the administration is constantly vigilant. English local authorities have, however, at least the advantage of being untrammelled by a purely legalistic conception of the budget. In France the budget is a definite legislative act, conferring powers on the executive, and is at the same time the means of control by the supervising authority, and the basis of the accounting.

261

(5)

So far, except for the reference to the obligation placed by the Local Government (Scotland) Act, 1947, on Scottish authorities to prepare separate estimates for capital and revenue expenditure, the terms 'estimate' and 'budget' have been used without qualification. From now on it will be necessary to distinguish between (a) the revenue budget, (b) the long-term capital programme, and (c) the annual capital budget. The terms 'estimates' and 'budget' will be regarded as synonymous.

The revenue budget is what is usually meant when local authorities refer to their 'budget' or their 'estimates'. It is by far the most important, because it is the vehicle for fixing the amount of the rate. In the case of trading undertakings the distinction between revenue and capital is that normally made by commercial concerns, i.e. that between revenue account transactions and those related to the acquisition and disposal of fixed assets. The revenue budgets of the non-trading activities relate to the transactions of the rate fund, the deficiency of which is charged to the local rate. They may or may not include items referring to the acquisition or disposal of fixed assets but they include the charges for the service of debt on assets acquired by borrowing.

There is nothing in the Rating and Valuation Act, 1925, to prevent local authorities from preparing a revenue budget or levying a rate more often than once a year, but in practice nearly all authorities compile an annual budget, and most of them levy an annual rate, often payable in two or more instalments. The remainder levy a half-yearly rate, but in fixing the rate for the second half of the year are content to carry out a revision of the budget prepared for the first half year, rather than to make a new budget for the second half year. Thus local revenue budgets may be regarded as annual events normally taking place before the year begins.

Long-term capital programmes, the significance of which is considered in some detail later in the chapter, are programmes of projected capital works for a period, e.g. three or five years ahead. For the purpose of our discussion they may be taken to refer to capital expenditure met from loan, though those authorities in the fortunate position of being able to meet a proportion of capital works from revenue may also include these items in the long-term capital programme. A long-term capital programme is merely a statement of provisional intention. It authorizes neither expenditure nor the raising of funds, and is likely to be subject to appreciable modification.

The annual capital budget is compiled before the beginning of the year. In contrast to a long-term programme, it shows the capital expenditure for only one year ahead. It is naturally more precise than a long-term capital programme, and is reflected in the revenue budget in so far as it is expected to involve charges to revenue in that year. But it does not itself confer authority to spend and, as is explained later, it has limited significance compared with the revenue budget.

Another kind of budget, the cash budget, does not figure prominently in local government. It is the estimate of cash receipts and payments during a period. The chief financial officer normally watches the cash balances, regulating temporary investment and borrowing in the way most advantageous to his authority. But in times of severe stringency or trade depression, the cash position of an authority may well become a critical matter for the finance committee. Therefore though cash budgets do not raise administrative questions within the scope of this book, their importance should not be overlooked.

There is yet another kind of budget—the long-term forecast on revenue account. This is not treated further in the pages which follow because its preparation raises no particular organizational problems. It follows closely the lines used for the annual revenue budget, but is prepared in a very much simplified form, being intended as an indication of the trend of the authority's finances rather than a definite plan of action.

The author has found that a long-term revenue forecast, though of only a tentative nature, can be an instrument of first-rate value to the local authority. Indeed it is difficult to see how a local authority faced with the need for wholesale expansion or replacement of services can manage its financial affairs without paying regard to its future financial position. A long-term capital budget, invaluable though it may be, is only concerned with part of the story. A long-term revenue forecast on the other hand is comprehensive, embracing the effect on future rates of the trends of both capital and revenue expenditure. It thus reflects the cost to rates of new capital items, and also projected developments of services and anticipated additional expenses not connected with capital expenditure. It is the document which gives the local authority the clue to what it can afford and hence to the pace of development of all kinds. The attitude of the local authority to the current year's budget may very well be determined in the light of the picture presented by the forecast. Forward looks are of great significance in financial affairs. A recent Select Committee commented: 'If both the total and the balance of expenditure are to be effectively controlled, it is essential that policy decisions should be taken with full knowledge of what the policy will cost not only next year, but, if possible, the following year and the year after that. Only in the light of such knowledge can the review of current policy be effectively pursued. Money must be voted and allocated annually, but an obsession with annual expenditure can stultify forward planning.'[1]

(6)

The budget should not itself be made the vehicle for the determination of new policy, such as the institution of new services, expansion of existing services, or the adoption of capital projects. All policy decisions affecting the budget should as far as possible be settled beforehand, even though they cannot operate until budgetary provision has been made. If items not yet approved in principle by the authority have to be included in the budget, they should be either segregated or otherwise distinguished, and must have individual specific approval before they are expended.

But if the revenue budget is not instrumental in making policy, it is a means of giving effect to it. Thus it is by means of the budget that the local authority restricts or expands borrowing and spending in accordance with prevailing economic policy, central or local. In fact, an orderly long-term policy can seldom be achieved unless accompanied by proper budgetary control and advance planning. A local authority anxious to replace gas lamps by electric lamps, to expand a fleet of vehicles, to provide a number of recreation grounds, to execute arrears of road-resurfacing, to carry out a programme of river cleansing, or to improve its buildings can often avoid borrowing by carefully planned revenue budgetary provisions over a period of years. Good budgetary practices are also an encouragement to local authorities to keep buildings and plant in working order and thus avoid the inevitable financial embarrassments of arrears of maintenance work. Again, the very problems of revenue budget making, if properly tackled, of themselves induce orderly policy. For instance,

[1] *Sixth Report from the Select Committee on Estimates, Session 1957–8.* Cmnd. 254, p. XI.

if budgetary stringency impels a general review of charges for services provided by the authority, the council may be led to look at the possibilities of adopting general principles of the kind advocated in the chapter on the collection of income, e.g. that charges for games in parks should cover the working expenses, the local authority bearing the capital charges.

A good revenue budgeting procedure is thus of great value to a local authority in the formulation of policy, though it must not itself be the medium through which new policy is decided. What help is it to the administration? First of all, by providing a plan of work and a means of control, it encourages methodical procedures and helps to foster a sense of responsibility. The budget also compels large numbers of officers at least once a year to review their aims and the methods of attaining them. The budget, however, not only helps the official in his administrative work; it also helps him in his task of bringing home to the members the financial implications of proposed policy changes. A good officer will always think of the effect of proposals on the budget, and if the budgeting technique is sound, it will be easier to gauge the effects than if it is faulty. Similarly, an authority in the habit of preparing a long-term capital programme helps its officers to judge the consequences of a new government policy, e.g. on education buildings, or road works.

Another use of the revenue budget is that of providing the local authority with its sole opportunity of looking at its activities as a whole. This is most important to a body with such varied aims and with such a loose administrative structure. It has not infrequently happened that the presentation of the budget has touched off a desire to hold a systematic enquiry into some aspect or aspects of the council's administration. In the absence of any counterpart to either the Public Accounts Committee, or the Select Committee on Estimates, local authorities are apt to escape the salutary influence of periodical probes: anything which focuses the attention of the authority on the value of these exercises is therefore to be welcomed. The possibilities in local government of the use of investigating committees are discussed in a later chapter. The point to note at the moment is the effect of the budget in acting as a catalyst to hasten enquiry.

(7)

Among the decisions of the council vitally affecting future revenue budgets, the most important are those about major capital projects. By budgetary planning, coupled with a willingness on the part of the council to levy a rate for capital expenditure from revenue, a few modest capital projects can be financed from current taxation. But these will be so small a proportion of the total that the term 'capital expenditure' is used here to indicate expenditure to be defrayed from loan. Should the capital expenditure met from revenue be appreciable, the amount should be included in the budgetary statements discussed below.

Of all classes of expenditure, the service of debt is the most intractable. In an emergency, even though staff may be reduced and services withdrawn, loan charges must continue to be paid for the period of the loan, which may vary from a few years for the purchase of plant to eighty years for the acquisition of land. Local authorities became acutely aware in the less prosperous nineteen thirties of the burden of loan charges on debts contracted at high interest rates in the boom of the early twenties. Further, a complete year's loan charges are not normally due until the year following the taking up of the loan. Borrowing thus not only spreads the burden over a period, but also enables the initial impact to be postponed —features which exercise at times a dangerous fascination. The administrative machinery should therefore be such that the council cannot defray expenditure by borrowing, except after the closest scrutiny and in the fullest knowledge of the effect on the finances of the authority.

The first stage at which such scrutiny can be made occurs when a project is included in a long-term capital programme. Though such a programme has nothing of the precision of a revenue budget, it has many merits. It gives the local authority an idea of the capital commitments ahead, it helps the council to sort out priorities and it provides data for the provisional phasing of expenditure. It enables the local authority to take into account the ultimate effect on the revenue budget of loan charges and maintenance costs, and to fix an approximate total of capital expenditure for the next few years. A long-term programme also helps to secure justice for competing schemes. Many capital schemes can be completed within a single year, others take two or three years, whilst a few are part of a far-reaching plan, e.g. a major scheme of reorganization of schools intended to be spread over many years. Unless all the schemes in mind are brought together, there will be a tendency to accept those put forward for immediate adoption to the detriment of later, and possibly more meritorious projects.

Some kind of forward planning is also imperative if peak loads for technical staffs are to be avoided. Inflated technical staffs, engaged to cope with a sudden rush of work, eventually involve both embarrassment to the local authority and hardship to individuals. Moreover, a local authority should surely consider the cumulative burden on revenue every time a decision is made about a capital scheme. Few local authorities are able to adopt all the schemes put forward, and a proper choice can be made only in the presence of complete data.

Long-term capital programmes will be inexact for they will not materialize exactly as expected; and they will need frequent revision. But they seem to the author to be an almost indispensable feature of rational financial management. The features which tend to discourage the preparation of capital budgets—the inevitable approximations, the tendency to over-optimism about the amount of work likely to be done, the dependence for realization on the central government's policy—are of small account compared with the positive value of the information they yield.

(8)

Inclusion in a long-term capital programme or even an annual capital budget should not of itself imply even provisional approval to a scheme. Every capital project should come to the council for specific consideration. The next stage in the life history of a capital scheme, after its appearance in the long-term capital programme, is, therefore, its submission to the council for adoption. The larger schemes may come to the council for individual approval twice: first for approval in principle, perhaps as an independent item or maybe as part of a larger scheme; and secondly as an application for loan sanction. For smaller schemes there may be no 'approval in principle' stage. Both kinds of occasion—submission of a scheme for approval in principle, and a recommendation to make application for loan, (or for a supplementary loan for an existing project)—would justify the issue of reports from the officers on the lines described in the chapter on the chief financial officer as financial adviser, though *full* reports might not be necessary on both occasions. To wait until the proposal crystallizes into a specific recommendation to take up a

267

loan would be fatal, for in those cases where a proposal comes on two occasions, the vital decision is normally made when the scheme is approved in principle. After this point the scheme can be abandoned or postponed only at the cost of wastage of architectural and other professional work.

The need to obtain the sanction of the central government to the raising of loans guards against sheer recklessness, and against charging revenue expenditure to capital account. It also gives some guarantee that schemes which are clearly beyond the resources of the authority will not be carried out. But it does not compensate for the absence of proper local scrutiny. A very considerable discretion is left to local authorities in the initiation of capital projects, though this discretion may have at times to be curbed in the interest of national economic policy.

So important is it for local authorities to protect themselves from the risk of becoming prematurely committed to a project, that many authorities have not been content to rely on practice or internal regulation, but include in the standing orders themselves a requirement that financial details shall accompany all proposals committing the council in principle, as well as specific proposals for application for loan sanctions. To complete the precautions there should also be a standing order applying the same procedure to a notice of motion moved on the floor of the council as to a recommendation moved by a committee. This can be accomplished by requiring that every notice of motion with financial implications should stand adjourned until the proposal has been through the normal procedure for financial business—a safeguard applying as much to additional revenue expenditure as to the capital expenditure under discussion in this section.

(9)

Having studied the principles underlying local budgets, and having stepped aside to consider the arrangements for approving new capital schemes, we can now proceed to more detailed aspects of budgets. The remainder of this chapter will be devoted to the form of the budget, both capital and revenue.

What should be the form of a local revenue budget? Local authorities answer the question in a variety of ways, both the form and the size of the local budget differing materially from place to place. An IMTA research team found in 1954 that, of two counties each spending £3 million per annum, one had a thirty-one page volume, the other a ninety-eight. Similarly of two county boroughs, one spending £6 million produced a volume of 330 pages and the other with an expenditure of £18 million had only 130 pages.[1] The number of published pages is an imperfect guide because the authorities with slim budgets may buttress them with more extensive internal documents. None the less, the printed document is the approved budget, and it is on the basis of this that officers account to committees and committees account to the council. Size, therefore, though in some ways misleading, is significant. Basically, a local authority budget is an authorization to spend monies on defined objects. One may, therefore, expect that either in the budget itself, or in a supporting document, the authorized headings will be set out in some detail. The general pattern of the headings will coincide with those to be used in the final accounts, so that as the standard form of accounts referred to in an earlier chapter comes into operation, there should be a high degree of uniformity between local budgets as well as between local accounts. This uniformity will not extend to the degree of detail, because the standard form of accounts leaves discretion with local authorities as to the amount of detail which they may print. In addition, local circumstances will be reflected in amplifications of the standard form: completely standardized budgets would be undesirable because a budget, being an internal instrument of control, must be fashioned to the needs of the authority. Authorities who print the abstract of accounts in abbreviated form, e.g. by confining the detail to what in the terminology of the standard accounts is called 'standard grouping', may show more detail in their estimates, partly for budgetary purposes, and partly so that the accounts and the budget together give a detailed picture of the finances of the local authority.

From the budgetary point of view, the arguments in favour of considerable printed detail are: inclusion in the published budget is the simplest, and probably in the long run the most economical way of recording details which must be noted somewhere for the purpose of compiling and administering the estimate; the details are necessary for the elected member to gauge the nature of the services to be provided; detailed headings cannot be used as easily as broad estimates to cover up either over-provision or transfers between recurring and non-recurring items; and, finally, such a budget provides

[1] See *The Use of the Revenue Budget as a means of Financial Control* (Institute of Municipal Treasurers and Accountants, 1954), p. 15.

a more satisfactory way of controlling subordinates because each detailed head can be made the responsibility of a single officer. On the other hand, detailed estimates can be condemned as leading to over-estimating through the introduction of a margin on many items instead of a few, and hence to unnecessary applications for supplementary estimates and for virement. They can be represented as wasting money and administrative time and encouraging members to pay too much attention to unimportant matters. The ideal might well be an abbreviated budget for the members, and a more detailed document for departmental use on the grounds that members and officers are concerned with different aspects. The author's opinion is that all in all, and particularly because of the nature of the member's responsibility, there is much to be said in favour of a reasonably detailed published budget in English local government.

(10)

For each item of income and expenditure there will be shown the estimate for the forthcoming year, that for the current year (probably both the original estimate and a revised estimate) and possibly figures for the previous year, or even years. Expenditure will be shown gross, 'contra' items such as sales or appropriations from funds being shown separately as receipts. Services will be grouped under the committee responsible for them, and the items will be totalled to show the cost for each division of service as well as that for services and committees. Some authorities show against each item a 'plus and minus' column indicating the variation between the proposed estimate and that of the current year, a useful way of focusing the attention of the committee. Expenditure on common services—architectural, typing, printing, etc.—should be shown in the first place as part of the estimates of the committee administering them, the estimated recharges to the 'customer' services being shown as income. These recoupments will appear as expenditure in the accounts of other committees. The alternative, of charging common services directly to the using committees, robs the administering committee of a bird's-eye view of operations and may well mask variations in cost by diffusion throughout the services. Moreover, the officers responsible for common services should be required to account in the aggregate to a single committee.

To make the budget more significant, some authorities group expenditure into ordinary and extraordinary or non-recurring. A few show sums included for new services, or for expansion of services, separately from those representing the maintenance of services at the existing level. Many authorities also adopt the salutary practice of marking by an asterisk or otherwise, those items—they should be few and exceptional for reasons already explained—included provisionally in the budget because they represent new policy yet to be determined.

Contingencies are best provided in one lump sum, for to allow a separate contingency item for each committee will be to encourage excessive provision. The contingency item can be used to cover expenditure, the magnitude of which will be governed by available supplies rather than by the intentions of the authority. Thus many authorities with complements of teachers, policemen and firemen below the numbers they wish to have, and would willingly pay for, allow for the possibility of an unexpected inflow by a lump sum rather than by inflation of the estimates of the individual committees. Similarly a local authority may provide loan charges on new schemes in one central pool, for whilst an experienced officer may be able to forecast with reasonable accuracy a global figure, to estimate the progress of individual projects may be more difficult, and may lead to too large a total provision.

A good feature of budgeting in industry is the emphasis on the connexion between the physical and financial aspects, figures of expected output being used wherever they are available as the basis of the estimates. In calculating the money needed to attain the expected output, industrialists usually use those carefully prepared estimates of the resources required for each unit, which the accountant calls standard costs. Local government committees, too, are coming to realize that they are making estimates not only to spend set sums of money, but also to employ a given number of people, supply home helps for so many hours, or provide for so many children in the homes of the authority. These quantities are the foundation of the budget which can be interpreted and administered only by reference to them. Modern budgetary practice, therefore, requires that relevant statistics shall accompany the budget, and wherever significant units are available they should be used. For example, a children's committee might expect its budget to show particulars of the staff of various kinds at various grades and details of the places available and likely to be occupied at each of their homes, together with the number of staff at each home, the ratio of children to staff and the unit costs. The number of boarded-

271

out children estimated for, and the number expected to be placed in the homes of other local authorities should also be stated.

In addition to the normal classification, the budget may also be classified subjectively, showing either in total or for each committee, the expenditure on salaries and wages (sub-divided over the various categories of employees), the cost of various types of goods to be purchased, and the amount to be spent on rents, rates and printing and stationery. This subjective analysis is particularly significant when figures are drawn together for the whole authority, for it gives the council important clues to trends, and at the same time supplies valuable data for policy decisions at budget time. If, for example, the council know the total of the printing and stationery bill, they can gauge what would be the effect of a percentage cut of, say, ten per cent; or if some expense such as telephone charges or national insurance contributions is increased after the budget has been made, the additional cost can be readily calculated.

The revenue budget must be comprehensive and must include all the accounts attached to the rate fund. Expenditure from reserves and renewals accounts must not be allowed to escape examination at budget time because it is not a direct charge upon the rates. Thus the budget should include properly classified and detailed estimates of the amount to be spent from the housing repairs fund just as if the repairs were a direct charge to the housing revenue account. It is illogical to control highways repairs because they fall directly on the highways accounts, but not repairs and maintenance of houses because they happen to be met from accumulated monies. All reserves, renewals and similar funds should therefore be subject to budgetary control, the precise form of the estimates depending on the nature of the fund. If the housing account has been made self-balancing and does not therefore affect the rate levy, its income and expenditure should none the less be made the subject of annual budgetary review.

(11)

One of the most vital budgetary documents is the report—or reports —of the chief financial officer to the finance committee at the stage when the committee is considering its recommendations to the council. The exact form of the report will be determined by tradition, the relations between the chief financial officer and his committee and, above all, by the local budgetary procedure, a topic taken up in the next chapter. The general lines of such reports will, however, be much the same everywhere, and it will therefore be convenient to consider them as part of the discussion on the form of the budget.

However strong the leaning of the chief financial officer towards short reports, he can scarcely avoid being expansive on this occasion. The finance committee will be interested in both the long-term trends and the immediate problem of settling the rate for the ensuing year. He can therefore be fairly expected to deal with such matters as the state of the local authority's working balances, reserves, renewals, and capital funds; the extent to which working balances have been drawn upon, or added to, in recent years; changes of magnitude expected in the future, e.g. in government grants or rates of interest and in particular the effect of capital programmes on future revenue estimates. He will set out and explain, service by service, the differences between the estimates for the forthcoming year and those for the current year. Significant trends in unit costs will also be shown.

Finally there are the summaries of the budget presented to the council. These should be fashioned to give an over-all view to the members who cannot be expected to take a detailed interest in the estimates of committees other than those upon which they serve. Summaries should show income and expenditure committee by committee for two or three years, both in amount and rate poundage, together with clear information about general grants, precepts from other authorities, balances brought forward from previous years, adjustments to working balances, and allocations to renewals and other funds. Either in the form of a finance committee document or a report from the chief financial officer the salient points of the budget should be summarized in a succinct way, aimed at giving the members a brief but comprehensive picture of the situation. This accompanying report is of particular importance because in local government, as we have seen, objective measures of output, unit or otherwise, are hard to find. So many intangibles have to be weighed, and so many subjective judgments made, that statistical summaries have to be supplemented by narrative, as detached and impartial as the subject matter allows. A final summary on a single sheet is also useful to the members.

Summaries prepared for the council may also be of value in informing the press and public, to whom the main outlines of the budget have to be explained. To explain and justify the amount of the local tax to those from whom it is to be compulsorily collected is the task of the members. The chief financial officer can, however, help in presenting the facts, and he may well prepare, in addition to the summaries and reports referred to above, a popular leaflet giving a non-technical analysis of the content of the rate and the council's financial position. The leaflet may be in the form of tables, diagrams, or even pictures, and may be issued either separately or sent out with the demand notes. It should reach those who pay their rates through a landlord, including the occupants of council houses, as well as the direct ratepayer.

(12)

Having studied the form of the revenue budget we must now consider that of the long-term capital programmes, and of the annual capital budget. The requirements of a long-term capital programme are:

(*a*) The programme should be for a period of years long enough to be significant, but not so extended that the figures become mere conjectures. Periods of three to five years are probably the ideal.

(*b*) The programme should include all the capital expenditure foreshadowed, including that of trading undertakings. To omit the latter, as is sometimes done because it does not affect the rate fund budget, is to make the programme of little use as an instrument for determining borrowing policy, or spreading the load of architectural and other technical work.

(*c*) Schemes included in the programme should be carefully classified. A common method, which may not suit every authority, is to show for each year of the programme the estimated cost of:

(*i*) schemes in progress
(*ii*) schemes out to tender
(*iii*) schemes approved by both council and central government
(*iv*) schemes approved by the council but awaiting central government sanction
(*v*) schemes not yet approved by the council.

(*d*) The programme should show the approximate annual loan charges and running costs.

(*e*) Summaries should show the analysis of each year's total capital expenditure between:

(*i*) cost of land acquisition
(*ii*) building work
(*iii*) other work or purchases.

This analysis is of utmost importance in deciding the practicability of the programme.

(*f*) A joint report of the officers concerned should make clear to the committee the demands the schemes would make on the council's administrative resources, and the extent to which they could be met by the existing organization.

Consideration of the capital programme will begin by the submission to a central committee, usually the finance committee, of the estimates of operating committees. The central committee will make recommendations to the council. In so far as the decisions relate to a tentative programme, and do not commit the council to expenditure they are of less importance than those taken on the revenue budget. But in so far as they determine the council's general attitude to the pace and direction of spending they are of great significance, and may become matters of acute controversy, because they settle, if only provisionally, the priorities of schemes, every one of which will have its supporters. A finance committee, confronted with the first draft of a capital programme, has invariably to consider adjustments before presenting the recommended programme to the council, usually by way of putting schemes back to a later year than that to which the operating committee has aspired. If the finance committee shows to the council both the original and the amended figures, any dissatisfied committee can raise complaints at the council meetings. Decisions on capital programmes may be of great practical importance. For instance, a council may be under pressure from committees to provide both a new library and a new town hall, but may not feel able to go forward with both schemes simultaneously. In this case the order in which the projects appear in the accepted capital programme may well settle a difficult local problem. Again, capital programmes are important to the administration because they give the clue to the number of architects, structural and heating engineers likely to be required in the next few years. They may also give an indication of the volume of new constructional work likely to be assigned to the council's direct labour organization.

(13)

Annual capital estimates are theoretically the natural complement to the long-term capital programme, though they are often used by authorities who do not compile long-term capital programmes as

275

well as by those who do. Indeed, in Scotland, formal annual capital estimates are obligatory: in England, though not required by law, they are becoming increasingly common and are often now printed together with the revenue budget. Even if there are no formal capital estimates, as happens in some English authorities, the chief financial officer has to estimate the capital expenditure for the purpose of computing the loan charges and maintenance expenses for the forth-coming year from his knowledge of the decisions of the council. In such cases he is, in effect, preparing informal capital estimates for office use.

Annual capital estimates relate to a single year, and include expenditure on both projects already begun and new schemes expected to be begun in the forthcoming year. To be of maximum value, the annual capital budget should also show the effect of each scheme on revenue in the current and first complete year. The majority of schemes will normally already have been decided upon by the council, many of them being covered by loan sanction: others will be awaiting sanction. A few of the schemes may not yet have received even the approval of the council. The schemes will be classi-fied in the annual capital budget in much the same way as in the long-term capital programme. Capital estimates, whilst usually over-optimistic, are sufficiently accurate to form the basis for calculating the impact on the forthcoming revenue budget.

Annual capital budgets on these lines are valuable in so far as they focus attention on schemes about to mature, and bring home to the council the volume of schemes contemplated for immediate develop-ment. Though most of the projects will be at such an advanced stage of consideration that their inclusion is almost automatic, a finance committee seeking to retrench may have to suggest deletions or postponements for these items as well as for items not yet sanctioned.

Capital estimates have not the significance or precision of the revenue estimates for three reasons. First, they are not authorizations of expenditure: authority for each scheme will have to be given by specific resolutions. Secondly, they are far less accurate because the pace of capital expenditure cannot be predicted as easily as that of revenue. Thirdly, if they prove to be inaccurate, the revenue budget for the year will be only marginally affected because of the delayed impact of loan charges on new capital schemes. But they are suffi-ciently accurate to allow of significant comparisons between actual and estimate. A local authority should be concerned to see that schemes do not lag behind the programme, as well as to watch that expenditure does not run ahead. This will be mainly accomplished by keeping track of the progress of individual schemes in the manner described in the chapter on the chief financial officer as accountant.

CHAPTER XX

BUDGETARY PROCEDURE

(1)

IN this chapter, which is devoted to the procedure for preparing a revenue budget, only a few of the arrangements in operation can be described, and many interesting exceptional instances will have to be ignored, e.g. the case of the chief financial officer to a district council 'who prepares the whole of the budget, presents it direct to the finance committee and himself makes the budget speech at the council meeting'.[1]

Though arrangements in individual authorities must be varied to suit local circumstances, there are some general principles which should be observed. They are:

(*a*) Operating committees and departments should in the first instance be allowed to stake claims for their wants, providing they are reasonable and practicable, and the council should be made aware of the costs of granting their requests. If the local procedure does not provide for these initial claims to reach the council, they should be recorded in an office document. The disadvantage of allowing the committees to ask for what they want is that the total claims may be sufficiently above the current rate of spending to alarm the public and if, as sometimes happens, the committees in their zeal put forward unreal figures, the practice becomes unworkable. But, in the author's opinion, these disadvantages do not justify supression of the departments' needs as visualized by the heads of departments.

(*b*) The council must accept the proposition that the sorting out of these claims is an intricate task, unsuitable for the floor of the council chamber, and that a handful of members—in practice the finance committee—must sift the draft estimates and make firm recommendations to the council in the knowledge that they are likely to carry the council with them.

(*c*) The scrutiny of draft budgets must be done in full knowledge of the facts, and in order that justice shall be done between the competing claims of departments, draft budgets should be compiled

[1] *The Use of the Revenue Budget as a means of Financial Control* (Institute of Municipal Treasurers and Accountants, 1954), p. 26.

on a uniform basis. This implies integration of the financial arrangements of the authority, interdepartmental co-operation and the existence of a chief financial officer, impartial, and closely acquainted with the affairs of the authority, who can provide the members with all the relevant information.

(*d*) The council itself must be the final arbiter, not only in determining the rate level but in settling unresolved disputes about the budget between the finance committee and other committees.

(2)

Before the actual preparation of the revenue budget begins, new policy affecting it, especially that of capital schemes, must be settled. There may well also be other matters to be arranged such as modifications of existing levels of work, determination of road improvement programmes, or completion of negotiations affecting the finances of the authority. A systematic review of all charges made by the authority is another invaluable preliminary, the usual practice of allowing questions of income to be dealt with as a by-product of the budget itself being far less satisfactory. The revenue budget process proper will begin in November, December or January according to the extent of the services of the authority, but outlying units in counties may need to begin work on the budget in September or October. County officials may have to consult 'district councils, education divisional executives and excepted districts, area health committees, governors and managers of schools, children's homes and welfare sub-committees, road safety committees, standing joint committee, magistrates' courts committee, and of course many government departments regarding capital programmes. In addition, some counties have joint committees with neighbouring counties or county boroughs'.[1] One of the essentials of good budgeting is that ample time should be allowed for unhurried consideration at all stages, so that the earlier, within reason, the budget starts, the more satisfactory is likely to be the final result.

The compilation of a budget should be a joint task between the chief officers of the departments and the chief financial officer, the duty of the latter being to put his special skill and experience at the disposal of his colleagues. Some information must clearly emanate from the finance department, such as loan charges, taxation charges,

[1] *The Use of the Revenue Budget as a means of Financial Control* (Institute of Municipal Treasurers and Accountants, 1954), p. 26.

apportionments of central charges, or computation of specific grants, but many estimates will be made jointly in the light of the department's judgment of its needs and circumstances and the finance department's experience. The exact procedure will depend on the extent to which the accounting is decentralized; even within a single authority the part played by the finance department will vary according to the size and organization of the departments.

If the draft budget is not being tailored at an early stage in the light of knowledge of the possible total amount to be allowed to the department, the chief financial officer's duty is to help the department to stake its claim. When the time arrives for pruning the estimates, the chief financial officer must help the department to amend the figures in a way that does the least injury to the service, an aspect of the budget to be dealt with in more detail later. One important function of the chief financial officer is to see that over-much attention is not paid to the previous year's figure. Whilst comparisons with past periods are significant and valuable, to make the previous year automatically the starting point for the new year's calculation is unsound. The chief financial officer will constantly need to warn committees against assuming that figures which do not exceed the previous year are necessarily justifiable. Committees have long been only too susceptible to the notion. Samuel Pepys when preparing his defence of the naval estimates in 1668 wrote of 'studying all we could to make the last year's swell as high as we could'.

The draft revenue budget should be an accurate reflexion of the departmental requirements, based where possible on estimates of physical needs and related to a measured output of service. Sometimes whole divisions of service are subject to unit measures of output such as the mileage of roads to be maintained, the number of hours for which home helps are to be supplied, or the number of meals to be served. The chief financial officer will help both his own and the other departments if he makes sure that the forms used for the preparatory budget work clearly show how all the figures have been calculated, for both the operating committee seeking to justify its figures before the finance committee, and the finance committee deciding what cuts to recommend, find their tasks facilitated if the detailed make-up of the estimates is readily available.

It is at budget time that the fully-fledged departmental finance officer (as opposed to just a finance clerk) comes into his own. He assembles the information from the various sections of his department, consults section heads, discusses the figures with his colleagues in the finance department and finally settles the draft budget with the head of his department. His colleague in the finance department may for this purpose be a sectional accountant, the chief accountant or the deputy chief financial officer or even the chief financial officer according to the size of the authority, and he himself may be the head of the department, the chief clerk or some other officer. In those cases where the finance officer is not the head of the department, his duty of acting as the principal link between his department and that of the chief financial officer does not preclude discussions between the finance department and other officers in the operating departments. Indeed, budget time is often the occasion when the officers of the finance department come into closest touch with departmental staffs from chief officers downwards. A far-seeing departmental finance officer uses the opportunity of budget time to make contact with all the activities in his department, to drive home to the technical and other staffs the importance of financial control, to co-ordinate financial practices and to bring to the attention of his chief any weaknesses in the department's control of income or expenditure. He will find it advantageous to draw in to the budget discussions as many of those officers who are to have responsibility for spending it as he can. A school caretaker is much more likely to watch his fuel consumption keenly if he feels he has had a say, if only indirect, in deciding the amount which should be allowed to him. Besides, a finance officer following the best practice will build up his budget by aggregation of units each of which is as far as possible identified with an individual.

(3)

It will be useful at this stage to discuss some of the features which a draft revenue budget should *not* exhibit. The first is that of hasty computations unsupported by detail and arithmetically unreliable. Calculations should be agreed between the department and the chief financial officer, so that consideration at later stages can be confined to the underlying policy. Secondly, a good draft budget should be free from unreal assumptions, e.g. over-optimistic estimates of the number of staff likely to be available, or of dates on which loan sanctions are likely to be received, contracts signed or builders set to work. These false assumptions would in any case have to be put right later, when they become confused with policy cuts and cause misunderstanding and possibly ill-feeling. Then there are those deliberate understatements of income or over-statements of expenditure inserted in the hope of creating a hidden 'cushion'. These are bound to come to light and be resented by members. They shake the confidence of the operating committees, the finance committee and the finance department in the department's standard of conduct, especially if the department, having been guilty of the creation of a hidden reserve, later in the year puts forward the 'saving' as a justification for a supplementary estimate on some other head.

(4)

Having considered the officer's work on the draft revenue budget, our next duty is to consider the role of operating committees and their chairmen. There are many ways of associating the members with the budget. Even before the office draft is prepared, the general trend of income and expenditure, and any special features, will have been discussed with the chairman by the head of the department, the chief financial officer also being sometimes present at the discussions. Many chief financial officers use budget time as the occasion for seeing all the chairmen and chief officers in turn, when the opportunity will be taken to discuss not only the draft budget but any other features of the committee's policy or administration having financial significance. In an authority large enough to make it impossible for the chief financial officer to keep in close personal touch with day-to-day affairs, these annual surveys of departmental finances can be particularly valuable features.

Whatever the exact procedure, discussions at a very early stage, between the head of the operating department and his chairman will be the general rule. No general rule governs the next stage, that of consideration of the draft budget. If the local practice is that individual committees do not formally consider their budgets until the members know what the committee's allocation is likely to be, the next step, following the preparation of the draft, is governed by considerations set out later in connexion with the budget of the authority as a whole. If, however, each committee is to make its claim regardless of the probable aggregate position, then the draft budget will probably be presented at this point to the operating committee either by the head of the department or by the chief financial officer or jointly. Attached to the budget should be the statistical data already referred to, and possibly a report calling attention to the salient points.

A report drawn up by a departmental head will tend to emphasize the responsibilities of the department and the need for a more generous allocation of funds from the council. It may even hint that the committee has not been dealt with too liberally in the past. If the report is made by the chief financial officer it is more likely to be devoted to pointing to increases in the allocations the committee has had in previous years, with suggestions that in view of the over-all position the committee should not be too sanguine in its expectations.

A joint report, if submitted, should not be allowed to rob the head of the department of the chance to say what he thinks his department's real requirements are, but a departmental head who makes extravagant statements renders a disservice to his department. He makes it hard for his committee to decide the real merits of the department's claims, and may induce them to put forward inflated estimates, thus exposing them to the risk of the finance committee dealing with their estimates more severely rather than less severely. Experienced chief financial officers know how radically chief officers differ in this respect.

Whether the committee amends the draft or not depends very much on tradition. If it has been carefully compiled in full knowledge of the committee's policies, amendments at committee may well be confined to minor changes. Committees of large authorities, especially counties controlling comprehensive services such as health and education, may refer the estimates to a sub-committee, either in addition to, or in substitution for, examination by the chairman. If the tradition is for this examination to be intensive it may well be that the sub-committee will suggest considerable changes. In general, however, draft estimates are not subject to extensive alteration by operating committees because they are based on prior knowledge of the committee's wishes.

In the smaller authorities the procedure may be more informal than that described above, whilst in the large authorities it may be more elaborate; but whatever the size of the authority the same principles should be applied. In counties with divisional executives or excepted districts, budgets will probably first be presented to the local committees, having been prepared by the local staff in conjunction with the headquarters staff of both the operating department and the finance department. At this stage, the chairman of the local committee or the main committee may or may not be consulted. The effect of local committees is to introduce another stage into the budgetary process rather than to affect the principles.

(5)

A revenue budget is not made by simply collating the draft budgets of the various services. Inevitably departments would like to do more than the council will permit, and the total allocations to departments have to be brought down to the amount the council is prepared to raised by taxation. This pruning process is the duty of the finance committee. To carry it out the members must have all the relevant information in a concise, significant and unbiased form. The supply of this information is an important task of the chief financial officer, calling for his services both as financial adviser and as accountant.

Unlike his colleagues, the heads of the operating departments, the chief financial officer can see the affairs of the authority as a whole. We have noted in earlier chapters how desirable it is for the staff of the finance department to keep abreast of events, to be acquainted with the aspirations and aims of departments and committees, and to be recognised as belonging to a team of officers assisting the council to carry out its policy, and not as unsympathetic critics. It is at budget time that the correct attitudes bear most fruit. A chief financial officer who is known to be impartial, having neither pet services nor pet aversions among the departments, who is both interested in the development of the services and fearless in exposing any departmental manoeuvres designed to take advantage of more scrupulous officers, will carry the confidence of the council and its officers. No member—not even the chairman of the finance committee—can pretend to a detailed knowledge of the council's financial activities, though members should know the trends and the special features.

Chairmen of finance committees and sub-committees, setting out to scrutinize the draft budgets, must start with the chief financial officer's observations, and must depend to a very large extent on his ability to direct their attention to the significant items in the estimates. The chief financial officer's approach must therefore be unimpeachable. His aim must be not merely to assist the council to keep expenditure to the chosen level, but to give proper weight to the merits of the various services, to try to dissuade the council from adopting short-term expedients, to encourage them to keep their buildings, machinery and installations in proper working order, and to discourage them from fluctuating policies, embarrassing both to those who run, and those who use the services. The council will also look to him for advice on acceleration of debt redemption, defrayment of capital expenditure from revenue and like matters.

The chief financial officer has also technical functions in connexion with the aggregate budget—such as computing the rate product, calculating lump-sum provisions covering more than one service, or making allowance for precepts, government grants or allocations to capital and other funds. An integrated financial system is invaluable in budgeting for it makes sure that the estimates of all departments are the product of a pooling of knowledge, that they are compiled on uniform lines, and that the chief financial officer comes to his exacting duty of helping the finance committee in its critical survey of budgets armed with full knowledge about their contents.

(6)

Difficult though the task of the chief financial officer may be, the real anxieties of the final determination of the shape of the budget must fall upon the members in council and committee. They have to make the decisions: the chief financial officer assembles information, makes calculations, and points out possibilities, consequences and trends. We must therefore now proceed to study the aggregate revenue budget from the point of view of the members of the local authority in council and committee. The responsibilities of the finance committee are described in general terms below, and the actual procedure is discussed in the next section.

Even where substantial agreement is reached between committees through budget conferences, the operation of the machinery of the political parties or otherwise, there may still be residual differences of opinion at a late stage in the budget making. One committee will not agree to the reductions the finance committee suggests, another reluctantly agrees but wishes to call attention to the frustrating effect of curtailing its allocation, and a third contends that the proposed allocation is contrary to the council's declared policy. In any case small gaps remain to be bridged, even after sacrifices have been made and substantial agreement reached. The finance committee, upon whom falls the task of trying to reduce these disharmonies to the minimum, has thus to contend with many prickly questions of policy.

In addition there are other aspects of the global figures to be considered. The amount of work visualized in the budget as a whole may need adjustment because it exceeds the capacity of the engineering, architectural, direct labour, or other departments providing common services; there may be inconsistencies of view between committees about standards of building maintenance, making allocations to renewals funds and so forth. The amounts of working capital and contingency provision have to be determined; allowance must be made for surpluses or deficiences brought forward from previous years; and the finance committee may have to consider the effects of alternative policies, e.g. an increased rate of sixpence as compared with one of a shilling.

All in all then, it is not surprising that budget making looms large both in the public eye and in the administration, or that there are many ways of setting about the final stages. Local practice is governed by deeply entrenched traditions, the result of the interplay of personalities and parties in the past, and often the process of arriving at a consensus of opinion is informal and defies close analysis. To attempt to lay down general rules is more difficult than for the largely administrative work of making the draft budget. Complex matters of this kind are not so susceptible to radical reform as are administrative or technical practices. None the less there are some fundamentals to be borne in mind by all authorities, and some precautions they can ignore only at their peril. They are set out below.

(7)

If the custom is for the operating committee to pass forward draft budgets adjusted to conform with a policy already informally determined, the aggregation stage is confined to minor tidying up, technical adjustments and the resolution of the odd outstanding dispute. The discipline and restraint between committees required to achieve these advance informal understandings are easier to achieve in a small authority because members will be acquainted with the business of all the committees: they may 'sit in' at the meetings of committees other than their own. Some small authorities are even able to supply all the members of the authority with the draft estimates for all departments before any of them are presented to a committee. Whatever the exact procedure, before the members can have an idea of their policy, the draft aggregate estimates must have been brought together by the chief financial officer and discussed with his chairman, and perhaps other leading members, in sufficient detail for a provisional decision on the rate level to have been made, by either tacit understanding or informal discussion. Having informally studied the picture as a whole, the members may feel that there should be no change in the rate poundage, that one is inevitable or that it should be restricted to a prescribed figure; they may feel themselves pledged to make a reduction, or perhaps to spend more on some kind of service than another, e.g. a public scare during the year about an infectious disease may make it politic to increase expenditure on cleaning of waterways. All the influences must of course have crystallized sufficiently for the members to have an idea of their rate fixing policy. Much the same results can be achieved by party discipline, the leaders of either the majority party or of all parties, conferring and coming to tentative conclusions which the members are expected to honour in committee. All these variations have their difficulties: in particular they imply that the decision, being based on provisional and informal discussions, is only a broad conclusion and may require modification. The larger the authority and the greater its range of activities, the more difficult it is for these informal arrangements to be worked satisfactorily, and the more necessary a formal procedure becomes, although, as we shall see, the effective decision will always be taken, subject to the council's ratification, by the 'Ruling Few'.

In those local authorities—and they are in the majority—where the alternative course is pursued (i.e. where the operating committees present to the finance committee estimates of the kind which in the ordinary run of events will have to be pruned), the first stage in the reduction may be intensive study of the draft estimates by the chairman of the finance committee in conjunction with the chief financial officer. Having come to some provisional conclusion, the chairman may then leave the chief financial officer to discuss with the heads of departments ways of bringing the estimates down to the level he has in mind. He may himself consult the other chairmen or he may leave the chief officers of the departments to draw in their chairmen at the appropriate stage. Local authorities differ in their willingness to allow chief officers to 'negotiate' reductions in draft estimates. Whatever the procedure the effect of any proposed cuts must be worked out in some detail, so that the officers, and later the committees, can visualize the effect on the services. Some authorities assign this role of detailed examination to a sub-committee, instead of to the chairman.

In due course, a recommendation will be presented to the finance committee either by the chairman or by a sub-committee. Subsequent procedure differs between authorities. Some finance committees make a recommendation to council without further consultation with the operating committees, and may have virtual power to amend departmental estimates without further ado. They may even omit much of the preliminary 'missionary' work designed to induce departments, and hence committees, to accept reductions. Other finance committees call together the chairmen of the committees or send the estimates back to committees for reconsideration, with or without the finance committee chairman as a persuading or cajoling agent. Unresolved differences would then be reported to council.

Such divergencies of opinion do in fact occur from time to time; so do occasions when a council makes alterations in its finance committee's allocations. But alterations of any kind must in practice be few and confined to principle. A budget is a complex instrument and for a council to meddle in detail with the allocations would bring chaos to the administration. All councils have to accept the fact that, whatever the procedure, however great the opportunities for consultations, however sincere the willingness to compromise, the effective decisions about budgeting will in the end be made by a few influential persons—normally the finance committee—making firm recommendations which are unlikely to be upset. There is in every organization a limit beyond which attempts to secure compromise by discussion and persuasion cannot be taken: a decision has to be made, and the finance committee must be sufficiently in touch with feeling in the council to be able to anticipate its view. Party discipline may help, and may give those who make the recommendations a sharper appreciation of the council's wishes, but it cannot relieve them of their responsibility.

(8)

This chapter being concerned with the compiling of a budget and not with its contents, it would be inappropriate to consider the amount of contingency allowances, the calculation of working balances and similar matters. Nor would it be relevant to discuss the techniques of retrenchment. It is however within our subject matter to consider the administrative implications of different ways of making reductions in draft budgets. The finance committee may decide to recommend the council to impose a percentage reduction in some item of expenditure, e.g. ten per cent off printing and stationery, or to halt all expansions of staff; they may 'freeze' services at their existing level; they may make an over-all percentage reduction in the allocation to committees; they may make lump sum cuts in allocations, leaving the details to be determined by the committees themselves, or they may examine the operations of committees and themselves suggest where the savings could be made. The budgeting procedure should be such that whatever method the committee adopt, the relevant information is available. Thus, as was mentioned earlier, a subjective analysis of expenditure will at once show the effect of a percentage reduction in printing and stationery and a properly arranged timetable, allowing adequate time at each stage, will make either lump sum or detailed cuts equally feasible. No local authority should be forced by inadequate machinery into rough and ready means of adjusting its budget.

Sound budgetary procedure does much towards the making of a good budget, and in particular it enables the authority to avoid acting in ignorance and protects it from unwittingly prejudicing a service. Further, if the finance committee have readily available detailed knowledge of departmental activities, even lump sum reductions will not be made blindly, but with some knowledge of the ways in which the departments could effect the adjustments. This is a good feature, for lump sum cuts, not based on the knowledge that they are practicable, or put forward without appreciation of their effects on the services, are incompatible with the theory of the members' acquaintance with administration upon which local government is based.

There is, however, an important proviso to the contention that the finance committee should be able to indicate where the savings can be made: the last word on the distribution of the money should be with the individual committees, subject to their proposals being in accord with the council's policy and budgetary practices: the finance committee may or may not wish to suggest possible items of reduction, but they should not be in a position to dictate, or even to induce the council to override the judgment of the operating committees on the distribution of their allocation. However, once the committee has decided how the money should be spent, then the budget should be made on that basis, and any later alterations should rank as a modification of the budget. To allow committees to suspend a decision about the use of the funds allowed by the council would be to defeat one of the aims of the budget, i.e. that it is an approved plan of action.

(9)

One day in March or early April (later in Scottish authorities as is explained in the next section) the chairman of the finance committee presents the budget to the council. In about half of the counties and a third of the county boroughs the meeting will have been called specifically to settle the rate.[1] The recommendations presented by the chairman will have been discussed, formally or informally, between the chairmen and often between committees, and a document embodying the recommendation will have been in the hands of the members some days before the council meeting. Budget day itself therefore is unlikely to be news. In local government the moment of surprise in budget making takes place earlier when the press find out the nature of the proposal to be made by the finance committee. Up to the time that the finance committee decides upon a policy its deliberations are confidential, though inevitably matters for speculation and conjecture among the public.

Whether the documents circulated to the members in advance of budget day contain all the supporting detail will depend upon the practice of the authority. Some authorities preface recommendations and resolutions to be put to the council with full explanations on the lines discussed in the last chapter: others give bare details. If the facts and figures have not been included in papers sent out before the meeting, the chairman has to give them in his speech, thus making his budget speech more detailed—and inevitably heavier—than it otherwise might have been. In any case, the budget speech will not only lack the element of surprise which gives drama to budget day in parliament, it will also lack variety.

The chairman of a finance committee cannot ring changes between a number of different taxes. He has only one tax—the local rate—and all he can do is to lower or raise the rate—usually by a few pence in the pound. Budget day in the town hall has therefore little of the glamour of budget day in the House of Commons. But it is an important occasion, if only because it is the only time when the council's attention is directed to its activities as a whole—or nearly as a whole, for trading undertakings do not always prepare budgets.

There may be an element of excitement if the budget is presented

[1] *The Use of the Revenue Budget as a means of Financial Control* (Institute of Municipal Treasurers and Accountants, 1954), p. 33.

with differences of opinion between the finance and some other committee or committees still unresolved. Whilst the right of any committee to make its views felt in the council itself must be preserved, regular disagreements at the final stage of the budget making would suggest defects in the arrangements of the local authority or in the spirit in which they operate. In practice the recommendations of finance committees are rarely upset, most divergencies of opinion between committees having been adjusted beforehand. Motions by individuals to alter the recommendations, unsupported by committees or caucuses, are even less likely to be successful than attempts by dissatisfied committees, though there is nothing to prevent a member from submitting proposals for increasing or decreasing the proposed rate, or for altering the distribution providing he follows the procedure laid down in the standing orders.

Budget speeches differ markedly. Chairmen may look to the chief financial officer to supply the data for the speech; occasionally they may expect the chief financial officer to draft part of it. Most chairmen, however, by the time budget day arrives have a working knowledge of the current financial position, and expect the chief financial officer to supply technical details only, though a chief financial officer who is on the right terms with his chairman may be able to offer helpful suggestions.

By one means or another, on budget day the council must be given a clear bird's-eye view of its financial position. Working balances, contingencies, the trend of expenditure and income, the state of renewal and capital funds, the effect of current economic conditions (e.g. interest rates), the impact of central government policy, such as alterations in the basis of grants in aid, impending legislative changes —all these need to be touched upon either in the chairman's speech or in the documents. Many chairmen strike a constructive attitude by dwelling on the improvements in the services and the administration made possible by the budget. A still more familiar note in budget speeches is the reminder to committees that the estimates allow little elbow-room for supplementary estimates.

(10)

As we have seen in Scotland, unlike England, there are more detailed statutory regulations governing budget procedure. These provisions are based on the principles already discussed and commended here. Of themselves they do not suggest radical differences in the Scottish and English approach to budgeting, except that the existence of statutory provisions in Scotland should ensure a higher minimum standard of good budgeting in every authority. In fact, however, Scottish practice has features of its own. The financial year ends on May 15, but the new rate is not levied until July or August, the authority financing itself in the meantime from working balances or bank overdraft. During this interval, expenditure on existing services, and even on new services, is incurred on the strength of draft estimates.

A second peculiarity is the practice among some of the larger authorities of 'double consideration of the budget'. The following short description of the way the method works in Edinburgh can be taken as typical. Departments compile draft estimates in February and March, submitting them to operating committees for approval. They are considered by an experienced sub-committee of the finance committee. The sub-committee holds meetings with representatives of the operating committees and their officials, and usually manages to secure agreement to the total allocations before the budget is submitted to the full finance committee. The budget, still considered as a preliminary budget, is then presented to the council who debate it and send it back to the committees for reconsideration. The final budget then passes again through the same stages as the preliminary budget, amendments to the original figures being made in the light of any instructions given by the council, of the fuller knowledge of the outcome of the accounts for the previous year, and of any changes in prices or other conditions. Major policy questions are settled at the time of the preliminary budget.

What are the merits of this procedure? Some disadvantages are obvious, such as the laborious process, and the inevitable (expensive) delay in levying the rate. But it has its advantages, summarized by Sir John Imrie, former City Chamberlain of Edinburgh, as follows: 'The system may look cumbersome, but it is not so in practice. It has many advantages, the principal being that in single chamber assemblies, such as Town Councils are, an opportunity occurs for thinking again and for giving the ratepayers a chance to make any observations to their Town Councillors if they so wish. It is found that advantage is not infrequently taken of this opportunity through the medium of the columns of the local press. All that has been written, however, emphasizes another budgetary requirement— that the financial plan of local activities should be carefully prepared, carefully reviewed and receive the utmost publicity as the ratepayers are directly concerned.'[1] This detailed consideration, with its opportunities for public discussion and second thoughts on the part of the members, does at least do something to answer the charge that the fusion of legislative and executive functions in one body implies an absence of independent criticism.

(11)

A final aspect of revenue budget-making calling for consideration is that of budgets for the trading undertakings of local authorities: the two public utilities remaining with them—passenger transport and water—and miscellaneous trading activities such as catering or entertainments. Some authorities treat the water undertaking as part of the rate fund for budgetary purposes, but in general local authorities do not bring any of these undertakings into the annual rate fund budgetary procedure, for they are self-supporting, and their finances can be left out of consideration when the rate is fixed. If they need rate subsidy—normally a temporary phenomenon—this is often given in arrear on the basis of closed accounts, losses being temporarily carried forward, so that for rate-making purposes local authorities may not need budgets even for those undertakings expected to make a loss. Neither are annual budgets for trading undertakings at present regarded by local authorities as necessary to authorize expenditure in the same way as they are for non-trading concerns financed from an annually determined tax.

Budgeting is, of course, used to help in the determination of policy, but it is not annual budgeting of the kind discussed earlier in this chapter. Forecasts of the income and expenditure of a water undertaking are the basis of applications to Parliament for powers to carry out large-scale water works, settlement of long-term development plans, applications to vary charges, the management of renewals and reserve funds, arrangements for renewal of equipment, and the fixing of tariff policy. Similarly, transport undertakings should not embark upon renewals or extensions of a fleet of buses without the guidance of a long-term budget, and they are compelled to submit forecasts for at least two years ahead whenever they make applications to the traffic commissioners for permission to alter fares. All these are, however, budgets prepared irregularly for specific purposes. Their

[1] *Budgeting in Theory and Practice* by J. D. (now Sir John) Imrie (Students' Society lecture, Institute of Municipal Treasurers and Accountants, 1948-9 Session), p. 239.

weaknesses are that, not being part of a regular routine, they are most likely to be compiled in a rough-and-ready fashion, and may not be produced when they should be, e.g. a transport undertaking may well be tempted to introduce new routes, or build a garage, without the careful attention to profitability which the existence of regular budgets would induce.

This is, however, only the beginning of the matter, for modern industrial practice is to use budgets for other purposes besides the making of forecasts upon which policy can be made. They are employed (*a*) for setting up standards by which in the short run, performances can be critically compared with the intention: and (*b*) for authorizing fixed or standing charges which do not vary except, over a long period, with output. Both these features are relevant to the trading undertakings of local authorities in varying degrees. For instance, a catering or entertainment establishment, after considering the probable demand on different patterns of charge, decides the policy which appears to be most remunerative, e.g. in the case of a catering undertaking the style and price of meals to be provided, or in an entertainment establishment the type of show and the charges to be made.

A budget can then be constructed showing both income and expenditure, performance being regularly compared with estimates. Divergencies would be investigated, appropriate action taken, and if necessary the budget adjusted. By comparing results with predetermined standards, the efficiency of a catering undertaking can be gauged by such measures as the ratio of the various kinds of costs—wages, food, etc.—to the total costs and to the income. A water undertaking, which normally is more stable, will have less use for these dynamic techniques, known to industry as 'flexible budgeting'. On the other hand it should find an annual budget invaluable for authorizing expenditure, as in the case of rate fund services, much of which is relatively fixed. In such an undertaking it is in practice the only way of ensuring that item by item the expenses are regularly examined and the chief officer's mandate for continuing or varying them conferred. A distinction should be made between so called 'fixed' charges and those which should vary directly with the output. In settled undertakings, such as water, the annual budgets would have many of the characteristics of a rate fund undertaking because so many of the expenses are relatively stable, but this should not prevent the constant scrutiny of individual items from the point of view of profitability.

The annual budget would be the occasion for a critical examination of all expenses, any tendencies of overheads to increase in proportion to the whole expenditure being noted and, where possible, checked. Overhead charges may need to be varied during the year if there is a marked change in output. Otherwise they should be regarded as the ceiling till the next budget, applications to engage additional staff or incur other increased expenditure not being entertained during the period of the budget. The remark often heard, that it is easier for a trading undertaking to secure extra staff or better buildings than the rate fund services is illuminating. A budget is also useful in helping an authority to determine what capital expenditure can be met from revenue. An unwise or erratic policy in this respect can have disconcerting effects on tariff policies.

The case the author put forward in 1936 in 'Local Authorities: Internal Financial Control' for a re-examination of the attitude of local authorities to budgets for trading undertakings has now become even stronger, because of the improvements in budgeting techniques in other comparable concerns. All the nationalized industries, for example, make extensive use of budgets. Local authorities too should employ trading budgets not only to help them settle long-term policy, but also to assist in adapting short-term policy to current circumstances, to lay down standards of cost and to gauge the extent to which the standards have been adhered to. It is not sound administration to depend on the preparation of occasional budgets for specific purposes. Still less should an authority look only to the evidence of closed accounts for its financial management data.

CHAPTER XXI

ADMINISTERING THE BUDGET

(1)

A BUDGET is a plan of action made at the beginning of a financial year. Whether the plan materializes or not depends on control of the day-to-day operations and ultimately upon the committees to whom they are responsible. Our next task is therefore to study the ways of preparing and using statements comparing performance with intention. As in other aspects of our subject, a distinction has to be made between the needs of committees and those of officers. The former have a watching brief: they are concerned to know if all is well. If it is, they need trouble no further. The latter—the officials—need an administrator's tool. Thus it is sufficient for the libraries committee to know that the librarian is keeping within his estimates, but the librarian himself must know, before he places each order for books, that by so doing he is not likely to overrun his estimates by the end of the year.

In a well-run authority where confidence exists between members and officers, there is much to be said for reporting to committees during the year only material deviations from the estimates. The committee can then concentrate on what is or may become adrift, and as to the departments, the mere suggestion that such a report is imminent will often induce remedial efforts. Committees working on this plan month by month may also demand a comprehensive statement on a positive basis once or more during the course of the year, and finance committees will expect to be kept in touch with the trend of expenditure of the authority as a whole, if only as a guide to the scope for granting of supplementary estimates without total overspending. But few authorities would go to the length of compiling a comprehensive statement every month showing the aggregate position.

(2)

Departments need statements different from those submitted to the committees and council. First of all, information has to be supplied much more promptly, for it is compiled to influence the actions of those responsible for incurring the liabilities. They want to know how they stand *before* they issue an order or engage an employee. Secondly the statements must be in greater detail. Local authority budgetary control is mainly achieved by matching the expenditure and income item by item against the estimates. Departmental statements must therefore be 'broken down' not only into the detailed estimate heads shown in the budget but often into still greater detail. The budget will set out the expenditure on supplies to primary schools in one heading, but the education department will exercise control school by school, and the headteacher item by item. Many items will be controlled partly by the monetary allocation, partly by cumulative 'man hour' statements, and partly by physical quantities. For some items, simple control of the quantities will be the main method used, and if a manpower budget has been prepared, it will be found to be invaluable for making comparisons during the year, especially if it is comprehensive and has been expressed in man hours where that measure is appropriate. The information has not only to be sorted down to the detailed estimate heads but also to be brought home to the persons responsible. The estimate for each school, for instance, will be divided into those heads for which the headteacher is entirely responsible, and those such as heating, for which the caretaker has to take prime responsibility. Also, the statements have to be considered together with costing and other types of financial data. For instance, the expenditure for repairs to school meals vehicles to date has to be interpreted in conjunction with statements showing the cost of individual vehicles. Some expenditure, e.g. that on school meals themselves, will be controlled more on the strength of costing information than on statements showing expenditure against estimate. This applies especially to items lending themselves to unit costing control.

The practical problems can be summarized under two heads. First, that of the statements themselves: what should be the contents of these statements? How should they be produced? How frequently are they needed? Secondly, what means are there of ensuring that they are heeded?

(3)

How should statements be compiled? Practically all accounts of local authorities being of income and expenditure and not of receipts and payments, the budget will be on this basis too. Accounts and budget will, as we have already seen, follow the same pattern of analysis, though the budget might be in more or less—usually more —detail. The problem then is to produce interim figures of expenditure. This is a more roundabout task than might be imagined because, although the final accounts are on the basis of income and expenditure, most chief financial officers keep their accounts throughout the year on a cash basis, and convert them at the end of the year by the addition of liabilities and accrued income. Items passing through stores and credit income are the main exceptions. Cash accounts can be converted into expenditure accounts at any time by rule of thumb methods, e.g. by adding a sum which is known by experience to represent approximately the liabilities incurred but not discharged at the date to which the statement relates. The results of this somewhat crude process are often found to be more satisfactory than might be imagined. Alternatively the value of the outstanding liabilities can be ascertained by the evaluation of the invoices or delivery notes for goods delivered but not paid for.

But there is a further step. Adequate control of some kinds of expenditure requires not only liabilities, but also commitments to be taken into consideration. To control the cost of repairs to buildings for instance, the value of the work commissioned must be known as well as the value of the work executed. In England, the general practice is not to enter these commitments in the books of account of local authorities as is done in many American and Canadian cities.[1] They have to be added as a memorandum to the expenditure statements. An authority keeping its ledgers on a cash basis (the usual method) would thus, in effect, have to add both liabilities and commitments to arrive at complete figures. Few authorities go to the length of converting comparative statements into complete commitment statements, but the officers of all authorities *must* have the complete figures for some items, usually those for which there is a lump sum provision covering many individual transactions which could be spent at any time during the year—e.g. purchase of library books, school supplies or the repairs of buildings.

In deciding the basis of the statements, one can thus be selective, using the most elaborate method, that of commitments, only for a small minority of items. The selective approach can be carried further, because some items can be controlled on physical quantities, whilst, as has already been mentioned, others—schools meals is the

[1] The author found when visiting North America in 1954 that local authorities there were divided on the value of the practice.

outstanding example—lend themselves best to control by a costing system, related to the budget but not really part of it. There is therefore little point in sticking slavishly to exhaustive statements showing the comparison between 'estimate' and 'actual' item by item.

If all expenditure and income were spread equally over the year, a simple proportional sum would suffice to indicate whether performance to date is in line with the plan. The position is in fact very different. Local expenditure consists of four classes: (a) expenditure which takes place regularly each week or month; (b) that which is made at longer intervals, e.g. quarterly half-yearly or annually, such as taxes, rates or rents; (c) seasonal expenditure—a large class including lighting and heating, costs of bathing establishments, roads resurfacing and many others; (d) expenditure of irregular incidence, e.g. purchase of police uniforms. Akin to class (d) are such items as provisions for contingencies, claims for compensation under planning legislation, snow removal expenses, or grants from county councils to rural districts for sewerage and water schemes. Expenditure on these may not materialize at all.

To show the expenditure to date side by side with a proportion of the estimate computed on a simple time basis is only significant for the first class of items. The others require more elaborate treatment if the statement is to be more than a rough guide. Class (b), which consists of fixed liabilities, can be dealt with most simply by using the proportion of the estimates to date and ignoring the actual expenditure, unless it is likely to differ from the estimate for the year, in which case a new figure would be calculated. Class (c)—seasonal expenditure—is more difficult, but can be dealt with in several ways, the most satisfactory being to compute from past years' experience what proportion would normally have been spent at the date of statement and to show this figure against the actual expenditure. For class (d)—irregular expenditure—there is no perfect solution though sometimes the transactions can be itemized and watched individually. A practice in vogue in some authorities is to exclude items from both columns until there is some expenditure, and then to regard the amount spent as both the appropriate part of the estimate and the expenditure, i.e. to insert the same figure in both columns.

Most chief financial officers are unwilling to take any method to its logical conclusion and there are many compromises in operation, the size of the local authority being the main determining factor. Whatever the method of production, statements should be in a form suitable to the recipient, e.g. a school caretaker should not be expected to wade through a complicated accounting tabulation to find out his heating and lighting costs: the relevant figures must be abstracted and set out in simple form.

(4)

The statements will normally be produced by the chief financial officer as part of his accounting service to the departments, though the task of converting the initial cash statements into income and expenditure or commitments statements, may fall on the departments who usually have the data available. Alternatively the chief financial officer may add the commitments from information supplied by the departments, probably through the medium of copy-orders. Any part of the work done by a department would be done in a manner agreed with the finance department, and would form part of the official records. The developments of machine accounting makes the production of comparative data easier, and the tendency will be for chief financial officers to be called upon to produce much more in the future.

Then there is the question of the frequency of the statements. Elaborate analysis of the kind under discussion is expensive to produce. The local authority should therefore be selective in deciding the frequency of production. Some items, e.g. wages in an engineering, cleansing or parks department, may warrant daily or weekly statements, whilst quarterly information may suffice for rents, rates and taxes. In practice, to avoid a complicated differentiation between items, local authorities usually select a very few items for weekly comparison and put the rest on a monthly, or less frequent treatment. Items of irregular incidence which are put on a simple memorandum commitments basis, will in effect be controlled transaction by transaction, and the periodical statements will merely be the opportunity for an overriding scrutiny. Statements for those trading undertakings using the flexible budgeting technique described in the last chapter fall into a special category as the budget serves in the main as the pointer to changes in policy. They will probably be called for monthly.

Finally there is the problem of the use of the statements. One of the principles of financial administration advocated throughout this book is that of laying upon departments a clear responsibility for the control of their own income and expenditure. Among the obligations thus laid upon the head of a department, none is more important, or indeed more specific than that of strict compliance with the budget. The main purposes of budgeting statements produced during the year will therefore be to help the heads of departments to carry out their responsibilities, to help to instil in officers responsible for expenditure a proper awareness of budgetary procedure, and to overcome the lukewarm attitude to financial data sometimes found in local government. The chief financial officer has not only to put the statements in the hands of the right people at the right time, but also to try to ensure that the staff understand them and are interested in applying the lessons they show, for the real control is always in the system and not in the form or contents of statements. He himself can exercise only a watching brief, and even the heads of departments are largely in the hands of their subordinates.

A departmental finance officer can be invaluable in the control of expenditure. He knows the department and its staff and at the same time understands the financial implications. Comparative statements should pass through him to the spending officers, and he should have the means of ensuring that the lessons of the statements are regarded. He will himself watch the over-all position in the department, call the attention of the head of his department to any untoward features, and take the initiative in reporting to committee matters needing their attention, e.g. likely overspendings. He will also act as the link with the chief financial officer's accountancy or financial control staff who will be watching events from the side lines. As the intermediary between the chief financial officer and the spending officers, the departmental finance officer must insist that the information is presented to the latter in a form that they understand: it is he who must protect the caretaker against being overwhelmed with abstruse or irrelevant data.

Given the prompt supply of significant information in suitable form, together with some training and encouragement, technical staffs, foremen and others at ground level can achieve remarkable feats of budgetary control. A highway superintendent who watches his road surfacing expenditure by means of graphs constructed to allow for seasonal variations in expenditure, a school caretaker who carefully charts the variations of his daily fuel consumption from his allowance, and the superintendent of a children's home who always knows his provision costs to date, are examples of what can be achieved.

301

(5)

In determining how far to go with the preparation of data of the kind under discussion, common sense must be the guiding rule. It is never easy to determine the precise point where the trouble and expense of preparing data ceases to be compensated by economies, and not uncommon to find comprehensive schemes abandoned in favour of simple, sometimes almost rule of thumb, arrangements. In any case the scale of operations has to be borne constantly in mind. Even within a sizeable health department, for instance, it may not be worth while to break down the records of expenditure of such activities as clinics or day nurseries to individual establishments except for a narrow range of selected items such as food purchases. The remainder of items will normally continue at an even rate, and there will probably be sufficient control if the estimates are watched for the service as a whole, providing such simple administrative controls as keeping records of fuel consumption on the spot are in operation. Any wrong tendency will probably emerge from general observation, and the harm done by a matron occasionally kicking over the traces may be less costly than an over-elaborate set of records.

If in a small authority the departments have such close personal knowledge that they are capable of administering their budgets without documentary help, there is no justification for comparative statements. Similarly, in a larger authority, a chief financial officer might well decide to give more attention to those services where budgetary control is defective; and in any authority there is little point in preparing statements unless they are to be used. The fact that even within a single authority the policy about the production of statements is apt to be varied from time to time, suggests how difficult it may be to come to a conclusion. Finally, the use of these statements has to be considered in conjunction with that of other financial records of which there will be a number. For instance, an engineer will need, in addition to information about the progress of expenditure compared with his budget, many statements outside the scope of this chapter—job costs, plant accounts, idle time of plant, progress of capital works, rate of absorption of overheads on rechargeable works and so forth.

302

(6)

A local authority budget is not a device for raising, on hit-and-miss principles, sufficient taxation to maintain the services for a year or half-year. It is a plan, worked out in considerable detail, for stable local services, and a local authority should have little difficulty in constructing a workable budget which can, and will, be adhered to. But though services normally run evenly, there will be unforeseen items such as snowstorms, floods, litigation and very occasionally new expenditure imposed during the year by legislation or even by public opinion. For instance, a street accident may bring an irresistible outcry for road works not in the budget. There may be wages awards, increases in prices, and variations in interest rates to contend with—all items beyond the control of the authority. Moreover, there will be some miscalculations for 'Fallibility must attend calculations which range over sixteen months in advance'.[1] There will thus be deviations, though they should be only marginal. For this reason every well-administered authority makes provisions for supplementary estimates and *virement*, on the lines of those operating in the central government, and if they are wise the members treat them as serious matters.

In Scotland, the law affords some small guidance, for the Local Government (Scotland) Act, 1947, provides that expenditure outside the estimates shall not be incurred unless specifically authorized by the council itself, after a report by the finance committee, but expenditure to meet emergencies can be incurred subject to subsequent report to the finance committee and ultimately to the council. There is also a provision to cover continuing expenditure prior to the making of the rate. The Education (Scotland) Act, 1946, refers specifically to supplementary estimates, and provides that savings under one head may not be used to defray expenditure under another without the consent of the authority. In England the machinery of control during the course of the year is at the discretion of each local authority.

Supplementary estimates brought about by tendencies affecting the departments as a whole—rising prices, wage awards, etc.—are often initiated by the chief financial officer. But other applications will normally come from departments and will be subject to much the same procedure as the original estimates—discussion within the

[1] May's *Parliamentary Practice*, 12th edition, p. 452.

department and with the chief financial officer's staff (who may be able to give an indication whether they are likely to be accepted by the finance committee), submission to the operating committee, approval by the finance committee and finally ratification by the council. There will be local variations; thus some finance committees have power to approve without submission to council, and in many authorities, either by prescription or tradition, small sums can be agreed to by the chief financial officer. To concentrate the attention of the committees on the items of significant size is a good practice because it not only saves time but helps to establish supplementary estimates as matters of consequence. No applications coming before the finance committee are more difficult to consider equitably than supplementary estimates, chiefly because they come before the committee piecemeal at different times of the year, thus making it impossible to judge their relative merits. Moreover, they may not always be judged in the same atmosphere; an application for a supplementary estimate may well have an easier passage in July than in October, when the council is becoming conscious again of the problem of rate fixing. On this topic the remarks of Hilton Young can hardly be bettered. He said:

'Because of the long forecast that has to be made in preparing the estimates, Supplementary Estimates may often be a necessity, but they are always a necessary evil. The House and taxpayer have the right to expect that the estimates and the scheme of the Budget shall be rigidly adhered to by those who have to administer them. Public control of public expenditure depends for its efficiency in large measure on the financial scheme for the year being presented to the House and considered and approved once and for all and as a whole. To allow the scheme, once approved, to be treated as something still fluid and liable to extensive modifications must infinitely weaken effective control, and Supplementary Estimates are the most harmful way of doing so. To make anything but the most restricted use of them must deprive the whole system of supply of its meaning and utility. Whilst admitting, therefore, that they are occasionally necessary in the case of emergencies unforeseen and unforeseeable, we should remember that they are always harmful. They are a diseased excrescence on the year's finance, and the success in finance of the Ministry may be measured by their ability to do without them.'[1]

[1] Extract from *The System of National Finance* by E. Hilton Young (John Murray, 1924), p. 76.

Supplementary estimates fall into five classes: (a) unavoidable new expenditure—emergencies, unexpected engineering obstacles, calamities, duties imposed on the authority by statute during the year and so forth; (b) applications because of increased costs beyond the control of the authority, such as rising prices or wage awards; (c) genuine oversights; (d) attempts to secure reinstatements of items deleted at budget time; (e) fads, fancies and afterthoughts of members or officers. In judging the strength of the applications, a finance committee would be more sympathetic to items falling under (a), (b) or (c). Indeed some of these items may be inescapable. But, in the main, applications should be resisted, for supplementary estimates disturb the balance of the finances, and at the same time help to weaken the financial discipline. Some authorities decline to make a specific contingency provision on the grounds that it encourages supplementaries, and that any genuinely unavoidable extra expenditure should be met out of incidental 'savings'. This leads naturally to the second piece of machinery for modification of the budget—*virement*.

(7)

'*Virement*' means the transfer of monies between headings, so that over-expenditure on one head is met either by under-expenditure on another, or from increased income. The tradition of meticulous calculation of the original figures leaves only a limited scope for this exercise, but there will always be some opportunity for it. and most local authorities allow *virement* either formally or informally. But it would be dangerous to allow departments or operating committees to carry out *virement* without requiring approval, because encouragement would be given to the creation of hidden cushions with the intention of diverting the excess provision to other purposes. Often the chief financial officer has power to agree to the smaller items, whilst the larger are submitted to the finance committee and sometimes also require ratification by the council.

In the central government the Treasury do not regard 'savings on sub-heads which are largely unrelated to the general run of the Vote' as available to meet excesses elsewhere on the vote.[1] A local authority likewise can rarely afford to allow fortuitous savings—let alone deliberately created surpluses—to be used for other items in a departmental budget. These windfalls are usually needed to cover un-

[1] *Fourth Report from Public Accounts Committee, 1950–1, H.C.* 241, para. 11.

avoidable overspendings in the local authority as a whole. Besides, to allow them to be transferred to other items would be to open a wide door to manipulation of the budget. But savings brought about by a department's own good management and economy are in a different category. The local authority may well be more liberal in its attitude to these, not only because they are a convenient and unexceptional way of finding the money for additional expenditure, but because they offer a financial incentive to efficiency. Local authorities should take advantage of incentives of this kind, which are unhappily few in local government. Naturally the attitude of local authorities to both supplementary estimates and *virement* will vary with the current financial position. In times of stringency they will tend to be less sympathetic and may have to decline applications which in happier days might well succeed.

(8)

An interesting feature of the budgetary system of the central government is the Select Committee on Estimates. This committee, established on the recommendation of the Select Committee on National Expenditure (1918), examines each year a group of departmental estimates, and reports to the House of Commons if any economies consistent with the policy implied in the estimates can be effected. The committee is composed of Members of Parliament and reflects the political constitution of the House.

Is there room for such a committee in local authorities? Or for an equivalent of the Select Committee on Public Accounts which, with the aid of the Comptroller and Auditor General, examines the Appropriation Accounts, calls for witnesses, and makes reports going beyond mere accounting matters into the realms of policy, purchasing techniques and so forth?

There are notable differences between the central government and local authorities, and arguments based on these differences can readily be adduced against a local estimate or public accounts committee. The central government committees are a check by the House on the government. In local government there is no separate 'government', for as we have seen in earlier chapters, the council both evolves policy and supervises its execution. If such committees were established in local government, the members would be, at least in theory, scrutinizing their own actions. Not only would the enquiry lack independence, but the members would in fact be purporting to examine something with which they are—or should be—familiar. But the possibilities of this type of committee should not be cast aside too lightly. The absence of any systematic examination of departmental activities, on the basis of either estimates or closed accounts, is certainly a weakness. Departmental estimates are normally brought into critical focus only when the authority is seeking to confine its rate within a prescribed limit or at periods when there is a cry for economy. Scrutiny, if it takes place at all, is thus spasmodic, and may be haphazard. Departmental estimates and accounts may well escape close examination by the members for decades, provided the services run smoothly or are not accidentally brought into the public limelight. In a small authority, over-provision or over-lapping of services and elaborate administration may well be noticed by the members. But in a larger authority members could hardly claim that such scrutiny as they can give in the ordinary course of their duties is an effective substitute for systematic enquiry. The theory that members supervise administration must only be applied in a broad sense : if there is no separate 'executive' there is certainly an 'administration' to be watched. Finally, the impossibility of instituting a truly independent enquiry, so far from supporting the case against the type of committee under consideration, might well be regarded as a point in favour, on the grounds that the concentration of responsibility in the hands of members has its dangers. Enquiries which cannot in the nature of things be completely objective are surely better than no enquiries at all.

The present author commended the idea of such committees in 'Local Authorities: Internal Financial Control' in 1936. Further support was given to the idea by the IMTA Research group in 1954, who recommended that the committee's enquiries should extend to the staffing and organization of the departments and the practices of the authority in such matters as financial administration, methods of tendering and the distribution of duties between departments.[1] The group thought that notwithstanding the absence of a central executive, or of an official comparable to the Comptroller and Auditor General, a public accounts committee in local government could do valuable work because the members with their close knowledge of the local administration would be able to initiate enquiries.

The spread of organization and methods investigations is gradually accustoming local authorities to the idea of self criticism. Is it

[1] *The Use of the Revenue Budget as a means of Financial Control* (Institute of Municipal Treasurers and Accountants, 1954), pp. 57–8.

therefore too much to hope that serious consideration may be given to the establishment of estimates committees or accounts committees? It would be unwise to expect a sudden widespread use of such committees and equally unrealistic to expect them to make dramatic discoveries or yield drastic savings. Indeed one condition of success would be the recognition that they would be an imperfect device, hampered by the nature of local authority organization and liable to be misunderstood. Their proceedings might also attract premature publicity which would make it difficult for the local authority to take up any recommendations they might make. If these shortcomings were frankly recognized at the time of their establishment, committees of this kind might well make a positive, if modest, contribution to local efficiency.

CHAPTER XXII

INTERNAL RULES

(1)

PREVIOUS chapters have described the financial organization needed by a local authority. This chapter and appendix E are devoted to answering two final questions: to what extent should financial procedures be laid down in written rules and what should be the content of such rules?

Internal rules of procedure can take several forms: standing orders made by the council; 'regulations' or 'instructions' issued either by the council or by committees; rules embedded in resolutions of the council or its committees; manuals of instruction for the guidance of officers; conditions of appointment of officers; and finally inter-departmental correspondence.

The term 'rules' is used in the present chapter to cover all these various classes of written prescriptions each of which is discussed in the section immediately below. The reader must however bear in mind that the phraseology used to indicate the various sorts of rules differs from place to place. For instance, some authorities have 'Instructions to Committees' which might be regarded as equivalent either to standing orders or to regulations. The classification which has been adopted in this chapter is therefore only general.

(2)

Of these various kinds of rules those in most common use are standing orders and regulations. The term 'standing order' implies a rule of the most formal kind made by the council itself. The Local Government Act, 1933, prescribes certain features of internal procedure which must be regulated by standing order, only one of which is financial—the making of contracts.[1] However, most authorities have some other financial standing orders, and these standing orders may or may not be supplemented by regulations which are concerned with more detailed points than are thought appropriate for standing

[1] Scottish authorities must also have internal rules to govern the matters standing referred to the finance committee, or delegated to that committee (*Local Government (Scotland) Act, 1947*).

orders. In the majority of authorities there are no other internal financial rules. These two forms of rules are discussed in more detail later and appendix E sets out in outline a code of standing orders and regulations designed to give effect to the principles advocated throughout this book.

No separate discussion of the third kind of rule—resolutions—is called for because this method can only be adopted for incidental matters. If the resolutions were systematic and extensive they would constitute a set of regulations. The disadvantage of laying down even incidental points in this way is that resolutions tend to be overlooked or mislaid: most local government officers have had the experience at some time or other of searching for an elusive resolution.

Manuals, like standing orders and regulations, are systematic codes, but at a lower level: they deal with departmental procedure and clerical processes. They are discussed later in the chapter.

Some financial rules can also be inferred from prescriptions of officers' duties as can be seen from the chapters on the chief financial officer and the operating departments. Rules derived from officers' conditions of appointment can only cover a small part of internal financial procedure, and they do not warrant further discussion.

Rules laid down in inter-departmental correspondence will only relate to points of detailed procedure, often to matters needing clarification. Like resolutions, they could not be elaborated into a complete code without becoming something other than they purport to be: they would in fact become manuals of instruction. Though they do not need treatment here, no sensible chief financial officer overlooks the possibilities of securing compliance with some small point of procedure or of clearing up a matter of doubt by means of a courteously worded memorandum to his fellow chief officers.

(3)

A local authority must under the Local Government Act of 1933 and that of 1958 adopt rules prescribing the procedure for entering into contracts and the process of receiving and paying out monies. These are the only incidents of financial administration which must be formally regulated. For the rest, a local authority may either govern its financial procedure by a written code or it may rely on custom or tradition; a code, if adopted, may be either detailed or broad, complete or incomplete. There is no code which applies automatically unless expressly excluded, in the same way that Table A applies to limited companies[1] though there are some rules recommended by the Ministry of Housing and Local Government.[2]

In practice very few local authorities are without some kind of financial rules additional to those required by law, but they are often too sketchy to be regarded as a 'code'. There are many authorities with no written rules to govern the annual budget, the consideration of capital expenditure and other important aspects of financial administration. At the other end of the scale there are a few authorities with minutely worked out codes in which an attempt has been made to cover every contingency, e.g. one set of regulations makes it incumbent upon the chief financial officer to see that the audit staff are not themselves engaged in compiling the records and also sets out the method upon which salary payments shall be calculated for 'broken periods'. In between come the majority with formal rules for major financial procedures only.

(4)

The absence of rules does not necessarily imply an absence of financial control. Most observers of local government can quote instances of adequate control existing side by side with scanty written rules. Chief financial officers have been known to say that the need for rules had not been felt, a state of affairs usually due to forceful members of the finance committee, to the outstanding personality of the chief financial officer, or to a good local tradition of inter-departmental co-operation in financial matters. These factors are closely related, a good tradition being invariably the result of an intense interest shown by dominating personalities in financial questions in the past. All are factors the importance of which it is difficult to exaggerate and one at least is usually prominent in authorities where financial control is adequate.

Unless they are operated in the right spirit, the most complete rules are doomed to be at the best a partial success. But to recognize that financial rules, however well constructed, may be completely ineffective in the hands of a weak committee is not necessarily to advocate reliance on oral tradition. Elections involve constant changes in membership. A strong finance committee may be replaced by an ineffective one, either because influential members have failed to secure re-election or because they have been placed by the

[1] See *Companies Act, 1948*, Section 8.
[2] See the 'Model' Standing Orders last revised in 1957.

council on other committees. A committee eager to carry out financial duties to the full may give way to one whose main interest lies elsewhere. In these circumstances internal rules can be at least some bulwark against the appearance of undesirable customs. Moreover, where financial control is dependent on a strong personality, either as chairman or chief financial officer, his passing invariably brings a reaction. Written rules should protect local authorities from the bad effects of fluctuations of this kind.

Formal rules also make the practice of the authority more intelligible. New members of the council and new officers, who are of limited use to an authority until they are acquainted with its procedure and practices, can at once see what is expected of them; officers can readily sense their roles and understand their duties; and, perhaps most important of all, the council knows who is responsible for the various incidents of financial administration.

Another virtue of a written code is that it makes for uniformity between different departments and periods and guards against the insensible discarding of safeguards, one of the greatest dangers the financial administration has to face.

Accidental lapses and deliberate abuse are also more likely where there are no rules. For instance, it is not unknown for committees to attempt to present direct to the council proposals which should have received the consideration of the finance committee. A daring chairman of a spending committee can flout custom when he could not infringe a standing order.

Among other virtues of written rules are: they facilitate the assessment of the responsibilities of officers' posts; they provide a starting point for the review of financial methods; and they help the critical comparison of performances. The advantages to auditors, both internal and external, are also considerable. The auditor knows more accurately what is the task of those whose work he is auditing; he finds it easier to bring shortcomings into focus; and his time is saved by the greater uniformity of method than is likely to exist under even the best unwritten traditions. Finally, local authority work is constantly increasing in complexity and volume. Unwritten understandings, satisfactory for small operations, may be unwisely retained after they have become inadequate. Haphazard practices, the defects of which may not be noticed in days of prosperity, may be of little avail in times of depression when there is a desperate desire for economy.[1]

[1] See I. Q. Holmes, *Local Government Finance in South Africa* (Butterworth, 1949), p. 204.

In English local authorities only the council can look at questions from the point of view of the authority as a whole. This of itself raises a strong presumption in favour of at least some formal machinery which helps to keep financial affairs in perspective and guards against uneconomical administration or disproportionate development of particular services.

(5)

This presumption in favour of written prescriptions rather than an oral tradition suggests that local authorities without codes should take suitable opportunities of installing them. Sometimes there is an obvious occasion, such as general overhaul of internal rules following an adjustment of boundaries, a change in status or a new statutory provision such as the requirement in the Local Government Act, 1958 that an authority should make safe and efficient arrangements for the receipt and payment of monies. Or some untoward event may have disclosed weaknesses which a written code would have guarded against. Thus the Newcastle upon Tyne Enquiry of 1945 was followed by the overhaul of the city's financial code.

Some local authorities carry out an annual review of all the internal rules of the authority, a practice which has much to commend it. But the review must not be perfunctory. Each officer should be asked to state whether the internal rules need revision on any points connected with his work. Thus an opportunity is presented not only to make modifications which have become desirable by new legislation—additional services, development of services, redistribution of duties and so forth—but also to correct any shortcomings which have become apparent throughout the year. The best sets of rules need constant critical scrutiny and, if necessary, adjustment, if they are to be effective tools of administration. Upon the chief financial officer falls the duty of watching that the financial rules are always up to date.

Every set of internal rules should at least affirm, in broad but unmistakable general terms, the principle of integration of financial arrangements and of control of financial matters by the finance committee. Provision should also be made for the procedure to be followed in the making and enforcement of the annual budget, the regulation of supplementary estimates, the approval of capital expenditure, the submission to the council of new projects which would involve additional calls on the public purse, the contracting of liabilities, the payment of accounts, the collection of income and internal audit. All these matters are fundamental to a proper system of control and most of them are included in the model standing orders issued by the Minister of Housing and Local Government already alluded to. The desirability of internal rules at least elaborate enough to cover these points would be generally agreed, but how much further local authorities need to go is a matter of dispute. In any case, even if there were agreement about the scope of the rules, there could be no uniformity in their content. A model code of universal application is out of the question because if financial administration is to function properly it must be fashioned to fit the precise circumstances of the local authority.

In Appendix E an attempt has been made to bring together, in classified form, the main points which the author thinks should be covered and to distinguish between what might be included in standing orders and what could best be inserted in regulations. The distinction is for general guidance only because every local authority will have its own notions about the relative importance of the various financial safeguards. Most of the financial procedures suggested in the appendix for inclusion in internal rules have been dealt with in previous chapters to which the reader is referred for discussions of the underlying principles and alternative procedures.

These points are not set out in the form of specimen rules because it is the object of the rule, not its actual form, which is our primary concern. 'Model' rules would in any case be of limited use, for in nearly every case they would require adaptation to fit local habits of phraseology. Further, by limiting the appendix to the substance of the rules, verbiage has been saved and the appendix made more compact and clear.

(6)

Our next task is to consider the merits of the issue of manuals of staff instructions. Such manuals cover the details of procedure not dealt with in the standing orders or regulations. Their aims are to secure sound financial work and uniformity between departments where it is desirable. For example, departments should not be allowed to interpret differently the council's regulations about car allowances to officers or the treatment of charges made by suppliers for containers. The manual should be part of the council's official arrangements and the standing orders of the council should make compliance with it compulsory. Its contents would be settled after thorough discussion with the departments and revised as circumstances changed. Matters besides accountancy procedure in the narrower sense would be covered, e.g. certification and payment of accounts, the control of income, the custody of stores and stores accounts, management of school funds, financial control within the departments, procedure for effecting insurances and making claims, and the purchasing routine. Notwithstanding the need for uniformity, there are aspects of administration such as the custody of stores and the keeping of stores accounts, for which modified instructions would be needed for different departments. Indeed, most departments will have some aspects of their work which justify an individual procedure.

The advantages of manuals of instruction can be briefly summarized as follows:

(a) Experience shows that the mere fact of codifying the arrangements of itself leads to improvements, economies and better understanding.

(b) They help to guard against the dangers and disadvantages of staff changes and the accidental dropping of safeguards due to inadequate instruction of newcomers.

(c) They are one of the simplest and most effective methods of defining individual responsibilities.

(d) They are the chief practical instrument in preventing duplication, for the council's rules should provide that only records prescribed by the manuals should be allowed. Any suggested record or procedure has therefore to stand the test of consideration for inclusion in a manual, a feature which of itself discourages unnecessary records.

(e) An additional argument in favour of the use of office manuals is the increasing tendency to mechanization. This demands uniformity of procedure but breaks down operations, not only mechanical, but clerical, into small stages, often unintelligible in themselves and therefore likely to be wrongly done unless the staff have the clearest instructions about each operation. Moreover, information gathered from many sources has to be fed into the machines in common form, a result much more likely to be attained if instructions are written. Written instructions are in any case unavoidable for the advanced machine work itself. No machine room can be planned or operated without them. Indeed one of the lessons to be learnt from modern mechanization is the value of codification of work.

315

(*f*) They are the ideal instrument for relating the broad rules laid down in standing orders to the varying circumstances of the departments. Each department is taken in turn and the best way of applying the general principles worked out in conjunction with the department.

(*g*) They also provide auditors, both external and internal, with a complete record of departmental procedures and newcomers with authoritative instructions. Audit staff can be more readily trained and work loads of auditors more easily assessed. Moreover, if the details of the operations are carefully set out in writing, lower grade audit staff can be used on some jobs than would otherwise be the case.

(*h*) Many details of domestic procedure, which need to be laid down clearly, but which are too minute to warrant inclusion in regulations can be accommodated in manuals. In fact an authority operating manuals hardly needs regulations: the standing orders and the manuals together should provide the complete code.

The disadvantage of manuals is that their compilation and constant revision absorbs a great deal of time of highly paid officers. Procedures have not only to be studied, examined and agreed upon, but also to be committed to writing, not always an easy task if the operations are complex and numerous. A compromise is to codify procedures, but only to revise the code infrequently. There is a school of thought which contends that it is worth while to draw up such a code even if it is not kept up to date. 'In some (American) offices full procedure manuals are written out, but opinion differs widely as to whether it is worth while to keep them up to date, or whether their real value consists in the original investigation which was necessary to produce them. In many companies they are maintained for the chief accounting procedures, but not for all office routines.'[1]

(7)

Whether a manual of procedure is worth while in any particular authority, depends on the general administrative arrangements. Where the chief financial officer is, as he should be, charged with the responsibility for the form of all financial records (whether kept in his own department or not), a manual devised, of course, in consultation between departments can be more easily produced than if he has imperfect control. A very small authority will hardly need to go to the lengths of codifying procedure.

[1] *Productivity Report*, 'Management Accounting' (Anglo-American Council on Productivity, 1950), p. 54.

The author's opinion is that the compilation of a manual is beneficial and that the advantages discussed above are not merely theoretical. References in earlier chapters of the book have already brought into focus some ways in which manuals and written codification of procedures can be made to contribute to the efficient running of the financial system and in one case, that of purchasing, an indication of the contents of a manual has been given. It would be outside the scope of this book further to consider the actual administrative detail which manuals would be expected to contain. The exemplification of internal rules in Appendix E therefore stops at the level of financial regulations. But just as there is no hard and fast distinction between standing orders and regulations, so there is no sharp dividing line between matters for inclusion in regulations and those appropriate to manuals. As has been mentioned above, a local authority which adopts manuals of instruction may well be able to incorporate much that would otherwise be put into regulations and promote the remainder to the status of a standing order, thus avoiding having rules at three levels: standing order, regulation and administrative manual. In any case manuals of instruction have an advantage over regulations because they can be more readily amended and kept up to date. To alter an instruction in a manual, agreement between departments and ratification of the finance committee, often only formal, are all that are needed, whereas the modification of regulations is a more involved process.

(8)

This discussion of the uses of manuals brings our study to an end. It is an appropriate if not a spectacular note to finish on inasmuch as it emphasizes the severely practical aim of the book. A final consolation for the student is that, though the procedures recommended have been designed for local government as it is, they would in the main still apply if it were radically changed. The tasks of controlling the purse, or of integrating financial arrangements, might become simpler, but they would not be much different. The student and practitioner would have little or nothing to unlearn. Moreover, the humbler the operation, the less likely it is to be disturbed by changes at the top. Manuals of instruction and the day-to-day procedures they codify may well outlast a council's practice in constituting its finance committee or determining the allocation of the rate between committees.

APPENDIX A

THE WORK OF ENGLISH LOCAL AUTHORITIES[1]

AMENITIES AND ENVIRONMENTAL

Town and Country Planning
Parks, Pleasure Grounds
Baths
Provision and Cleansing of Public Highways
Public Lighting
Refuse Collection and Disposal
Sewerage and Sewage Disposal
Smallholdings and Allotments
Road Safety
Land Drainage
Clean Air

SOCIAL

(a) *Public Health*
Ambulances
Health Centres
Midwifery Service
Home Help and Nursing Services
Child Welfare
School Health
Tuberculosis and Mental Health (other than Provision of Institutions)
Welfare of the Blind and Otherwise Handicapped
Cemeteries

(b) *Old People*
Provision of Homes

(c) *Children*
Care of neglected children
Day Nurseries

EDUCATIONAL AND CULTURAL

Primary, Secondary and Technical and other Further Education
Libraries
Art Galleries and Museums
Assistance to Drama and Music
Youth and Youth Employment

[1] An alternative classification of services of local authorities will be found in *Local Government in Britain* published by HMSO, 1957 (pp. 12–13).

318

CONTROL FUNCTIONS

Police
Fire Protection and Civil Defence
Regulations of Weights and Measures
Public Health (Notification of Infectious Diseases, Vaccination,
  Prevention of Nuisances, Inspection of Food and Drugs)
Regulation of Building
Registration of Births, Deaths and Marriages and of Electors

HOUSING

Provision of Houses
Making Loans for House Purchase and Grants for Improvements

TRADING

Water Supply
Public Transport
Markets
Restaurants
Entertainments
Aerodromes
Property

APPENDIX B

STATUTORY PROVISIONS RELATING TO FINANCIAL

ADMINISTRATION

320

INTRODUCTORY NOTE

This appendix sets out the rules about internal financial procedure made by the central government and embodied in Acts or in orders issued under the authority of Acts. The length of the appendix is due to the lack of uniformity among the various classes of authority rather than the extent of the provisions. In a few respects all English provincial local authorities are subject to the same statutory obligations, but for the most part, even though the same statute—the Local Government Act, 1933—may apply, the various classes of authority are governed by different sections.

With the exception of the provisions about receipts and payments included in the Local Government Act, 1958, the English statutory rules have been on the statute book for many years, though they may have been re-enacted. In Scotland, on the other hand, a general overhaul of financial sections has taken place. In 1943 the Jeffrey Committee, reporting on the consolidation of local government and public health legislation in Scotland, recommended that most of the provisions relating to finance and accounts could not usefully be re-enacted without expansion and amendment, and their recommendations were embodied in the Local Government (Scotland) Act, 1947. The Committee had three aims in mind:

(a) to abolish as far as possible the inconsistencies between different classes of authorities;

(b) to bring the provisions up to date. They said in their report:

'Secondly, a number of provisions of the existing law are not in accord with modern practice, and, in view of the scale on which local authorities are now required to transact business, some of those provisions are, we understand, so unworkable that local authorities are forced to disregard them or to resort to expedients of doubtful validity in an attempt to reconcile practice and legal requirements. This is particularly the case in connection with payments into or out of the county or burgh fund and the operation of bank accounts.

'The present position is unsatisfactory and compares very unfavourably with that under the special legislation which the cities and some others of the large authorities have found it necessary to obtain. We felt accordingly that it would be futile to confine our attention to an endeavour merely to reproduce the existing law. It is clearly of the utmost importance that the methods by which moneys are to be paid into and out of a local authority's funds and the system on which their banking accounts are operated should be carefully regulated, but if the requirements in regard to these matters are such that strict compliance with them would unduly impede the business of the authority, those requirements ought to be modified in the light of the best modern practice.'[1]

[1] *Local Government and Public Health Consolidation (Scotland) Committee First Report*, Cmd. 6476 (1943), pp. 20 and 21. The possibilities of alteration and

(c) to cover by statutory regulations some additional aspects of financial administration.

The English and Scottish codes show the following principal differences:

(a) The Scottish Act provides, so far as is desirable, a uniform code for all types of authority.

(b) All Scottish local authorities must appoint a finance committee charged with the tasks of advising the council on financial matters, and of supervising the financial arrangements of the authority.

(c) A system of budgeting is laid down which ensures that sufficient rates are made for all proposed expenditure on both revenue and capital account. The Act provides for emergency or other unforeseen expenditure and requires the finance committee to submit to the council a report on the budget.

(d) Requirements about rate funds and bank accounts have been brought into line with modern financial practice.

(e) In Scottish burghs, there must be appointed an honorary treasurer (equivalent to the chairman of the finance committee in England) who is to 'exercise general superintendence over the finances of the council'. He holds office for three years.

(f) Accounts are to be kept on an income and expenditure basis, and a balance sheet prepared.

(g) The Secretary of State for Scotland is given power to prescribe the qualifications of chief financial officers. Regulations under this section have been issued and are considered in the chapters on the chief financial officer.

The opportunity might have been taken in the Local Government Act, 1958, to provide English local authorities with a statutory code similar to that of the Local Government (Scotland) Act, 1947. But the view of the Ministry was that to provide statutory provisions similar to those operating in Scotland would be to run counter to the recommendations of the Manpower Committee which had emphasized the need to leave local authorities free to order their internal affairs.[1] Some financial officers dissent from this attitude in the belief that the Scottish Act merely dealt with safeguards so vital that local authorities cannot afford to be without them, and that to regulate them by statute is not to interfere with local administration but to provide an essential framework. That there are matters of financial procedure important enough in the view of the Ministry to warrant statutory provision is shown by the section in the Local Government Act, 1958, altering the law about the making of payments.

consolidation of the English financial provisions had been considered by the Chelmsford Committee who decided against alteration of the existing law on the grounds that suggestions to do so would be controversial and beyond the terms of reference of the committee. See *Local Government and Public Health Consolidation Committee. Interim Report.* Cmd. 4272 (1933), pp. 50 and 51.

[1] See *Reports of the Local Government Manpower Committee.* Cmd. 7870, 1950; 8421, 1951.

No one would ask for detailed regulation by statute. The mere fact that provisions tend to remain on the statute book after they have become out of date of itself suggests that the method of control by statutes should be employed sparingly. Local authorities, becoming in many other ways more bound by rules made in Whitehall, want as little statutory regulation of internal management as possible, whilst central departments find it almost impossible to make rules applicable to the varying circumstances of local authorities. But at some point a precaution does become so essential that it should be laid down by statute. It is a matter of opinion when this point has been reached.

1

FINANCE COMMITTEES

(I) COMPULSORY APPOINTMENT

(a) English Provincial County Councils

Local Government Act, 1933—Section 86

(1) A county council shall appoint a finance committee consisting of such number of members of the council as they think fit for regulating and controlling the finance of the county, and shall fix the term of office of the members of the committee.

(b) London County Council and Metropolitan Borough Councils

London Government Act, 1939—Section 60

(1) The county council and every borough council shall appoint a finance committee consisting of members of the council for regulating and controlling the finance of the county or borough, as the case may be.

(2) The number of members of the finance committee and their term of office shall be such as may be fixed from time to time by the appointing council.

(c) Scottish Authorities

Local Government (Scotland) Act, 1947—Section 113

(1) Every local authority shall have a finance committee whose duties shall include:

(a) advising the authority on financial matters;

(b) subject to the directions of the authority, supervising the recovery of moneys due to the authority and generally the whole financial arrangements of the authority; and

(c) exercising such other functions as are by this Act or any other enactment or any statutory order imposed on the finance committee.

(2) Subject to the provisions of this Act, the finance committee of every

local authority existing at the commencement of this Act shall be the finance committee of the authority, and any local authority having no such committee at the commencement of this Act shall appoint such committee within six weeks after the commencement of this Act.

(3) Subject to the provisions of this Part of this Act, of any administrative scheme thereunder and of section eighty-six of the Education (Scotland) Act, 1946, every local authority shall make provision by standing orders or otherwise with respect to the matters standing referred to the finance committee and the functions of the authority delegated to that committee.

(*d*) *County Boroughs, Non-County Boroughs, Urban and Rural Districts*

No statutory provision.

(II) FINANCE COMMITTEE NOT TO INCLUDE PERSONS OTHER THAN MEMBERS OF THE LOCAL AUTHORITY

(*a*) *English Provincial Authorities* (*i.e. County Councils, County Boroughs, Non-County Boroughs, Urban and Rural District Councils*)

Local Government Act, 1933—Section 85 (3)

A committee appointed under this section (*other than a committee for regulating and controlling the finance of the local authority or of their area*) may include persons who are not members of the local authority : provided that at least two-thirds of the members of every committee shall be members of the local authority.

(*b*) *London County Council and Metropolitan Boroughs*

It will be seen from Section 60 of the 1939 Act quoted on page 323, that the finance committee must consist of members of the council.

(*c*) *Scottish Authorities*

Local Government (Scotland) Act, 1947—Section 116

(1) Save as otherwise provided in this Act or any other enactment or any statutory order with respect to any committee or sub-committee:
  (*a*) a committee appointed by a local authority and a sub-committee thereof shall consist wholly of members of the authority; and
  (*b*) a local authority shall determine the number of members of a committee appointed by the authority and shall fix the term of office of members of the committee.

(2) Every member of a committee appointed by a local authority who at the time of appointment is a member of the authority shall, upon his ceasing to be a member of the authority, also cease to be a member of the committee.

(III) LOCAL AUTHORITIES PROHIBITED FROM DELEGATING POWER OF ISSUING
PRECEPTS, OR LEVYING RATES AND RAISING LOANS

(a) *County Councils, County Boroughs, Non-County Boroughs, Urban and Rural District Councils*

Local Government Act, 1933—Section 85 (1)

A local authority may appoint a committee for any such general or special purpose as in the opinion of the local authority would be better regulated and managed by means of a committee and may delegate to a committee so appointed . . . . any functions . . . . except the power of levying, or issuing a precept for, a rate or of borrowing money.

Note—A number of statutes provide for the compulsory appointment of committees for particular services. It is usually provided that the functions of the authority relating to the service shall stand referred to the committee except the power to borrow money or to levy or issue a precept for a rate. See for example National Health Service Act, 1946, 4th Schedule, Part II Section 3.

(b) *London County Council and Metropolitan Boroughs*

London Government Act, 1939—Section 67

(1) . . . . .

Provided that a local authority shall not delegate to a committee a power of levying, or issuing a precept for, a rate or of borrowing money, or, in the case of the county council, any power exercisable by the council under subsection (1) of section 2 of the Local Authorities (Financial Provisions) Act, 1921.

(2) A committee appointed by a borough council shall not incur any expenditure in excess of the amount allowed by the council.

(Subsection (2) is unique; no other local authority is subject to this statutory provision).

(c) *Scottish Authorities*

Local Government (Scotland) Act, 1947—Section 124

(1) Notwithstanding anything in this Act or any other enactment or any statutory order, a local authority shall not delegate to any committee, nor shall any committee of a local authority have, the power of raising money by rate or loan, and any function the delegation of which is expressly prohibited by any enactment or statutory order shall not be delegated by a local authority to a committee.

(2) The preceding subsection shall apply in the case of a joint committee or a joint board constituted for the purposes of a combination under this Act or any enactment repealed by this Act, and also in the case of delegation of functions by a county council to the town council of a small burgh or a district council or a joint committee of such councils in like manner as it applies in the case of a committee of a local authority.

2

ANNUAL BUDGET

(I) OBLIGATION TO MAKE AN ANNUAL BUDGET

(a) *English Provincial County Councils*

Local Government Act, 1933—Section 182

(1) Before the commencement of every financial year a county council shall cause to be submitted to them an estimate of the income and expenditure of the council during that financial year, whether on account of property, contributions, rates, loans or otherwise.

(2) The council shall estimate the amounts which will be required to be raised in the first six months and in the second six months of the financial year by means of precepts.

(3) If before the expiration of the first six months of the financial year it appears to the council that the amounts estimated at the commencement of the year will be larger than is necessary or will be insufficient, the council may revise the estimate and alter the said amounts accordingly.

(b) *London County Council*

London Government Act, 1939—Section 116

(Apart from slight differences in wording, this provision is identical with Section 182 of the 1933 Act).

(c) *Scottish County Councils*

Local Government (Scotland) Act, 1947—Section 177

(1) Before or as soon as may be after the commencement of each financial year every county council shall cause to be prepared:

(a) estimates in respect of that year of receipts and sums receivable and of expenditure relating to the several accounts of the council (showing separately capital expenditure) whether on account of property, contributions, rates, loans, public utility undertakings or otherwise; and

(b) estimates of the sums required to be raised to meet the deficiency on the several accounts of the council in respect of annual expenditure; and

(c) a report on the said estimates by the finance committee of the council for submission to the council.

(2) The county council shall consider as early as practicable in each financial year the estimates for that year and the report on the said estimates by the finance committee of the council, and shall revise such esti-

mates, approve the estimates as so revised, authorize the expenditure included therein, and fix for that year:

(a) the amount required to be requisitioned in accordance with the provisions of this Act by the council from the town council of each burgh within the county for any purpose;

(b) the amount estimated to be required to be raised by the council by levying in accordance with the provisions of this Act the county rate and any other rates within the landward area of the county for the purpose of meeting expenditure payable out of the same, the amount in respect of each rate being stated separately;

(c) in the case of a county council carrying on a public utility undertaking, the amount estimated to be required to be defrayed out of the annual revenue of each such undertaking; and

(d) the estimated amount of the capital expenditure of the council for each purpose:

Provided that:

(i) the council, at any time after they have revised the estimates and before they have determined the amount per pound of the rates for the year, may, if they find it necessary, again revise any estimate and alter the amount included therein;

(ii) the council shall fix the amounts under paragraph (a) of this subsection in time to enable them to comply with the provisions of subsection (4) of section 214 of this Act.

(3) No expenditure shall be incurred by or on behalf of a county council unless:

(a) previously authorized in accordance with the estimates approved by the council; or

(b) otherwise previously authorized by the council; or

(c) if not so authorized, necessarily incurred in circumstances of emergency:

Provided that:

(i) any expenditure on salaries, wages and other recurring annual expenditure prior to the approval of estimates by the council may be authorized in accordance with standing orders or by resolution of the council, but any other expenditure under paragraph (b) of this subsection shall not be authorized by the council except on consideration of a report thereon by the finance committee of the council; and

(ii) any expenditure under paragraph (c) of this subsection shall forthwith be reported to the appropriate committee and to the finance committee of the council and as soon as practicable thereafter reported by the finance committee to the council with a view to being approved by the council.

(4) A county council may make standing orders for the purpose of carrying the provisions of this section into effect, so however that such orders shall not be inconsistent with the provisions of any enactment with respect to matters to which this section relates.

(d) Scottish Burghs

Local Government (Scotland) Act, 1947—Section 181 (as amended by the Valuation and Rating (Scotland) Act, 1956)

(1) Before or as soon as may be after the commencement of each financial year every town council shall cause to be prepared:

(a) estimates in respect of that year of the receipts and sums receivable and of expenditure relating to the several accounts of the council, including the common good (showing separately capital expenditure), whether on account of property, contributions, rates, loans, public utility undertakings or otherwise; and

(b) estimates of the sums required to be raised to meet the deficiency on the several accounts of the council in respect of annual expenditure; and

(c) a report on the said estimates by the finance committee of the council for submission to the council.

(2) The town council shall consider as early as practicable in each financial year the estimates for that year and the report on the said estimates by the finance committee of the council, and shall revise such estimates, approve the estimates as so revised, authorize the expenditure included therein and fix for that year:

(a) the amount estimated to be required to be raised by the council by levying in accordance with the provisions of this Act the burgh rate and any other rate within the burgh for the purpose of meeting expenditure payable out of that rate, the amount in respect of each rate being stated separately;

(b) in the case of a town council carrying on a public utility undertaking, the amount estimated to be required to be defrayed out of the annual revenue of each such undertaking; and

(c) the estimated amount of the capital expenditure of the council for each purpose:

Provided that the council, at any time after they have revised the estimates and before they have determined the amount per pound of the rates for the year, may, if they find it necessary, again revise any estimate and alter the amount included therein.

(3) No expenditure shall be incurred by or on behalf of a town council unless:

(a) previously authorized in accordance with the estimates approved by the council; or

(b) otherwise previously authorized by the council; or

(c) if not so authorized, necessarily incurred in circumstances of emergency:

Provided that:

(i) any expenditure on salaries, wages and other recurring annual expenditure prior to the approval of estimates by the council may be authorized in accordance with standing orders or by resolution of the council, but any other expenditure under paragraph (b) of this subsection shall not be authorized except on consideration of a report thereon by the finance committee of the council;

(ii) any expenditure under paragraph (c) of this subsection shall forthwith be reported to the appropriate committee and to the finance committee of the council and as soon as practicable thereafter reported by the finance committee to the council with a view to being approved by the council.

(4) A town council may make standing orders for the purpose of carrying the provisions of this section into effect, so however that such orders shall not be inconsistent with the provisions of any enactment with respect to matters to which this section relates.

(e) Scottish District Councils

Local Government (Scotland) Act, 1947—Section 185

(1) Before or as soon as may be after the commencement of each financial year every district council shall cause to be prepared:

(a) estimates in respect of that year of the receipts and sums receivable and of expenditure relating to the several accounts of the council (showing separately capital expenditure) whether on account of property, contributions, rates, loans or otherwise; and

(b) estimates of the sums required to be raised to meet the deficiency on the several accounts of the council in respect of annual expenditure; and

(c) a report on the said estimates by the finance committee of the council for submission to the council.

(2) The district council shall consider in or before the month of June the estimates for the current financial year and the report on the said estimates by the finance committee of the council, and shall revise such estimates, approve the estimates as so revised, authorize the expenditure included therein and fix for that year:

(a) the amount required to be requisitioned by the council from the county council in accordance with the provisions of this Act; and (*b*) the estimated amount of the capital expenditure of the council for each purpose.

(3) No expenditure shall be incurred by or on behalf of a district council unless:

(*a*) previously authorized in accordance with the estimates approved by the council; or

(*b*) otherwise previously authorized by the council; or

(*c*) if not so authorized necessarily incurred in circumstances of emergency:

Provided that:

(*i*) any expenditure on salaries, wages and other recurring annual expenditure prior to the approval of estimates by the council may be authorized in accordance with standing orders or by resolution of the council, but any other expenditure under paragraph (*b*) of this subsection shall not be authorized except on consideration of a report thereon by the finance committee of the council;

(*ii*) any expenditure under paragraph (*c*) of this subsection shall forthwith be reported to the appropriate committee and to the finance committee of the council and as soon as practicable thereafter reported by the finance committee to the council with a view to being approved by the council.

(4) A district council may make standing orders for the purpose of carrying the provisions of this section into effect, so however that such orders shall not be inconsistent with the provisions of any enactment with respect to matters to which this section relates.

(*f*) *County Boroughs, Non-County Boroughs, Metropolitan Boroughs, Urban and Rural Districts*

No provision.

(II) OBLIGATION TO LEVY SUFFICIENT RATES
(in effect this makes a budget necessary)

(*a*) *All Provincial English Local Authorities*

(defined in the Act as 'any body having power to levy a rate or to issue a precept to a rating authority'—this definition would include *ad hoc* authorities such as Joint Boards of various kinds)

Rating and Valuation Act, 1925—Section 12 (1)

Every local authority shall make such rates or issue such precepts as will be sufficient to provide for such part of the total estimated expenditure to be incurred by the authority during the period in respect of which the rate is made or precept is issued as is to be met out of moneys raised by rates, including in that expenditure any sums payable to any other authority under precepts issued by that authority, together with such additional amount as is in the opinion of the authority required to cover expenditure previously incurred (whether within six months before the making of the rate or issue of the precept, as the case may be, or not), or to meet contingencies or to defray any expenditure which may fall to be defrayed before the date on which the moneys to be received in respect of the next subsequent rate or precept will become available.

(b) *London County Council and Metropolitan Boroughs*

The London Government Act, 1899, Section 10 (2)

' . . . the general rate . . . shall be assessed, made, collected and levied as if it were the poor rate and all enactments applying or referring to the poor rate shall, subject to the provisions of this Act as to audit, be considered as applying or referring also to the general rate.'

Article 1 of the Consolidated Order Amendment Order dated February 26, 1866, provides as follows:

'The clerk shall . . . in each year estimate the probable amount of the expenditure in the relief of the poor and other charges by the Guardians on behalf of the Union . . . .'

London County Council (General Powers) Act, 1933—Section 67 (2)

The general rate from time to time made by a borough council may include such an amount as will be sufficient in the opinion of the borough council to cover expenditure incurred before the making of the rate.

(c) *Scottish Authorities*

Local Government (Scotland) Act, 1947—Section 212

(1) It shall be the duty of every rating authority to levy such rates as will provide sufficient funds to meet such part of the total estimated expenditure to be incurred by the authority during the financial year in respect of which the rate is levied (after taking account of any balance or estimated balance at the end of the last financial year) as is to be met out of moneys raised by rates (including in that expenditure any sums payable to any other local authority under requisitions issued by that authority), together with such additional amount as is in the opinion of the rating authority required to cover expenditure previously incurred or to meet contingencies so far as the same fall to be met out of rates.

(2) It shall be the duty of every requisitioning authority to issue to the rating authority a requisition for payment of such sum as will provide sufficient funds to meet such part of the total estimated expenditure to be incurred by the requisitioning authority during the financial year in respect of which the requisition is issued (after taking account of any balance or estimated balance at the end of the last financial year) as is to be met out of moneys raised by rates levied by the rating authority and out of grants payable to the rating authority under Part III of the Local Government (Scotland) Act, 1929, so far as such grants, if any, are properly applicable to such

expenditure, together with such additional amount as is in the opinion of the requisitioning authority required to cover expenditure previously incurred or to meet contingencies so far as the same fall to be met out of rates and out of such grants.

(3) In levying a rate or issuing a requisition for the purposes of this section, account shall be taken only of expenditure to which such rate or the sum in such requisition is properly applicable, and in taking account of any balance or any expenditure previously incurred for the purposes of this section, due regard shall be had to the incidence of the rate to which such balance or expenditure properly relates.

(III) MISCELLANEOUS

(a) English Non-County Boroughs and Urban District Councils: duty to supply County Councils with estimates in respect of certain roads

Highways Act, 1959—Section 237 (3)

The council of a non-county borough or urban district shall, on or before the fifteenth day of December in each year, submit to the county council for their approval a detailed estimate of—

    (*a*) the cost, for the ensuing financial year, of the maintenance of every county road for which the council of that borough, or of that district, as the case may be, are, by virtue of the said section 4, the highway authority, and;

    (*b*) the cost, for the ensuing financial year, of any reasonable improvement connected with the maintenance of any such road;

and on any such estimate being approved by the county council, either with or without modifications, the amount to be paid by the county council under this section in respect of the maintenance and improvement shall be the amount of that estimate, or of that estimate as amended by any supplementary estimate submitted to and approved by the county council, or such less sum as may have been actually expended thereon by the council of the non-county borough or of the urban district, as the case may be, during the said financial year: ...

(b) Scottish Authorities

Dates by which requisitions to be sent and rates fixed

Local Government (Scotland) Act, 1947—Section 194 (1)

The Secretary of State may, if at any time after consultation with associations representing the different classes of local authorities concerned he considers it practicable for the said local authorities to comply, make regulations prescribing a date early in the financial year by which the local authorities concerned shall approve their estimates for that year and fix the amounts to be raised by each rate and the amount to be defrayed out of the annual revenue of each public utility undertaking, and prescribing earlier dates by which requisitions are to be sent by requisitioning authorities to rating authorities, and such regulations may contain such incidental, supplemental and consequential provisions as appear necessary for the purpose of giving full effect thereto, and on such regulations being made the provisions of this Act so far as relating to the matters dealt with in the regulations shall have effect subject to the provisions of the regulations and be modified accordingly:

Provided that nothing in these regulations shall be deemed to prevent a county council or a town council if they find it necessary from again revising any estimate and altering the amount included therein at any time before they have determined the amount per pound of the rates for the year.

Regulations made under this subsection may apply to all local authorities generally or to any particular class of authority.

(c) Scottish Education Authorities

Education (Scotland) Act, 1946—Section 86

The estimates (including supplementary estimates) of capital and revenue expenditure relating to education shall be in the prescribed form, and approval by the education authority of those estimates and authorization of the expenditure included therein shall be sufficient authority to the education committee to incur, on purposes falling within the description of any head in the prescribed form, expenditure not exceeding in amount the total under that head in the estimates so approved. Savings under one head may not be used to defray expenditure under another head without the consent of the education authority.

3

FUNDS AND PAYMENTS THEREFROM

(I) ESTABLISHMENT OF FUNDS

(a) English Provincial County Councils

Local Government Act, 1933—Section 181

(1) All receipts of a county council, whether for general or special county purposes, shall be carried to the county fund, and all liabilities falling to be discharged by the council, whether for general or special county purposes, shall be discharged out of that fund.

(2) Separate accounts shall be kept of receipts carried to, and payments made out of, the county fund—

(a) for general county purposes;

(b) for each special county purpose, except that, where as respects any two or more special county purposes the part of the county chargeable is the same, one separate account may be kept as respects both or all of those purposes;

and the account for general county purposes shall be called the general county account, and an account for any special county purpose shall be called a special county account.

(Section 180 dealing with general and special expenses has not been reproduced here.)

(b) London County Council

London Government Act, 1939—Section 118

(This provision is identical with Section 181 of the 1933 Act except that it begins '(1) Subject to the provisions of the London County Council (Finance Consolidation) Act, 1912, all receipts of the County Council . . .' Section 115, like Section 180 of the 1933 Act, deals with general and special expenses).

(c) Scottish County Councils

Local Government (Scotland) Act, 1947—Section 176

All receipts of and sums receivable by a county council from whatever source shall be credited to and form part of the county fund, and all expenditure of the council shall be defrayed out of that fund:

Provided that, unless the council by resolution otherwise determine, this section shall not apply in the case of receipts and sums receivable and expenditure relating to any funds or property held by the council as trustees for any purpose under any deed of trust or other document.

(d) English Provincial Boroughs

Local Government Act, 1933—Section 185

(1) All receipts of the council of a borough, including the rents and profits of all corporate land, shall be carried to the general rate fund of the borough, and all liabilities falling to be discharged by the council shall be discharged out of that fund.

(2) An account, called the 'general rate fund account' shall be kept of all receipts carried to, and payments made out of, the general rate fund:

Provided that, where any such receipts are receipts for the benefit of a part only of the borough, or any such payments are payments in respect of expenditure with which a part only of the borough is chargeable, a separate account shall be kept of receipts and payments in respect of that part of the borough.

(3) If the general rate fund is more than sufficient for the purposes to which it is applicable, the surplus thereof may be applied under the direction of the council for the public benefit of the inhabitants and improvement of the borough.

(e) Metropolitan Boroughs

London Government Act, 1939—Section 121

(1) All receipts of a borough council shall be carried to the general rate fund of the borough, and all payments falling to be made by the council shall be made out of that fund.

(2) An account, called the 'general rate fund account', shall be kept of all receipts carried to, and payments made out of the general rate fund,

and where the receipts are receipts for the benefit of a part only of the borough, or the payments are payments in respect of expenditure with which a part only of the borough is chargeable, a separate account shall be kept of receipts and payments in respect of that part of the borough.

(3) If the general rate fund is more than sufficient for the purposes to which it is applicable, the surplus thereof may be applied under the direction of the borough council for the public benefit of the inhabitants and improvement of the borough.

(f) Scottish Burghs

Local Government (Scotland) Act, 1947—Section 180

All receipts of and sums receivable by the town council of a burgh from whatever source shall be credited to and form part of the burgh fund, and all expenditure of the council shall be defrayed out of that fund:

Provided that, unless the council by resolution otherwise determine, this section shall not apply:

(a) in the case of the receipts and sums receivable and expenditure relating to the common good of the burgh; or

(b) in the case of receipts and sums receivable and expenditure relating to any funds or property held by the council as trustees for any purpose under any deed of trust or other document.

(g) English Urban District Councils

Local Government Act, 1933—Section 188

(1) All receipts of the council of an urban district shall be carried to the general rate fund of the district, and all liabilities falling to be discharged by the council shall be discharged out of that fund.

(2) An account, called the 'general rate fund account', shall be kept of all receipts carried to, and payments made out of, the general rate fund:

Provided that, where any such receipts are receipts for the benefit of a part only of the district, or any such payments are payments in respect of expenditure with which a part only of the district is chargeable, a separate account shall be kept of receipts and payments in respect of that part of the district.

(h) English Rural District Councils

Local Government Act, 1933—Section 191

(1) All receipts of the council of a rural district, whether in respect of general or special expenses, shall be carried to the general rate fund of the district, and all liabilities falling to be discharged by the council, whether in respect of general or special expenses, shall be discharged out of that fund.

(2) Separate accounts shall be kept of receipts carried to, and payments made out of, the general rate fund of the district:

(a) in respect of general expenses;

(b) in respect of each class of special expenses, except that where, as

respects any two or more classes of special expenses, the part of the district chargeable is the same, one separate account may be kept as respects all expenses of both or all those classes;
and the account kept in respect of general expenses shall be called the general district account and an account kept in respect of any class of special expenses shall be called a special district account.

(Section 190, dealing with general and special expenses has not been reproduced here.)

(i) Scottish District Councils

Local Government (Scotland) Act, 1947—Section 184

All receipts of and sums receivable by a district council from whatever source shall be credited to and form part of the district council fund, and all expenditure of the council shall be defrayed out of that fund. Receipts and sums receivable and expenditure for the purposes of this section shall include those relating to any funds or property held by the council as trustees for any purpose under any deed of trust or other document.

(j) Scottish Authorities—Fee Funds

Local Government (Scotland) Act, 1947—Section 188

(1) All fees, commissions, discounts allowed on payment of accounts and expenses payable to or recovered by any officer of a local authority in respect of any business relating to the authority whether by reason of his office or otherwise (except personal outlays incurred by the officer and such fees, commissions, discounts and expenses as the officer is in pursuance of an express provision of his agreement with the authority entitled to retain for himself) shall be accounted for and paid to the county fund, the burgh fund or the district council fund, as the case may be, and:

(a) such part as may be approved by the Secretary of State of all the said fees and commissions so accounted for and paid shall form a fund to be known as the 'fee fund' of the authority which may be applied for any purpose relating to the authority or the area of the authority for which, in the case of a burgh having a common good, the common good may be applied; and

(b) all such fees and commissions (except the part thereof carried to the fee fund) and all such discounts and expenses so accounted for and paid shall be carried to the credit of the respective accounts of the authority to which they relate.

(2) Where at the commencement of this Act a local authority or an officer of the authority on behalf of the authority holds moneys derived from any such fees, commissions, discounts and expenses as aforesaid, such moneys shall be paid to the county fund, the burgh fund or the district council fund, as the case may be, and form part of the fee fund of the authority.

336

APPENDICES

(II) OPERATION OF FUNDS

(a) *All English Authorities*

Local Government Act, 1958—Section 58

(1) Every local authority shall make safe and efficient arrangements for the receipt of moneys paid to them and the issue of moneys payable by them, and those arrangements shall be carried out under the supervision of the treasurer:

Provided that in the case of a local authority of which the treasurer at the passing of this Act is not a whole-time officer (that is to say, a person who devotes substantially the whole of his time to his employment by the authority) the said arrangements shall at any time when the treasurer is not a whole-time officer be carried out under the supervision of such officer of the authority as may be designated by them as their chief financial officer.

(2) . . .

(3) In this section 'local authority' includes the council of a metropolitan borough.

(b) *Scottish County Councils*

Local Government (Scotland) Act, 1947—Section 178

(1) It shall be the duty of the county treasurer to see that all receipts of and sums receivable by the county council falling to be credited to the county fund are duly credited to and form part of that fund and that all expenditure of the council falling to be defrayed out of the county fund is so defrayed:

Provided that nothing in this subsection shall be deemed to prevent the county council or any duly authorized committee of the council giving directions with respect to the payment or recovery of sums claimed to be due to the council or with respect to the payment of sums claimed to be due by the council.

(2) The county council shall cause to be kept in the books of any one or more incorporated or joint stock banks such bank accounts in name of the council, not being more in number than are necessary, as the council may determine, and, save as otherwise provided in any regulations that may be made by the Secretary of State, there shall be paid into the said bank accounts all sums received by the council, and out of the said bank accounts all payments due to be made by the council.

(3) The county council may give directions with respect to keeping, paying moneys into, and operating on, the several bank accounts.

(4) No payment shall be made out of the county fund if the expenditure in respect of which it is made has been incurred contrary to the provisions of subsection (3) of the immediately preceding section, except where it is made in pursuance of the specific requirement of any enactment or statutory order, or of a decree of a competent court.

(5) Save as otherwise provided in any regulations that may be made by

337

the Secretary of State, all payments due to be made out of the county fund shall be made in pursuance of an order of the finance committee of the county council signed by two members of that committee present at the meeting of the committee at which the order is made, and countersigned by the county clerk, and the same order may include several payments, and all cheques for payment of moneys issued in pursuance of such an order shall be signed by the county treasurer or by such other officer of the county council as the council or the finance committee may appoint for the purpose.

(6) Regulations made under this section shall be laid before each House of Parliament as soon as may be after they are made.

Note—The Secretary of State has made Regulations under Sections 178 (5) and 182 (5) (see page 339) providing for specified payments of a recurring or routine nature or payments incurred in circumstances of emergency to be made without an order signed by two members of the finance committee and countersigned by the clerk. The payments so made, other than salaries, wages or allowances to officers in terms of their appointment must be reported to the finance committee as soon as practicable after the date of payment (S.I. 1948, No. 714 (S. 52)—The Local Government (Payment of Accounts) (Scotland) Regulations, 1948).

Local Government (Scotland) Act, 1947—Section 179

Every county council shall in each year make payment of the following salaries, fees, outlays and expenses so far as the same were immediately before the commencement of this Act by law or usage payable by the council:

(1) the salaries, fees and necessary outlays of procurators fiscal in the sheriff court;

(2) the expenses of searching for, apprehending, subsisting, prosecuting or punishing criminals;

(3) the expenses connected with upholding, repairing, enlarging, renting, furnishing, insuring, lighting, cleaning or warming any courthouse, and all taxes and rates legally chargeable thereon;

(4) the expenses connected with the holding of the court for striking the fiars prices for the county;

(5) all expenses occasioned by damage done to property within the county by tumultuous or riotous assemblies and all expenses properly incurred in the prevention of riots;

(6) any other expenses or payments directed by any Act to be defrayed out of the county general assessment.

(c) Scottish Burghs

Local Government (Scotland) Act, 1947—Section 182

(1) It shall be the duty of the town chamberlain to see that all receipts of and sums receivable by the town council falling to be credited to the burgh

fund are duly credited to and form part of that fund, and that all expenditure of the council falling to be defrayed out of the burgh fund is so defrayed, and where the burgh fund does not include the common good that all receipts and sums receivable relating thereto are duly paid to the common good and all expenditure relating thereto is defrayed out of the common good:

Provided that nothing in this subsection shall be deemed to prevent the town council or any duly authorized committee of the council giving directions with respect to the payment or recovery of sums claimed to be due to the council or with respect to the payment of sums claimed to be due by the council.

(2) The town council shall cause to be kept in the books of an incorporated or joint stock bank one bank account or where necessary two bank accounts in name of the council or where additional accounts are considered necessary such additional accounts in name of the council as the Secretary of State may authorize, and, save as otherwise provided in any regulations that may be made by the Secretary of State, there shall be paid into the said bank account or accounts all sums received by the council and out of the said bank account or accounts there shall be paid all payments due to be made by the council.

(3) The town council may give directions with respect to keeping, paying moneys into, and operating on, the bank account or the several bank accounts.

(4) No payment shall be made by a town council if the expenditure in respect of which it is made has been incurred contrary to the provisions of subsection (3) of the immediately preceding section, except where it is made in pursuance of the specific requirement of any enactment or statutory order or of a decree of a competent court.

(5) Save as otherwise provided in regulations that may be made by the Secretary of State, all payments due to be made by the town council shall be made in pursuance of an order of the finance committee of the council signed by two members of that committee present at the meeting of the committee at which the order is made, and countersigned by the town clerk, and the same order may include several payments, and all cheques for payment of moneys issued in pursuance of such an order shall be signed by the town chamberlain or by such other officer of the town council as the council or the finance committee may appoint for the purpose.

(6) Regulations made under this section shall be laid before each House of Parliament as soon as may be after they are made.

Note—Regulations made under Section 182(5) are referred to on page 338.

(d) Scottish District Councils

Local Government (Scotland) Act, 1947—Section 186

(1) It shall be the duty of the treasurer of the district council to see that all receipts of and sums receivable by the council falling to be credited to the

district council fund are duly credited to and form part of that fund and that all expenditure of the council falling to be defrayed out of the district council fund is so defrayed:

Provided that nothing in this subsection shall be deemed to prevent the district council or any duly authorized committee of the council giving instructions with respect to the payment or recovery of sums claimed to be due to the council or with respect to the payment of sums claimed to be due by the council.

(2) The district council shall cause one bank account to be kept in the books of an incorporated or joint stock bank in name of the council, and, save as otherwise provided in any regulations that may be made by the Secretary of State, there shall be paid into the said bank account all sums received by the council and out of the said bank account there shall be paid all payments due to be made by the council.

(3) The district council may give directions with respect to keeping, paying moneys into, and operating on, the bank account.

(4) No payment shall be made out of the district council fund if the expenditure in respect of which it is made has been incurred contrary to the provisions of subsection (3) of the immediately preceding section, except where it is made in pursuance of the specific requirement of any enactment or statutory order or of a decree of a competent court.

(5) All payments due to be made out of the district council fund shall be made by means of a cheque signed by two members of the council and by the clerk or treasurer of the council, and one cheque may be used for the purpose of making several payments.

(6) Regulations made under this section shall be laid before each House of Parliament as soon as may be after they are made.

4

TREASURER

(I) APPOINTMENT

(1) Honorary Treasurer (Chairman of Finance Committee) in Scottish Burghs
Local Government (Scotland) Act, 1947—Section 30

(1) The town council of every burgh shall elect a town councillor to the office of honorary treasurer of the burgh, and the person so elected shall, subject to the directions of the council, exercise general superintendence over the finances of the council and shall be convener of the finance committee appointed by the council under this Act.

(2) Subject to the provisions of this Act relating to filling casual vacancies in the office of honorary treasurer, the term of office of the honorary treasurer shall be from the day of his election to that office until the first Tuesday of May in the third year after the day of his election, and during that period, notwithstanding anything in this Act, he shall not,

so long as he continues to hold the office of honorary treasurer, be due to retire as a town councillor.

(3) The town council of every burgh in which there is not at the commencement of this Act an honorary treasurer shall elect a town councillor to be honorary treasurer of the burgh at the first meeting of the council held after the day of the annual election of town councillors in the year nineteen hundred and forty seven or at any adjournment of that meeting.

(4) A person shall not at any one time hold the offices of magistrate of a burgh and honorary treasurer of the burgh, and where a person holding the office of magistrate is elected to the office of honorary treasurer, he shall be deemed to have resigned from the office of magistrate, or where a person holding the office of honorary treasurer is elected to the office of magistrate, he shall be deemed to have resigned from the office of honorary treasurer.

(2) Appointment of Treasurer
(a) English Provincial County Councils

Local Government Act, 1933—Section 102

(1) Every county council shall appoint a fit person to be the county treasurer, and may pay to the person so appointed such reasonable remuneration as they may determine.

(2) The county treasurer shall hold office during the pleasure of the county council.

(3) A vacancy in the office of county treasurer shall be filled within four months after its occurrence.

(4) The offices of clerk of the county council and county treasurer shall not be held by the same person or by persons who stand in relation to one another as partners or as employer and employee.

(b) London County Council

London Government Act, 1939—Section 71

(1) The county council shall appoint a fit person to be the county treasurer, and may pay to the person so appointed such reasonable remuneration as it may determine.

(2) The county treasurer shall hold office during the pleasure of the county council.

(3) A vacancy in the office of county treasurer shall be filled within four months after the date on which it occurs.

London Government Act, 1939—Section 72

The offices of clerk of the county council and county treasurer shall not be held by the same person or by persons who stand in relation to one another as partners or as employer and employee.

(c) Scottish Counties

Local Government (Scotland) Act, 1947—Section 77

(1) Every county council shall appoint a county treasurer who shall be

341

the chief financial officer of the council and may pay to him such reasonable salary as they may determine.

(2) Regulations may be made by the Secretary of State prescribing the qualifications which shall be required to be possessed by any person appointed to the office of county treasurer by a county council, and after the date of the regulations or after such later date as may be therein prescribed a person shall not be appointed to that office unless he possesses such qualifications.

(3) The county treasurer shall hold office during the pleasure of the county council, so however that he shall not be removed from office except by a resolution of the council passed by not less than two-thirds of the members of the council present at a meeting of the council the notice of which specifies the consideration of the removal from office of the county treasurer as an item of business.

Note—The Secretary of State has made regulations under Sections 77 (2) and 85 (2) (see page 343) prescribing the qualifications to be possessed by any person appointed to the office of county treasurer by a county council or to the office of town chamberlain by a town council (S.I. 1948, No. 2547) (S. 195)—The Local Government (Qualifications of County Treasurer and Town Chamberlain) (Scotland) Regulations, 1948 and S.I. 1950, No. 1913 (S. 128)—The Local Government (Qualifications of County Treasurer and Town Chamberlain) (Scotland) (Amendment) Regulations, 1950.

Local Government (Scotland) Act, 1947—Section 78

(1) Every county council shall appoint a county collector who shall be the collector of rates levied by the council and may pay to him such reasonable salary as they may determine.

(2) The county collector shall hold office during the pleasure of the county council, so however that he shall not be removed from office except by a resolution of the council passed by not less than two-thirds of the members of the council present at a meeting of the council the notice of which specifies the consideration of the removal from office of the county collector as an item of business.

(d) English Boroughs

Local Government Act, 1933—Section 106

(1) The council of every borough shall appoint fit persons to be . . . treasurer . . .

(2) . . . the council may pay to an officer appointed under this section such reasonable remuneration as they may determine, and, subject as aforesaid, every such officer shall hold office during the pleasure of the council.

(3) A vacancy in the office of town clerk or of treasurer shall be filled within twenty-one days after its occurrence.

(4) The offices of town clerk and treasurer shall not be held by the same person or by persons who stand in relation to one another as partners or as employer and employee.

(e) Metropolitan Boroughs

London Government Act, 1939—Section 76

(1) Every borough council shall appoint fit persons to be . . . borough treasurer. . . .

(2) A borough council may pay to an officer appointed under this section such reasonable remuneration as it may determine, and every officer so appointed shall hold office during the pleasure of the council.

(3) A vacancy in the office of town clerk or of borough treasurer shall be filled within twenty-one days after its occurrence.

(4) The offices of town clerk and borough treasurer shall not be held by the same person or by persons who stand in relation to one another as partners or as employer and employee.

(f) Scottish Burghs

Local Government (Scotland) Act, 1947—Section 85

(1) Every town council shall appoint a town chamberlain of the burgh who shall be the chief financial officer of the council and may pay to him such reasonable salary as they may determine. Any reference in this Act to the treasurer of a local authority shall in its application to a town council be construed as a reference to the town chamberlain.

(2) Regulations may be made by the Secretary of State prescribing the qualifications which shall be required to be possessed by any person appointed to the office of town chamberlain by a town council, and after the date of the regulations or after such later date as may be therein prescribed a person shall not be appointed to that office unless he possesses such qualifications.

(3) Subject to the provisions of this Part of this Act relating to officers holding office at the commencement of this Act, the offices of town clerk and town chamberlain shall not, except with the sanction of the Secretary of State, be held by the same person or by persons who stand in relation to one another as partners or as employer and employee.

(4) The town chamberlain shall hold office during the pleasure of the town council, so however that he shall not be removed from office except by a resolution passed by not less than two-thirds of the members present at a meeting of the council the notice of which specifies the consideration of the removal from office of the town chamberlain as an item of business.

Note—Regulations made under Section 85 (2) are referred to on page 342.

Local Government (Scotland) Act, 1947—Section 86

(1) Every town council shall appoint a burgh collector who shall be the

collector of rates levied by the council and may pay to him such reasonable salary as they may determine.

(2) The burgh collector shall hold office during the pleasure of the town council, so however that he shall not be removed from office except by a resolution of the council passed by not less than two-thirds of the members of the council present at a meeting of the council the notice of which specifies the consideration of the removal from office of the burgh collector as an item of business.

(g) English Urban and Rural District Councils

Local Government Act, 1933—Section 107

(1) Every district council shall appoint fit persons to be ... treasurer.

(4) The offices of clerk of the council and treasurer shall not be held by the same person or by persons who stand in relation to one another as partners or as employer and employee.

(h) Scottish District Councils

Local Government (Scotland) Act, 1947—Section 94

(1) Every district council shall appoint a clerk of the council and a treasurer of the council and such other officers as the council think necessary for the efficient discharge of the functions of the council, and may pay to the clerk, treasurer and other officers appointed under this section such reasonable salaries as the council may determine.

(2) The clerk, the treasurer and every other officer appointed under this section shall hold office during the pleasure of the council, so however that neither the clerk nor the treasurer shall be removed from office except by resolution of the council passed by not less than two-thirds of the members of the council present at a meeting of the council the notice of which specifies the consideration of the removal from office of the officer as an item of business.

(3) A clerk or a treasurer of a district council may, and if required by the council, shall, appoint a person approved by the council to act as his depute, and if either of the said offices is vacant or the holder of the office is unable to act and there is no depute acting, the district council may appoint a person to act temporarily in the office for a period not exceeding six months, with power to the council to renew the appointment for a further period not exceeding six months, and all things required or authorized to be done by or to any such officer may be done by or to the depute or person appointed to act temporarily in the office, and any reference in this Act or any other enactment or any statutory order to the principal officer shall include a reference to the depute or person acting in the office.

(4) Nothing in this section shall be deemed to affect the provisions of any enactment or statutory order requiring the appointment of any officer for the purposes of that enactment or order.

(II) SPECIFIC DUTIES IMPOSED ON THE TREASURER
(*other than those dealt with under 'Operation of Funds' above*)
(1) *Abstract of Accounts*
(*a*) *English Provincial Boroughs*

Local Government Act, 1933—Section 240
(*c*) After the audit of the accounts for each financial year the treasurer of the borough shall print an abstract of the accounts for that year.

Note—The subsection refers to accounts not subject to district audit.

(*b*) *Other Authorities*

No provision.

(2) *Compulsory Lodgment of Monies in Bank*
(*a*) *Scottish Authorities*

See Sections 178, 182 and 186 of the Local Government (Scotland) Act, 1947, reproduced under III (II) 'Operation of Funds'.

Local Government (Scotland) Act, 1947—Section 194(2)
The Secretary of State may make regulations—
(*a*) for requiring local authorities to take steps periodically to satisfy themselves as to the balances on bank account and in the hands of officers of the authorities . . .

Note—The Secretary of State has made Regulations under Section 194(2) (*a*) providing for the certification by the auditor of the sums held in the bank in the name of the local authority, and the cash balances held by the County Treasurer, Town Chamberlain, or Treasurer of the District Council (S.I. 1948, No. 713 (S. 51)—The Local Authority (Control of Bank and Cash Balances) (Scotland) Regulations, 1948).

(*b*) *Other Authorities*

No provision.

(3) *Income Tax Assessments*
All authorities

Income Tax Act, 1952—Section 362
(2) The chamberlain or other officer acting as treasurer, auditor or receiver for the time being of any body of persons chargeable to tax shall be answerable for doing all such acts as are required to be done under this Act for the purpose of the assessment of such body and for payment of the tax, and for the purpose of the assessment of the officers and persons in the employment of such body . . .

(3) Every such officer as aforesaid may from time to time retain out of any money coming into his hands, on behalf of the body, so much thereof as is sufficient to pay the tax charged upon the body, and shall be indemnified for all such payments made in pursuance of this Act.

(4) *Admission of Freemen in English Boroughs*

The duty of receiving any fees, fines, etc., payable on admission of freemen is laid upon the treasurer by Section 263(2) of the Local Government Act, 1933.

(III) SPECIAL DUTIES OF TREASURERS OF ENGLISH COUNTIES AND QUARTER SESSIONS BOROUGHS

(*a*) Duty to pay costs in criminal cases ordered to be paid out of local funds and to attend or be represented at every court of assize or quarter sessions for the purpose of making payments. (Costs in Criminal Cases Act, 1952—Section 11)

(*b*) Duty of recovering costs in criminal cases from the treasurer of the county or borough in which the offence was committed.

(Criminal Justice Act, 1925—Section 14 (4))
(Administration of Justice (Miscellaneous Provisions) Act, 1938—
Section 11 (4))

(*c*) Duty to make payments out of the county or borough fund in respect of jury service and to attend or be represented at every court of assize or quarter sessions to make the payments. To receive and pay into the county or borough fund that part of the expenses which is attributable to other than criminal business and is recoverable from the Supreme Court.

(Juries Act, 1949—Sections 3-7)

(*d*) A county treasurer is required to observe the orders of the court of quarter sessions or justices for the payment of costs in criminal proceedings.

(Local Government Act, 1888—Section 67)

(*e*) A county treasurer is required to keep separate accounts of the county police.

(County Police Act, 1839—Section 23)

(*f*) A county treasurer is required to send orders for payment to treasurers of quarter sessions boroughs of costs of criminal proceedings at the Assizes in respect of offenders committed for trial from the borough and for any contributions which the borough may be liable to contribute from the county rate.

(Municipal Corporations Act, 1882—Section 153)

(IV) STATUTORY DUTIES WHICH USUALLY FALL ON THE CHIEF FINANCIAL OFFICER THOUGH NOT SPECIFICALLY IMPOSED ON HIM BY STATUTE

(*a*) *All Local Authorities*

(*a*) Certification of debt returns (Local Government Act, 1933—Section 199 (2), London Government Act, 1939—Section 141 (3) (metropolitan boroughs), Local Government (Scotland) Act, 1947—Section 264 (2)).

(*b*) Certification of annual return of income and expenditure (1933

Act—Section 244 (applies to London as well as to provincial authorities), 1947 Act—Section 297).

(c) Receipt of sums certified by the district auditor to be due from any person and certification that a sum payable or a certificate of a district auditor has not been paid (1933 Act—Sections 232 and 233 (2) (apply also to London)).

(d) Receipt of all money due from any officer (1933 Act—Section 120 (2), 1939 Act—Section 87 (2))

(e) Preparation of the financial statement for submission to the district auditor (1933 Act—Section 222 (1) (applies also to London)).

(f) Making up of accounts subject to district audit and the deposit of accounts for inspection (in Scotland, the making up of accounts for audit, deposit for inspection and deposit of audited accounts for inspection) (1933 Act—Sections 223 and 224 (1) (apply also to London), 1947 Act, Sections 200 and 204).

(g) The preparation of the abstract and the submission of accounts, vouchers, etc. for audit in the case of accounts subject to district audit (Audit Regulations, 1934, Articles 6 and 7). Similarly the duty of submitting accounts, vouchers, etc. to professional auditors appointed under Section 239 of the 1933 Act will normally be allotted to the treasurer.

(h) In Scotland, the rectification of the accounts as directed by the Secretary of State (1947 Act—Section 202).

(b) Scottish Authorities

Local Government (Scotland) Act, 1947—Section 175

(1) Every local authority shall cause to be kept such accounts as shall secure that sums raised by rates or requisition or other sums received by the authority are not applied to purposes to which such sums are not properly applicable, and, in particular without prejudice to the said generality, that all sums required by the authority for the repayment of any sum borrowed for a specific purpose by the authority and to meet interest on the sum so borrowed are debited to the account to which the expenditure for that purpose is chargeable, and that capital moneys are not applied to any purpose other than a purpose to which capital moneys are properly applicable.

(2) Every local authority shall cause the accounts of the authority (including those relating to funds or property held by the authority in trust) to be kept in such manner as to show in respect of the financial year to which the accounts relate:

(a) all receipts and payments of the authority during that year;

(b) any revenue and expenditure relating to revenue in respect of that year not received or paid in that year; and

(c) any capital moneys due but not paid to or by the authority in that year.

347

All such receipts and revenue of, and capital moneys due to, a local authority are in this Part of this Act in relation to the authority referred to as receipts and sums receivable, and all such payments and expenditure relating to revenue of and capital moneys due by a local authority are in this Part of this Act in relation to the authority referred to as expenditure.

(3) Every local authority shall cause the accounts of the authority to be kept in such a manner as to comply with any provision relating thereto contained in any enactment or statutory order.

Local Government (Scotland) Act, 1947—Section 189

(1) Immediately after the end of each financial year the local authority shall cause the accounts of the authority for that year to be brought to a balance and a balance sheet prepared with respect thereto.

(2) The accounts and balance sheet shall be made up so as to exhibit a complete statement showing with regard to each account:

   (a) the assets and liabilities;
   (b) the amount set aside by the authority during the year for the repayment of debt by way of periodical contributions to any sinking fund, to a loans fund as hereinafter provided for or otherwise;
   (c) the amount of the sums borrowed and the sums received from the sale or alienation of property;
   (d) the amount of annual revenue, the amount of rates collected and the amount of all sums in arrear or remaining unpaid at the close of the accounts; and
   (e) the amount of all sums paid and sums remaining unpaid in respect of any expense incurred during the year, distinguishing capital expenditure from expenditure out of annual revenue.

(3) The accounts of each local authority shall be completed and signed by such person or officer of the authority and before such date as the Secretary of State may prescribe.

Note—Regulations issued by the Secretary of State under powers conferred by Sections 189 (3) and 200 (1) of the Local Government (Scotland) Act, 1947, prescribe the form of abstract of accounts and provide that the abstract shall be completed and signed by the County Treasurer, Town Chamberlain or Treasurer of the District Council before October 31st each year.

   The County Council (Abstract of Accounts) (Scotland) Regulations, 1952, S.I. No. 1723.
   The Town Council (Large Burgh) (Abstract of Accounts) (Scotland) Regulations, 1952, S.I. No. 1720
   The Town Council (Small Burgh) (Abstract of Accounts) (Scotland) Regulation, 1952, S.I. No. 1724.
   The District Council (Abstract of Accounts) (Scotland) Regulations, 1952, S.I. No. 1722.

Local Government (Scotland) Act, 1947—Section 190

Every local authority shall cause the abstract (prepared in accordance with the provisions of section two hundred of this Act) of the accounts of the authority for each financial year as audited in accordance with the provisions of Part X of this Act together with the auditor's report thereon to be laid before a meeting of the authority to be held not later than the thirty-first day of December first occurring after the end of the financial year to which the said accounts relate or such later date as the Secretary of State may in any particular case approve, and the said accounts shall, if and as approved by the authority, be signed by the chairman of the meeting and by the clerk of the authority and shall be deposited with the clerk of the authority or such other officer as the authority may designate for the purpose.

Local Government (Scotland) Act, 1947—Section 200

(1) An abstract in duplicate of the accounts of the local authority which shall be in such form and shall be made up, balanced and signed in such manner as the Secretary of State may prescribe shall be deposited in the office of the authority . . .

Local Government (Scotland) Act, 1947—Section 297

(1) Subject to the provisions of this section, a return shall be made to the Secretary of State for each year of all sums levied or received in respect of any compulsory rates, taxes, tolls or dues and of the expenditure of any such sums:

Provided that nothing in this subsection shall extend to:

(*i*) rates, taxes, tolls or dues levied for the public revenue of the United Kingdom; or

(*ii*) tolls or dues taken by any statutory undertakers carrying on business for profit or by any company within the meaning of the Companies Act, 1929, as revenues of their undertaking; or

(*iii*) tolls or dues taken by prescription or otherwise as private property.

(2) The returns required to be made under this section shall:

(*a*) be in such form and contain such particulars as the Secretary of State may direct;

(*b*) be for the year ending the fifteenth day of May or for such other period of twelve months as the accounts are in use to be made up for;

(*c*) be sent to the Secretary of State in the month of July immediately after the end of the year to which the return relates;

(*d*) be made:

(*i*) in the case of a return by a local authority, by the clerk of the authority;

(*ii*) in the case of any other return where the power to levy the rate, tax, toll or due is vested in a corporate body, by their clerk, or if there is no clerk by the treasurer or other person whose duty it is to keep the accounts of that body, and in any other case by the person or body of persons in whom that power is vested.

(3) Where under the immediately preceding subsection a return is required to be made by the clerk of an authority or by the clerk to a corporate body, the return shall be certified by the treasurer or other person whose duty it is to keep the accounts of the authority or corporate body.

(4) Where under any enactment whether passed before or after the commencement of this Act, any annual return relating to any rate, tax, toll or due (other than such as are levied for the public revenue of the United Kingdom) is required to be made to a Minister, a return under this Part of this Act need not be made, so however that where such annual return is made to a Minister other than the Secretary of State a duplicate thereof shall in like manner be sent to the Secretary of State, and any person failing to send such duplicate shall be subject to the like penalty as a person failing to make a return under this Part of this Act.

(5) The duplicate abstract of accounts of a local authority or of a joint board to which this Part of this Act applies which is required by Part X of this Act to be sent to the Secretary of State by the auditor of the accounts of the authority or board shall, if the Secretary of State so directs, be deemed to be the return made by the clerk of the authority or board under this Part of this Act with respect to the sums levied or received and expenditure included in the accounts:

Provided that if for any reason the said duplicate abstract of accounts is not received by the Secretary of State by the thirtieth day of September in any year, the Secretary of State may, notwithstanding any such direction, require the clerk of the authority or board to furnish to him within one month after the date of the requirement a return under this Part of this Act, and the provisions of this Part of this Act shall, subject to any necessary modifications, apply with respect to the return so required.

5

CONTRACTS

(*a*) *All English Provincial Authorities*

Local Government Act, 1933—Section 266

(1) A local authority may enter into contracts necessary for the discharge of any of their functions.

(2) All contracts made by a local authority or by a committee thereof shall be made in accordance with the standing orders of the local authority,

and in the case of contracts for the supply of goods or materials or for the execution of works, the standing orders shall:

    (a) require that, except as otherwise provided by or under the standing orders, notice of the intention of the authority or committee, as the case may be, to enter into the contract shall be published and tenders invited; and

    (b) regulate the manner in which such notice shall be published and tenders invited:

Provided that a person entering into a contract with a local authority shall not be bound to inquire whether the standing orders of the authority which apply to the contract have been complied with, and all contracts entered into by a local authority, if otherwise valid, shall have full force and effect notwithstanding that the standing orders applicable thereto have not been complied with.

(b) *London County Council and Metropolitan Boroughs*

London Government Act, 1939—Section 160

(Apart from slight differences in wording this provision is identical with Section 266 of the 1933 Act)

(c) *Scottish Authorities*

Local Government (Scotland) Act, 1947—Section 336

    (1) A local authority may enter into any contract necessary for the discharge of any of their functions.

    (2) A local authority shall not grant any obligation, contract any debt, enter into any contract or agreement or execute any deed unless the same shall have been authorized by the authority or by a committee thereof or a person duly empowered by the authority, and in the case of contracts for the supply of goods or materials or for the execution of works, standing orders of the authority shall:

    (a) require that, except as otherwise provided by or under the standing orders, notice of the intention of the authority or committee or person, as the case may be, to enter into the contract shall be published and tenders invited; and

    (b) regulate the manner in which such notice shall be published and tenders invited:

Provided that a creditor in any such obligation or debt or a person entering into a contract or agreement with a local authority or a person transacting on the faith of a deed executed by a local authority shall not be bound to inquire whether the same has been duly authorized as aforesaid, and all such obligations, debts, contracts, agreements and deeds granted, contracted, entered into or executed by a local authority if otherwise valid shall have full force and effect, notwithstanding that the same have not been duly authorized in accordance with the provisions of this section.

6

GENERAL STATUTORY PROVISIONS RELEVANT TO FINANCIAL ADMINISTRATION

(i) MEMBERS NOT TO BE APPOINTED TO A PAID OFFICE

(a) *All English Provincial Authorities*

Local Government Act, 1933—Section 122

A person shall, so long as he is, and for twelve months after he ceases to be, a member of a local authority, be disqualified for being appointed by that authority to any paid office, other than to the office of chairman, mayor or sheriff.

(b) *London County Council and Metropolitan Boroughs*

London Government Act, 1939—Section 89

A person shall, so long as he is, and for twelve months after he ceases to be, a member of a local authority, be disqualified for being appointed by that authority to any paid office, other than to the office of chairman or deputy chairman in the case of the county council, or to the office of mayor in the case of a borough.

(c) *Scottish Authorities*

Local Government (Scotland) Act, 1947—Section 101

It shall not be lawful for a local authority or for a committee or sub-committee of the authority (including any committee or sub-committee to which section fifty-two of this Act applies) or for a joint committee or joint board containing persons appointed by the authority to appoint to any paid office in the gift or disposal of the authority or of the committee or sub-committee or of the joint committee or joint board, as the case may be, a person who is or has within six months prior to the date of appointment been a member of the authority or a person who is or has within six months prior to the date of appointment been a partner in business of the person who is or has within the said six months been a member of the authority.

(ii) RIGHT OF MEMBERS TO INSPECT DOCUMENTS AND ACCOUNTS

(a) *English Provincial Authorities*

Local Government Act, 1933—Section 283 (3)

(3) The accounts of a local authority and of the treasurer of a local authority shall be open to the inspection of any member of the authority, and any such member may make a copy thereof or an extract therefrom.

(b) *London County Council and Metropolitan Boroughs*

London Government Act, 1939—Section 173

(4) The accounts of the county council and of the county treasurer shall

be open to the inspection of any member of the county council, and the accounts of a borough council and of the borough treasurer shall be open to the inspection of any member of the borough council, and any member of the county council or of a borough council may make a copy of, or take an extract from, the accounts so open to his inspection.

(c) *Scottish Authorities*

No provision.

(III) MEMBERS AND CONTRACTS

(a) *All English Provincial Authorities*

Local Government Act, 1933—Section 76 (as amended by the Local Government Act, 1948, Section 131 and the Local Government (Miscellaneous Provisions) Act, 1953, Section 15)

(1) If a member of a local authority has any pecuniary interest, direct or indirect, in any contract or proposed contract or other matter, and is present at a meeting of the local authority at which the contract or other matter is the subject of consideration, he shall at the meeting, as soon as practicable after the commencement thereof, disclose the fact, and shall not take part in the consideration or discussion of, or vote on any question with respect to, the contract or other matter:

Provided that this section shall not apply to an interest in a contract or other matter which a member may have as a ratepayer or inhabitant of the area, or as an ordinary consumer of gas, electricity or water, or to an interest in any matter relating to the terms on which the right to participate in any service, including the supply of goods, is offered to the public.

(2) For the purposes of this section a person shall (subject as hereafter in this subsection provided) be treated as having indirectly a pecuniary interest in a contract or other matter, if

(a) he or any nominee of his is a member of a company or other body with which the contract is made or is proposed to be made or which has a direct pecuniary interest in the other matter under consideration; or

(b) he is a partner, or is in the employment , of a person with whom the contract is made or is proposed to be made or who has a direct pecuniary interest in the other matter under consideration:

Provided that:

(i) this subsection shall not apply to membership of, or employment under, any public body;

(ii) a member of a company or other body shall not, by reason only of his membership, be treated as being so interested if he has no beneficial interest in any shares of that company or other body.

(2A) Where a member of a local authority has indirectly a pecuniary interest in a contract or other matter and would not fall to be treated as having such an interest but for the fact that he has a beneficial interest in shares of a company or other body, then, if the total nominal value of those shares does not exceed five hundred pounds or one hundredth of the total nominal value of the issued share capital of the company or body, whichever is the less, so much of subsection (1) of this section as prohibits him from taking part in the consideration or discussion of, and from voting on any question with respect to, the contract or other matter shall not apply to him, without prejudice, however, to the duty of disclosure imposed by the said subsection (1):

Provided that where the share capital of the company or other body is of more than one class, this subsection shall not apply if the total nominal value of all the shares of any one class in which he has a beneficial interest exceeds one hundredth part of the total issued share capital of that class of the company or other body.

(3) In the case of married persons living together the interest of one spouse shall, if known to the other, be deemed for the purposes of this section to be also an interest of that other spouse.

(4) A general notice given in writing to the clerk of the authority by a member thereof to the effect that he or his spouse is a member or in the employment of a specified company or other body, or that he or his spouse is a partner or in the employment of a specified person, shall, unless and until the notice is withdrawn, be deemed to be a sufficient disclosure of his interest in any contract, proposed contract or other matter relating to that company or other body or to that person which may be the subject of consideration after the date of the notice.

(5) The clerk of the authority shall record in a book to be kept for the purpose particulars of any disclosure made under subsection (1) of this section, and of any notice given under subsection (4) thereof, and the book shall be open at all reasonable hours to the inspection of any member of the local authority.

(6) If any person fails to comply with the provisions of subsection (1) of this section, he shall for each offence be liable on summary conviction to a fine not exceeding fifty pounds, unless he proves that he did not know that a contract, proposed contract, or other matter in which he had a pecuniary interest was the subject of consideration at the meeting.

(7) A prosecution for an offence under this section shall not be instituted except by or on behalf of the Director of Public Prosecutions.

(8) The county council, as respects a member of a parish council, and the Minister, as respects a member of any other local authority, may, subject to such conditions as the county council or the Minister, as the case may be, may think fit to impose, remove any disability imposed by this section in any case in which the number of members of the local authority so disabled at any one time would be so great a proportion of the whole as to impede the transaction of business, or in any other case in which it appears to the

county council or the Minister, as the case may be, that it is in the interests of the inhabitants of the area that the disability should be removed.

(9) A local authority may by standing orders provide for the exclusion of a member of the authority from a meeting of the authority whilst any contract, proposed contract or other matter in which he has such an interest as aforesaid is under consideration.

(10) In this section, the expression 'shares' includes stock and the expression 'share capital' shall be construed accordingly.

(b) London County Council

London Government Act, 1939—Section 51

(1) A member of the county council shall not vote on, or take part in the discussion of, any matter before the council in which he has, directly or indirectly, by himself or his partner, any pecuniary interest.

(2) A member of the county council shall not vote on any resolution or question which is proposed or arises under the Housing Acts, 1936 and 1938, if it relates to premises in which he is beneficially interested, and if any person votes in contravention of the provisions of this subsection, he shall in respect of each offence be liable on summary conviction to a fine not exceeding fifty pounds, but the fact of his having voted shall not invalidate the resolution or proceeding of the county council.

(c) Scottish Authorities

Local Government (Scotland) Act, 1947—Section 73 (as amended by the Local Government Act, 1948, Section 131, the National Assistance Act, 1948, 7th Sch., Part III and the Local Government (Miscellaneous Provisions) Act, 1953, Section 15).

This provision is similar to Section 76 of the 1933 Act (see page 353) apart from minor differences in wording, the omission of a provision corresponding to Section 76 (7), and a revision of subsection (8) as follows:

(8) In any case in which the number of members of a local authority disabled by the provisions of this section at any one time would be so great a proportion of the whole as to impede the transaction of any particular item of business, the Secretary of State may, on the application of the authority or otherwise and subject to such conditions as he may think fit to impose, remove any disability imposed by this section as respects such business or, with the consent of the authority and after such inquiry as he may direct, himself transact the business on their behalf—any business so transacted being of full force and effect and binding upon the authority —and the Secretary of State may also, on any such application or otherwise and subject to such conditions as he may think fit to impose, remove any disability in any other case in which it appears to him that it is in the interests of the inhabitants of the area that he should do so:

Provided that notwithstanding anything in this section every member' of the authority may take part in the consideration or discussion of and vote on the question whether any such application shall be made or any such consent granted.

(d) Metropolitan Boroughs

London Government Act, 1939—Section 52 (as amended by the Local Government Act, 1948—Section 131 and the Local Government (Miscellaneous Provisions) Act, 1953—Section 15).

Apart from minor differences in wording this provision is the same as Section 76 of the 1933 Act.

(IV) OFFICERS AND CONTRACTS

(a) All English Provincial Authorities

Local Government Act, 1933—Section 123

(1) If it comes to the knowledge of an officer employed, whether under this Act or any other enactment, by a local authority, that a contract in which he has any pecuniary interest, whether direct or indirect (not being a contract to which he is himself a party), has been or is proposed to be, entered into by the authority or any committee thereof, he shall, as soon as practicable, give notice in writing to the authority of the fact that he is interested therein.

For the purposes of this section an officer shall be treated as having indirectly a pecuniary interest in a contract or proposed contract if he would have been so treated by virtue of subsection (2) or subsection (3) of section seventy-six of this Act* had he been a member of the authority.

(2) An officer of a local authority shall not, under colour of his office or employment, exact or accept any fee or reward whatsoever other than his proper remuneration.

(3) If any person fails to comply with the provisions of subsection (1) or contravenes any of the provisions of subsection (2) of this section, he shall for each offence be liable on summary conviction to a fine not exceeding fifty pounds.

(4) References in this section to a local authority shall include a reference to a joint committee appointed under Part III of this Act.

* See above under Members and Contracts.

(b) London County Council and Metropolitan Boroughs

London Government Act, 1939—Section 90

(1) If it comes to the knowledge of an officer employed by a local authority that a contract in which he has any pecuniary interest, whether direct or indirect, not being a contract to which he is himself a party, has been, or is proposed to be, entered into by the authority or by any committee thereof, he shall, as soon as practicable, give notice in writing to the authority of the fact that he is interested therein.

(2) For the purposes of this section, a person shall, subject as hereinafter provided, be treated as having indirectly a pecuniary interest in a contract or proposed contract if:

(*a*) he or any nominee of his is a member of a company or other body with which the contract is made or is proposed to be made; or

(*b*) he is a partner, or is in the employment, of a person with whom the contract is made or is proposed to be made:

Provided that:

(*i*) this subsection shall not apply to membership of, or employment under, a public body;

(*ii*) a member of a company or other body shall not, by reason only of his membership, be treated as being so interested if he has no beneficial interest in any shares or stock of that company or other body.

(3) In the case of married persons living together the interest of one spouse shall, if known to the other, be deemed for the purposes of this section to be also an interest of that other spouse.

(4) If any person fails to comply with the provisions of this section, he shall in respect of each offence be liable on summary conviction to a fine not exceeding fifty pounds:

Provided that proceedings for an offence under this section shall not be instituted except by or with the consent of the Director of Public Prosecutions.

London Government Act, 1939—Section 91

(1) An officer of a local authority shall not, under colour of his office or employment, exact or accept any fee or reward whatsoever other than his proper remuneration.

(2) If any person acts in contravention of the provisions of this section, he shall in respect of each offence be liable on summary conviction to a fine not exceeding fifty pounds:

Provided that proceedings for an offence under this section shall not be instituted except by or with the consent of the Director of Public Prosecutions.

(*c*) Scottish Authorities

Local Government (Scotland) Act, 1947—Section 102

(1) If it comes to the knowledge of an officer employed by a local authority under this Act or any other enactment or any statutory order that a contract in which he has any pecuniary interest whether direct or indirect (not being a contract to which he himself is a party) has been or is proposed to be entered into by the authority, he shall as soon as practicable give notice in writing to the authority of the fact that he is interested therein:

Provided that this subsection shall not apply to an officer other than the clerk or treasurer of the authority, unless the contract relates to a matter in connection with which the officer is employed by the authority and the officer is normally consulted by the authority or by members thereof in connection with such contracts.

For the purposes of this subsection an officer shall be treated as having indirectly a pecuniary interest in a contract or proposed contract if he would have been so treated by virtue of subsection (2) or subsection (4) of section 73 of this Act had he been a member of the authority.

(2) An officer of a local authority shall not under colour of his office or employment exact or accept for himself any fee or reward whatsoever other than his proper remuneration.

(3) The provisions of subsections (5) and (6) of section 73 of this Act shall subject to any necessary modifications apply in the case of an officer of a local authority as they apply in the case of a member of the authority, so however that the book mentioned in the said subsection (6) shall be open to the inspection only of any member or the clerk of the authority.

(4) If any person fails to comply with subsection (1) or contravenes any of the provisions of subsection (2) of this section he shall be liable on summary conviction to a fine not exceeding fifty pounds.

(5) References in this section to a local authority shall include references to a committee or sub-committee of the authority (including any committee or sub-committee to which section 52 of this Act applies) or to a joint committee or joint board.

(v) OFFICERS LIKELY TO BE ENTRUSTED WITH THE CONTROL OF MONEY

(a) All English Provincial Authorities

Local Government Act, 1933—Section 119

(1) A local authority, other than a parish council, shall, in the case of an officer employed by them, whether under this or any other enactment, who by reason of his office or employment is likely to be entrusted with the custody or control of money, and may in the case of any other officer employed by them, either require him to give, or themselves take, such security for the faithful execution of his office and for his duly accounting for all money or property which may be entrusted to him, as the local authority think sufficient.

(2) A local authority, other than a parish council, may, in the case of a person not employed by them but who is likely to be entrusted with the custody or control of money or property belonging to the local authority, take such security as they think sufficient for the person duly accounting for all such money or property.

(3) In the case of the treasurer of a parish council, the parish council shall either require the officer to give, or may themselves take, such security for the faithful execution of his office as may be directed by the county council.

(4) A local authority shall, in the case of persons not employed by them, and may in any other case, defray the cost of any security given or taken under this section, and every such security shall be produced to the auditor or auditors at the audit of the accounts of the local authority.

Justices of the Peace Act, 1949—Section 28
(1) Where a justices' clerk does not duly pay to the Secretary of State or other person entitled thereto any sums received by him by reason of his office (other than sums received on account of his salary or expenses as justices' clerk), or a person employed to assist a justices' clerk does not duly pay to the clerk or some person on his behalf any sums received in the course of that employment, the responsible authority shall pay the amount of those sums to the Secretary of State or other person entitled to receive them from the clerk.

(2) A county or borough council shall have the same power under subsection (2) of section 119 of the Local Government Act, 1933 (or in the case of the London County Council subsection (2) of section 86 of the London Government Act, 1939), to take security with respect to the sums referred to in the foregoing subsection as they have with respect to money belonging to the council which is entrusted to the custody or control of a person not employed by them.

(b) *London County Council and Metropolitan Boroughs*

London Government Act, 1939—Section 86
(1) A local authority shall, in the case of an officer employed by the authority who by reason of his office or employment is likely to be entrusted with the custody or control of money, and may in the case of any other officer employed by the authority, either require him to give, or itself take, such security for the faithful execution of his office and for his duly accounting for all money or property which may be entrusted to him, as the authority thinks sufficient.

(2) A local authority may, in the case of a person not employed by the authority but who is likely to be entrusted with the custody or control of money or property belonging to the authority, take such security as it thinks sufficient for his duly accounting for all such money or property.

(3) A local authority shall, in the case of persons not employed by the authority, and may in any other case, defray the cost of any security given or taken under this section, and every security so given or taken shall be produced to the district auditor at the audit of the accounts of the authority.

(c) *Scottish Authorities*

Local Government (Scotland) Act, 1947—Section 98
(1) Every local authority in the case of each of the treasurer, the collector, and such other officers as the Secretary of State may prescribe shall,

and in the case of any other officer employed by them may, require the officer to obtain in name of the authority from any company accepted by the Court of Session as cautioner for a judicial factor appointed by the court security for the faithful execution of his office and for his duly accounting for all money or property which may be entrusted to him to such amount as the local authority think sufficient, not being less in the case of a treasurer or a collector of a county council or a town council than one thousand pounds.

(2) The provisions of the foregoing subsection shall apply in the case of an officer of a local authority holding office at the commencement of this Act, except in so far as security has been provided by him which complies with that subsection.

(3) If any officer of a local authority fails to provide security in accordance with subsection (1) of this section within three months after the date on which the authority have required him to do so, he shall be deemed to have resigned from his office at the expiration of the said period of three months.

(4) A local authority may, in the case of a person who is not employed by them but who or whose employees are or are likely to be entrusted with the custody or control of money or property belonging to the authority, require such person to obtain in name of the authority or themselves take from any such company as aforesaid such security as they think sufficient for all such money or property being duly accounted for.

(5) The local authority shall defray the premium in respect of any security taken under this section.

(6) Every such deed of security shall be delivered to and remain in the custody of the clerk of the authority or other officer designated by the authority for the purpose and shall be produced by the clerk or other officer to the auditor at the audit of the accounts of the authority, and the auditor shall in each case report whether in his opinion security of a sufficient amount has been provided and whether the premiums payable have been duly paid.

Note—The Secretary of State has made Regulations under Section 98 (1) prescribing the officers, other than the treasurer and the collector, required to provide security for the faithful execution of their offices and for duly accounting for all money or property which may be entrusted to them (S.I. 1948, No. 2282 (S. 182)—The Local Government (Security by Officers) (Scotland) Regulations, 1948).

(VI) ACCOUNTABILITY OF OFFICERS

(a) *All English Provincial Authorities*

Local Government Act, 1933—Section 120

(1) Every officer employed by a local authority, whether under this Act or any other enactment, shall at such times during the continuance

of his office, or within three months after his ceasing to hold it, and in such manner, as the local authority direct, make out and deliver to the authority, or as they direct, a true account in writing of all money and property committed to his charge, and of his receipts and payments, with vouchers and other documents and records supporting the entries therein, and a list of persons from whom or to whom money is due in connection with his office, showing the amount due from or to each.

(2) Every such officer shall pay all money due from him to the treasurer of the county, borough, district or parish, as the case may be, or otherwise as the local authority may direct.

(3) If any such officer:

(a) refuses or wilfully neglects to make any payment which he is required by this section to make; or

(b) after three days' notice in writing, signed by the clerk of the authority or by three members thereof, and given or left at his usual or last known place of residence, refuses or wilfully neglects to make out or deliver to the authority, or as they direct, any account or list which he is required by this section to make out and deliver, or any voucher or other document or record relating thereto, or to give satisfaction respecting it to the authority or as they direct;

a court of summary jurisdiction having jurisdiction where the officer is or resides may, on complaint, by order require him to make such payment or delivery or to give such satisfaction.

(4) Nothing in this section shall affect any remedy by action against any such officer or his surety, except that the officer shall not be both sued by action and proceeded against summarily for the same cause.

(b) *London County Council and Metropolitan Boroughs*

London Government Act, 1939—Section 87
(Apart from minor differences in wording, this provision is identical with Section 120 of the 1933 Act.)

(c) *Scottish Authorities*

No provision.

(VII) RESTRICTION OF PERSONAL LIABILITY OF OFFICERS IN SCOTLAND

Local Government (Scotland) Act, 1947—Section 103
(1) An officer of a local authority shall not be personally liable in respect of any act done by him in the execution of any enactment or statutory order relating to a function of the authority and within the scope of his employment, if he acted reasonably and in the honest belief that his

duty under such enactment or statutory order required or entitled him to do it:

Provided that nothing in this subsection shall be construed:

(a) as relieving a local authority from any liability in respect of acts of their officers, or

(b) as exempting any officer of a local authority from being surcharged in accordance with the provisions of Part X of this Act.

(2) Where an action has been brought against an officer of a local authority in respect of an act done by him in the execution or purported execution of any such enactment or statutory order and the circumstances are such that he is not legally entitled to require the authority to indemnify him, the authority may nevertheless indemnify him against the whole or a part of any damages or expenses which he may have been ordered to pay or may have incurred if they are satisfied that he honestly believed that the act complained of was within the scope of his employment and that his duty under such enactment or order required or entitled him to do it.

Section 201—*Power of Secretary of State to disallow illegal payments and surcharge on interim report of auditor.*

Proviso (b) 'a surcharge shall not be made under this section upon an officer of a local authority by reason only of his signing a cheque or order in respect of any illegal payment, if he satisfies the Secretary of State that before signing the cheque or order he advised the authority in writing that in his opinion the payment was illegal;'

APPENDIX C

Organization Chart of a Finance Dept

(SHOWING ONE FORM OF ORGANIZATION FOR A CHIEF FINANCIAL OFFICER'S DEPARTMENT OF MODERATE SIZE)

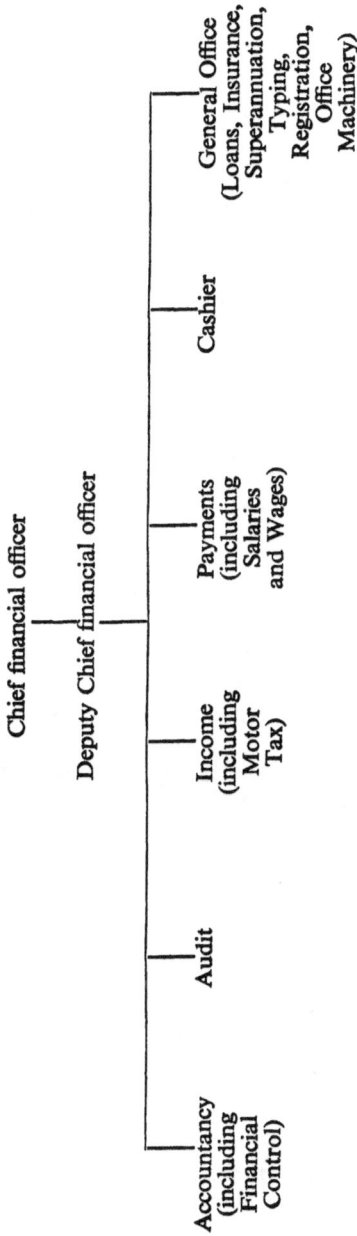

Chief financial officer

Deputy Chief financial officer

- Accountancy (including Financial Control)
- Audit
- Income (including Motor Tax)
- Payments (including Salaries and Wages)
- Cashier
- General Office (Loans, Insurance, Superannuation, Typing, Registration, Office Machinery)

APPENDIX D

EXAMPLE OF JOINT REPORT

Date

To the Chairman and Members of the Baths Committee:

1. The capital cost of the scheme for new central baths, plans and details of which will be submitted to the committee, is estimated as follows:

		£
(a) Site to be appropriated from the Estates Committee		100,000
(b) Buildings		300,000
Plant and Services		
(c) Filtration plant		22,000
(d) Heating and ventilation		65,000
(e) Electrical services		11,000
(f) Furniture and fittings		2,000
(g) Professional fees		25,000
		£525,000

The total of £525,000 is £25,000 more than the amount the committee had provisionally in mind.

2. The land is already in the Council's possession and is included at the District Valuer's valuation.

3. Loan sanctions will be needed as follows:

	£
30 years (buildings and professional fees)	325,000
15 years (other items)	100,000

4. The estimated expenditure and income of the baths for the first complete year of operation is:

Expenditure

	£
Salaries and wages	12,500
National insurance	420
Superannuation	200
Repair and maintenance of buildings	400
Fuel and light	12,000
Rates	9,500
Water	750
Cleaning materials	1,000
Repair and maintenance of plant	360
Equipment, tools and materials	350
Provisions	2,400

364

Clothing and uniforms	100
Laundry	1,000
Insurances	100
Departmental establishment charges	1,300
Debt management	400
Debt charges—Interest	21,250
Principal	17,500
Appropriation charges—Interest	1,665
Principal	3,000
Total expenditure	£86,195

Income

Sales—Café		4,000
Fees and charges—		
Swimming bath	20,500	
Swimming bath, schools	2,400	
Spectators	1,200	
Galas, etc.	1,860	
Slipper baths	2,250	
		28,210
Miscellaneous income		340
Total income		£32,550

5. The rate charge is therefore £53,645, equivalent to a rate in the £ of $3 \cdot 35d$ on the current rate product.

6. Estimates have been prepared on the basis of existing costs. The staff complements have been estimated in conjunction with the Establishment Officer.

7. Increased charges have been assumed for the new baths. They compare with the existing scale as follows:

	Present		*Proposed*	
	s.	*d.*	*s.*	*d.*
Adults: Sundays	1	3	2	0
Weekdays	1	0	1	6
Children: Weekdays		8	1	0
Schools		4		8

8. In arriving at the estimated income we have had to make an arbitrary assumption about the number of bathers during the year. This has been put at 265,000. No allowance has been made for any decrease in income at the council's existing bath.

9. The chief financial officer would draw attention to the magnitude of the scheme, the cost to rates (£53,645) being more than the whole cost of the Children's Service (£51,450) or the Welfare Service (£46,210).

10. No cost would fall to be met in the current year. The new bath is included in the council's long-term capital forecast. The proposal, if agreed to by the Baths Committee must, under the Council's standing orders, be submitted to the Finance Committee.

————Baths Superintendent

————Chief Architect

————Chief Financial Officer

APPENDIX E

Outline Standing Orders and Regulations

CONTENTS

INTRODUCTORY NOTE

A. STANDING ORDERS

INTRODUCTORY NOTE

The reader's attention is drawn to the following points, some of which are elaborated in the chapter on internal rules:

(a) No categorical distinction can be made between standing orders and regulations but the general dividing line is that the former should include the broader statements of principles and the latter the administrative prescriptions. In the exemplification which follows the marginal matters have been included as standing orders. Thus the tendency has been to lengthen the standing orders section at the expense of the regulations.

(b) If an authority uses manuals of instruction, regulations will probably not be needed.

(c) This appendix should be read in conjunction with the appropriate chapters of the book.

(d) These specimen standing orders and regulations show only the substance of the point to be covered, leaving the actual form for local decision.

(e) The appendix should be read as a whole. Thus though there is a section headed 'Duties of the finance committee', specific tasks of the committee are referred to under other headings, e.g. 'Revenue Budget'.

A. STANDING ORDERS

Duties of finance committee
The finance committee to:

advise the council on the financial aspects of all proposals;

control and co-ordinate accounting methods and financial business;

watch generally over finance and accounts and, if necessary, hold conferences with other committees;

carry out investigations and call for relevant supporting documents;

submit to the council regulations for the control and management of the finances of the authority (or alternatively approve manuals of instruction);

settle financial matters in dispute between departments;

allocate expenditure between capital and revenue;

deal with cases of irregularity in financial or stores transactions;

make recommendations to the council on borrowing transactions;

manage all funds and investments;

allocate central establishment charges;

control the finance department;

receive the report of the external auditors and take any necessary action;

superintend the collection of all income accounts in consultation, if necessary, with the other committees;

write off bad debts, institute legal proceedings for recovery, etc.;

supervise the making of payments (see section on payment of accounts below);

effect all insurances and settle claims.

Financial duties of operating committees
Operating committees to be responsible for the following duties and to

be required to nominate an officer of the department to act as departmental finance officer to assist in their discharge:

supervising the expenditure and keeping it within the amount allocated; allocation of costs to proper heads of account;

certification of invoices and passing to the chief financial officer for payment;

initiation of income collection;

paying to the chief financial officer all monies received and safeguarding cash collections and imprests;

making arrangements for custody, control and checking of stores, small plant and tools, and for notifying the chief financial officer of discrepancies;

supplying the chief financial officer with all data needed for accounting and financial control purposes;

keeping financial records in a form agreed with the chief financial officer and conforming with instructions in the manuals;

effectively controlling vehicle and plant operation.

Duties of chief financial officer
The chief financial officer to:

supervise (subject to the control of the finance committee) the finance and accounts of the authority;

act as financial adviser to the council and its committees;

keep the finance committee in touch with all proposals of committees which would materially affect the finances of the council;

report annually to each committee and to the finance committee the results of the internal audit;

report annually on the financial organization of the authority.

Financial reports
A committee recommending to the council a new scheme involving expenditure, whether it is to be defrayed from capital, revenue, or accumulated monies of any kind to submit a detailed report showing the amount to be raised by loan, the amount to be charged against the current rate, future rates or other account. Where the scheme is to be carried out in stages, the report to indicate the total cost of the full scheme.

Such reports to be considered by the finance committee before being considered by the council, and the finance committee to report whether it approves or does not approve. The report to include general observations and relevant statistics, e.g. loan debt on existing and similar works.

A member of the council intending to move a resolution involving expenditure to give notice to the finance committee in order that a concurrent report may be presented.

There should be a comparable order for other proposals affecting finances, e.g. proposals to alter scales of charges.

Urgent proposals

Chairman of finance committee to have power to sanction urgent expenditure, not otherwise authorized, subject to subsequent report to the council, such report to include full details of the circumstances.

Revenue budget

Committees to prepare and send to the finance committee, by a specified date and in a form prescribed by the latter committee, details of anticipated expenditure for the remainder of the current year, and a forecast of expenditure for the forthcoming year.

The finance committee chairman to have power to attend the budget meetings of all committees and other meetings when annual or supplementary estimates are to be considered.

Chairmen of committees to be allowed to attend the finance committee while the estimates of their committees are being considered.

The finance committee to be required to confer with other committees in cases of dispute.

The finance committee to submit the aggregate estimates to the council together with their recommendations. In cases of unsettled disputes between the finance committee and a spending committee, both sets of figures to be shown.

No amendments to be in order at the council meeting at which the estimates are considered, if the effect would be to increase the amount of an estimate.

Supplementary estimates

Where a committee wishes to incur expenditure not originally included in the estimates, a report to be forwarded to the finance committee. Supplementary estimates not to be considered unless the matter is one of urgency. The procedure laid down for the original estimates to apply as far as possible to supplementary estimates.

Virement

Consent of finance committee and council to be obtained for diversion of budgetary provision from one purpose to another.

Annual capital budget

Annual estimates of capital expenditure to be prepared by operating committees and submitted to the finance committee by a prescribed date, the estimates to distinguish between expenditure approved and not yet approved. The finance committee to consider the estimates, confer with the operating committees, if necessary, and submit recommendations to the council.

Long-term capital forecast

The committees to prepare and submit to the finance committee by a prescribed date estimates showing the proposed capital expenditure for, say, five years ahead distinguishing between expenditure approved and not yet approved. The finance committee to consider the estimates, confer with the operating department, if necessary, and submit recommendations to the council.

Loan expenditure

Except with the consent of the finance committee no expenditure chargeable to loan should be incurred unless borrowing powers are available.

Purchasing and contracting

Committee to have power to allot contracts the value of which does not exceed £   (Any exceptions to be stated, e.g. power of committees to allot maintenance contracts without limit).

Officers to have power to allot contracts the value of which do not exceed £   .

The general rule to be that competitive tenders or quotations are obtained for purchasing of supplies, contracting and sub-contracting.

Supplies to be on an annual basis except where this would be detrimental.

Every contract to comply with the standing orders.

Where the value of goods to be purchased exceeds £   , but does not exceed £   , tenders to be invited by local advertisement, and where the estimated value is over £   advertisement to be inserted in trade journals as well as locally.

Tenders to be sent in plain envelopes marked 'Tender for ———' to the Clerk of the authority in whose custody they are to remain until the time of opening.

All tenders to be opened at one time in the presence of the chairman of the appropriate committee or a person designated by him, and the Clerk to the authority or a person designated by him. The chairman to initial the tenders.

Tenders other than the lowest not to be accepted except upon a report by the appropriate officer. The full details in such circumstances to be reported to the finance (or general purposes) committee.

Circumstances in which exceptions to the requirement that all contracts over a specified value should be advertised are to be allowed, to be defined, e.g. emergencies, supply of proprietary apparatus or appliances and machinery, goods or materials where effective competition is prevented by government control, goods or materials which it is considered desirable to procure locally. The standing orders to specify the exact procedure to be followed for these exceptions, e.g. tenders to be received from selected firms, either at the discretion of the committee or from an approved list.

Where exceptions are likely to be numerous, the standing orders to provide a procedure for the compilation of a list, e.g. advertising in appropriate local and trade journals inviting suppliers to have their names placed on the list.

Any tenderer withdrawing a tender may be disqualified from tendering for   years.

Contracts which are to be under seal to be defined, e.g. those over a certain amount or those not to be performed within one month. In addition, a still further distinction may be drawn between contracts which are to be in writing and those which must be sealed.

All written contracts to contain the following clauses:

> Fair wages; inspection of wages books; cancellation for offences under the Prevention of Corruption Acts and similar offences; security for non-performance, and a clause specifying that so far as practicable goods should be manufactured within the Commonwealth; the chief financial officer to review the contract settlement before the architect's or technical officer's final certificate is given.

Any departure from the standing orders relating to contracts to be reported to the council or referred to the general purposes committee; in all cases the details to be included in the report to the council of the committee concerned.

Allocation and nomination of sub-contracts to be made in accordance with the instructions of the committee responsible for the contract.

All extras and variations to contracts to be authorized by resolution.

Appropriate committee to be warned by chief officers where the expenditure on a contract is likely materially to exceed the estimate.

Final certificates for payment to be promptly submitted and supported by all relevant documents.

Central purchasing

Classes of goods which are to be purchased centrally to be specified (the details may be left to regulations or manuals) whether they are to be bought by a central purchasing department or otherwise.

Direct labour

(These standing orders will vary according to the extent to which the local authority wishes the direct labour department to compete with outside tenderers and whether committees have an option to employ direct labour or not.)

Nature of work to which the orders relate to be defined, e.g. building maintenance, building construction, street lighting.

Definition of classes of work to be carried out automatically by direct labour without an estimate of cost before the work is begun, e.g. jobs not exceeding cost of £100.

Definition of classes of work to be carried out by direct labour but only after the submission of an estimate, e.g. jobs to cost between £100 and £1,000.

Limit above which competitive tendering is to be required, e.g. £1,000. In cases where the direct labour department is to tender in competition with other tenderers, the tender to be forwarded to the Clerk and dealt with as if it were an outside tender. The tender to include an appropriate amount of overhead expenses.

On completion of the work, a complete statement of the cost, including overhead expenses, certified by the chief financial officer, to be presented to the appropriate committee and to the finance or general purposes committee. The statement to show, in addition to the final ascertained cost, the amount of the tender submitted by the departmental officer in the first instance and the detail of approved variations.

Where direct labour works are carried out on an extensive scale, standing orders to make special provision for the purchase of materials, e.g. the requirements as to advertising not to apply, but the principle of competitive tendering to be maintained as far as possible.

Payment of accounts

Accounts to be scheduled and submitted to the appropriate committee (this may be the finance committee or the operating committees). The approved list of accounts signed by the chairman to be the authority for payment, or (for any accounts first paid by the chief financial officer from an imprest or advance account) the authority for the reimbursement of the imprest account. (The operation of the imprest account to be governed by regulations.) Lists of invoices approved for payment to be deposited for the inspection of members of the council.

Collection of income

Recommendations of committees dealing with existing or new sources of income not to be considered by the council until a report has been submitted by the finance committee.

B. REGULATIONS

Proposals for expenditure and other reports affecting finances

Heads of departments to give adequate notice of submission of such reports and to supply the chief financial officer with all information necessary for the chief financial officer to advise the committee. Joint reports by the officers to be submitted where possible. (One council requires all new schemes to be considered by an informal committee of all the officers concerned before it is submitted to a committee.) Reports to show financial effects in full.

Annual budget

The dates for the submission of the draft estimates to the chief financial officer to be laid down, also the dates for submission to operating committees, consideration by the finance committee and for the finance committee's submission to the council. Estimates to include transactions on revenue account and capital, repairs, reserve and contingency funds.

The estimates to show separately ordinary expenditure, extraordinary expenditure and loan charges. Items which have not been approved in principle by the council to be shown as provisional sums or to be specially earmarked in some other way.

Accounts

The chief financial officer to be responsible for keeping the accounts of the council. The form of subsidiary records to be laid down by the chief financial officer after consultation with heads of departments. The chief financial officer to supply committees and heads of departments promptly with all the financial information they need for the control of operations. The chief financial officer regularly to report to the committees on their financial position.

Audit

The internal audit to extend to accounting for receipts, initiation of charges and collection of sums due, custody of stores, utilization of transport and equipment, allocation of costs, and verification that such allocations accord with labour, materials and other resources applied, charging of expenditure against budget heads, checking and certification of payments, control and disbursement of petty cash, efficiency of all accounting arrangements, including proper allocation of duties between accounting officers and compliance with the accounting manual and the council's purchasing instructions.

Chief financial officer to have access to all documents and records relating in any way to finance, and to be entitled to have such explanations as he considers necessary. The chief financial officer to be notified of all irregularities or suspected irregularities.

Payment of accounts

Timetable for passing forward of invoices to be laid down. The nature of primary records in which accounts submitted for payment are to be recorded to be prescribed (register of periodical payments, contract register, etc.)

Verification in the operating departments to cover the following points:
the supply of the goods, and the correctness of quantity and quality;
the deduction of cash and trade discounts; accuracy of prices;
allocation to head of account and financial year; legality and authorization.

Heads of departments to designate the officers (if any) authorized to certify invoices on their behalf.

Classes of accounts to be paid from the chief financial officer's imprest or advance account to be defined, e.g. wages, contract accounts, payments to earn discount, accounts for purchase of property (For reimbursement of imprest accounts see under standing orders).

Purchasing and contracting

Local authorities, being compelled by the Local Government Act, 1933 to have standing orders to govern purchasing and contracting, usually make their orders comprehensive, leaving little to be covered by regulations. This appendix follows the common practice and therefore the only points left to be suggested for regulations are:

Goods to be ordered on official order forms. Person signing orders to be responsible for ensuring that estimate provision is available.

Relations between central purchasing officers and using departments to be defined.

At a still lower level there are however very many points of departmental procedure to be provided for. Purchasing and contracting has therefore been selected to illustrate the kind of details which should go into a manual of instruction. This has been done in the last section of the first chapter on purchasing and contracting, to which the reader is referred.

Salaries and wages

The regulations to stipulate the records to be kept in departments and the times by which information for payment of salaries and wages should be transmitted to the chief financial officer. The form of all records to be settled by the chief financial officer who should be notified of all appointments, resignations, transfers, etc.

Petty cash accounts

Amounts of petty cash imprests to be fixed by the chief financial officer. Reimbursements to be made at regular intervals on submission of vouchers. Payments to be limited to small items of expenditure and any other items approved by the chief financial officer.

Insurances

Chief financial officer to be responsible for covering all risks. Heads of departments to notify the chief financial officer of all risks and of all losses or other claims. Chief financial officer, in consultation where necessary with the head of department and with the Clerk, to negotiate all claims. An annual list of insurances to be submitted by the chief financial officer to the heads of departments. The list to be reviewed and returned.

Inventories

Inventories to be prepared and kept up to date by the heads of departments. The inventories to be in approved form and open to audit.

Stocks and stores

The heads of departments to be responsible for the custody and control of stores. Stocktaking to be continuous, records of discrepancies being submitted to the chief financial officer. Substantial surpluses or deficiencies to be reported to committee. Maximum and minimum levels of stores to be laid down where appropriate.

Properties

The terrier of properties maintained by the Clerk (or Estates Officer) to be open to audit.

CIRCULAR NO 4/59 OF THE MINISTRY OF HOUSING AND LOCAL GOVERNMENT

WHITEHALL, LONDON, S.W.1

26*th January*, 1959

SIR,

LOCAL GOVERNMENT ACT, 1958
Arrangements for handling Receipts and Payments

1. As from April 1st next the existing enactments imposing detailed procedures for paying money into and out of the funds of county, borough and metropolitan borough councils will be replaced by the provisions of section 58 of the Local Government Act, 1958; and the new provisions will also apply to the councils of urban and rural districts. Each authority will be required to make safe and efficient arrangements for the receipt of moneys paid to them and the issue of moneys payable by them. The section requires that these arrangements must be carried out under the supervision of the Treasurer, except that if the Treasurer at the passing of the Act— that is July 23, 1958—was not a whole-time officer, the arrangements, while such conditions remain, are to be supervised by the person designated by the authority as their Chief Financial Officer. In making appointments to the office of Treasurer authorities will no doubt in the light of the new statutory requirements satisfy themselves that the supervisory duties required by these provisions can be properly discharged, bearing in mind that, except in the case of authorities which had on July 23, 1958 a Treasurer who was not whole-time, it is the Treasurer who must perform them.

2. The limitations imposed by existing enactments have not prevented the evolution of efficient and workable financial arrangements, though they have much influenced their form. The new provisions will enable all authorities to review present rules and adopt the procedures best suited to their particular needs. Rules and procedures can probably best be included as financial regulations in the Council's Standing Orders, but some authorities may prefer simply to record the arrangements in the minutes of the Council or Finance Committee.

3. It is the clear intention of the new provisions that the duties of supervision shall be carried out by the authority's chief financial officer, whether or not he has been officially designated as Treasurer. The range of this officer's responsibilities often appears in standing orders, financial regulations, minutes of the Council or conditions of employment; and the duties required of him by section 58 do no more than underline the

importance of, and accord statutory recognition to, a procedure which is essential to any system of sound financial control.

4. In view of the responsibilities which today fall on the chief financial officer of any local authority with a large budget it is plainly desirable that, wherever practicable, authorities should appoint a whole-time treasurer with appropriate professional qualifications as the chief financial officer, investing him with adequate authority, and supporting him by sufficient trained staff; though it is recognized that this is not usually practicable for the smaller district councils. When authorities are seeking candidates for appointment to this office the Minister suggests that they should consider doing so from a wide field, since only so can a strong and diverse body of financial experience be built up. There is naturally a bias in favour of an appointment from those already serving the local authority, but there is a real advantage to local government as a whole if a wide experience can be encouraged, and a field open to the best candidate should serve the authority's own interest well.

5. Basic to a sound system of financial administration is a Finance Committee with clearly defined responsibilities for regulating and controlling the finances of the authority. This need does not depend upon express statutory provision.

6. It is hoped that the observations in the appended Memorandum will be of assistance to authorities in devising arrangements to comply with the new statutory requirements.

7. A copy of this Circular is enclosed for the Chief Financial Officer of the Authority.

I am, Sir,

Your obedient Servant,

F. L. EDWARDS,

Under Secretary.

The Clerk of the Authority.

MEMORANDUM

A. General

1. The new legislation provides an opportunity for all local authorities to carry out a complete review of their arrangements for financial control and security; and it is desirable that any revised procedures which may be decided upon should in turn be re-examined periodically. The need for overhaul may arise from a variety of causes such as alteration of areas or functions and, above all, from improvements in office routines and altering techniques which may result from mechanization or O and M studies. A periodical and thorough review of the whole system—say once in every 5 years—might usefully be undertaken by Finance Committees and Chief Financial Officers. Such a periodical overhaul does not of course dispense with the need for constant consideration of these questions.

2. Paragraph 13 of the Memorandum which accompanied the Accounts (Boroughs and Metropolitan Boroughs) Regulations, 1930, contained a comprehensive statement of the principles to be observed in the allotment of accounting duties, and it may be useful to recapitulate it here:

13. The Regulations do not contain any provisions which would limit the discretion of a Council in regard to the officers it employs or the the duties it assigns to each. But, in view of the important bearing which wise allotment of duties has upon the efficiency, economy and security of the account keeping, it is thought desirable to refer here to the principles which appear to be of chief value in this connection.

   i. That the duty of providing information, calculating, checking and recording the sums due to or from the Council should be separated as completely as possible from the duty of collecting or disbursing these sums.

   ii. That officers charged with the duty of examining and checking the accounts of cash transactions should not themselves be engaged in any of these transactions.

   iii. That responsibility for the maintenance of current supervision of all accounts and records relating thereto should rest upon one chief financial officer, even when a separate departmental accountant is employed, as the efficiency of internal audit depends largely upon its independence. And that the officer charged with this duty of supervision should have access at any time and authority to apply any test or check to the accounts and records.

   iv. That responsibility for the organization of efficient accounting systems should also rest upon this officer. But that he should in all cases consult the chief officer of the department concerned as to the form and manner of keeping any records, statements or accounts which have to be kept in that department, due regard being paid on the one hand to the provision of prompt, reliable and complete information for the preparation and verification of accounts and, on the other hand, to the avoidance of unnecessary delay or increase of cost in the execution of work.

B. Payments out of local funds

3. The fundamental principles here are:—

(a) A reliable procedure for dealing with payments is of little value if it is not linked with an equally sound system at the earlier stage for ensuring that the financial implications of proposed expenditure are properly considered, and for controlling the liabilities entered into.

(b) The Finance Committee and the Council annually chart the Council's financial course by approving the budget and determining the rate or precept. They need to continue their supervision throughout the year to ensure that budgetary limitations are observed and that advance express approval is sought to expenditures outside, or in excess of, budget estimates.

(c) The nature of the annual budget is such that time is seldom available for detailed consideration of all new or exceptional projects included within it; and it is particularly desirable that Finance Committees should give further specific consideration to expenditure of this nature before it is finally approved, whether or not it has already been included in the annual budget. For County Councils and Metropolitan Borough Councils the provisions of section 86 (2) of the Local Government Act, 1933, and section 60 (3) of the London Government Act, 1939, required such a review by the Finance Committee before any liability exceeding £100 was incurred. Those statutory provisions have now been repealed so that more up-to-date arrangements embodying the same principle can be applied by every type and size of authority to appropriate categories of new or exceptional expenditure.

(d) A way of ensuring that goods and services continue to cost no more than they should is to throw their provision open to competitive tender under conditions which ensure that all those tendering have sound knowledge of the amount and frequency of the supplies required.

(e) The responsibility for certifying that invoices are in accordance with supplies received and that the amounts claimed are in every respect properly payable is necessarily shared between departments. The several responsibilities of each must be clearly defined; and the fact that the various checks have been applied should each be legibly recorded on the face of the document.

(*f*) The control over goods is at all stages as important as the control over cash. The best safeguard against fraud and misappropriation of cash or goods is in the separation of duties; and to be effective this separation must not be allowed to break down in times of pressure, e.g. during holiday periods and meal breaks. The control over capital goods purchased involves keeping inventories up-to-date.

4. In local government the units are so diverse that it is out of the question to expect uniformity of practice in applying these principles. Each local authority must decide for themselves how best to apply them to their own circumstances. In the very small authorities members must themselves take an active part in the arrangements for the release of moneys, whilst in the large authorities such a procedure is impracticable.

5. The system of dual or triple signing of individual cheques in accordance with a Council resolution to pay is one which is adopted by some small authorities. It provides a substantial measure of security against improper payments if it is combined with a scrutiny by members of accounts, an examination to ensure that cheques are drawn only in accordance with the Council's resolution to pay, and a satisfactory procedure for meeting urgent payments between Council meetings.

6. The larger authorities will rely mainly on internal checks and separation of duties to ensure that all accounts for payment are adequately examined and properly authorized and that adequate safeguards exist to prevent an improper claim being passed for payment or a cheque being wrongly issued. Where separation of duties cannot easily be secured, a requirement of counter-signature of cheques is sometimes adopted but is not necessarily fully effective. Its best use is where limited to cheques of large amounts.

7. Some Councils, where detailed examination of all accounts by members would be impracticable have evolved a useful system of review by appointing a Committee to make a judicious selection of items from statements submitted and calling for special reports from their Chief Officers setting out the complete history and all relevant details of the transactions leading up to the payment of the items selected.

8. There are other obvious safeguards which, in accordance with good accounting practice, should be provided for in the arrangements adopted. These include such matters as control of access to blank cheques and of the preparation, signing and despatch of cheques; prompt examination of paid cheques; and frequent and independent reconciliation of cash books with bank pass books. These matters are of particular importance where the arrangements provide for a single signature on cheques.

C. Payments into local funds

9. Whilst it is unlikely that the new statutory provisions will call for any marked changes in arrangements for paying moneys into local authority funds, it is recommended that these arrangements should be reviewed and incorporated in the standing orders, financial regulations or minutes of the Council, subject to any alterations which the review may show to be desirable. In some cases modification of present arrangements may be required so that supervision by the Treasurer can be fully effective.

10. Here again a sound system for paying moneys into Council funds needs to be associated with satisfactory arrangements for calculating and recording sums due to the Council; and those operations should be performed independently of the staff charged with the duty of collection.

11. The standing orders, financial regulations or minutes should include detailed instructions as to the control of sums received by officers in the course of their official duties and as to the frequency with which they bank such receipts. These instructions should be in terms which will not leave room for any belief that exceptional items can be handled differently.

12. It is usual to provide that writing off any sums due requires the approval of the authority or of a committee thereof; and it is also usual to require regular reports to them of arrears.

13. Guidance in the preparation of detailed rules can be obtained from a study of the provisions concerning collection and payment of Council moneys which appear in the Accounts (Payment into Bank) Order 1922, the various Rate Accounts Orders, the Accounts (Boroughs and Metropolitan Boroughs) Regulations, 1930, and the Memorandum which accompanied the Regulations.

D. Bank Accounts

14. Arrangements for handling receipts and payments necessarily extend to the Council's banking arrangements, including not only the terms agreed for management but also the number of accounts to be opened, the manner in which they are to be operated, and the name or names in which they are to stand. Accounts to be operated by officers will normally be designated as an account of the officer of the Council, and not as an account of the individual; and for such accounts overdrafts should require the express authorization of the Council communicated to the bank. The Banks have requested that any instructions given to them for the opening and operation of accounts should be authorized by resolution of the Council and that a certified copy of such resolution be supplied.

(Crown Copyright. Reproduced by kind permission of H.M. Stationery Office.)

TABLE OF STATUTES

ORDERS

INDEX

Abernethy, W. L., 150
Accounts, 28, 29, 120–2, 162, 163, 295, 345, 347, 374
Accountability of officers, 360, 361
Accounting:
  centralization, 126–30
  data for committees, 122
  data for departments, 123–5
  duplication of records, 130
  organization, 130, 131
  see also Cost accounting
American city manager, 16
American local government, 14
Anglo-American Council on Productivity, 146, 166, 316
Annual returns of income and expenditure, 346, 347
Anstey, E., and Mercer, E. O., 100
Approval of projects in principle, 266, 267
Attorney-General v. de Winton, 61, 62, 197
Audit, external, 69, 148, 150, 347
Audit, internal, 145–61, 374
  approach, 155, 156
  and external audit, 148–50
  independence, 153, 154
  and machine accounting, 141–3
  nature of, 145–7
  organization, 158–60
  and organization and methods, 151–3
  post-war conditions, 147, 148
  programmes, 157, 158
  reports on audits, 160, 161
  staff, 154, 155

Banking of monies (Scotland), 345
Bell, R. W., 117
Borough audit, *see* Audit, external
Bridges, Lord, 39
British Transport Commission, 73, 89
Budgeting in Public Authorities (R.I.P.A. Study), 258
Budgeting, general, 26, 29

Budget, principles:
  capital programmes, 266, 267
  capital projects, 267, 268
  distinctive local government features, 261
  kinds of, 262–4
  and policy, 215, 216, 264, 265
  purposes, 258–60
  statutory provisions, 260, 261, 325, 326–33
Budget, form of:
  capital budget, 275–7, 370
  capital programme, 274, 275, 371
  publication with accounts, 121
  reports and summaries, 272, 273
  revenue budget, 268–72
Budget, procedure, 278–95, 370, 371, 373, 374
  chairman's speech, 290, 291
  drafting procedure, 279, 280
  features to be avoided, 281, 282
  implications of cuts, 288, 289
  principles, 278, 279
  revision (committees), 285–8
  revision (officers), 284
  Scotland, 291, 293
  submission to committees, 282, 283
  trading undertakings, 293–5
Budget, statements during year:
  form, 297–9
  nature of, 297
  need for, 296
  use of, 300–2
Budget, administration:
  estimate committees, 306–8
  revised budget and final accounts, 121
  supplementary estimates, 303–5, 370
  virement, 305, 306, 370
Building Contracts of Local Authorities (R.I.P.A. Study), 242, 245
Burgh collector (Scotland), 343

Capital programmes, *see* budgets
Capital budgets, *see* budgets
Central control of local authorities, 14–16, 46, 47

386

Cost accounting, potentialities in local
  government, 166–70
problems, 164–6
standard costing, 168, 169
County collector (Scotland), 342
County financial officers' associations,
  82
County police, 346
Coventry, 160, 185, 191
Criminal cases (costs of), 346

Davison, E. H., 34
Debt management, *see* Chief financial
  officer's department (organization)
Debt returns (certification of), 346
Departments of local authorities:
  co-ordination (need for), 21
  and direct labour works, 254, 255
Departmental finance officers, 184–95
  attendance at finance sub-committees,
    51, 52
  budget, administering, 301
  budget making, 280, 281
  dual responsibility, 189–91
  duties, 186–8, 369
  and payments, 201, 249
  qualities needed, 191
  relations with chief financial officer,
    190, 191
  relations with finance department, 186
  relations with other officers, 187–9
  status, 185, 186, 191, 192
  training, 193
Departmental financial work, 184–95
  accounting data needed, 28, 123–5
  budget, administering, 296, 297, 300–2
  budget, making of, 278–89
  budget, supplementary estimates, 303,
    304
  budget, value of, 265
  budget, virement, 305, 306
  collection of income, 216, 217, 222,
    223
  financial responsibility, sense of, 34,
    109
  insurance, 174, 175
  organization of financial work, 185–
    93

payments of accounts, 199–204
payment of wages, 210
purchasing and contracting, 229–41
scales of assessment, 218, 219
Departmental heads:
  certification of bills, 201
  and direct labour, 255
  financial duties, 194, 195
  relations with chief financial officer,
    108–10, 114, 115, 119, 194
  technical training, 21
Direct labour work, 275, 285, 372, 373
  control of, 123, 254–7
  nature of, 253
  purchasing for, 232
District Audit, *see* Audit, external
Drury, John, 199, 204
Duplications of records, 130
Dutch local government, 17

Edinburgh, 235, 292, 293
Establishment committees, 20
Establishment work, 22, 36, 92, 182,
  209
Estimates, *see* budget
Estimate committees, 306–8

Finance committees:
  budgets (capital), 275
  budgets (cash), 263
  budgets (general), 285–9
  budgets (supplementary estimates),
    303, 304
  collection of income, 216
  duties, scope of, 49, 106, 107
  duties, nature of, 44–7, 368
  as a functional committee, 20, 39, 49
  insurance, 174
  loans, 172
  manuals of instruction, 317
  meetings, data needed, 50
  meetings, procedure, 50
  member, nature of interest, 33
  members selection, 41–4
  need for, 39, 40
  payments, 51, 208
  relations with chief financial officer,
    106–8